Randolph County, Illinois Veterans

Lest We Forget

Sgt. Carl E. Thomas, taken at Coulterville, IL, 1947.

Bobby Dement, Japan

Gary Birke in the "bush" near Pleiku, Vietnam as a rifleman with B Co., 1st/35th Infantry, 4th Infantry Division, 1969

Turner®
PUBLISHING COMPANY

Publishers of America's History
412 Broadway, P.O. Box 3101
Paducah, KY 42002-3101
270-443-0121

Copyright © 2003 Randolph County Genealogical Society
Publishing Rights: Turner Publishing Company

Turner Publishing Company Staff:
Editor: Randy W. Baumgardner
Designer: Ina F. Morse

This book was compiled and produced using available information. Turner Publishing Company and the Randolph County Genealogical Society regret they cannot assume liability for errors or omissions.

This book or any part thereof may not be reproduced without the written consent of the author and publisher.

Library of Congress Catalog Control No.: 2003110283
ISBN 978-1-63026-967-8

Elmer Shemonic

Table of Contents

Foreword	4
Dedication	7
Sponsors	8
Special Thanks	9
Randolph County, Illinois Veterans	11
A Salute To Those Killed in Action	171
"TAPS"	174
The History of the Service Flag	175
Served Our Country, Too	176
Revolutionary War Veterans Buried in Randolph County	181
Picture Album	182
Old Glory	189
A Witness At Nuremberg	190
Articles from the Chester Herald Tribune paper	192
Index	200
These Boys	208

1954, M-33 radar. Capt. Seljc on top giving class. The first antenna is called an acquisition antenna. It spins about 40 rpm The other antenna is on top of a tracking van with four operators inside it. To the left of that is a partsvan.

Foreword

The histories recorded in this book are from living veterans willing to share their stories, and from family members of deceased veterans who had records of a loved one that had served in the military. One of the major concerns when we began this project was realizing it would be an impossible task to get the history or even the name of every Randolph County Veteran, due to the large number of men and women who served from this county. We found this realization to be well-founded when faced with the many large volumes of only the discharges that have been recorded. Many were never recorded. In order to get all names and histories possible, we have relied on veterans and their families to provide the information for this book.

When first approached to do this book, another concern we had was that there may not be enough histories forthcoming to produce a sizeable volume, since most veterans do not discuss the difficult days, weeks or months of hardship they endured during conflicts they were involved in, many of which gave new meaning to their lives and freedom to the lives of all who live in this country.

The valor, courage and character of the men and women in these stories should remind us that freedom is not without cost. President Harry S. Truman said, "Freedom is still expensive. It costs money. It costs blood. It still calls for courage and endurance, not only in soldiers, but in every man and woman who is free and who is determined to remain free."

Some of these stories are of people who died before we were born; some are from those we've known, who have now passed on; some are from people you've never heard of; some are of those who have been called heroes; others do not contain specific acts of heroism; but all those listed in these histories have worn the uniform of the United States of America, in one war or another, and fought in their individual way for the way of life we enjoy today.

We are so very fortunate that veterans of World War II, Korea and Vietnam have shared their stories and experiences with us, and to the families of all deceased veterans, our sincere thanks for taking the time to research and put the military history of your loved one(s) on the pages of this book. Our way of life rests upon the foundation that has been cemented in place by the blood of all soldiers who have fought on the battlefields at Concord Bridge, Vicksburg, Beaches of Normandy, Islands of the Pacific, Persian Gulf, Afghanistan, and

Iraq. They have left home and families to serve their country, so we might live in a land where our ideas and way of life are not enforced by guns and bullets. Many times this nation has placed its trust in our service men and women; they have never let us down.

As we go to print with this book, thousands of our men and women are on the front lines of a war now being fought in Afghanistan and Iraq. We hope the military histories of those serving there will be written by someone at a later time, when these veterans return and are willing to share their stories, because every war has its own stories and every generation has its own heroes. Our blessings should be counted on a daily basis, and we should never fail to give thanks for those who have been the protectors of all we hold dear.

Virginia Mansker, President
Randolph County Genealogical Society

DEDICATION

With deep gratitude and respect, we, the members of the Randolph County Genealogical Society, proudly dedicate this book to all veterans of Randolph County, Illinois.

The stories and experiences you have shared will leave a deep and lasting impression on those who read this book and on all who enjoy the freedom and privileges for which you endured and gave so much.

We will be forever grateful and never forget the price you paid and the sacrifices you made for our way of life.

In times of great difficulty, the achievements and victories you have won for this nation have been gained by both valor and tragedy, many paying the ultimate price.

The men and women, throughout history, who have been a part our Armed Forces have preserved the ideas we cherish and the high cause to which our nation was originally dedicated.

We cannot honor you by going back to where you stopped; however, we sincerely hope this publication will honor you by keeping what you did on the pages of Randolph County history for future generations.

Book Committee:
Virginia Mansker, President
June James, Treasurer
Mildred (Midge) Dobyns
Dale Fulton
Danny James

Sponsors

Our sincere appreciation to the following sponsors, without whose support this publication would not have been possible.

American Legion Auxiliary Post 487	Chester
American Legion Joseph Park Post 622	Prairie du Rocher
American Legion Post 6632	Red Bud
American Legion Post 396	Sparta
American Legion BBK Post 480	Steeleville
American Legion	Chester
Chester V.F.W.	Chester
Sparta V.F.W.	Sparta
Buena Vista Bank	Chester
Chester National Bank	Chester
First National Bank	Sparta
First State Bank	Red Bud
North County Savings Bank	Red Bud
Jane and George Boyd	Sparta
Spencer F. Brown	Chester
Mike Brush	Murphysboro
Patty Burke	Texas
Larry Burton	Chester
Don and Mildred Dobyns	Ava
Carolyn Dorf and Family	Tilden
Dr. & Mrs. Steven Dorf and Stefanie	
Tom, Sharon and Ashley Bates	
Edward Fisher	Chester
Marion Frazer	Percy
William D. Frazer	Evansville
Donald and Carolyn Holder	Baldwin
Dr. Michael P. Holub	Chester
Danny and June James	Chester
Ralph and Bonnie Kipp	Chester
Jeffrey Kerkhover	Chester
Daniel Limbaugh	St. Louis
Richard Mann	California
Sherry J. Mansker	Springfield
Virginia L. Mansker	Rockwood
Victor Mohr	Red Bud
Harry Montroy	Evansville
Mary Park	California

Ron Stork	Sparta
Karen Athmer Wagner	Chester
Richard W. Witbart	Steeleville
Eagles Club	Chester
Chester Women's Club	Chester
Chester Rotary Club	Chester
Sparta Rotary Club	Sparta
Sparta Chamber of Commerce	Sparta
Randolph County Board	Chester
Randolph County Genealogical Society	Chester
County Office Supply	Sparta
Farmers National Realty	Steeleville
Gilster-Mary Lee	Chester
Dave's Food Center	Steeleville
Horrell Distributing Company	Red Bud
Rozier's Country Market	Chester
Reid's Harvest House	Chester
Randolph County Farm Bureau	Sparta
Nurnberger Insurance	Sparta
McDaniels Bookbinding	Chester
Steeleville Pharmacy	Steeleville
Victor Drugs	Chester
Don and Paul Koeneman, Attorneys at Law	Chester
Schuwerk, Brown and Arbeiter	Chester
Welge, Pechacek, Schroeder, McClure	Chester
Village of Ellis Grove	
Village of Prairie du Rocher	
Village of Rockwood	
Village of Ruma	

SPECIAL THANKS

County Journal Newspaper	Jack Bivens
North County News	Marion Frazer
Randolph County Tribune	Eugene Guebert
Sparta News Plaindealer	Larry Mudd
Steeleville Ledger	Jack Watson
Brian Snider, KSGM	Jack Sheppard, WHCO
Randolph County Clerk's Office Staff	

Randolph County, Illinois Veterans

GILBERT KENNEDY ADAMS, a veteran of the Spanish American War, he was born October 5, 1876, in Sparta, Illinois, son of Robert and Mary McHenry Adams. He served with Company G, 40th Infantry USV from June 20, 1898 until June 24, 1901. He died June 29, 1947, at Sparta, Illinois and is buried in Caledonia Cemetery.

HAROLD W. ADAMS, U.S. Army WWI, enlisted May 25, 1918, discharged December 3, 1918, served with Battery A, 1st Field Artillery Regiment. He was born May 26, 1900 in Walsh, Illinois and died May 12, 1939.

JOHN D. AGNEW, Sergeant, born October 29, 1825, enlisted in the Civil War February 14, 1865, and served with Company F, 153rd Illinois Infantry. He was promoted to sergeant July 1, 1865. John became ill with rheumatism in camp near Tullahoma, Tennessee.

Mustered out at Memphis, Tennessee September 21, 1865 and was honorably discharged at Camp Butler, Illinois September 21, 1865. He died in Randolph County on December 29, 1895 and is buried in Mount Summit Cemetery near Rockwood, Illinois.

ROGER L. AHRENS, Staff Sergeant, entered service for Korean War June 11, 1952, in U.S. Air Force. Basic training at Lackland AFB, Texas; Radio School at Keesler AFB, Mississippi; shipped to Korea, stationed at Kimpo and Siwon March

S/Sgt. Roger Ahrens

1953-April 4, 1954. Assigned to Fordland AFB, Missouri until discharged June 10, 1956. He attended Southern Illinois University, Memphis State, worked in steel industry in Phoenix, Pittsburgh, St. Louis, Memphis and Dallas. Roger retired in 1996 and now lives in Richardson, Texas. He was born November 21, 1933, in Chester, Illinois, the son of Bert and Hulda Winkleman Ahrens.

JOHN R. AKIN, Gunner's Mate 1/c, was inducted into service, June 12, 1942, in a splendid ceremony at Soldier's Field, in Chicago, Illinois, along with 5,000 others. He was in Gunner's Mate School at Great Lakes Naval Station for four months, then to Melville, Rhode Island for nine weeks learning to be a motor torpedo boat sailor. He then was transferred to Pearl Harbor; then to Treasure Island Naval Transfer in San Francisco; and was at Bremerton, Washington by the end of April 1943.

At Bremerton, on a blind date, May 26, 1943, he met a wonderful young lady and 38 days later, on July 4, 1943, they were married, and are still married.

July 1943, two PT Boats came down from Alaska, "under their own bottoms" (naval slang for under their own power). At the end of November, after being restored to combat readiness, the boat and crew went to the South Pacific aboard a Norwegian tanker.

He was then assigned to Pearl Harbor, in an experiment to determine if PT Boats could destroy mine fields using depth charges, due to the possibility that waters between islands in the Philippines had been mined by the Japanese.

Returned to USA in February 1945 and spent time on shore patrol in Boston and San Francisco until the end of the war. John was discharged October 1, 1945, and went home to Shelton, Washington to his wife and son.

He was born in Tilden, Illinois, July 9, 1920, son of Charles J. and Ernestine Moody Akin.

JOHN R. ALLEN, Corporal, was born March 21, 1839, in Randolph County, Illinois. He served two and a half years in the Civil War. He enlisted June 11, 1861 and was assigned to the 22nd Regiment, Company II, Illinois Volunteers. John was wounded at Chickamauga, Georgia, on September 21, 1863, and his right leg was amputated. He was discharged February 17, 1864.

He married Mary McClinton April 29, 1864. Returned to Sparta, Illinois after the war and was a grocer. John was elected mayor in 1889. His parents were Andrew and Sarah Jane Hill Allen. He died August 26, 1890.

DALE ALLISON, Painter 1/c, served in the Navy during WWII and was stationed on Guam 1945-46. He was born in Chester, Illinois, the son of John and Lizzie Smith Allison. He returned to Chester and retired from Farm Fresh Dairy. Dale now lives in Blairsville, Georgia.

HARRY JONES ALLISON, Aviation Radioman, of Chester, Illinois, entered WWII in February 1943. He served in the Navy and was proud to serve his country until he was killed in action October 1944. He is listed on the tablets of the missing at Manila American Cemetery. His parents were Royce and Loretta Jones Allison of Chester, Illinois.

REUEL ALLISON, Sergeant, served in the 4th Marine Division during WWII. Entered service July 22, 1943. He served as a drill instructor at Camp Pendleton,

Sgt. Reuel Allison

California and participated in the battle of Iwo Jima, February 19, 1945. He was among the many Marines who watched proudly as the American flag was raised atop Mount Suribachi, as a signal the island now belonged to the Marines. Reuel was discharged November 3, 1945 and returned to Chester. He was the son of John and Lizzie Smith Allison. He died August 4, 1995.

RICHARD ALLISON, Specialist 4, entered the Army July 13, 1965 and served in Korea from December 1965 until April 17, 1967, with Company C, 13th S&S Battalion. He had his basic training at Fort Leonard Wood, Missouri, and education training at Fort Belvoir, Virginia. He is the son of Reuel and Ruby Jungwaelter Allison, of Chester, Illinois. After discharge he returned home and continued his job as a land surveyor. He later retired from Menard Correctional Center as a casework supervisor.

ROYCE BRIGGS ALLISON, SK2/c, served in the Navy during WWII, aboard landing crafts in the Pacific Theater. Commonly called by the name of "Briggs", he is the son of Royce and Loretta Jones Allison, of Chester, Illinois.

FREDERICK A. ALLMEYER, Private First Class, U.S. Army, entered service on October 2, 1968 and served with Company D, 1st Battalion, 12th Infantry, 4th Division. He lost his life in Viet-

Pfc. Fredrick Allmeyer

nam on June 6, 1969 from wounds received in combat. He was awarded the Bronze Star for heroism in ground combat and the Purple Heart, posthumously. He was born in Chester, Illinois, April 12, 1948, the son of Martin and Emma Ebers Allmeyer.

ELMER H. ALMS, son of Mr. and Mrs. William Alms, of Steeleville, Illinois, spent three years in the Air Force Ground Group during WWII. He was in France, Germany and England. Alms was honorably discharged in October 1945.

JAMES HARVEY ANDERSON, Private, enlisted on November 8, 1861 in Captain Ashley Pierre's Company E, 30th Regiment, Illinois Infantry and served in the Civil War. He was discharged at Smyrna Campground, Georgia November 13, 1864. James has always been a legend in his family - bigger than life. He was 5'10", dark complexion, with gray eyes and auburn hair when he signed up.

According to family legend he was captured, put in a Civil War prison camp along with his brother, George, and worked as a cook. He saved up cayenne pepper from the kitchen and used it to help him and his brother escape. He put the pepper in their tracks so the dogs couldn't pick up their scent. I haven't been able to prove the prison camp story, but from his pension records, I know he was at Vicksburg, Mississippi in 1863 and Kennesaw Mountain, Georgia in 1864.

In 1863 he served as a brigade wagoner and teamster under General Leggett. During his service he contracted many illnesses, including scurvy, stomach disorders and he also had blindness in one eye. He never recovered his sight in that eye and he had pains in it for the rest of his life.

James was born in Sparta, Illinois. He was the son of Noble and Elizabeth (Price) Anderson.

WILLIAM WESLEY ANDERSON, Sergeant, born near Chester, Illinois, December 12, 1837, was of a family of one brother and four sisters. On June 30, 1861, he enlisted in Company F, 18th Regiment, Illinois Volunteers and was mustered in at Bird's Point, Missouri (across the river from Chester). He gave his age as 23, and occupation as farmer. His unit fought in the Battle of Fort Donelson, where he lost his clothing. His pay was reduced $7.20 for this loss, also 55 cents for the loss of a cartridge box belt, and two cents for a tompion.

He suffered a gunshot wound in the right thigh on the first day of the Battle of Shiloh. His application for pension, dated April 24, 1888, stated, "I was wounded on the sixth day of Aprile 1862 at the Battle of Shiloh, and I was one of the Color Gards of the 18th Ills Inf and was in Line of Battle and ingaged in the fight, when I riceaved my Wound." (Spelling and Punctuation as in original document.) His obituary states he seized the regimental flag as it fell from the hands of a mortally wounded color bearer, and then William was shot. He was furloughed home until May 1862, then returned to find himself in Company C, which was then sent to Jackson and Bethel in Tennessee and Little Rock, Arkansas, in time to take part in the fight when Little Rock was taken.

He was promoted to sergeant in December 1863, and was reduced to ranks on March 31, 1865, for clearing a week's leave only with the quartermaster and not his captain. When mustered out December 16, 1865, at Pine Bluff, Arkansas, he decided to remain in the south. He died August 15, 1935, at age 97 years, eight months and is buried in Oak Grove Cemetery at Searcy, Arkansas.

CHESTEEN R. ANDREWS, Private First Class, served in WWII (1944-45) in the 42nd Rainbow Division with Task Force Linden, Alsace. He was married with two children, when drafted in 1944. Trained as an infantryman, assigned to 42nd Rainbow Division, 232nd Regiment, and along with two other regiments formed Task Force LINDEN.

Pfc. 1/c Chesteen Andrews

The Task Force was to perform blocking action to a very strong German offense on the southern part of the Siegfried Line. They were over run by German forces, he and a few members of his squadron holed up in an old bunker. Realizing the only way to survive was to surrender, they were captured in January 1945. A prisoner of war until May 1945 when liberated by Russian forces, and they worked their way back to American forces. In one short year, he had been drafted, trained, captured and liberated. He never talked about the months as a prisoner of war, but he did ask for "pie or cake" for every meal once he got home.

On the way back to the American lines, they came upon a freshly killed horse. Chesteen, being the son of a butcher, made sure the group had fresh meat.

He returned to farming, also worked at the Mental Health Center in Chester, Illinois, until his death, September 2, 1980. Andrews was born in Rockwood, May 9, 1919. He was the son of Edward and Carrie Woods Andrews.

LLOYD T. APPEL, Sergeant, U.S. Army, active service January 26, 1954-

January 4, 1956. Completed basic training at Camp Chaffee, Arkansas, then sent to Germany from July 1954 to December 1955. He served with Headquarters Battery, 60th Field Artillery Battalion. He was in active reserves until May 1956 and inactive until January 1962.

He was born December 29, 1931, the son of Arnold and ___ Pierce Appel.

ALBERT R. ASBURY, Private First Class, born March 15, 1918, in Jones Ridge, Illinois, entered military service December 3, 1943, during WWII. He served in Field Artillery, Battery A, 413th Battalion, in Central Europe. Asbury received a Bronze Service Star and Good Conduct Medal. He was discharged November 22, 1945 at Jefferson Barracks, Missouri. He was the son of Samuel and Sarah Christian Asbury of Rockwood, Illinois.

ANDREW C. ASBURY, Private, born at Jones Ridge, Illinois, son of Samuel and Sarah Christian Asbury, entered the service February 26, 1941, in East St. Louis, Illinois. He was assigned to Battery F, 56th Coast Artillery. Asbury served five months and 14 days, and was then discharged from Letterman General Hospital, San Francisco, California, August 2, 1941.

DONALD RAYMOND ASBURY, E-4, enlisted in the Air Force on August 14, 1961. Donald took his Airman basic from St. Louis, Missouri. He went to Sheppard AFB, Texas for his air freight special courses from September 1961-January 1962. He spent a total of four years, seven months and two days of active duty. Donald spent two years, one month and 25 days overseas. He was awarded the Air Force Longevity Service Medal (August 14, 1961-August 13, 1965) and the Air Force Good Conduct Medal. Donald was discharged April 5, 1966. He was discharged from the Reserves on August 13, 1967. His hometown is Rockwood, Illinois (Randolph County) Donald was born May 20, 1944.

DONALD T. ASBURY, FT3, 3/c Petty Officer, entered the Navy in July 1961 and served with the FT Division Missile Launch in Vietnam. He was engaged in research and development on the Polaris Missile System, aboard the USS *Ob-*

Petty Off. Donald T. Asbury

servation Island EAGLE 154, sailing out of Cape Canaveral, Florida. When not test launching the missiles he supervised and assisted newly commissioned nuclear subs in their initial test firings. Donald was born September 10, 1941 in Chester, the son of Alto Harry and Cleva (Willis) Asbury. He returned home and taught school. Donald currently owns a jewelry store.

ERVIN RAY ASBURY, E-4, entered the Air Force August 29, 1978. Ervin took six weeks of basic training in October 1978. Then he took 18 weeks of an aerospace ground equipment course in February 1979; one week of ground shelter heater, 1H-1 in November 1979. Ervin took one week of NCO orientation course, phase 1 in June 1981, then had a week of MD-4/MD-4M motor generator sets, November 1981. Ervin's last duty was with the 314th FMB (MAC). He earned the Air Force Training Ribbon and the Air Force Longevity Service Award Ribbon. Ervin was discharged May 1, 1981, from Little Rock AFB, Arkansas. He was born July 26, 1960.

HARRY ALBERT ASBURY, Technical Sergeant, was born in Jones Ridge, Illinois, September 30, 1909, to Thomas C. and Mattie Christian Asbury. Entered WWII November 2, 1943, and served in Northern France, Rhineland and Central Europe with Company A, 716th Railway Operation Battalion, as communications installer, establishing telephone switchboards and lines under hazardous conditions.

A lasting experience was being quartered in General Field Marshall Rommel's home for a period of time, where he became acquainted with Mrs. Rommel and her son.

He received two Overseas Service Bars, European African Middle Eastern Theater Ribbon w/3 Bronze Stars, WWII Victory Medal and Good Conduct Medal. Qualified as expert with M-1903 rifle. Discharged November 30, 1945, from Camp Grant, Illinois.

Retired from Chester Mental Health Center. Harry died September 2, 1982.

HOWARD LAVERN ASBURY, E-2, U.S. Army, 1952-54, served with the 68th Engineer Company. He earned the National Defense, Korean Service w/2 Bronze Stars, United Nations Service and Korea Unit Citation medals and ribbons. He was born September 5, 1931, in Rockwood, Illinois.

JACK HAROLD ASBURY, Boatswain Mate 2/c, Chester, Illinois, born April 23, 1931 to Harry and Cleva Willis Asbury. He served in the U.S. Coast Guard during the Korean Conflict from August 1, 1951-August 1, 1954. He served aboard several vessels dealing primarily with inland navigation, life safety and marine patrols. Primary duty as boatswain was to supervise deck crews in the performance of their duties. As an educator, he retired in August 1986 as assistant regional superintendent of an educational service region for Randolph/Monroe counties. Jack now lives in Sparta, Illinois.

KEVIN BRUCE ASBURY, Lieutenant Commander, U.S. Coast Guard, June 1, 1978-June 1, 2002. He was born in April 1960 at Percy, Illinois, the son of Jack H. and Lela Hartman Asbury. He graduated U.S. Coast Guard Academy in 1982 with a bachelor of science degree in marine engineering and a master's degree in mechanical engineering. He served aboard several Coast Guard ocean vessels as chief engineer officer. The ships were involved in "at sea" inspections, drug smuggling and ice patrols. He retired July 2002 and now lives with his wife and daughter in Vergennes, Illinois.

MITCHELL WILLIAM ASBURY, E-3, U.S. Navy, 1969-73. He was born in Red Bud, Illinois, December 25, 1949. He served with Air Antisubmarine Squadron thirty-one, Bainbridge, MD. Asbury was discharged May 4, 1973 and served in the reserves until 1975.

MURRAY RICHARD ASBURY, Seaman 2/c, entered the U.S. Navy March 31, 1944 for a two year enlistment. He was discharged from Great Lakes Naval Hospital November 20, 1944. Asbury was born November 17, 1906, at Cora City, Illinois, the son of Samuel and Sarah Christian Asbury of Rockwood, Illinois.

RALPH O. ASBURY, Private First Class, enlisted in the Illinois National Guard in 1951. He was activated and went to Korea with the 894th Searchlite Battalion. Prior to departing Korea for the United States, Ralph met his brother, Howard, in Pusan, Korea.

Howard and Ralph Asbury

They were both discharged in June 1954 and both worked at Laclede Steel, Alton, Illinois. Ralph retired after 36 years. Both were born in Rockwood, Illinois; Ralph on January 7, 1934 and Howard about 1931. Howard died August 1995. Their parents were Roy Lee and Mabel Lorentz Asbury.

SAMUEL RICHARD ASBURY, Private E-1, U.S. Army, 1961-63, served as wheel vehicle mechanic. He was born in Rockwood, Illinois on November 21, 1940.

HERMAN ASSELMEIER, Sergeant, born February 16, 1931 in Maeystown, Illinois, son of Herman and Clara Fauss Asselmeier. He served in the USMC with Weapons Company, 2nd Battalion, 5th Marines, 1st Marine Division from February 1951-February 1954, Korean Conflict. He served with 81st Mortars, ATT to Easy Company, 2nd Battalion, 5th Marines, 1st Marine Division.

VERNON W. ASSELMEIER, Corporal, U.S. Army, served with Company G, 8th Infantry Regiment, 4th Division during the Korean War. He was born in Valmeyer, Illinois and lived in Chester, the son of Herman H. and Clara Fauss Asselmeier. He enlisted in 1951, stationed

Cpl. Vernon Asselmeier

in Budingen, Germany, occupational duty until 1953. He continued service in the Army Reserves until 1956. Returning to Chester, he retired as chief of security, Menard Psychiatric Center. He died August 11, 1992.

JACK ATCHISON, 2nd Lieutenant, enlisted in the Army Air Corps at Jefferson Barracks, Missouri, October 8, 1940. He was accepted into the Air Cadets March 18, 1943 and was assigned to Rankin Aeronautical Academy, Santa Ana, California. Jack received his commission and silver wings at Stockton Field, California on February 8, 1944.

2nd Lt. Jack Atchison

First pilot assigned to a B-17 Flying Fortress, Hobbs Air Base, New Mexico. Deployed with 15th Air Corps, 327th Bomber Squadron, based at Ramatali Air Base, Foggia, Italy. He was killed in flight action November 30, 1944 in Italian Theatre and buried in Foggia, Italy. The body was removed to Evergreen Cemetery, Chester, Illinois in 1949.

Jack was born April 14, 1917 in Mt. Summit, Randolph County, Illinois, the son of Omar and Kate Holloman Atchison. He was the first commissioned officer from Chester to have lost his life in WWII.

MILTON "PETE" OMER ATCHISON, E-9 Master Chief, began his military career by enlisting in the Navy Seabee's at age 17, on February 21, 1945. After training at Great Lakes, Rhode Island, Camp Parks and Treasure Island, California, then sent overseas to Philippine and Admiralty Islands.

E-9 M.C. Milton Atchison

Pete spent 16 months in military, then became an active reservist with CBMU531 and 140th Naval Reserve units out of Cape Girardeau, Missouri. Retired at age 60 from the Reserves.

He was born April 19, 1927 to Omer and Kate Holloman Atchison in Chester, Illinois. He returned to operate a filling station and served many years as Chester's fire chief.

THOMAS EVERT ATCHISON, 1st Lieutenant, was born in Mount Summit,

Sgt. Herman Asselmeier

1st Lt. Thomas Atchison

Illinois, August 25, 1920, to Omar and Kate Holloman Atchison. Enlisted in U.S. Coast Guard in 1940. During WWII he served as chief gunner's mate in both Atlantic and Pacific Theatres, in submarine patrols in North Atlantic, participated in invasion of Philippines, Iwo Jima, Okinawa and Ie-Shima in South Pacific.

A staff sergeant in 1948, he was promoted to 1st lieutenant. He served in Korea as an artillery officer. Completed 10-1/2 years in military, then entered University of Illinois in 1953 to earn a degree of juris doctorate in 1957. Owned and operated law offices in Chester until his death, October 13, 1981. Buried in Evergreen Cemetery in Chester.

ARTHUR FRANKLIN "ART" ATHMER, Sergeant, U.S. Army, served with Headquarters Battery, 4th Division Artillery, 5th Army from March 26, 1951-February 11, 1953. He served in the Reserves from 1953-66.

Sgt. Arthur F. Athmer

He was stationed in Germany during the Korean Conflict. In the Reserves he served in Headquarters Battery, 927th Field Artillery, 102nd Infantry Division, then in 1959 to Headquarters Battery, 4th Battalion, 34th Artillery, 102nd Infantry Division.

Art was born in Chester, Illinois, the son of Ben and Lena Johnson Athmer. Art served as an Illinois state policeman from 1955 until his retirement as a master sergeant in December 1984. He died at home in Chester on March 29, 1997.

OLIVER C. AUBUCHON, Seaman 2/c, U.S. Navy, son of Eli and Barbara Aubuchon, was born in Prairie du Rocher, Illinois on May 29, 1924. He enlisted in the U.S. Navy in 1943 and was discharged as a seaman second class in 1946. He married Dorothy Amsler in 1945 and worked for Allied Chemical. He died February 8, 1980.

S/M 2nd/c Oliver Aubuchon

VERNON LEON BAGWILL, Private First Class, entered the U.S. Army January 29, 1944, served with Company B, 137th Infantry in WWII as a squad leader in Germany.

Pfc. Vernon L. Bagwell

He received the ETD Ribbon, Victory Ribbon, Occupational Ribbon, Unit Citation, Purple Heart and Good Conduct Medals. Discharged November 28, 1945.

Vernon returned to Southern Illinois and started a taxi service in Coulterville. He later owned a school bus service and opened a Shelter Care Home. Vernon died October 28, 1990. He was born in Willisville, Illinois, the son of Edward and Martha Welch Bagwill.

ALBERT BAKER, Private, served in Company H, 50th Regiment of Captain John Snyder's Pennsylvania Veterans Infantry in the Civil War from March 11, 1865 until discharged July 13, 1865. He was born in Randolph County in 1845 and died in Ruma, Illinois April 18, 1881, at the age of 36 years, three days. Baker is buried in New City Cemetery in Red Bud, Illinois.

HENRY BARGMAN, Technician 4, U.S. Army, July 1943-February 1946, was

T/4 Henry Bargman

born in Chester, Illinois August 24, 1912, son of Fred and Minnie Neely Bargman. He entered service, took basic training at Cape Cod and was assigned to Company F, 534th EB&SR. Bargman spent first winter in Florida.

He shipped out of California on Liberty ship and arrived in New Guinea 22 days later. He built APO with the help of eight natives. He spent a couple of months in Japan before arriving in Seattle, Washington on January 1, 1946. Bargman was discharged from Jefferson Barracks on February 2, 1946.

GLEN M. BARTENS, E-3, enlisted into the Army in March 1964. Glen took his basic training at Fort Leonard Wood, Missouri. Then he went to Fort Bliss, El Paso, Texas for missile training. His next duty was at Fort Dix, New Jersey and from there Glen was sent to guard a missile base near Stuttgart, Germany until his discharge in November 1965. Glen was with Battery B, 3rd Missile Brv., 71st Artillery USAR EUR. He served in the Vietnam Era. His hometown is Steeleville, Illinois and his parents are Arnold and Sylvia (Roettjer) Bartens.

NORLYN D. BARTENS, Spc., U.S. Army, 1985-89, born Steeleville, Illinois, the son of Glen M. and Rose M. Liefer Bartens. After basic training at Fort Dix, New Jersey, additional training at Fort Belvoir, Virginia for power generation equipment repair. He was stationed at Fort Huachuca, Arizona, followed by two and one-half years at Giessen, Germany. After discharge he served with the Sparta National Guard in Company B, 133rd Signal Battalion for three years.

ARTHUR M. BAUER, Private First Class, entered the U.S. Marine Corps, July 2, 1940, to serve in WWII. Born in Evansville, Illinois on August 24, 1915, his parents were Anton and Ida Gross Bauer.

Pfc. Arthur M. Bauer

Arthur participated in assault and capture of Kwajalein and Atoll in the Marshall Islands. Served in the South Pacific, including both Western and American Samoa, Hawaii, Marshall Islands, New Caledonia Island and Guadalcanal. For his honest and faithful service he received the Honorable Service Lapel Button.

He married Marilyn Burk. He died August 3, 2000.

JOHN H. BAUER, Private First Class, served in WWII with Company I, 3rd Infantry Division in the U.S. Army. He was drafted into the Army December 15, 1942 and was sent to Wyoming for infantry training and shoe repair.

Pfc. John H. Bauer

He did guard duty in California and New York before boarding a troop ship to Casablanca and Tunis in North Africa. From there to Naples, Italy and then to Paris, France where he was assigned to 3rd Infantry on front line.

Participated in battles of Rome-Arno, Rhine, Munich, Nürnberg, through Germany and Salzburg, Austria. Being a scout and taking prisoners was scary.

He received the Combat Infantryman Badge SS w/rifle, five Overseas Service Bars, European-African-Middle Eastern Theater Ribbon w/3 Bronze Stars, Good Conduct Medal, Bronze Arrowhead and WWII Victory Medal. Bauer was discharged December 8, 1945.

John was born in Evansville, Illinois on July 5, 1922. His parents are Anton and Ida Gross Bauer. He now resides with his wife, Leora (Becker), in Evansville, Illinois.

OLIVER I. BAUER, Private First Class, served in WWII in Company C, 81st CML Mortar Battalion, in the U.S. Army. He entered service November 10, 1942 and saw action at Normandy, Northern France, Rhineland, Germany, Central Europe and Ardennes, Belgium.

Pfc. Oliver I. Bauer

His service earned him the European-African-Middle Eastern Theater Ribbon w/ Silver Battle Star, three Overseas Service Stars and the Good Conduct Medal. He was discharged September 3, 1945.

Oliver is the son of Anton and Ida Gross Bauer. He was born at Evansville, Illinois August 4, 1920. He is now a resident of Three Springs Lodge Nursing Home in Chester, Illinois.

JOHN D. BAUMAN, Sergeant First Class, was born in Kaskaskia, Illinois, August 22, 1930, to Louis W. and Veronica Schmerbauch Bauman. He graduated from Southeast Missouri University in 1952 and also entered into service in 1952.

He served as chief clerk in Headquarters Company, 5th Infantry Division until discharged in 1954. Returning home he went to law school at Washington University in St. Louis, Missouri, graduated with a doctorate degree in 1957.

ERNEST J. BEATTIE, Technical Sergeant, was inducted into the Army March 14, 1945, after being rejected by other branches due to poor vision. After basic and amphibious training for invasion of Japan, shipped out to Philippines and was put in Military Police Unit. Before getting to the Philippines, Japan surrendered, so their first mission was to clear Japanese who didn't surrender from the hills.

T/Sgt. Ernest J. Beattie

Discharged December 2, 1946 after 14 months overseas, he later joined a Reserve Unit in Sparta and when the Korean War broke out, he was called back. He helped reactivate Fort Leonard Wood, Missouri and served about a year.

Ernest was born in Sparta, Illinois on November 14, 1926, the son of Leon and Essie Smith Beattie. His service included both WWII and Korean War.

A. WILLIAM BECK, Corporal, U.S. Army, 1949-53, served with the 9604th Signal Corps Research from a base in Alaska. After enlistment and basic train-

Cpl. A. William Beck.

ing he attended school for electronic technician and monitored nuclear weapons. He was born in Percy, Illinois, the son of George and Hulda Caupert Beck.

ADAM H. BECKER, Sergeant Chief Plotter, was inducted into WWII at Scott AFB, December 17, 1942. Assigned to 122nd C.A. Battalion. Basic training in California, then to Brisbane, Australia, then to Milne Bay, New Guinea, also to Lar-Finch Afen and Hollandia. Achieved rank of "buck" sergeant at time of discharge on January 16, 1946.

Sgt. Adam H. Becker

Adam was born in Evansville, Illinois November 14, 1920. He returned there to work as head mechanic at International Shoe Company, then began a 26-year career as a rural mail carrier, from which he retired. His parents are Fred and Hilda Zippel Becker.

DOUGLAS CHARLES BECKER, Private, U.S. Army, served with the 25th Infantry Division, July 18, 1967-July 17,

Pvt. Douglas C. Becker

1969. He served in Vietnam and earned the Vietnam Service and Vietnam Campaign medals, two Overseas Bars, Purple Heart and Rifle Expert Medal. He was born November 29, 1947, the son of George E. and Charleene Fehringer Becker, Red Bud, Illinois.

DOUGLAS W. BECKER, Sergeant, of Evansville, Illinois, served in the U.S. Army. He was killed in Unzhurst, Germany, August 9, 1944, at the age of 21 years, five months, three days. His body was returned home in 1948, to be buried in Sauer Cemetery, near Evansville, Illinois.

FRED W. BECKER, Corporal, was inducted into the Army during WWI, and served as a cook. He served in France and Germany. He was inducted September 4, 1917 and discharged July 24, 1919.

Cpl. Fred W. Becker

A barber before entering service, he returned to Evansville, Illinois to operate a barber shop for over 50 years. He always cooked Sunday dinner. His daughters were not too thrilled because he always "made a lot of dirty pots and pans." Fred was born in Evansville, Illinois on April 6, 1893, the son of Adam and Catherine Meier Becker.

GEORGE E. BECKER, Sergeant, served in WWII in Company D, 132nd Infantry, in Guadalcanal, Bougainville, North Solomon and Philippine Islands. Squad leader of a machine gunnery group that used water-cooled machine guns in combat, in the above areas. He also had overseas duty in Australia, New Caledonia and the Fiji Islands.

Sgt. George E. Becker

Becker was awarded three Bronze Stars for these campaigns, Asiatic-Pacific Theatre Ribbon, American Defense Ribbon w/7 Overseas Bars and the Philippine Liberation Ribbon w/Bronze Star. He was discharged September 1, 1946.

The son of George and Anna Botterbrodt Becker, he was born in Evansville, Illinois, September 6, 1918.

RONALD T. BECKER, joined ROTC at the University of Missouri at Rolla. Upon his graduation he entered the U.S. Army in 1970 in the Ordinance Division. He was stationed at Aberdeen Proving Grounds, Maryland.

Ronald T. Becker

In November 1970 he was sent to Nürnberg, Germany. He was assigned as a mechanical maintenance officer and achieved the rank of first lieutenant and was transferred to Headquarters and D Company, 126th Maintenance Battalion, 4th Armored Division. He was honorably discharged in 1972 and started work with Caterpillar Inc. as a mechanical engineer in vehicle test and development.

He presently resides in Peoria, Illinois with his wife, Kathy (Birk), whom he married in 1969. They are the parents of four children: Jennifer, Patricia, Brad and Katie.

TYRUS "TY" BECKER, Specialist 4, served his country from March 1968 thru March 1970. He served with the A Company, 3rd Battalion, 7th Infantry, 199th Infantry Brigade while in Vietnam from May thru August 1969 was booby trap instructor for 199th Infantry.

Sp/4 Tyrus Becker

He was awarded the Purple Heart and two Bronze Stars. From August 1968 thru August 1969 he served as point man for A Company for eight months. Ty saw action in the TET and Pineapple Battles.

Ty is the son of Tyrus and Lucille (Hunter) Becker, born April 18, 1948 at Red Bud, Illinois. After serving his country, Ty worked at UMWA & LU 925.

EBENEZER MADISON BEEN, 2nd Lieutenant, born April 29, 1834 in Preston, Illinois, the son of James Allen and Margaret Anderson Cox Been. He served in Company "C", 154th Illinois Infantry in the Civil War.

2nd /Lt. Ebenezer M. Been

He attended McKendree College and was a surveyor prior to service. Returned home, continued surveying and farming after the war. He died November 4, 1885, near Preston, Illinois.

WILLARD BEISNER, Corporal, served in WWII in the Pacific Theatre in the 890th CML Company. He entered the

Cpl. Willard Beisner

service in 1943 and died of burns and injuries from a phosphorous bomb on the island of Guam, September 11, 1945. His parents were Herman and Linda Beisner of Chester, Illinois.

STEPHEN CARROLL BELCHER, Specialist 5, enlisted in the Army in September 1968. He spent three years as a combat medic, 13 months of which were patrolling the 38th Parallel on the DMZ in South Korea, two months in Germany and 18 months at Fort Riley, Kansas. Stephen was with the 2nd Battalion (M), 9th Infantry, 2nd Infantry Division (Medical Platoon HHC 2/9 Infantry). Stephen served during the Vietnam War. He was discharged in 1971. His hometown is Anna, Illinois, Union County. He is the son of Carroll Greg and Dorothy Lee (Conant).

WILLIAM E. BELL, Staff Sergeant, served in WWII (1940-45) in DMD 4th General Hospital Unit, in the New Guinea,

S/Sgt. William E. Bell

Luzon, Philippine Campaigns. He was awarded three Bronze Stars for these campaigns, also the Good Conduct Medal. His parents are Arthur and Lulu Moile Bell of Tilden, Illinois. He married Nola V. Fucton, October 9, 1946.

LELAND E. BERGFELD, Yeoman 1/c, son of Rollie and Grace McIntyre Bergfeld, of Percy, Illinois, enlisted in the Coast Guard August 4, 1942. Completing recruit training in Alameda, California, he transferred to Seattle Base Annex.

Yeo. 1st/c Leland E. Bergfeld

In April 1943 he reported to San Francisco as a member of the commissioning crew of Coast Guard-manned Navy auxiliary cargo transport, USS *COR CAROLI* (AK-91) and deployed to shuttle military cargoes between island bases in South and Central Pacific. During his 26 month tour he participated in the capture and occupation of Guam.

In June 1945 he transferred Stateside and proceeded to DCGO, Cleveland, Ohio, and served there until discharged January 10, 1946.

CLARENCE LEONARD BERTRAM, Private First Class, U.S. Army, 1951-53. He served with Company B, 44th Armored Infantry Battalion and was stationed at Fort

Pfc. Clarence L. Bertram

Richardson, Anchorage, AK from October 1952-October 1953. He was born March 16, 1930 in Waterloo, Illinois, Monroe County, the son of Arthur Joseph and Pauline Meier Bertram.

GLEN M. BESHER, Corporal, was drafted into the Army on September 10, 1952. He served with the 868th Field Artillery Battalion. Glen served in the Korean Conflict. He did his basic training at Camp Chaffee, Arkansas and AIT training in heavy artillery at Fort Bragg, North Carolina.

Cpl. Glen M. Besher

He was immediately sent overseas to Baumholder, Germany. There he served as a "T-10" driver for the "280 Atomic Weapon". He served in Germany until he was discharged on June 9, 1954.

Upon returning home, he returned to his occupation as a dairy farmer. Glen was born in Red Bud, Illinois on May 14, 1931 to Robert H. and Fern (Gulley) Besher.

CHARLES R. BEST, Lieutenant Colonel, born September 16, 1919 in Wayne County, Illinois, son of Van W. and Sarah Petty Best. He went in the draft from Chester on July 6, 1941. He was an artillery battery commander in combat during WWII (ETO) with 1st and 9th Armies. He was separated from the Army in February 1946 and joined the Reserves at Belleville, Illinois where he served as battalion commander until 1963.

MICHAEL L. BIERMAN, U.S. Navy Seabees, petty, officer 3, took six weeks boot camp at Gulfport, Mississippi in September 1969. Then Mike took temporary duty for four months at NAS Miramar, San Diego, California. After that he had a month of military training at Port Hueneme, California. He was then shipped to Chu Lai, South Vietnam for seven months with CBMU 301.

Mike came back to the States and spent his last year at Naval Construction Regiment, Davisville, Rhode Island. He was honorably discharged in December 1971. His parents are Hugo H. and Wynona L. (Bollman) Bierman.

EZRA G. BIEVENUE, Technician Fifth Grade, enlisted in the Army March 14, 1942. He served with 2012th Ordinance Maintenance Company AF in WWII. Bievenue participated in battles in Algeria-French Morocco, Tunisian, and Rome-Arno.

T/5 Ezra G. Bievenue

He was awarded the European-African-Middle Eastern Theater Ribbon w/3 Bronze Battle Stars, one Service Stripe, Good Conduct Medal, Meritorious Unit Award GO 157 Headquarters AAFSC 45. Discharged October 22, 1945.

His brothers Elroy, Howard and Clinton, were all in the service. Ezra was born April 2, 1919 in Prairie du Rocher, Illinois, the son of Raymond and Jennie Thiery Bievenue. He died September 28, 2001.

JARROD R. BIRCHLER, Sergeant, enlisted in the Marines December 5, 1997. Jarrod took his Marine combat training at Camp Pendleton, California in January 1998. Then he went to Fort Leonard Wood, Missouri for his (MOS) military occupational specialty. He reached his first duty station at Camp Lejeune, North Carolina in April 1998. He went to Europe with the 26th Marine Expeditionary Unit from July-December 2000.

Sgt. Jarrod R. Birchler

Jarrod returned to Fort Leonard Wood, Missouri for advanced MOS training. He is currently stationed in Okinawa, Japan (since March 2002). Jarrod is with the Support Company, 9th Engineer Support Battalion, 3rd Force Service Support Group Division. He is now detached and in the process of going to Thailand.

His hometown is Sparta, Illinois. He is the son of Gerald D. and Donna J. (Wingerter) Birchler.

GARY J. BIRKE, Specialist 5, served in Vietnam as a rifleman with B Company, 1st/35th Infantry of the 4th Infantry Division near Pleiku, Vietnam and earned a

Spc/5 Gary J. Birke

Combat Infantryman's Badge. He also served as a gunner on the gun truck, "Devil Woman", with the 8th Transportation Group near Qui Nhon.

Gary J. Birke on gun truck. *Gary J. Burke cleaning 50 cal. machine gun.*

He was born July 11, 1949, in Red Bud, Illinois, son of Edward and Vera Laurent Birke. He entered service April 10, 1969 and was discharged April 9, 1971.

JACKIE B. BIVENS, Sergeant, son of Everett F. and M. Lucille Newton Bivens, was born in Fairfield, Illinois on November 23, 1931, enlisted in the USMC February 1951 and was discharged in February 1954.

Sgt. Jackie B. Bivens

He was assigned sea duty from 1951-53, accompanied two Mediterranean cruises, Nova Scotia and Guantanamo Bay, Cuba maneuvers, transferred to Camp Lejeune, North Carolina, 8th Battalion, 2nd Division and 2nd Battalion, 3rd Division, Japan, to beef up forces for signing of peace.

His awards include the Good Conduct, National Defense, Korean Service, United Nations Service and Navy Occupation w/ European Clasp medals.

ROBERT T. BLAIR, U.S. Army WWI, enlisted May 19, 1918 and was discharged January 15, 1919. He served with the 3rd Regiment, Company M. He was born September 18, 1895 in St. Louis, Missouri and lived in Chester. Robert died April 26, 1941 in an auto accident. He is buried in Caledonia Cemetery, Sparta.

FRANCIS J. BLECHLE, First Sergeant, born March 28, 1922, Chester, Illi-

1st/Sgt. Francis Blechle

nois, to Theodore Sr. and Minnie Steinkeuhler Blechle. He was drafted into WWII on February 10, 1943, to become a member of the 29th Division of the 115th Infantry. Blechle trained at Fort Wheeler, Georgia and shipped out to England aboard *Queen Mary* in July, to Scotland, then to England for more training.

In June 1944 he went to Plymouth, England and boarded ships. Once on the ships in the English Channel, they were told in a memo from Supreme Headquarters of the Allied Expeditionary Force, they were headed on a 'Great Crusade' to eliminate Nazi tyranny over people of Europe. Memo signed by Dwight D. Eisenhower. So many ships (as far as you could see) heading out to sea, is a sight he would long remember.

Their platoon hit Omaha Beach about 11:00 a.m. June 6, 1944. They were pinned down the rest of that day and night. They moved ahead the next day, with only one man dead, and the rest thinking they might end up the same way. He was on one side of a hedgerow, Germans on the other side, close enough he could hear them talking. He pulled the pin on a grenade, had his rifle ready, but they didn't come.

Pushed ahead through small towns in Normandy for 13 days. On day 12 a piece of shrapnel hit Blechle in the left leg. He spent two months in a hospital in England, before rejoining his outfit near St. Lo, France. All the men he knew earlier were dead or injured.

On patrols he helped capture Germans and gathered information for intelligence. Went into Brest, southern France, where on day eight, he stepped on a land mine, which blew off the heel of his left foot. He was hospitalized from December 1944 until discharged September 19, 1947. Blechle came home with the Purple Heart w/Oak Leaf Clusters and Silver Star.

He worked from 1948-81 as manager, VFW Club in Chester, Illinois. Remembering D-Day can bring a tear to the eyes of Francis "Specs" Blechle.

JAMES C. BLECHLE, R/4, entered service November 3, 1942 and served with the 296th O.M. Salvage Repair Company in England and France from December 12, 1943 until December 24, 1945. He was

R/4 James C. Blechle

discharged January 12, 1946. James was born November 19, 1919, in Chester, Illinois, the son of Theodore Sr. and Minnie Steinkuhler Blechle.

WALTER C. BODEKER, Private First Class, the oldest of five brothers who served in the military, joined the Army November 10, 1942. He served in Normandy, Northern France, Rhineland and Central Europe, with Detachment A, 1227th M.P. Company. Honorably discharged December 9, 1945.

Pfc. Walter C. Bodeker

Walter was born June 30, 1920, in Walsh, Illinois, the son of Arthur and Beulah Abel Bodeker. After service he came home to Randolph County, worked at International Shoe Company, steel mill in Granite City and retired from Security Hospital in Chester, Illinois, January 1982. He loved to sing, play guitar, boating and camping by the river. Walter died February 1, 1982.

GERALD L. BOLLINGER, Staff Sergeant, U.S. Air Force, 1949-53, served with the 605th TacCon Squadron, 502nd TacCon Group, 14th Air Force. After basic training at Lackland AFB, Texas; Communications Specialist School, Francis E. Warren AFB, Cheyenne, WY; assigned April 1950 to Pope AFB, Fort Bragg, North Carolina.

In September 1950 he landed in Pusan, Korea and was assigned to 5th Air Force Headquarters, furnishing communications and directing air traffic throughout the entire Korean area of conflict.

In February 1952, replacement troops enabled him to rotate back to the United States, to 35th Comm. Squadron Command, Hamilton AFB, California. He was discharged September 11, 1953.

He was born in Ellis Grove, Illinois, the son of Floyd L. and Agnes Marie Bean Bollinger. His immigrant grandfather, Heinrich M. Bollinger, from Zurich Switzerland, was killed in the Revolutionary War, near Lincolnton, North Carolina, February 5, 1776.

EVERETT F. BOLLMAN, Corporal, served in WWII. Had basic training at Fort Bliss, Texas, with 533rd A.W. Battalion. He was then sent overseas. Landed at Casablanca, North Africa in March 1943, then to Sardinia and Tulon, France to Alsace Lorraine area. He joined the 63rd Infantry Division. Had a rough winter, 1944-45, including Battle of the Bulge. Was captured in Heidelberg on March 28, 1945. He and four others were assigned to guard a castle for six days, then back to battle.

Cpl. Everett F. Bollman

Bollman was seriously wounded April 11, 1945 and spent the remainder of his time in a hospital in England and Percy Jones Hospital, Battle Creek Michigan.

He was inducted September 26, 1942 and discharged December 1, 1945. After 31 months overseas and nine months in the hospital, he was discharged with 100% disability.

Everett was born in Welge, Illinois, the son of Fritz and Lena Waltemate Bollman.

TERRY L. BOLLMAN, Commander, U.S. Navy, June 19, 1970-July 1, 1992, was born August 26, 1948 in Chester, Illinois, the son of Fritz and Mabel Rieckenberg Bollman. Terry was commissioned an ensign, Supply Corps, U.S. Navy from NROTC, University of Illinois in 1970.

Terry L. Bollman

He served as supply officer aboard the nuclear missile sub, USS *George C. Marshall* and the guided missile cruiser USS *Wainwright*. Additional duty stations included OICC, Bangkok, Thailand and commander, DCASPRO RCA, Moorestown, New Jersey.

Currently he is the business operations director, DD(X) Program, Northrop Grumman Corporation, Pascagoula, Mississippi.

OLLIE S. BOONE, U.S. Army WWI, enlisted September 25, 1918 and was discharged May 20, 1919. He served with Company A, 416th Service Battalion, Quartermaster Corporation. Ollie was born August 12, 1895 in Sparta, Illinois, the son of William Boone. He died May 30, 1940 from a gunshot wound and is buried in Rosedale Cemetery, Sparta, Illinois.

WILLIAM PAUL BOURNER, U.S. Army, June 1969-June 1971, was born in

William P. Bourner

Sparta, Illinois, September 3, 1949, the son of Robert and Oleta Carlyle Bourner. He was stationed at Fort Leonard Wood, Missouri his full two years in the Army. He worked in the printing plant.

JOHN R. BOWLIN, Seaman 2/c, of Sparta, Illinois, son of Walter and Ella Mae Wilson Bowlin, served in the U.S. Navy during WWII. He was in the military from January 5, 1945 until October 19, 1945. He served aboard the USS *Braruis*, and many sailors aboard the ship were lost during several severe typhoons, in the South Pacific around the Philippines and Luzon.

ROBERT J. BOWLIN, Sergeant, born in Sparta, Illinois, the son of John R. and Wanda Rose Bowlin, entered the service February 20, 1968 and served in Vietnam until January 7, 1969, when he died from wounds received.

Sgt. Robert J. Bowlin

He received the Army Commendation Medal, August 18, 1968; Silver Star, January 1969; also a Silver Star, August 22, 1969; Oak Leaf Cluster, January 7, 1969; along with the Purple Heart. The letter awarding him the Silver Star and Purple Heart, posthumously, reads as follows:

"Specialist 4 Bowlin distinguished himself by heroic actions on August 22, 1968, while serving with Company D, 3rd Battalion, 22nd Infantry in the Republic of Vietnam. Company D came under an intense mortar and rocket attack, followed by a massive communist ground assault. When an enemy rocket struck near Bowlin, seriously wounding many men, with complete disregard to his own safety, he moved through the bullet swept area to aid the wounded soldiers. When the enemy advanced they met heavy fire from Specialist 4 Bowlin's weapon. His valorous actions helped to thwart a large hostile force, and saved several lives. His personal bravery, aggressiveness and devotion to duty are in keeping with the highest tradition of the military service and reflect great credit upon himself, his unit, the 25th Infantry Division and the U.S. Army."

The letter announcing this award was dated January 13, 1969.

GEORGE STEWART BOYD, served in the Army during WWI. He was born in

Wedding of George S. Boyd

Randolph County on April 9, 1893, the son of George W. and Mary Ann Houston Boyd. He died in September 1977 in Sparta, Illinois. He married Ruth Rachel Holmes while still in the Army.

WILLIAM GEORGE BOYD, U.S. Army, HHC Americal Division, Chulai, Republic of Vietnam. George was a college student at SIU-C until enlistment in January 1967. He served in Chulai, Vietnam. Boyd was discharged in October 1969.

William George Boyd

George was born January 13, 1947 at Sparta, Illinois, the son of Clyde Byron and Marion Mae (Fulton) Boyd. After service he was briefly employed by Sparta Printing, until he began working for Illinois Power in Baldwin where he is in his 33rd year of employment.

He is married to the former Jane Wiley. They have one daughter, Rachel and husband, Neil Giffhorn of Waterloo, Illinois.

BILLY JOE BOYSTER SR., Specialist 4, U.S. Army, December 1975-May 1982, was born in Pana, Illinois June 21, 1957, the son of Daniel and Ola Metcalf Boyster. He enlisted, completed his basic training at Fort Jackson, South Carolina and Fort Gordon, Georgia, then to Fort Benning, Georgia for AI training. He served 25 years in the National Guard. He served at Wildflickin, Germany for 20 months with D Company, 54th Engineers Combat and transferred to Fort Ord, California October 1980-May 1982, with A Company, 14th Engineers Combat.

DONALD BRANT, Chief Petty Officer, enlisted into the Navy in 1954. He was discharged in 1958. Donald re-entered the Navy in 1960. He retired in 1979 after 29 years of serving his country. In his duty on a long list of ships, he was a boiler technician and a Navy recruiter for five years in Kansas City, Missouri.

Chief Petty Off. Donald Brant

He has seen the world and became King Neptune in crossing the Equator. Brant was in Vietnam and the Cuba Blockage.

His family includes his wife Phyllis and children: Angela, Jackie and Donald Jr. They all enjoyed a good life as a military family. Donald returned to Chester, Illinois. He worked for the city of Chester, retiring again after 17 years.

DONALD R. BRANT JR., E-6, U.S. Navy, March 21, 1985-June 24, 1994, served in Helicopter Training Squadron 8 and 18, Naval Construction Battalion. Also served as personal leading petty officer for Naval Reserve Center, Chicago and Detroit. He served in Desert Shield/Storm.

Brant earned two Naval Achievement Medals, Expert Rifle and Pistol, Navy Unit Commendation and was Naval Reserve, "Sailor of the Year".

He was born in San Diego, California, June 21, 1965, the son of Donald R. Sr. and Phyllis P. Coleman Brant.

E-6 Donald R. Brant Jr.

HOWARD N. BRANT, was drafted into the U.S. Army, January 13, 1949 and sent to Camp Breckenridge, Kentucky. He was assigned to the 526th Regiment, 101st Division, where he received his basic training. On April 20, 1949, he was sent as a replacement to the Far East Command through Fort Lawton, Washington. He arrived there on June 16, 1949. He was assigned to the 19th Regiment, 24th Division at Beppu, Japan.

Howard N. Brant

When Korean police action was needed the 24th Division was sent to Korea July 2, 1950. He was committed to combat on July 8, 1950. Howard was wounded by shrapnel in Fusan August 11, 1950 and he was transferred to a hospital in Fusan, Korea. From that hospital he was transferred to hospitals in Fukioka, Osaka and then to Tokyo, Japan. On August 29, 1950, Howard was evacuated by air to Fairfield Air Base, then to Great Lakes Illinois Naval Base Hospital. He arrived there September 1, 1950. He was discharged from this hospital for active duty March 9, 1951 and he was assigned to 5016th ASU at Fort Riley, Kansas.

Howard was sent to Camp Atterbury, Indiana on April 16, 1951 where he spent time on light duty or was in the hospital until he received a Honorable medical discharge on November 30, 1951. He is a native of Chester, Illinois.

BRANT BROTHERS, Four sets of brothers aboard the guided missile destroyer *Barney* (DDG-6) make an unusual lineup as they salute the officer-of-the-deck. It is believed to be the largest collection of brothers attached to one ship during peacetime.

Brant Brothers

From left they are: Chief Machinist Mate Roland E. Brant, age 36; Boilerman 2/c Donald R. Brant, 27; Seaman Richard D. Brant, 21. Others are Colonna, Melton and Munroe brothers. The Brant brothers are natives of Chester, Illinois. Chief Brant a veteran of 16 years, youngest brother, Richard, three years service, Donald a veteran of nine years, has been aboard 10 months.

FREDRICK CHARLES BREITHAUPT, Private, Civil War, served in the 5th Regiment of Illinois Cavalry Volunteers, Company K. He enlisted September 6, 1861, at Sparta, Illinois, at age 19. His parents were Heinrich Dietrich Wilhelm and Catharina Maria Mehring Breithaupt. Born February 8, 1839, near Eilvese, Hanover, Germany, he immigrated to the United States, arriving here November 20, 1858.

Pvt. Fredrick C. Breithaupt

After enlistment, he joined Captain Farnan's Company K at Camp Butler, Illinois, November 21, 1861. On March 3, 1862, the 5th Cavalry left St. Louis for Pilot Knob, Missouri. A march was then made to Doniphan, and on April 1, they engaged in a skirmish in which they captured the Confederate camp. April 17 the unit moved to Pocahontas, Arkansas, and on June 27 began a march to the Mississippi River. They joined General Curtis at Jacksonport on the 29th, and arrived in Helena, Arkansas on July 13.

While Charles was ill during October and November of 1862, their unit was attacked and 78 men were captured. Injured in an accident, taking care of cavalry horses May 15, 1863, he spent time in several hospitals, and on August 1, 1863, he was transferred to Company B, 5th Regiment Veteran Reserve Corps, by General Order #289. He was discharged November 22, 1864.

After living in Kansas during the 1870s, in 1883 he purchased 160 acres near New Palestine in Randolph County, and lived there until his death, June 11, 1925. He is buried in New Palestine Cemetery.

CLINTON F. BREMER, Electrician Mate 1/c V6, was in WWII December 15, 1942 until April 9, 1946. After boot camp and Service School at Great Lakes Naval Center, had special training at USN. Algonac, Michigan on magnetic compass adjustment. Spent 26 months in New Orleans, adjusting compasses on various ships that came into port, then at Higgins shipyard on landing crafts that were being built. From New Orleans, to Fleet Service School, Norfolk, Virginia for training on gyro compasses, then assigned to USS *Vixen*, flagship of Atlantic Fleet. Clinton was discharged April 9, 1946, at St. Louis, Missouri. He was born March 4, 1921 the son of Richard C. and Anna L. Albert Bremer.

ALLEN D. BRENNING, E-5, served with the 4th Infantry Division in the Central Highlands. He was awarded the Bronze Star for valor on two separate occasions. While serving in Cambodia, he was awarded the Silver Star for gallantry in action. Al was awarded the Purple Heart for wounds received on June 22, 1970.

He spent the remaining time in service as the range instructor at Fort Leonard Wood, Missouri. Al was with Company C, 1st of the 12, 4th Infantry Division.

E-5 Allen D. Brenning

Al was born July 13, 1949 in Chester, Illinois, the son of Albert and Oneta (Eggemeyer) Brenning.

ELMER L. BRENNING, Corporal, was drafted then he enlisted for 18 months. From March 1946 until September 1947 he served at Elgin Field, Florida, with the First Experimental Guided Missiles Group on V2 rockets. He had to make out the morning reports and also worked in technical supply. He saw two rockets launched and one rocket burned out.

Cpl. Elmer L. Brenning

His duty was also to send reports to Washington and one on the Sound Barrier being broken. They also had these V2 rockets in Texas. He believes this is the UFO that landed in Roswell, New Mexico, because it all happened at the same time.

After returning home he worked on the family farm, retired from General Motors after 30 years. He was born October 3, 1927 in St. Louis, Missouri to __ Brenning and __ Harsman.

ALFRED O. BROCKMEYER, Technician Fifth Grade, served in the Army during WWII. He had 12 weeks training in Nebraska, then to Hawaii, as an automotive mechanic. He was inducted in November 1942 and discharged in December 1945.

Alfred is a member of American Legion, Steeleville and V.F.W. Post in Chester. He is a lifelong member of St. Paul's

T/5 Alfred O. Brockmeyer

Lutheran Church, Wine Hill. A flag pole and flag were put in St. Paul cemetery in memory of him and in honor of all veterans. His parents were Fritz P. and Anna Dierks Brockmeyer.

FRITZ E. BROCKMEYER, Private First Class, born August 17, 1921, in Steeleville, Illinois, the son of Fritz and Anna Dierks Brockmeyer. He enlisted June 14, 1944 in the U.S. Army in Chicago. Boot

Pvt. 1st/c Fritz E. Brockmeyer

camp at Camp Pendleton, California, then to Guam invasion and Battle of Iwo Jima. He served with the 3rd Marine Division during WWII. He was wounded at Iwo Jima and sent to a hospital in Hawaii. He was there when the war ended. Fritz was discharged June 9, 1946. He died September 12, 1983.

IRWIN C. BROCKMEYER, Corporal, U.S. Army, served during the Korean

Cpl. Irwin C. Brockmeyer

conflict from January 1952-December 1953. He is the son of Fritz P. and Anna Dierks Brockmeyer Sr. of Steeleville, Illinois. After basic training he served in Germany with the Medical Detachment Artillery. He is a member of the American Legion, Steeleville; VFW, Chester, Illinois; and St. Mark Lutheran Church, Steeleville.

WILLIAM BROCKMEYER SR., Private, served two enlistments in the Union Army during the Civil War. He enlisted August 13, 1861 and was discharged December 31, 1863. He re-enlisted January 1, 1864 and was discharged December 31, 1866.

Pvt. William Brockmeyer Sr.

William was born October 14, 1839, in Germany. He came to the United States in 1861, just as the war began. He immediately joined the Army to fight for his adopted country, with Company I, Illinois Infantry. He was hospitalized in Georgia during his second enlistment. He came back to Steeleville, Illinois, to be a farmer.

William died suddenly July 12, 1907 of a heart attack at home. Soldiers who had known him came long distances to pay their respects. There were 121 horse-drawn wagons in the funeral possession from the home to St. Paul's Church at Wine Hill.

DAVID O. BROWN, Corporal, son of John C. and Mary Short Brown, served in France during WWI. He returned to Percy, Illinois and became a partner with his brother, Richard Lee Brown, in dry goods store.

SPENCER F. "BUS" BROWN, Lieutenant, served in both WWII, 1945-46 and the Korean War, 1952-53, a construction battalion. He received training at Great Lakes Naval Center and Davisville, Rhode Island. He was on Kwajalein, in the

Lt. Spencer F. Brown

Marshall Islands, also at Port Hueneme and Naval Air Station, Memphis, Tennessee. Bus was born December 4, 1919 in New York City, NY. He is the son of W.C. and Jennie Smith Brown.

W. JOHN BROWN, 1st Lieutenant, born in Sparta, Illinois May 30, 1922, served during WWII, at Headquarters, Island Communications, Iwo Jima, in the Pacific. He was in cargo loading-off shore operations, and saw action in the battles of Iwo Jima and Saipan. Entered the service in December 1942 and was discharged in June 1955. His parents are J. Stanley and Geneva Stamm Brown.

GERALD M. BRUNHOFER, Corporal, U.S. Army, born July 17, 1931 in Evansville, Illinois, the son of Max

Cpl. Gerald M. Brunhofer in Alps

Brunhofer and Estelle, nee Brauer, served during the Korean Conflict from May 1952-April 1954, with C Company, 1st Battalion, 351st Infantry. He served 19 months in Trieste, Italy, with occupation forces, British, French and Yugoslav troops.

CHARLES L. BUATTE, Staff Sergeant, served in WWII with Squadron A, 9 3505th AAF Bu. as a gunner on B-17, flying 13 missions. He was shot down in Hamburg, Germany in 1944. He was wounded in his left leg. Charles was a

S/Sgt. Charles L. Buatte

POW for five months. He entered the service February 19, 1943 and was discharged September 24, 1945, from Scott AFB, Illinois. Charles, the son of Joe and Bessie Branom Buatte, was born May 31, 1923 in Sparta, Illinois. He retired from the Corps of Engineers in 1985.

DAVE BUATTE, Specialist 4, U.S. Army, 1965-67, was born in Chester, Illinois, the son of Charles and Grace

Spec/4 Dave Buatte

Jungewaelter Buatte. He was drafted, took basic training at Fort Leonard Wood, Missouri, and served a tour in Korea, occupational duty. After discharge, works for Corps of Engineers and will retire in 2004. He lives now in Bethalto, Illinois.

PHIL BUATTE, Private First Class, was drafted into the Army in October 1966.

Pvt. 1st/c Phil Buatte

Fort Leonard Wood, Missouri is where he took his basic training. Phil served in Vietnam from 1966-68. Chester, Illinois is Phil's hometown. His parents are Charles and Grace (Jungewaelter) Buatte. Phil works as a heavy equipment operator and lives in Richmond, Virginia.

EARL LOUIS BUECKMAN, Staff Sergeant, was inducted into the Army June 23, 1942, to serve in WWII. He served in Northern France, Rhineland, Central Europe and Battle of Bulge, with Battery C, 95th Division, 920th Field Artillery, Patton's 3rd Army.

S/Sgt. Earl L. Bueckman

Bueckman Brothers

Washing his car December 7, 1941, he heard news of Pearl Harbor on the radio. This changed his life for the next four years. The troop train he was traveling on from the Mojave Desert in California to final training in Pennsylvania and West Virginia, came through Chester, to give him a glimpse of his hometown.

He spent a year overseas before being discharged November 21, 1945. He was born in Chester, Illinois, May 15, 1918, to Henry and Sara Hartman Bueckman. Returning home he worked on the railroad, as a carpenter, and dairy farming. Bueckman died June 18, 1987 and is buried in Mount Hope Cemetery, Perryville, Missouri.

MELVIN W. BUECKMAN, Corporal, U.S. Army, son of Omer and Marga-

Melvin Bueckman in Japan

ret Barger Bueckman, born July 16, 1928 in Chester, Illinois. He served with the 24th M.P. Company, 24th Infantry Division in Korea. This division was first to enter Korea. In addition to fighting North Koreans and Chinese, the weather was about 120° in the summer and 30° below in the winter. He participated in "April Offensive", "Iron Triangle", "Nomad" and "Pipedream" battles. Upon return to the United States, he was assigned to be under four Atomic tests at Nevada Test Sight.

ORVILLE C. BUECKMAN, Carpenter's Mate 2/c, V-6 USNR, served in the CBs during WWII. He enlisted on August 6, 1943 and was stationed in the

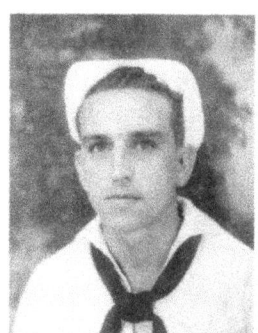
C.M. 2nd/c Orville C. Bueckman

Pacific, U.S. Fleet Hospital 107 in New Caledonia. He was born in Chester, Illinois, September 12, 1912, the son of Henry and Sara Hartman Bueckman. After discharge on October 16, 1945 he returned to Chester, to pursue a lifelong career as a carpenter. Bueckman died September 29, 2001 and is buried in St. John's Lutheran Cemetery in Chester.

WILLIAM J. BUESCHER, Private, U.S. Army, WWI, Company G, 22nd Engineers, June 24, 1918-July 16, 1919. He was born in Steeleville, Illinois, the son of William and __ Redecker Buescher. He

Pvt. William J. Buescher

was a farmer. William enlisted at 22 years of age.

CHRISTIAN H. BUHRMESTER, Private, enlisted in the service for the Civil War, August 27, 1861, with Captain Ludwig, at Red Bud, Illinois. He re-enlisted, was mustered in by Captain Pucher, on September 3, 1861, at Camp Butler, Illinois, as a veteran, to muster out November 4, 1865, at Nashville, TN. He used his own horse and equipment, which he lost at Burnsville, Mississippi, September 16, 1862, and another horse, April 19, 1863, at Pontotoc, Mississippi. He served with Company M, 7th Illinois Cavalry. Christian was born November 13, 1842 in Hille, Germany and died December 28, 1894. He is buried in Trinity Lutheran Cemetery in Red Bud, Illinois.

CHRISTIAN BURBES, Private, served in the Civil War, December 4, 1864 until mustered out August 31, 1865, at Pilot Knob, Missouri. He served with Company L, 13th Cavalry, Illinois Regiment. Christian was born in Prussia. He resided in Holland, Illinois and Chester, Illinois.

He was married to Mary Chardong, December 19, 1865, in Chester, Illinois. His wife filed for a pension, January 21, 1872, as an invalid and again November 4, 1889 as a widow. His parents' names are unknown, but he gave his age as 46, in the 1880 census. He died December 30, 1882 and is buried in Evergreen Cemetery in Chester, Illinois.

JOHN WARREN BURKE, Sergeant, born in Ontario County, New York on November 3, 1840, to Dennis John and Mary Ellen O'Brien Burke, came via Iowa, Minnesota and Missouri to Randolph County, Illinois where he enlisted in the Civil War the 10th of September, 1861 at Sparta, Illinois. He was assigned to Company K,

5th Illinois Cavalry, and in the summer of 1862, they became a part of the Army of the Southwest, under General Curtis, and a part of Steele's Division reaching Helena, Arkansas in July.

From there they went to Vicksburg, Mississippi, and during the siege was a part of Grant's forces that held the lines from Hayne's Bluff to Black River against General Joseph E. Johnston. He re-enlisted as a veteran volunteer January 1, 1864, and after a 30 day furlough to Randolph County, re-joined his company at Vicksburg.

After spending about a year in various camps in Tennessee, on July 10, 1864, they were ordered to Alexandria, Louisiana, and from there was part of the cavalry that marched into Texas under General Custer. In early October, at Hempstead, Texas, the regiment received orders to be mustered out. Turning over horses, arms and equipment, they came home by way of Galveston, New Orleans, St. Louis to Springfield, Illinois, where they were discharged at Camp Butler on October 27, 1865.

HARLAN L. BURMESTER, Sergeant, U.S. Army Reserves, June 20, 1957-May 1, 1963, born September 23, 1937, the son of Victor and Melba Schnepel

Sgt. Harlen Burmester

Brumester. He trained at Fort Leonard Wood, Missouri and Fort Polk, Louisiana, then weekly training at Belleville, Illinois. Two weeks every year he went to Camp McCoy, Wisconsin. He was discharged in 1963.

WILLIAM LEWIS BURRIS, Private, Civil War, August 19, 1862-July 22, 1865, served with the 125th Illinois Volunteer Infantry. Shortly after enlistment, he contracted typhoid fever and was hospitalized in New Albany, Indiana in February 1864. He rejoined his regiment in Nashville, Tennessee. Cutting firewood, he cut the inside of his foot with an ax and never fully recovered from this accident. He was born April 7, 1837 in Barren County, Kentucky, the son of Zebedee D. and Mary/Polly Goodwin Burris. He died April 27, 1899 in Sparta, Illinois.

BRANDON L. BURTON, HM2, U.S. Navy, December 1993-December 2002, born June 9, 1969 in Watweka, Illinois, the son of Larry A. and Gaye Irwin Burton. Brandon enlisted in the Navy in 1993, attended Hospitalman "A" School in 1994, Field Medical School in 1996 and Surgical Technician "C" School in 1996.

HM 2 Brandon L. Burton

He was assigned to Balboa Hospital, San Diego, California, the Naval Hospital in Guantanamo Bay, Cuba 1996-99. He served aboard the USS *Austin*, LPD in 2000, with the 26th MEU. The remainder of his enlistment, he spent at Camp Lejeune, North Carolina, with the Medical Battalion Clinic and he instructed Special Marine Units in hand to hand combat. He was discharged in 2002. He now is a martial arts instructor and reality fighting competitor.

JOHN BUTLER, Private, born January 21, 1894, at Rockwood, Illinois, the son of James and Elizabeth Moore Butler, entered service at Chester, Illinois on May 27, 1918, and served in the 72nd Company, 18th Battalion, Infantry Replacement and the 137th Field Artillery, 38th Division, Training Troops, until December 26, 1918, when he was discharged at Camp Grant, Illinois. He died March 3, 1939 and is buried in Pleasant Ridge Cemetery near Rockwood, Illinois.

ROBERT F. BUTLER, Sergeant, joined the Merchant Marines at the beginning of WWII. He served aboard the USS *George Bandcroft*. Discharged only a short time, he was drafted in January 1945 and sent

Sgt. Robert F. Butler

to the Asiatic Pacific Theatre. He was in the Liberation of Philippines, in Company B, 727th Amphibian Tractor Battalion. Discharged August 7, 1946.

Butler was born in Chester, Illinois, the son of William F. and Abigale L. Brown Butler. He was the great-great-grandson of Revolutionary soldier, John Clendenin, the grandson of Civil War soldier, Sealsberry Brown and the nephew of WWI veteran George A. Murer.

CHARLES FREDERICK CAMPBELL, Major, USAF, was born May 27, 1929, in Morristown, New Jersey, the son of Charles W. Campbell and Laura R. nee Horn. He enlisted in the U.S. Air Force as an airman on November 11, 1950, and taught electronics at Keesler AFB, Mississippi. He did pilot training in 1952 at Stallings AB, Kinston, North Carolina; Perrin AFB, Texas; Foster AFB, Texas; and gunnery at Nellis AFB, Nevada.

Left: Charles Fred Campbell. Right: Maj. Charles F. Campbell (pilot, bottom step).

In 1953 he flew F-86s and F-94Cs in 27th FIS at Griffiss AFB, New York. In 1955 he flew F-89Ds at Elmendorf AFB, Alaska in 66th FIS until October 1957. Campbell flew B-47s at Plattsburg AFB, New York from December 1958 to May 1964 in the 528th and 531st Bomb Squadrons, then served as 380th Bomb Wing aircraft performance officer until July 1965.

Transferred to Turner AFB, Georgia in 1965 as 484th Bomb Wing performance officer for B-52s. Served in 4133rd Provisional Bomb Wing on Anderson AFB, Guam while our bombers were involved over Vietnam until 1967. Then transferred to SAC Headquarters, Offutt AFB, Nebraska where he served in the Directorate of Operations Plans until retirement in June 1971.

After retirement he completed seminary work at Concordia Theological Seminary, Springfield, Illinois and served as a pastor of St. John Lutheran Church, Chester, Illinois from 1975 to retirement in 1994.

CRAIG FREDERICK CAMPBELL, Lieutenant Colonel, born August 7, 1959, at Pittsburg AFB, New York. Was commissioned in 1983, command architect, Dir. Civil Engineer, Headquarters MAC, Scott AFB, Illinois; 1986, Air Force regional engineer, Continental European Region, Comiso, Italy; 1987, branch architect, 36th Civil Engineer Squadron, Bitburg AB, Germany; later chief of Construction Management.

Lt. Col. Craig Campbell

Completed master of public administration degree in 1990 and assigned as chief of Construction Management, Hurlburt Field, Florida until 1994. Then Environmental Compliance Program manager, Langley AFB, Virginia and chief of Southwest Asia Facility Requirements Team and executive officer, then squadron commander 20th Civil Engineer Squadron.

2001-02, Scott AFB, Illinois as deputy chief of Operation Division Directorate of Civil Engineering, Headquarters Air Mobility Command and deputy director of AMC Contingency Support Staff for Worldwide Operation. Served with Civil Engineer Chief of Joint Task Force, Southwest Asia during "Operation Enduring Freedom."

In June 2002, he assumed command of the 796th Civil Engineer Squadron at Elgin AFB, Florida. In December 2002, he began tour as Civil Engineer Deputy of Central Air Forces at Prince Sultan AB, Saudi Arabia, overseeing engineering movements to "Operation Southern Watch" and continuing "Operation Enduring Freedom" and planning future action.

Campbell is the son of Charles F. and June L. Kroutter Campbell of Chester, Illinois.

KENNETH D. CAMPBELL, Aviation Electronics Technician Mate 2/c, entered the Navy in WWII, April 1944. He served at Naval Air Station, Minneapolis, Minnesota as line maintenance PB fory.

T. Mate 2/c Kenneth D. Campbell

Discharged at Shelton, Virginia in 1946, he attended college to become a DVD, where he followed that occupation until retirement.

Kenneth was born September 21, 1922, in Coulterville, Illinois, the son of Verne and Blanche Hemphill Campbell. He died November 27, 1998 in Evansville, Wisconsin.

SAMUEL CAMPBELL, Private, served in the Black Hawk War under J. Briggs, during 1831 and 1832. He had come to the Evansville, Illinois area in 1807, with his parents, John and Nancy Campbell, from Abbeville, South Carolina. His death occurred in 1856 with burial in Kelly Cemetery, Evansville, Illinois.

CARL L. CARAWAY, Technical Sergeant, born May 21, 1915, in Eldorado, Illinois, served in WWII from 1940 until 1945. He was in the CCCs and enlisted in the Army for one year, then caught in the draft and stayed until the end. He saw action in the Battle of the Bulge. He retired from Menard Prison in Chester, Illinois. Carl passed away September 9, 1988.

T/Sgt. Carl L. Caraway

WILLIAM LOUIS CARLYLE, Private First Class, was with Electric Combat Engineers during WWII, and was in the Battle of the Bulge, where his arm was broken. He was in a hospital in Reims on V-E Day. Later sent to Percy Jones Hospital in Battle Creek, Michigan. He lost his left arm above the elbow. He entered service in September 1942 and was discharged in August 1945. Carlyle was born on Kaskaskia Island, January 11, 1925. His parents are William Oscar and __ Buatte.

THOMAS CARRICO, grandfather of Silas Hamilton of Chester, Illinois, was born in Virdin, Illinois in 1825. He enlisted in the Union Army August 13, 1862 and died March 14, 1863, in Union hospital in Cornith, Mississippi of dysentery, a disease which killed thousands of Civil War soldiers. His military career lasted only six months and a few days.

Thomas Carrico

Two grandsons, James Lyle and Oscar Myron Hamilton, both served in WWII. Oscar M. enlisted on June 6, 1941. After reaching rank of staff sergeant he entered Officers Candidate School in August 1942, getting a second lieutenant commission. He was in jungle fighting in New Guinea and the Philippines in 1944-45, then to

1st Lt. Oscar M. Hamilton

Japan. Stayed in Reserves another 19 years, leaving in 1965 with rank of major. He has Combat Infantryman Badge and a Bronze Star.

James Lyle was in Company A, 1687th Engineer Battalion, on the island of Aruba from February 1942-December 1943.

WILLIS C. CARTER JR., Seaman 1/c, served as clerk and sonorman 3/c aboard USS *Sylph* (PV-12) and USS *Burke* (APD-65) from September 21, 1943 to September 1944, during WWII. He was born October 17, 1926, in Coulterville, Illinois, the son of Willis and __ Purdy Carter. Awards received were WWII Victory Ribbon and American Area Ribbon.

Seaman 1st/c Willis C. Carter

DONALD S. CASETTA, Corporal, U.S. Army, 1951-1953. After basic training at Camp Stewart, Georgia, he was assigned to Fort Meade, MD, serving there until his discharge. He was born October 8, 1929 in Pinckneyville, Illinois, the son of Steve and Ella Hoelscher Casetta. He died April 21, 1982 and is buried at St. Mary's Catholic Cemetery, Chester, Illinois.

STEVE CASETTA, Private, born March 26, 1891, in Coal City, Illinois, entered WWI in June 1918 and served in France with the 96th Casual Company. He was discharged in May 1919 and returned to farming. Enlisted in WWII, served as a mechanic with Traveling Automotive Technicians. He again returned to farming near Chester, Illinois when discharged from WWII. The son of Donizio and Rosa Casetta, he died December 7, 1948, an appropriate day for an old soldier to die on.

JOHN BOYD CASHION, Corporal, born in Perry County, Missouri, on September 21, 1838, to Robert and Jane Clifton Cashion. He served in the 5th Illinois Cavalry, Company K of the Civil War, from September 10, 1861 until January 24, 1864. Participated in battles at Vicksburg, Mechanicsburg, Louisiana and Mississippi.

Cpl. John Boyd Cashion

After mustering out of service at Springfield, Illinois, he served in the Veterans Reserve Corps. Cashion died in Rockwood, Illinois, June 23, 1905. His brother, Ferdinand, entered the service at the same time, was wounded, and transferred out on May 16, 1864. Both are buried in Ebenezer Cemetery near Rockwood, Illinois.

ARTHUR H. CASTENS, Corporal, U.S. Army, October 2, 1952-September 4,

Arthur H. Castens (Germany)

1954, served with 291st Heavy Equipment Engineers, was drafted while working at the rock quarry. He was born December 12, 1928 in Campbell Hill, Illinois, the son of William and Ida Otten Castens.

IVAN L. CASTENS, Corporal, served in Korea in Company D, 135th Engineer Combat Battalion of the 44th Infantry Division from April 1951 until April 1953. He received basic training at Fort Leonard Wood, Missouri, then was assigned to Camp Cook, California, and from there to Fort Lewis, Washington, as post engineers. Ivan was born in Steeleville, Illinois. He was the son of Edith Castens.

PAUL W. CASTENS, Seaman 1/c, enlisted in the Coast Guard on May 4, 1942. He served as ship's cook aboard U.S. Coast Guard cutters *Goldenrod* and *Lantana*, with District Headquarters in St. Louis, Missouri during WWII. He was discharged October 15, 1945, and returned to Steeleville, Illinois.

Seaman 1st/c Paul W. Castens

He owned Castens Insurance Agency. Paul was born September 11, 1912, in Campbell Hill, Illinois, the son of Herman C. and Mary Castens. He died December 30, 1987.

JAMES D. CHANDLER, Specialist 5, U.S. Army, July 1967-July 1969, served with Company B, 65th Engineer Battal-

Spec/5 James D. Chandler

ion, 25th Infantry Division in Vietnam. He was born November 28, 1947 in Welge,

Illinois, the son of James Clyde and Esther Wisdom Chandler. He married Anita Bendorf and had two sons, Jimmy and Bret. He owned and operated Chandler Oil Company before his death May 10, 1996.

RALPH THOMAS CHAPMAN, E-4, enlisted into the Air Force June 14, 1964. Took his basic training at Lackland AFB. Then was stationed with the 18th Tactical Fighter Wing at Kadena AFB, Okinawa, as a warehousing specialist in supply for 18 months. He served in Vietnam.

E-4 Ralph T. Champman

He was then sent to Vandeburg AFB, California were he was assigned to 4392nd Strategic Air Command for 26 months. After his discharge June 15, 1968, he joined Operating Engineers Local 520 which is his present employment. He was born August 17, 1946 at Christian Welfare Hospital, East St. Louis, Illinois, the son of Ralph Lloyd and Isabelle (Caskey) Chapman.

ALBERT HAROLD CHOATE, Corporal, U.S. Army, was drafted in June 1950. He did his basic training at Fort Leonard

Cpl. Albert H. Choate

Wood, Missouri. He served in the Korean Conflict and was discharged from Fort Sheridan, Illinois in September 1952. Returning home, he farmed for a time and later, he drove a truck. His parents were Lawrence and Lelia Smith Choate.

GEORGE F. CHOATE, USMC, enlisted January 11, 1981. Completed boot camp at San Diego MCRD, California. He

George F. Choate

was stationed in Okinawa/Japan for a year and discharged in June 1984. He was born August 19, 1963 in Chester, Illinois, the son of Albert Harold and Rosalee Draves Choate.

JACK R. CHOATE, Corporal, born in Jackson County on December 23, 1932, served in Korea. The son of Lawrence and Lelia Smith Choate, he made his home in

Cpl. Jack R. Choate

Chester, Illinois after his time in service. He was a member of both the VFW and American Legion. These organizations provided a color guard at his funeral service, May 16, 1996. Burial was in Evergreen Cemetery in Chester, Illinois.

JASON DALE CHOATE, E/4 Senior Airman, enlisted in the Air Force in 1996.

E/4 Airman Jason D. Choate

He was with the 30th Transportation Squadron at Camp Vandenberg, California. Choate was discharged March 15, 2000. The son of Dale and Jean Allen Choate, he now lives in Steeleville, Illinois, with his wife and three children. He works at Chester Mental Health.

LINDA JEAN CHOATE, E-3 seaman, daughter of Dale and Jean Allen Choate, enlisted in the Navy October 9, 1995. Stationed in San Diego, California, she was an illustrative draftsman with the Navy Seabees. She was discharged in October 1998.

TAVIS MICHAEL CHOATE, Staff Sergeant, U.S. Army, enlisted on September 22, 1997 and completed basic training at Fort Leonard Wood, Missouri. Proceeded to Army Intelligence School at Fort Huachuca, Arizona. Then proceeded to Fort Stewart, Georgia in June 1998 and served as intelligence analyst.

S/Sgt. Tavis M. Choate

He has served at Fort Polk, Louisiana; National Training Center, Fort Irwin, California; Operation Joint Forge NATO, Bosnia Herzegovina; Fort Hood, Texas; Molesworth AFB, England; and Kuwait. He is currently in the Army. Tavis was born September 26, 1979 in Chester, Illinois, the son of Harold Alan and Tina J. Schultz Choate.

ALLEN A. CHUNN, Specialist 4, U.S. Army, October 31, 1957-October 30, 1959, was born in Evansville, Illinois on June 10, 1933, the son of Jesse and Della Griffith Chunn. After basic training at Fort Leonard Wood, Missouri, went to Fort Sill, OK, followed by Fort McClellan, Alabama for CBR training.

He was transferred to Baskins, Germany for 16 months. Returning to the States, he was transferred to Reserves for

Sp/4 Allen A. Chunn

six years. He worked in construction for Armco Steel Corporation, 20 years, then self-employed. He now lives in Hughes Springs, Texas.

ALLAN D. CHUNN, USN, October 12, 1972-June 30, 1993, was born in Sparta, Illinois on March 22, 1953, the son of Allen A. and Doris J. Bumann Chunn. As an aviation structural mechanic he served in several squadrons, ashore and afloat.

Allan D. Chunn

He served on the USS *Seattle* AOE-3; USS *Kitty Hawk* CV-63; and USS *Abraham Lincoln* CVN-72. Chunn served ashore at NAS Whiting Field, NAS Norfolk, NAS Pensacola, Florida, NAS Whidbey Island and NAS Lenmoore. He served in Operation Desert Storm. Allan retired June 30, 1993.

HERBERT L. CHUNN, Technician Fifth Grade, was born February 7, 1921,

T/5 Herbert L. Chunn

in Grantsburg, Illinois to Jesse and Della Griffith Chunn, He entered WWII on December 15, 1942, and was a truck driver delivering supplies to front line with 754th Tank Battalion. During the battle of Luzon, he met his brother, Wayne. He was on several islands during the Pacific Campaign, including North Solomons. Chunn was awarded two Bronze Stars, Good Conduct Medal and Meritorious Service Award. He was discharged December 26, 1945. Chunn died May 17, 1995.

IRA VICTOR CHUNN, Private First Class, entered the service in WWII on February 19, 1943, with U.S. Army Air Force. A fire fighter in China, India, Burma Theatre, he participated in air offensive of Japan, China, East Indies, India and Burma, with the 1505th AAF Base Unit.

Pfc. Ira Victor Chunn

Chunn received the Meritorious Unit Award, Victory Medal WWII, Good Conduct Medal, Distinguished Unit Badge, American Theatre Ribbon, Asiatic-Pacific Ribbon w/4 Bronze Stars and Soldier's Medal for pulling crew out of burning airplane that crashed. He was discharged on November 15, 1945.

He died February 7, 1985. Chunn was born in East Prairie, Missouri on March 22, 1923. He was the son of Jesse and Della Griffith Chunn.

JAMES ROBERT CHUNN, Sergeant First Class, U.S. Army, was born April 6, 1930 at East Prairie, Missouri, the son of Jesse and Della Griffith Chunn. He served from July 1948 to May 30, 1950, then in active Reserves until February 1953. Basic training and leadership at Fort Knox, Kentucky, he served in American Graves Registration at Granville and St. Pair, France, (Normandy) area. Transferred to Cherbourg France. He served with the

Sgt. 1st/c James Robert Chunn

102nd Infantry, active Reserve, during the Korean War.

JOSEPH A. CHUNN, First Sergeant, was born at Grantsburg, Illinois, on September 5, 1915, the son of Jesse and Della Griffith Chunn. He enlisted in the Army on April 18, 1942, during WWII. He served

1st/Sgt. Joseph A. Chunn

with the 817th Tank Destroyer Battalion in Northern France, Ardennes, Rhineland and Central Europe. Arrived at Omaha Beach in July 1944. He served as chief supply first sergeant. Chunn was wounded in the Battle of the Bulge in Belgium. He was in O'Reilly General Hospital until discharged August 14, 1946, with EAME Theatre Ribbon w/4 Bronze Stars, Good Conduct Medal and American Theatre Ribbon. Chunn died April 1, 1988.

MYRON L. CHUNN, Specialist 4, U.S. Army, served active duty from July 1, 1958-June 20, 1960; Reserves June 30, 1964.

Spec-4 Myron L. Chunn

He received basic training at Fort Leonard Wood, Missouri. Served at Fort Riley, Kansas and Augsburg, Germany. He was born November 9, 1935 in Evansville, Illinois, the son of Jesse and Della Griffith Chunn.

SYLVESTER WAYNE "WAYNE" CHUNN, Sergeant, served in WWII on Luzon in the Philippines (where he met his brother, Don) and on Guadalcanal with Company G, 152nd Infantry.

Sgt. Sylvester W. Chunn

He entered service on December 6, 1944 at Chicago, Illinois and was discharged on November 7, 1946 at Fort Sheridan, with Bronze Star, Asiatic-Pacific Theatre Ribbon w/Bronze Star, Victory Medal and Good Conduct Medal.

Wayne was born in East Prairie, Missouri on February 6, 1926, the son of Jesse and Della Griffith Chunn. Wayne died August 5, 1974.

CHARLES ERVIN CLELAND, Private, was inducted into WWI October 5, 1917. He served in Company D, 333rd Infantry, 84th Division, fighting in the trenches on the Verdun front in Meuse-

Pvt. Charles E. Cleland

Argonne, September 26-October 8, 1918. Cleland was captured by Germans and was a prisoner of war for some time. He was discharged May 29, 1919. Cleland was born in Cutler, November 30, 1893, the son of Robert James and Mary Margaret Ervin Cleland. He died November 10, 1973.

HARRY BURNS CLENDENIN, Private, born in Rockwood, Illinois, April 25, 1892, to Harvey and Maggie Morgan Clendenin, served in WWI in the Army Infantry, 311th Ambulance Company from April 29, 1918 until discharged June 5, 1919. He was in battles of St. Mihiel and Meuse-Argonne in France. He died March 27, 1986 and is buried in Ebenezer Cemetery near Rockwood, Illinois.

HARVEY CLENDENIN JR., Second Lieutenant, was born in Rockwood, Illinois, September 17, 1838, the son of Harvey and Lourancy Barber Clendenin. He served with the Union Forces in Company I, 80th Illinois Infantry, which was organized in Rockwood (Liberty), Illinois, July 28, 1862.

Mustered into service at Centralia, Illinois, August 15, 1862. He was appointed second lieutenant at Blue Springs, Tennessee, April 8, 1864. He suffered a shoulder wound on July 4, 1864 but died from typhoid fever on July 19, 1864, near Marietta, Georgia. After his body was brought home, he was buried in Ebenezer Cemetery, near Rockwood, Illinois.

JAMES C. CLENDENIN, Private, served in Company K, 5th Illinois Infantry. He is buried in Ebenezer Cemetery, near Rockwood.

MOSES WALTER CLENDENIN, First Sergeant, was a doctor in the Civil War. He served in Company A, 80th Illinois Infantry and was at Marietta, Georgia when Harvey Clendenin died. He was the son of John Heard and Mary Elizabeth Vickers Clendenin. He died May 30, 1864, and is buried alongside his wife, Lydia Wagoner, in the Reid Cemetery in Rockwood, Illinois.

FLORA B. CLEVENGER, Private First Class, enlisted in the Marine Corps

Pfc. Flora B. Clevenger

November 9, 1944, in Detroit, Michigan. Had boot training at Camp LeJeune, North Carolina, then stationed at Parris Island, South Carolina 1945-46. She was Navy personnel and assistant correspondence clerk for Service Company, Post Troops, Marine Barracks, during WWII. Flora was discharged May 2, 1946. She is the daughter of Robert and __ Travis Dyer. She was born July 10, 1923.

GARY L. CLEVENGER, Major, USAF, January 19, 1970-1990, was born in Red Bud, Illinois, November 19, 1946, the son of James L. and Shirley C. Andrews Clevenger. Gary served in the U.S. Air

Maj. Gary L. Clevenger

Force for 20 years as a comptroller, auditor, budget officer and financial officer. Retiring as a major, he worked for Crosswinds Youth Services in Florida. At the time of his death, on October 11, 2001, he was vice president of Business, Finance and Project Management.

HOMER LEE CLEVENGER, Sergeant, born September 4, 1920, in East St. Louis, Illinois, the son of James A. and Bernice Lawder Clevenger. He served in

Sgt. Homer Lee Clevenger

WWII with Fleet Marine Force, South Pacific, with 3rd Battalion, Marine Raiders, K Company. He trained for battles in the South Pacific, American Samo, New Caledonia Islands, Guadalcanal and other islands. Clevenger was at Bougainville on

November 1, 1943-June 12, 1944, then drill instructor at Parris Island, South Carolina until discharged in January 1946.

JAMES LAWDER CLEVENGER, Sergeant, served in WWII January 1943-January 1946, with 5th Anti-Aircraft

Sgt. James L. Clevenger

Group, in Camp Haan and Camp Irvin, California. He was born October 16, 1918, in Carbondale, Illinois. His parents were James A. and Bernice Lawder Clevenger.

LARRY D. CLEVENGER, CT-3, enlisted into the Navy in September 1965. He had his boot training at Great Lakes, Illinois. AIT at Communication School in Pensacola, Florida 1965-66. His tour of duty included Kamiseya, Japan 1966-68; also the Philippines. Sailed to Phu Bai Vietnam aboard the USS *Oxford*. While there Larry received the Vietnam Medal. He was honorably discharged in September 1969.

CT-3 Larry D. Clevenger

Larry was born in Murphysboro, Illinois July 5, 1947 to Homer and __ (Dyer) Clevenger.

ROY DUANE CLUSTER, Private First Class, was born January 19, 1921, at Murphysboro, Illinois, the son of Roy E. and Effa Parker Cluster. He was drafted into WWII service on September 9, 1944, during the dark days of fighting in Europe, leaving a wife, two small children and another on the way.

He served in Company F, 262nd Infantry, Heavy Weapons crewman 605, in Northern France and Rhineland Germany. Cluster was discharged December 27, 1945.

Roy returned to his previous employment with Missouri Pacific Railroad and later managed Murphysboro Lumberyard, then his own construction company. He died January 7, 1991.

JAMES COATS, Sergeant, served in WWII 1943-45, under General George Patton, in France, Belgium and Germany.

Sgt. James Coats

He was wounded in the knee during the 'breakthrough' in Battle of the Bulge. Now living in Schuline, Illinois, he was born October 31, 1921 in Morgantown, Kentucky, son of Theodore and Erthabelle Lacefield Coats.

CHARLES H. COFFEY JR., Private First Class, was born in Chester, Illinois

Pfc. Charles H. Coffey, Jr.

April 12, 1926. He served in the Army Air Corps during WWII, as a gunner on B-17s, and in Army Occupation of Germany. His parents were Charles and Myrtle Nichols Coffee. He died October 1, 1970.

CHARLES H. COFFEY SR., Private, born November 24, 1896, in Perryville, Missouri, the son of William and Margaret Barrett Coffey. He was a soldier in WWI

Pvt. Charles H. Coffey Sr.

from 1917-19, serving in the USMC in Cuba. He died in Perryville, Missouri, May 7, 1973.

DONALD B. COFFEY, Sergeant, served in the Korean War Era with 2nd 155 MM Gun Battalion, Force Troop F.M.F. He trained as machine gunner and projec-

Sgt. Donald B. Coffey

Coffey - 2nd 155 mm Gun Batt.

tionist. Coffey served in Vieques, Puerto Rico. He entered service February 8, 1951 and was discharged February 8, 1954. Coffey was born in Lacon, Illinois, April 5, 1931, the son of Charles Sr. and Myrtle Nichols Coffey.

DANIEL N. COLBERT, First Sergeant, enlisted in the Marine Reserves in January 1953, active duty June 1953. Served in MAG-33, 1st Marine Air Wing, during the Korean War, in Korea, and Japan 18 months. Attended University of Illinois, on staff flight instructor.

Sgt. Daniel N. Colbert

He flew weather research for University of Chicago and was chief pilot for Sheaffer Pen Company, from where he retired as senior systems analyst in 1992, after 32 years with company.

Daniel was born in Chester, Illinois September 1, 1935, the son of Daniel and Leila Barber Colbert.

LOUIS COLVIS, Cook, enlisted May 12, 1917, Jefferson Barracks, Missouri, to serve in WWI. He was in 44706th Cook Headquarters Company, 16th Infantry in Bathlemont, Rambucourt Sec-

Louis Colvis

tor, Broyes Sector, Cantigny Sector, Aisne-Marne Offensive, St. Jacque Sector, St. Mihiel offensive and Meuse-Argonne Sector in France. Born at Fort Gage, Illinois, the son of Jean John Louis and Celestine Verlin Colvis, was 28 years of age when he entered the service. He was discharged at Camp Grant, Illinois September 25, 1919.

CLEMENT C. CONWAY, Sergeant, born in 1790 in Kaskaskia, Illinois, served with the Illinois Militia in War of 1812. Known as "Fiddles" he was quartermaster sergeant, under Pierre Menard and Shadrack Bond. Great-grandfather to veterans Charles H. Coffey Sr. of WWI and to Donald B. Coffey of the Korean War Era. His parents were James and Priscilla Coleburn Conway.

JAMES P. COOP, Specialist 4, U.S. Army, October 4, 1960-September 28, 1962; Reserves October 3, 1966. Completed basic training at Fort Leonard Wood, Missouri. Sent to Aschaffenburg, Germany

Spec-4 James P. Coop

and drove a truck for the Combat Construction Engineers, Charlie Company, 9th Engineers. He returned home to his family farm and worked at Red Bud Furnace Company for 29 years. He was born September 7, 1937 at Belleville, Illinois, the son of Edward C. and Elsie Pautler Coop.

CALVIN LEE COPPLE JR., Specialist 4, U.S. Army June 18, 1981-June 18, 1985, was born in Pinckneyville, Illinois, August 22, 1962, the son of Calvin and Donna Saul Copple. He enlisted after high school and served in Germany with the 55th Engineer Battalion, Company C. After discharge he returned to Sparta and now lives with his wife and three children in Percy, Illinois.

GERALD THOMAS COSTLIOW, Seaman 1/c, entered the Navy June 5, 1943 during WWII. Served aboard USNTS, Farragut, Idaho: USS *Guardfish* (Flag CSD-82); USS *Devilfish* (SS-292); Submarine Division 103; U.S. Submarine Base Navy 128 and U.S. Submarine Base, Pearl Harbor. He was awarded the WWII Victory Medal, Pacific Asiatic Area Campaign Medal and American Area Campaign Medal. Discharged March 5, 1946, from Great Lakes Naval Center. Costliow was born August 8, 1925, in Chester, Illinois.

JAKE COTNER, served in WWI as a wagoner in Company G, 314th Ammo Training Division. He spent his adult life in the Rockwood, Illinois area. Cotner was born April 3, 1888, in Missouri. He died June 7, 1955 and is buried in Evergreen Cemetery in Chester.

CURTIS E. COWAN SR., Corporal, served in WWII May 1946-48 and Korean War 1950-51. He was a military policeman in the 2nd Division, serving one year in the Philippines after basic training at Fort Polk, Louisiana. He was born December 10, 1928 at Hamburg, Missouri, the son of Curtis R. and Essie M. Chitwood Cowan. After service he worked 10 years with the Department of Mental Health and Electrolux Company for 23 years. He now lives in Chester, Illinois. The eldest of his six sons, Curtis E., served in the Vietnam War.

ED COWAN JR., Specialist 4, Curtis E. Cowan Jr. was inducted into the Army June 13, 1969. He was discharged December 15, 1970. His 13-1/2 months in Viet-

Spec-4 Ed Cowan Jr.

nam was spent in Du Pho, a fire support base. He was with the 6th Battalion, 11th Artillery, Americal Division. Cowan returned home and went back to Spartan Printing Company. He is now working at Menard Correctional Center, Chester, Illinois. He was born September 18, 1949, the son of Curtis and Leona (Smith) Cowan.

JAMES EARL COWELL, Private First Class, born in Chester, Illinois, January 21, 1949, served in the Vietnam War. He entered service November 14, 1967, and was sent to Fort Leonard Wood, Missouri, then to Fort Benning, Georgia, then to Tacoma, Washington, from where he shipped out to Vietnam.

He was with C Company, 1st Battalion, 6th Infantry, and was in the battle of Que Son Valley. He received the Purple Heart, Bronze Star, National Defense, Combat Infantry, Vietnam Service, Good Conduct and Sharpshooters Medals. He was killed May 31, 1968. He was the son of Earl W. and Imogene Geppert Cowell.

EDWARD BERNELLE COX, Private, U.S. Army, SATC Fulton, Missouri, WWI, enlisted November 1, 1918 and was discharged December 14, 1918. He was born August 9, 1899, in Baldwin, Illinois, the son of W.A. Cox and Dora E. Preston Cox. He was a retail merchant. Cox died September 6, 1942 and is buried in Caledonia Cemetery, Sparta.

ROBERT D. CRAIG, Specialist 4, U.S. Army, served with Headquarters Company, 116th Engineer Group, took basic training at Fort Leonard Wood, Missouri, followed by Unit Supply Specialist Training

Sp-4 Robert D. Craig

School. He was assigned to Fort Lewis, Washington as personnel specialist, active service and four years inactive Reserves 1956-62. He was born in Tilden, Illinois, the son of Robert J. and Helen M. Hamilton Craig. He married Esther E. Gerlach on September 25, 1954.

SAMUEL CRAWFORD, Sergeant, served in J. Briggs Company of Illinois Militia, in the Black Hawk War in the summer of 1832 as a private. This company was later designated as Regiment 3, Brigade 3, Illinois Militia. He later joined W. Gordon's Company of Illinois Militia as a sergeant. His parents were Hugh and Annie Looney Crawford. He was born September 10, 1796. He died near Sparta, Illinois January 20, 1845 and is buried in Union Cemetery in Sparta.

DALE W. CRONIN, Private First Class, entered WWII February 3, 1943 at Scott Field, Illinois. He served with Company I, 18th Infantry as rifleman 745, in action in Normandy, Northern France, Ardennes, Rhineland and Central Europe. On November 9, 1944 he was wounded in action in Germany. He saved two wounded buddies by dragging first one, then the other to a foxhole, one survived, one did not.

He earned the Combat Infantry Badge, Purple Heart, European-African-Middle Eastern Theatre Ribbon w/Silver Battle Star, three Overseas Bars, Silver Star Medal, GO 35 145 Army Distinguished Unit Badge, w/2 Bronze Oak Leaf Clusters and Good Conduct Medal. He was discharged October 29, 1945, at Fort Sheridan, Illinois.

Pfc. Dale W. Cronin

Cronin was born in Pinckneyville, Illinois, October 9, 1922, the son of John and Minnie Stevenson Cronin. He died February 17, 2003. The thing that stayed with him throughout his life was the many days on the front lines going without food and water.

EDWARD R. CROW, Staff Sergeant E-5, entered active duty in the U.S. Air Force, October 1967, and served during the Vietnam War Era, but saw no war zone duty. He served as an aircraft control and warning operator.

Basic training was at Lackland AFB, San Antonio, Texas; Technical School, Keesler AFB, Biloxi, Mississippi. His permanent assignments were, Pickstown AFB, South Dakota; Richards-Gebaur AFB, Kansas City, Missouri; Wallace AFB, Luzon Island, Philippines; and Charleston AFB, Maine. Discharged from service in September 1971.

Crow was born in Murphysboro, Illinois, the son of Olen L. and Mary T. Schneider Crow. Ed now resides in Chester, Illinois and works as economic development director for the county.

HARRY H. CUNDIFF, Technician Fifth Grade, was inducted in Chicago, Illinois, and had 16 weeks basic training at Fort McClellan, Alabama, before being shipped out of New York on the *Queen Elizabeth*.

Ferried into Scotland and went by train to South Hampton, England. From there they crossed the English Channel to LeHavre, France, then continued on to Belgium, as a replacement after the Battle of the Bulge. He was then assigned to Mortar Squad of the 66th Infantry, 42nd Division, on the Brest Peninsula, containing the Germans cut off at the SUB PEHS at St. Nazaire.

Moved about in Germany, France, Austria and returned to the United States via Bremerhaven, Germany. Cundiff is the son of Leo and Annie Colbert Cundiff of Sparta. He served in WWII from September 1944 until discharged August 1946.

WILLIAM RAYMOND CUNNINGHAM, CMACN E-3, enlisted into the U.S. Navy-Seabees in September 1960. Raymond spent two years in Active Reserves, two years Active Duty and two years Inactive Reserves. He was

E-3 William R. Cunningham

with MCB#1. Raymond spent seven months in Porto, Spain and five months in Guantanamo Bay Cuba. Raymond was born August 3, 1939 in Sparta, Illinois, the son of Floyd L. and Pearl (Norvell) Cunningham. He still lives in Randolph County.

LOUIS J. CUSHMAN, Airman 2/c, USAF, born in St. Louis, Missouri August 14, 1942, the son of Ludwig "Louis" and Evelyn Novak Cushman. He served November 10, 1960 to May 19, 1964 with

A 2/c Louis J. Cushman

6937th Comm. Group (USA FSS). He served in Pakistan one year as an operation analyst specialist. He died May 6, 1970 in an auto accident.

LUDWIG A. CUSHMAN, Staff Sergeant, born in St. Louis, Missouri, October 31, 1913, to Joseph and Clara Lindner Cushman. He served in the Army during WWII with Company B, 544th Engineer

S/Sgt. Ludwig A. Cushman

Battalion and SR, on Luzon and New Guinea. Entered service April 23, 1942 and was discharged November 25, 1945, earning two Bronze Stars for Campaign per WDGO #33 + #40, 1945; also the Good Conduct Medal. He died May 2, 1982.

WILLIAM W. CUSHMAN, Specialist 4, entered the Army April 26, 1968. Took his basic training at Fort Leonard Wood, Missouri and his AIT training at Fort Ord, California. He was with Company D, 2nd Battalion, 12th Infantry, 25th Infantry Division while serving in Vietnam.

Sp-4 William W. Cushman

When he came back to the States he was stationed at Fort Dix, New Jersey. His medals included several Purple Hearts and the Bronze Star. He was discharged April 24, 1970.

William was born February 4, 1949 at Chester, Illinois, the son of Ludwig and Evelyn Novak Cushman. At the time of his death, on September 6, 1998, he was postmaster at Steeleville, Illinois.

MICHAEL DANIS, Private, served in the Revolutionary War from February 6 until March 13, 1779, under Captain Francis Charleville's company of Kaskaskia Volunteers, during George Rogers Clark's capture of Fort Sackville (Vincennes). His hometown was Kaskaskia, then known as Virginia Country. He was the son of Michael and Marie Barbe Pilet dit LaSonde Danis. He died near Kaskaskia.

CARL E. DAVIS SR., Private First Class, served in WWII with the 38th Field Artillery Battalion at Camp Carson, Colorado from March 14, 1946 until September 18, 1947. Recalled to Vietnam April

Pfc. Carl E. Davis, Sr.

30, 1968 and served as first class petty officer with Seabees in Vietnam, stationed at the same base as his son, Carl Jr., at the same time. Carl Sr. finished his tour with Seabees in Northern Ireland before discharge September 23, 1970. Davis was born October 12, 1928, in East St. Louis, Illinois, the son of James and Mae Schirmer Davis.

CARL EUGENE DAVIS JR., Lance Corporal, entered the military on July 29, 1966 was with the Headquarters & Maintenance Squadron II, Marine Aircraft Group II, 1st Marine Aircraft Wing, Fleet Marine Force Pacific. He was stationed near Da Nang, Vietnam, as an aviation crash tech-

L/Cpl. Carl E. Davis Jr.

nician. His duties involved maintenance and repair of A6A aircraft weapons delivery systems.

Davis received the National Defense Service Medal, Vietnam Campaign Medal w/device, Vietnam Service Medal w/star, Combat Action Ribbon, Rifle Marksman Badge and the Purple Heart Medal while serving his country. Carl was discharged November 13, 1969.

Carl was born July 15, 1948 in Pueblo, Colorado, the son of Carl Eugene Sr. and Alberta (Gross) Davis. Carl Davis Sr. served in the Navy Seabees. He and Carl Jr. were stationed at Da Nang during the same period. Carl Jr. was permanently retired and passed away September 21, 1985.

ORVILLE C. DAYTON, Seaman 1/c, the son of Edward and Martha Johnson Dayton of Rockwood, Illinois, was serving aboard the light cruiser *Helena* at Pearl Harbor December 7, 1941. Not heavily damaged, the *Helena* went on to participate in various sea battles of South Pacific.

He was participating in Operation Toenail Landing (landing 43rd Infantry on New Georgia Island, in Solomons), had completed mission, going back to port, when the convoy they were in was ordered to turn around to intercept a group of 10 Japanese destroyers, known as Tokyo Express. They met in battle of Kula Gulf. At 1:50 a.m., July 5, 1943, the *Helena* opened fire on enemy ships, at 2:04 a.m. the first torpedo hit the *Helena*, then taking two more torpedoes, she broke in two and sank in less than five minutes. Survivors were in the water until July 14, when some made it to Vella Lavella Island, helped by 'sky watchers' hiding on the island and were later rescued.

Orville was first reported missing, then declared dead.

EARL PAUL DECKER, Staff Sergeant, entered WWII April 5, 1945 and served with Post Operating Company, Camp Beale, California. He was discharged September 10, 1947. Decker was born in Chester, Illinois, the son of Adolph C. and Maria Kipp Decker.

EDWARD V. DECKER, Private First Class, was born in Chester, Illinois, the son of Adolph C. and Maria Anna Kipp Decker. He was one of the first 18-year-old men drafted from Randolph County

Pvt. 1st/c Edward V. Decker

in WWII. Assigned to 215th AAF Base Unit, based in Colvis, New Mexico; Miami Beach, Florida; and Atlanta, Georgia where he went to Blacksmithing School; then to Pueblo, Colorado to camouflage airplanes and load ammunition. He was discharged December 12, 1944 from Pueblo.

GEORGE F. DECKER, Technician Fifth Grade, served in WWII with the 5250th Technical Intelligence Company in

T/5 George F. Decker

Tokyo, Japan. He entered service from Chester, Illinois, July 5, 1945 and was discharged July 1, 1946. George is the son of Adolph C. and Maria Kipp Decker.

HARVEY HUGO DECKER, Technician Fifth Grade, was inducted September 9, 1944, in Chicago, with seven other men who boarded a bus at the Royal Restaurant in Chester, Illinois. He was in 3rd

T/5 Harvey H. Decker

Company Battalion, went to Cook School, Fort Frances E. Warren, Wyoming, graduated February 10, 1945.

Harvey Decker in the Philippines.

On May 5, he was on a ship bound for the South Pacific and arrived at Luzon, Philippines, June 6, 1945. The major battle was over, but still resistance until end of war.

He was an officers cook in New Guinea, but still had to go on patrol. Decker killed a Japanese sniper on one patrol. He was discharged January 6, 1946, with Overseas Service Bar, Asiatic Theatre Ribbon, Bronze Battle Star, Good Conduct Medal, Meritorious Unit Award GO 47 HQ, REP COMM and WWII Victory Medal.

Harvey is the son of Adolph C. and Anna Maria Kipp Decker.

VERNON C. DECKER, Private, was inducted December 6, 1944, at Fort Sheridan, Illinois; basic training in Texas; went overseas, landed in Manila in May 1945. He joined Company C, 148th Infantry, 37th Division July 5, 1945.

Pvt. Vernon C. Decker

Vernon was accidentally shot by a fellow soldier and spent time in various hospitals. He returned to the United States in September 1945. Released from Von General Hospital, Chicago and sent to Fort Campbell, Kentucky to join Company A, 10th Infantry, 5th Division.

Discharged from Fort Sheridan, August 1, 1946, with Victory Metal, American Theatre Ribbon, Asiatic-Pacific Theatre Ribbon, one Bronze Battle Star, Philippine Liberation Ribbon, one Bronze Battle Star and Good Conduct Medal.

He was born in Chester, Illinois, the son of Adolph C. and Maria Kipp Decker.

PRESTON J. DEFRENNE, served with Battery C71, Field Artillery, during WWI, as a saddler, maintaining harness, saddles and other leather equipment used by Horse Field Artillery. After the war he pursued a career as a cobbler. He was born August 9, 1878, in Prairie du Rocher, Illinois, the son of Joseph and Agnes LaChance DeFrenne. He died November 24, 1959.

ALFRED H. DEGENER, Yeoman 1/c, born in Red Bud, Illinois, the son of Fredrich and Ida Kleeman Degener. He served in the U.S. Navy, on both the USS *Wyoming* and USS *New Mexico* during WWI, from July 15, 1916 until July 14, 1920.

ALFRED J. DEGENER, RM3/c, served in the Navy during WWII, from June 5, 1943 until March 11, 1947. His parents are Alfred H. and Tillie Diechmann Degener, of Sparta, Illinois. He began service at Great Lakes Naval Training Center; went to Radio School at University of Wisconsin, Madison, WI; Communication School, Los Angeles, California; Advance Naval Base, Funa Futi, South Pacific; then to Norfolk, Virginia; and Newport, Rhode Island Naval Bases before being discharged at Chicago, Illinois.

DONALD WALDEMAR DEGENER, HM1/c, spent six years in the U.S. Navy during WWII. A native of Sparta, Illinois, he is the son of Alfred and Tillie Eichmann Degener. He entered at Great Lakes June

HM/1 Donald W. Degener

11, 1942, and served with both the 3rd and 2nd Marine Divisions.

Assignments: December 15, 1942, First Separate Medical Company, "C" Company, 3rd Medical Battalion, 3rd Marines Reinforcement, various South Pacific areas ending with Bougainville; March 4, 1944, rotated to Naval Base, Quantico, Virginia; January 17, 1945, was with Fleet Hospital 111 at Guam; mine sweeper, USS *Prime* (AM-279) from November 28, 1945 until assigned to the repair ship, USS *Delta* (AR-9) on May 29, 1946; March 5 until July 9, 1947, he was with Sub. Group Two, Phil. Group, Atlantic Reserve Fleet; COM. Florida Reserve Fleet; USS LMS (498); 2nd Amphibious Tractor Battalion, 2nd Marine Division before being honorably discharged June 10, 1948.

EDWARD VALENTINE DEGENHARDT, Gunner's Mate 2/c, was born September 23, 1913, the son of John and Ida Niederbracht Degenhardt. He enlisted January 1942 in the U.S. Navy from Coulterville, Illinois. He was assigned to Armed Merchant Vessel SS *Oklahoma* as gunner's mate. Sailed to Pearl Harbor, along West Africa, through Panama Canal. Ship was torpedoed and sank March 28, 1945, killing two-thirds of the crew, including Edward.

RALPH FRANK DEGENHARDT, Seaman 1/c, son of John and Ida Niederbracht Degenhardt was born in Coulterville, Illinois, October 14, 1926, and enlisted in the U.S. Navy in February 1945, during WWII. Had boot camp in Virginia, then served on USS *Medea*. Received Asiatic Theater Medal and Victory Ribbons. Served 15 months, recorded his honorable discharge May 1946.

BOBBY DEMENT, Sergeant, served in a heavy weapons company as 2nd gunner

Sgt. Bobby Dement in Japan

on 30 caliber machine gun. He was with Company D, 8th Cavalry Regiment in Korea. He entered the service in July 1950, and was discharged in July 1953.

Received the Korean Service, Combat Infantry, United Nations Service Medals w/2 Bronze Stars. Also the National Defense and Korean Presidential Citation medals.

Bobby was born November 5, 1931 in Cherry Valley, Arkansas, the son of John and Anne Siler Dement. After discharge he worked in food service for the Department of Corrections until he retired in 1991.

DONALD R. DERICKSON, Specialist 4, U.S. Army, served October 1959-February 1962. He completed basic training in Texas and was sent to Berlin for 21 months, including 93 day Kennedy exten-

Sp-4 Donald R. Derickson

sion. He worked in a hospital there, during which time the Berlin Wall was built. He was born in Murphysboro, Illinois, June 26, 1936, the son of Cardel B. and Rose Mary Hauner Derickson. He worked in the coal mines and now with the Chester Street Department.

FRANK E. DERICKSON, Staff Sergeant, U.S. Army, 1948-51 was stationed at Fort Lewis, Washington for 21 months, then Japan for four months. Then to Wŏnsan, North Korea on November 8,

S/Sgt. Frank E. Derickson

1950. He served with the 8th Army for nine months in Korea and returned to Camp Carson, Colorado for discharge on September 14, 1951. He was born August 8, 1928, in Murphysboro, Illinois, the son of Cordell and Rose Hauner Derickson.

JOSEPH S. DEROUSSE JR., Private, served in the Civil War in Company C, 154th Regiment of Illinois Infantry, which was organized at Camp Butler, Illinois February 21, 1865. He was called to service on February 16, 1865. Left by rail for Louisville, Kentucky, February 24, then on to Nashville, Tennessee, arriving there February 27.

Due to flooding the regiment held there until March 2, when they moved to Murfreesboro, Tennessee. Many of the men died from exposure while here. On May 15, they marched to Tullahoma, Tennessee, and remained there until June 11, then returned to Nashville, where the regiment was put on picket guard and garrison duty.

The regiment mustered out at Nashville, and were ordered to Springfield, Illinois. They were given final payment and discharged September 29, 1865. Private Derousse was from Kaskaskia, Illinois, the son of Joseph S. and Bernice Chamberline Derousse. He died January 11, 1892, and is buried at Evergreen Cemetery in Chester, Illinois.

RAYMOND H. DETTMER, Corporal, served in Company K, 32nd Infantry Regiment, 7th Division in the Korean Conflict from 1952-54. He joined the Army at an early age.

Cpl. Raymond H. Dettmer

Received training at Camp Cooke, California, then ordered to Korea. Landed at Inchon and within a few days moved to front line duty, serving as a rifleman. He later became a company clerk.

He received the Infantry Combat Badge, Korean Service Medal w/2 Bronze

Stars, United Nations Service Medal and the National Defense Medal.

Corporal Dettmer was from Chester, Illinois. His parents were Herman and Louise Wolff Dettmer.

LEONARD A. DIERKS, Sergeant, was born at Degonia, Illinois, April 12, 1932, the son of Ernest and Clara Ohlau Dierks. He was proud to serve his country in the Korean Conflict from October 1952 until August 1954. He served in Company A, 23rd Regiment, 4th Platoon of the 2nd Division.

Sgt. Leonard A. Dierks

Dierks participated in Out Post Harry On Line battle. He received basic training at Fort Knox, Kentucky in October 1952 and joined 2nd Division in May 1953. He was a gunner on 60mm mortar on line and later became a squad leader. Was on line when the truce was signed.

CHRISTOPHER ALLEN "CHRIS" DOBYNS, Private 2/c, enlisted in the Army February 3, 1991. While serving his country he earned the National Defense Medal, Army Service Ribbon, Sharpshooter Marksman Medal and also the Heavy Driver and Mechanic Badge.

Pvt. 2nd/c Christopher Dobyns

He served with the 591st Transportation Company USAR and was honorably discharged November 12, 1993 from Fort Dix, New Jersey.

Chris was born in Sparta, Illinois August 8, 1973, the son of Wayne Sr. and Sharon (Swartwood) Dobyns. He works at and lives in Sparta, Illinois. Chris served during Peace Time.

CLETUS R. "BUCK" DOBYNS, Staff Sergeant E/6, enlisted in the Army in 1959. He took his basic training at Fort Leonard Wood, Missouri. Was stationed at Fort Lewis, Washington. Then was shipped to Korea, 7th Division in December 1959. Came back to the States and went to Fort Benning, Georgia.

S/Sgt. Cletus R. Dobyns

Went back overseas to Germany, 2nd Armour Division. Came back to Fort Benjamin Harris, Indiana. Then in 1967 was shipped to Vietnam, stationed at Pleiku with the 4th Infantry Division. After his tour of duty he was honorably discharged in 1968.

Cletus was born September 3, 1941 at Modac, Illinois, the son of Arthur and Mary (Byers) Dobyns. After service he went to work at Sparta Printing Company where he retired from in 2001. Dobyns resides in Odin, Illinois.

DAMON A. DOBYNS, SP-E, entered the Army March 28, 1961. He took his basic training and AIT at Fort Leonard Wood, Missouri. Then he went to Fort Hood, Texas. From there Damon went to Germany for 30 days, then back to Fort Hood, Texas.

Spec/E Damon A. Dobyns

While serving his country Damon was with Company E, 17th Combat Engineers, 2nd Armor Division. He was discharged on March 27, 1964 from Fort Hood, Texas.

After Damon's return home he worked construction and then retired from the coal mine. He was born April 4, 1943 in Sparta, Illinois, the son of Arthur U. and Mary E. (Byers) Dobyns.

DAVID RAY DOBYNS, Specialist 4, entered the Army February 22, 1983. He took his basic training at Fort Leonard Wood, Missouri. David was a light wheel vehicle-power generator mechanic. While in service he received the Parachute Badge,

Sp/4 David R. Dobyns

Army Service Ribbon, Army Achievement Medal, Sharp Shooter Badge-M16 and Expert Qualification Badge-Hand Grenade. David was given a medical discharge. David was born December 12, 1963, the son of Damon and Carol (Garner) Dobyns. David still lives in Sparta.

DONALD DEAN "PEEWEE" DOBYNS, Specialist 4 E-4, enlisted into the Army on November 15, 1966 at the age of 17. Took his basic training and AIT at Fort Leonard Wood, Missouri. He was shipped to Germany in 1967 then volunteered for Vietnam. He entered the country August 1, 1968 and left there July 29, 1969. Was stationed at Pleiku and Ban Me Thuot with the 18th Combat Engineers,

Sp/4 Donald D. Dobyns

pulling security, armed with M-60 machine gun, disarming land mines with demolition squad, while helping build roads and bridges.

While in the service he was awarded Sharp Shooter Badge for M-14 Rifle and Expert Badge for M-60 machine gun, the National Defense Service Medal, Vietnam Service Medal w/2 Bronze Service Stars, Vietnam Campaign Medal w/device 60 and Vietnamese Cross of Gallantry w/palm.

After his tour in Vietnam he spent his remaining service time at Fort Carson, Colorado, where he was honorably discharged May 14, 1970.

He was born July 12, 1949 in Sparta, Illinois, the 12th child and the seventh son to serve his country, of Arthur U. Dobyns and Mary Eliza (Byers) Dobyns.

JERRY DAVID DOBYNS, E4, enlisted into the Navy August 31, 1963. Took his basic training at Great Lakes, Illinois. Jerry was a 623 Marine Mechanic. He was aboard the USS *Frontier* (AD-25) and was awarded the National Defense Service Medal.

E-4 Jerry D. Dobyns

He was honorably discharged from active duty February 16, 1966 from San Francisco, California and transferred to the Naval Reserves Station at Bainbridge, Maryland August 2, 1967. He was released from Naval Reserves on August 30, 1969.

Jerry was born August 16, 1946 at Sparta, Illinois, the fifth son of Arthur and Mary (Byers) Dobyns. He was the fifth son to serve his country. Jerry works as a butcher at Mad Pricer in Sparta and lives in Tilden, Illinois.

JOSEPH LEE DOBYNS, E-4, enlisted into the Navy January 4, 1991. Joe was with the LHA-4. He served aboard the USS *Nassau*. Joe was born January 1, 1969 and the first Randolph County baby in 1969. He is the fourth son of Wayne Sr. and

E-4 Joseph Lee Dobyns

Sharon (Swartwood) Dobyns. Joe is a truck driver and lives in Sparta, Illinois. Joe served during Peace Time.

OTIS LEE DOBYNS, Private First Class, was inducted into the Army December 15, 1942. Lee served his country during WWII, leaving the States on December 17, 1943 for Europe destination. This was European-African-Middle Eastern Theater, arriving December 25, 1943. Sailing on February 8, 1944 for the Asiatic-Pacific Theater arriving on March 12, 1944.

Pfc. Otis Lee Dobyns

Leaving for the States April 28, 1945 and arriving back on United States soils May 8, 1945. While serving his country, Lee belonged to the 1677th Ordnance, S&M Company Avn. He was an automotive mechanic 014.

Lee fought in the India Burma Co. 33 WD 45. He earned the Asiatic-Pacific Service Medal, Good Conduct Medal, WWII Victory Medal, American Theater Medal, along with the European-Africa-Middle Eastern Service Medal. He was issued a lapel button ASR score September 2, 1945. He was given a medical discharge November 9, 1945.

Lee was born in Sparta, Illinois, the son of Miles and Laura (Gowens) Dobyns September 8, 1920. Lee became an ordained minister with the United Pentecostal Church. He passed away June 23, 1992 at the Covenant Medical Center, Urbana, Il.

He is buried at Branchside Cemetery, Gays, Illinois.

ROBERT E. "BOB" DOBYNS, Private E-I, entered the service on September 11, 1966. Bob took his basic training at Fort Leonard Wood, Missouri. Then he went to Fort Benning, Georgia for his AIT

Pvt. E-1 Robert E. Dobyns

after which he went back to Fort Leonard Wood, Missouri. Bob was a cook and he was with the MOS/94B 20. He was discharged September 11, 1968. Bob spent his time in the States. He was the sixth son of Arthur and Mary (Byers) Dobyns to serve his country. Bob was born May 18, 1948 in Sparta, Illinois and still makes it his home.

VERNON A. "PETE" DOBYNS, Specialist 4, was drafted into the Army in 1963. Pete took his basic training at Fort Leonard Wood, Missouri. Then he went to Fort Ord, Texas for his AIT. Then he

Sp-4 Vernon A. Dobyns

was shipped overseas, spending three months in Germany and 13 months in Korea. Pete was with Company D, 2nd Armor Division (Hell on Wheels). He was discharged in 1969. After returning home Pete got a job as a butcher, which he did for 34 years. He's still alive and kicking, just not very high. Pete was born in Modoc, Illinois January 20, 1940, the son of Arthur U. and Mary E. (Byers) Dobyns.

WAYNE M. DOBYNS JR., Private First Class, enlisted in the Army in February 1983. Wayne was discharged February 1986. Wayne was born September 11, 1964, the son of Wayne Sr. and Sharon (Swartwood) Dobyns. Wayne works at Super Wal-Mart and lives in Sparta, Illinois.

Pvt. 1st/c Wayne M. Dobyns

WAYNE MYLES "SONNY" DOBYNS SR., Private First Class, enlisted into the Army January 29, 1954. Took his basic training at Fort Hamilton, New York. Then went to Fort Dixon, New Jersey for his AIT. Was discharged October 3, 1960. Sonny was born November 4, 1936 in Modoc, Illinois, the son of Arthur U. and Mary E. (Byers) Dobyns. He was the first of seven sons to serve his country. After the service Sonny did laborer work and retired from that occupation. He and his family live in Sparta, Illinois.

Wayne M. Dobyns Sr.

WILLIAM DAVID "BILL" DOBYNS, enlisted in the Army Air Force on April 7, 1943. While stationed at Fugi, Italy, with the 15th Air Force he flew 52 combat missions. He was awarded six bronze stars, the Presidential Citation w/ Oak Leaf Cluster and the Aerial Medal of Honor. Bill received his discharge September 29, 1945, at Buckley Field No. 2, on the point system before he was 21 years of age.

William D. Dobyns

After serving his country he was a lumberman by profession. At the time of his death he was assistant manager of Residential Builders Supply Company in Colorado.

Bill was born September 21, 1924 in Sparta, Illinois to Miles and Laura (Gowens) Dobyns. Bill died January 24, 1966 in Colorado. He is buried at Golden Cemetery, Golden, Colorado.

CHARLES RAY DORF, Corporal, of Tilden, Illinois, was among a contingent of 23 young men from Randolph County, who left for induction into the armed services on January 16, 1952. He received his basic training at Schofield Barracks, in Oahu, Hawaii, and was assigned to the 23rd Company, 20th Battalion, Hawaiian Infantry Training Center, and from there most of the men were sent directly to Korea. Charles was also sent to Germany and was assigned to the 8th Transportation Traffic Regulation Group. He was discharged in January 1954. His parents were Earl Sydney and Anna Marie Miller Dorf.

Group from Randolph County. Dorf is fourth from left in first row.

EARL EUGENE DORF, Seaman 2/c, served in WWII on the USS *Jason* in the Asiatic-Pacific Campaign from June 19, 1944 to November 1945. He entered service in October 1943 and was discharged in December 1945. He is the son of Earl Sidney and Anna Marie Miller Dorf, and was born in Tilden, October 31, 1924.

Seaman 2nd/c Earl E. Dorf

GEORGE & GLENN DOWNEN, were born twins in 1920 in Cora City, Illinois. Their parents are Snider and Clara Bunselmeyer Downen. George served in

George Dowen

the Air Force in WWII as an airplane mechanic. He later worked at Cole's Mill, in Chester and Perryville, Missouri Airport, then Anaheim, California post office for 22 years. He now lives in Chester, Illinois. Glenn, also served in WWII, in the Army Ordinance in the Pacific Area. Glenn returned to civilian life to be a jeweler.

JAMES K. DOWNS, Technician Fifth Grade, was born September 26, 1910, at

T/5 James K. Downs

Seymour, Indiana, to Arch and Annis Clark Downs. He entered the service in June

1942, and served with Harbor Defense, as Searchlight crewman, with Battery K, 95th Coast Artillery, during WWII. He was discharged in October 1945 and died at age 92 in November 2002.

ARNOLD G. DRAVES, Sergeant, served in the Air Force during WWII, with 2512th BU in Normandy, Northern France, Rhineland and Air Offensive Europe in England as airplane armorer. He enlisted August 20, 1941, at Peoria, Illinois. He received the European-African-Middle Eastern Ribbon w/4 Bronze Battle Stars and five Overseas Service stripes.

Discharged September 11, 1945, at Fort Sheridan, Illinois. Draves was born July 31, 1919, at Chester, Illinois, the son of Edward and Anna Gray Draves. He died in Florida, August 13, 1986 and is buried in Woodlawn Cemetery, Havana, Florida.

EDWARD DONALD DRAVES, Sergeant, was drafted January 30, 1952. He received basic training at Fort Riley, Kansas, then sent to Korea.

Sgt. Edward D. Draves

He was stationed on 38th Parallel for 10 months, with Mike Company, 38th Infantry, near P'yongyang. Of the 1,000 men that went up the hill known as 'Old Baldy', after first attacks, only 200 men capable of fighting were left, the rest were killed or wounded. These men re-took the hill, but few remained from the original unit. Discharged October 31, 1953, from Fort Riley, Kansas.

Returned to Rockwood, Illinois and he worked in timber and trucking. He was born April 26, 1931, the son of Edward and Anna Gray Draves.

EDDIE DRECZKA, Private, was born in Chester, Illinois August 14, 1890, the son of John and Nathalie Williams. He served in WWI somewhere in France from

Pvt. Eddie Dreczka

April 26, 1918 until discharged August 23, 1919.

VIRGIL RAY DRECZKA, E-2, U.S. Army, August 16, 1951-November 7, 1959, served with Company I, 86th Infantry Regiment, 10th Infantry Division. Drafted in August 1951 and sent to Fort Riley, Kansas.

E-2 Virgil R. Dreczka

On March 20, 1952, due to death of his father, he was given a hardship separation to return to the farm and transferred to ERC for eight years with no time lost. Discharged in November 1959.

He was born August 21, 1926, in Fort Gage, Illinois, the son of Stephen V. and Grace N. Leavitt Dreczka. He died October 13, 1986.

LEMUEL L. DUCLOS, Private First Class, was born in Prairie du Rocher, Illinois, December 12, 1926, the son of Louis and Pearl McClenahan. He entered WWII in April 1945 and served until November 1946, in 3rd and 9th Infantry, Company F, 38th Infantry Regiment, 2nd Infantry Division in WWII occupational.

In the Reserves, he was called up for Korea in September 1950 and served until October 1951. He was wounded in the 'big push' December 1, 1950.

Returned home, went to Air Condition-Refrigeration School on GI Bill. Re-

Pfc. Lemuel L. DuClos

tired January 17, 2002, from air condition, refrigeration business after a stroke. Also retired from Operating Engineers Local 520. He received the Purple Heart for wound received in Korea.

CLINTON DUENSING, Corporal, born March 6, 1921, in Breman, Illinois, the son of Elmer and Alma Siemers Duensing. He entered WWII service January 11, 1944, after working at Elmwood Ordinance Plant in Wilmington, Illinois.

Cpl. Clinton Duensing

Stationed at Fort Ord, California, then to Fort Sill, Oklahoma for additional schooling. Assigned to a Geoditic Computer 213. Sent to Hawaii and was injured on a night patrol. Returned to Percy Jones Hospital and was discharged April 16, 1946.

Moved to East St. Louis, Illinois and worked for U.S. Postal Service as a letter carrier, retiring in 1982. He died December 1, 1996.

RAYMOND HERMAN DUENSING, First Lieutenant, enlisted in the Army November 11, 1942, to serve in WWII. Stationed at Headquarters, European Theatre Operations USA in England, France and Germany, in Adjutant General Department.

Discharged February 12, 1946, with European-African-Middle Eastern Campaign Medal w/2 Bronze Stars, American Campaign WWII Victory Medal.

1st Lt. Raymond H. Duensing

He was born October 15, 1908, in Shiloh Hill, Illinois to Adolph and Emilie Brammer Duensing Sr. Returning home he owned and operated Duensing Hardware in Lake Jackson, Texas. Duensing died June 8, 2002.

WAYNE DUENSING, Corporal, U.S. Army, 1950-52, served with the 43rd Infantry Division, 43rd Quartermaster Company and Truck Platoon. He was a truck driver instructor and took care of the truck fleet. He received his leader's course from the 43rd Infantry Division, at Camp Pickett, Virginia. He was stationed at Sheridan Kaserne Base, Augsburg, Germany.

Cpl. Wayne Duensing

Returning home, he married Lois Gillison. They owned Wayne's Western Auto Store for 27 years in Steeleville. He was born August 25, 1927, in Bremen, Illinois, the son of Adolph and Olga Knoke Duensing. He died July 28, 2000.

CHARLES WILBERT DUFFIE, Sergeant, was drafted into the Army from Michigan in September 1945, as part of WWII Occupational Forces. He was a special vehicle operator and served 14 months in the Philippines and Asiatic-Pacific, receiving service ribbons for these areas. The son of Thomas and Mary Ann Watt Duffie, he was born in Cardiff, Alabama, August 9, 1915, and moved to Randolph County at the age of 7 years.

JAMES THOMAS DUFFIE, WWII Navy Veteran, was the son of Thomas and Mary Ann Watt Duffie. He was born in Coulterville, Illinois, November 21, 1926. He married Louise Cape and had six sons.

STEPHEN ALEXANDER DUNN, Company A, First Regiment, Washington Infantry Volunteers, Spanish American War, enlisted April 28, 1898 and was discharged November 1, 1899. He was born March 14, 1867, in Walsh, Illinois and died August 31, 1939. Dunn is buried in Union Cemetery, Sparta, Illinois.

GARY G. DURKEE, Colonel (Retired), graduated from the U.S. Military Academy at West Point, New York in 1958. He was a fighter pilot having flown some 14 different types of aircraft. Gary flew more than 100 missions into North Vietnam in the F-105 fighter bomber.

Col. Gary Durkee

Gary's decorations include: the Legion of Merit, Distinguished Flying Cross, the Meritorious Service Medal and the Air Medal. He retired as vice commander of Ramstein AB in Germany in 1988. He taught ROTC until shortly before his death October 1, 1993.

Gary was born in Ellis Grove, Illinois on October 28, 1935 to Louis and Naomi (Hermes) Durkee.

SHIRLEY RAY EASTON, Corporal, born July 4, 1931, to Thomas and Rosella Keeton Easton. He died in Rockwood, Illinois September 6, 1993. Easton is buried in Ebenezer Cemetery near Rockwood.

GEORGE DEXTER EATON JR., First Sergeant, served in Company K, 5th Regiment of the Illinois Cavalry during the Civil War. He enlisted August 31, 1862. He saw action at Mechanicsburg, Pennsylvania and Canton, Coldwater and Brownsville, Mississippi.

His parents were George E. and Eliza Ann Eaton. He was married to Margaret Grey in 1853. He died August 25, 1864, at Vicksburg, Mississippi of malaria fever, and is buried in the National Cemetery there, Section H, Grave 626.

BRUCE A. EBERS, Sergeant, U.S. Army, November 1980-November 1983 and November 1986-June 1996. Ebers was born April 4, 1962 in Randolph County, the son of Norman and Fern Wolter Ebers. He spent the majority of his first enlistment in Nitzingen, Germany as a tank driver and gunner. He was discharged and returned to active service three years later, stationed at Ramstein AB.

Sgt. Bruce A. Ebers

In 1990 he was reassigned to Fort Bliss, Texas and sent to Saudi Arabia/Iraq until April 1991. He returned to Texas until released from service in the summer of 1996.

HILMER H. EBERS, Technical Sergeant, entered the service May 26, 1942 and served with Company L, 13th Infantry, in Central Europe and Rhineland. He

T/Sgt. Hilmer Ebers

was discharged November 10, 1945 and returned to Steeleville, Illinois.

Hilmer was born July 18, 1913 in Steeleville. His parents were Albert and Minnie Clasen Ebers. His comments, "too many close calls to think about."

NORMAN A. EBERS, Private First Class, served in post WWII Army of Occupation in Japan, in the 364th Air Service Group. He was born in Steeleville, Illinois October 30, 1927, the son of Edmund and Lena Dierks Ebers.

Pfc. Norman A. Ebers

He entered service March 12, 1946 at Fort Sheridan, Illinois. Took basic training at Kessler Field, Mississippi; then to Fuchu, Japan. He was discharged September 2, 1927. Ebers was awarded the WWII Victory Medal and Army of Occupation Medal.

Norman was married to Fern Wolter and worked at AFCO, Red Bud, Illinois. Norman died July 11, 1998.

WILLIAM L. EBERS, SH2/c (E-S), Ship's Serviceman (Barber), served in the Vietnam War aboard three different destroyers: Richard S. Edwards DD-950, Halsey Powell, DD-686 and Rupertus DD-851, during two cruises in the Pacific. He entered the U.S. Navy April 1, 1966 and was discharged in December 1969.

While serving aboard the USS Rupertus in the Gulf of Tonkin, their ship

Sh2 William L. Ebers

was guarding the USS *Forrestal*, when aircraft exploded. They rescued sailors and pilots from the ocean.

He was born in Red Bud, Illinois, May 11, 1946. His parents are Hilmer and Cleo Pautler Ebers. He was a barber for 35 years and is now retired.

ANDREW DEAN EGGEMEYER, MOS 5, enlisted on February 18, 1986 in the Air Force. Andrew took his basic at Lackland AFB. Then he went to Keesler AFB for one year.

From Keesler he was sent to Offutt AFB from August 1987 until September 1997. Then on to McClellan AFB September 1997 until 2000. Lastly to Minot AFB, North Dakota 2000 to the present. Andrew served in Desert Storm and now he is in Operation Iraqi Freedom.

Andrew was born April 27, 1966 in Chester, Illinois, the son of Dennis and Susan (Springer) Eggemeyer.

CLYDE L. EGGEMEYER, Private First Class, BSM 8 PH, was born at Walsh, Illinois on November 21, 1922, the son of

Pvt 1/c Clyde Eggemeyer

Joseph and Theresa Rieckenberg Eggemeyer. He entered WWII service February 13, 1943 and served in the 7th Infantry, 3rd Division. He was killed in action March 27, 1945 at Metz, Germany. Clyde was awarded the Bronze Star and Purple Heart.

DAVID P.H. EGGEMEYER, Private, served from September 19, 1917-June 6, 1919 in WWI with Company M, 129th Infantry Division, in major offensives in Meuse-Argonne on the east side of the Meuse River. In this battle he was with 17th French Army Division.

Eggemeyer served under General J. Pershing. He saw action in Somme-Amuns sector with an Australian company. He was in Albut Sector with the 18th Division BEF;

Pvt. David Eggemeyer

Verdun Sector; and Meuse-Argonne Forest. He transferred to Mashville-Seaville, St. Hillaire, Chateau'd Audmoir November 11, 1918, then to Army of Occupation and served there until April 26, 1919. He was discharged at Camp Grant, Illinois June 6, 1919.

David was born in Chester, Illinois, the son of Fritz and Caroline Rabe Eggemeyer.

DONALD D. EGGEMEYER, Private First Class, U.S. Army 1948-51, was born June 3, 1929 in Chester, Illinois, the son of Otto and Grace Bockhorn Eggemeyer. He enlisted, completed basic training, stationed at Fort Campbell, Kentucky for a short period, transferred to Albuquerque, New Mexico where he spent the majority of his enlistment. He was discharged from Camp Attebury, Indiana.

Pfc. Donald D. Eggemeyer

Returning home he married Norma Jean Cotner and had three daughters: Donna, Joni and Tammy. He owned and operated Eggemeyer Construction Company. In 1970 he built Reaban's Restaurant, later called Mr. D's. He was in the restaurant business until 1982. In 1993 Don built Plank Road Mini Storage. He died December 19, 2000.

EDMUND EGGEMEYER, Corporal, U.S. Army 1952-54. After basic training he was sent to Korea, but because he had two brothers in Korea, he was sent to Japan. A United States law was passed limiting two brothers in combat area at the same time. After Floyd, the oldest brother rotated home Edmund, the youngest, was sent to Korea.

Cpl. Edmund Eggemeyer

He was born November 15, 1931 in Randolph County, the son of Arthur and Cora Runge Eggemeyer. Edmund died November 9, 1987.

ERNEST EGGEMEYER, Private, was born February 2, 1895 in Walsh, Illinois to August and Minnie Dieckhoff. He served with 6th Company, 106th Depot Brigade at Camp Custer, Michigan during WWI from

Pvt. Ernest Eggemeyer

September 4, 1918 until November 27, 1918. He died September 11, 1970 and is buried in Zion Lutheran Church Cemetery, Walsh, Illinois.

FLOYD EGGEMEYER, Corporal, U.S. Army 1951-53, completed basic training at Fort Campbell, KY and served in Korea from February 1952-February 1953 with the 25th Division as a welder and jeep driver in a combat area. He was discharged from Colorado, the oldest of three brothers that served in Korea.

He was born January 3, 1929 in Randolph County, the son of Arthur and Cora Runge Eggemeyer. He is now retired from Steelweld Equipment Company and lives in St. Clair, Missouri.

HAROLD W. EGGEMEYER, Technician Fifth Grade, was drafted into WWII March 18, 1942 and served as a tank driver with Senior Company, 707th Tank Battalion in Northern France, Ardennes, Rhineland and Central Europe. He was discharged September 23, 1945.

T/5 Harold W. Eggemeyer

Harold was awarded the Good Conduct Medal, Bronze Star, 60 106 28th Infantry Division Badge, European-African-Middle Eastern Theatre Ribbon w/4 Bronze Battle Stars, three Overseas Bars and one Service Lapel Button.

He was born September 26, 1911 in Randolph County, the son of Henry and Pauline Gremmels Eggemeyer. He returned home to work at Tri-City Grocery. He was always proud and felt it an honor to have served his country. He died April 2, 1988.

HARVEY F. EGGEMEYER, Private First Class, served with Squadron I, 3502nd

Cpl. Floyd Eggemeyer

Pfc. Harvey F. Eggemeyer

Army Air Force Base Unit during WWII. He entered the Army Air Force February 12, 1944 at Jefferson Barracks, MO. Took basic training in Mississippi and pilot training in Kansas City until discontinued. The balance of his time was at Luke Field, Arizona. Eggemeyer was discharged November 3, 1945 with the American Theatre Ribbon and WWII Victory Medal.

He was born in Sparta, Illinois, July 27, 1921, the son of Martin and Norma Degner Eggemeyer.

HERBERT W. EGGEMEYER, Private First Class, entered WWII December 4, 1942 and was assigned to Company G, 414th Infantry, 104th Division. He was wounded once in Belgium and twice in Germany. He also served in France and Rhineland.

Pvt. 1/c Herbert W. Eggemeyer

Eggemeyer received the American Theatre Ribbon, Good Conduct Ribbon, two Battle Stars, European-African-Middle Eastern Ribbon, and Purple Heart w/2 clusters during his service as an auto rifleman. He was discharged November 10, 1945.

He returned to Chester and married Clara Young. He was gas superintendent in Chester for 25 years. Eggemeyer was born in Walsh, Illinois on July 16, 1921, the son of Joseph and Theresa Rieckenberg Eggemeyer.

JAMES EARL EGGEMEYER, Private First Class, USMC 1953-54 active, 1955-57 Reserves. Jim was born December 3, 1933 in Chester, Illinois to Otto and Grace Bockhorn Eggemeyer. He enlisted in the Marine Corps. After boot camp and training at Camp Pendleton, California, he was stationed at Kodiak, Alaska. There he met Marlyss Blinn and they married in 1954.

In 1955 he returned to Chester and built the Bunny Wash Laundromat. In 1957 they moved back to Kodiak, Alaska and

Pfc. James E. Eggemeyer

Pvt. Phillip Eggemeyer

Pvt. 1/c Sylva Eggemeyer

opened their business, Eggemeyer's Furniture in 1963. It was destroyed by The Great Tidal Wave of 1964. They rebuilt in 1966. James and Marlyss reared five children. Jim died July 25, 1999 after suffering several years from Parkinson's disease.

MELBERT EGGEMEYER, Private First Class, signed up with Merchant Marines in 1944, just out of high school. He served six months and was drafted into WWII service April 30, 1946. He took basic training at Fort Bliss, Texas and was assigned to Company B, 738th Division Military Police and served as a military policeman in Manila, Philippines until discharged May 15, 1947.

Pfc. Melbert Eggemeyer

Melbert is the son of Lienald and Lydia (Eggemeyer) Eggemeyer of Sparta, Illinois.

PHILLIP EGGEMEYER, Private, was born in Benefield, Prussia, Germany, April 20, 1842. He volunteered for three years in Civil War service from August 3, 1861-July 4, 1865. He served with the 10th Infantry, Company I, at New Madrid, Missouri, Island #10, Lookout Mountain, Missionary Ridge, Tennessee, Kenesaw Mountain, Georgia and Sherman's March to the Sea.

In Atlanta his term was up. He re-enlisted for the remainder of the war. In a battle at Bentonville, North Carolina March 18, 1865, he was wounded with a musket ball in the chest. After two weeks in the hospital, he was discharged at Louisville, Kentucky July 4, 1865.

Two brothers, Fritz and Frederick, also served in the Civil War.

RAYNOLD EGGEMEYER, Private First Class, USMC, 1951-53, served from March 1952 to April 1953 in Korea, 361 days in combat. He was awarded the Korean Service Medal and two Battle Stars.

Pfc. Raynold Eggemeyer

He returned to the United States, Point Mugu Air Missel Test Center, Oxnard, California September 1953, then to 9th Marine Corps Standby Reserve. He was discharged September 12, 1959.

Raynold was born February 1, 1930 in Randolph County, the son of Arthur and Cora Runge Eggemeyer.

SYLVA L. EGGEMEYER, Private First Class, served in the Ardennes Campaign and the Rhineland Campaign during WWII. He entered service July 23, 1942 and served with Company F, 276th Infantry, 70th Division as a military policeman and combat infantryman.

He was injured in the vicinity of Geubiuingen, France February 6, 1945. He was discharged July 18, 1945.

Sylva was born in Walsh, Illinois, May 10, 1920. His parents are Joseph and Theresa Rieckenberg Eggemeyer. He returned to Chester and resided there until his death November 14, 1992.

He was awarded the European-African-Middle Eastern Theatre Ribbon, two Bronze Campaign Stars, Combat Infantry Badge, Good Conduct Medal and Purple Heart.

WILBERT EGGEMEYER, Technician Fourth Grade, served in the 3464th Ordinance B in the Philippine Islands, repairing vehicles that supported the battalion and servicing 105 guns.

T/4 Wilbert Eggemeyer

He was born in Walsh, Illinois. His parents are Eddie and Minnie Hapke Eggemeyer. He entered service February 6, 1945 and was discharged November 1, 1946.

HERMAN LOUIS EHLERS, Motor Machinist Mate 2/c, was born in Welge, Illinois November 22, 1925. He entered WWII February 4, 1944 and served on NTS Farragut, Idaho; RB Shoemaker, California; SLCU #2; USS LST-453; and USS *Remus* ARL-40. He was discharged April 19, 1946.

Ehlers received the American Area, WWII Victory, Asiatic-Pacific and Philippine Liberation medals.

VINCENT ADAM EICHENSEER, Chaplain, served in WWI from September 9, 1917 until June 6, 1919. He was assigned to the 129th Infantry as chaplain for his battalion. He was severely gassed on the battlefield, but he carried a fellow soldier, who had become unconscious from the gas, from the field. He had his knapsack shot out from under his head while sleeping.

Chaplin Vincent A. Eichenseer

He was in the Battle of the Argonne Forest, and was awarded the Purple Heart for his bravery and endurance under stress.

He was born in Red Bud, Illinois October 7, 1895, the son of John and Mary Wierschem Eichenseer. He died November 3, 1979, and the Purple Heart was buried with him.

WILLIAM ELSEY, Private, entered the Civil War August 20, 1861 and served with Company C, 30th Regiment. He was engaged in the Battle of Belmont on November 7, 1861, under the leadership of General Ulysses S. Grant.

Elsey was wounded and taken to Cairo, Illinois. He died from wounds December 22, 1861.

MARILYN L. ELZROTH, Private First Class, served as an Army WAC during WWII from February 5, 1944 until discharged December 8, 1945, at Fort Des Moines, Iowa. She was born December 10, 1923 in Christopher, Illinois. She was a photostat operator at the time of her enlistment.

She served as a clerk general with Headquarters 463rd AAFBU, Geiger Field, Illinois. She received the American Campaign Medal, Good Conduct and WWII Medal. Her hometown at the time of enlistment was Prairie du Rocher, Illinois.

ALVIN ERDMAN, Private, was born December 5, 1923 in Horse Prairie, Illinois. He entered WWII on March 13, 1943 and lost his life on May 31, 1944 at Anzie Beachhead Invasion, Salerno,

Pvt. Alvin Erdmann

Italy after being transferred from fighting in Africa.

He served with Battalion A, Company 34, 175th Field Artillery. His parents are Arnold and Lu Erdmann.

ARNOLD ERDMANN, Private, born August 24, 1894 in Horse Prairie, Illinois. He entered WWI on June 24, 1918 and was sent to France with Battery E, 119th Field Artillery. He was scheduled to go to the front line the next day, but in the middle of the night someone ran through the camp yelling, "the war is over."

Pvt. Arnold Erdmann

Arnold spent the next six months in France before being discharged April 30, 1919. He is the son of Rudolph and Caroline Hitzamen. He died August 30, 1989.

JAMES HARRY ERVIN, Captain, was born in Perry County, Illinois on July 31,

Capt. James H. Ervin

1919. He served in the U.S. Army for 30 years beginning in 1942. He was wounded in Europe in WWII and was in Korea and Vietnam.

He received two Purple Hearts and a Bronze Star. He was discharged in June 1972.

His name is in the Infantry Hall of Fame in Fort Benning, Georgia. He now lives in New Port Richie, Florida. He is the son of Lionel H. and Margaret E. Heppard Ervin.

LIONEL HARRY ERVIN, Master Sergeant, enlisted in the Air Force on June 23, 1947. He was a control tower operator. Lionel worked for the FAA as a control tower operator. He served his country in Vietnam at Pleiku.

M/Sgt. Lionel H. Ervin

Lionel retired in New Port Richie, Florida on May 31, 1968. He was born February 12, 1930, the son of Lionel H. and Margaret (Hippard) Ervin.

DONALD PAUL ESSELMAN, Sonar Man 2/c, U.S. Navy, March 27, 1951-April 20, 1955 and served aboard the USS *Bennington* and the USS *Taravia* with VF-72nd Squadron. He was awarded the National Defense Service Medal, Good Conduct Medal, Navy Occupation Service Medal w/European Clasp.

SN-2 Donald P. Esselmann

Returning home he married Lena Moranville and had four children. He was born March 27, 1933 in McBride, Missouri, the son of Patrick Louis and Lillian Anderson Esselman. He died December 11, 2001.

He said, "I am proud to have served our country. I also am proud to have served with the best men this country had to offer."

THEODORE W. FADLER, Staff Sergeant, served in WWII in the 317th T.C. Squadron after enlisting in the Army on October 15, 1942. He attended Aircraft Mechanic School to become a radio operator on a C-47 in India, Burma and China. He was a member of the WWII Air Commandos. Fadler was discharged November 11, 1945.

S/Sgt Theodore W. Fadler

He returned home, opened a welding business, until 1958, when appointed postmaster in Prairie du Rocher, Illinois. He received postmaster appointment in Red Bud, Illinois in 1976. Theodore was born July 26, 1920 in Lithium, Missouri, the son of Andrew and Frances Brown Fadler. He died November 1, 1993. He has a son, son-in-law and three grandsons who are veterans.

DOUGLAS FALKENHEIN, Specialist E-5, entered the military in September 1966 and was with the 2nd Battalion, 7th Cavalry, 1st Air Cavalry. He fought in the 1966 TET Offensive, Breaking Siege of Khe Sanh.

Spc/5 Douglas Falkenhein

Doug was a field medic with the 1st Air Cavalry and sent to the field shortly before the TET offensive began. Their battalion received heavy casualties trying to reinforce Marines in the city of Hue. Their division was also involved in breaking the siege of Khe Sanh. He was honorably discharged in September 1968.

He was born August 18, 1947 in Red Bud, Illinois, the son of Harold and Florentine (Koester) Falkenhein. Doug lives in Sparta, Illinois and works for the state of Illinois.

JOSEPH C. FAVIER, Specialist 5, served in Vietnam in Company E, 702nd Maintenance Battalion. He entered the service in September 1965. After basic training at Fort Leonard Wood, Missouri, he was sent to ASCOM AB where he was an airframe repairman, repairing helicopters and fixed wing aircraft.

Spc/5 Joseph C. Favier

Favier received the National Defense Medal. He was discharged at Seattle, Washington in July 1967. He is from Sparta, Illinois and the son of Clarence and Lillian Klien Favier.

ARNOLD DEAN FEAMAN, Seaman 1/c, entered WWII November 24, 1944 and went to Gunnery School at Great Lakes. He was shipped to Idaho, then to California.

Arnold boarded a ship and sailed to

Seaman 1/c Arnold Dean Feaman

Japan. Then he was on a tour of South Pacific before returning to the United States. He was discharged in July 1945.

He is the son of Arnold and Aleda Ahrens Feaman and was born at Fort Gage, Illinois on December 12, 1926.

CAROL P. FEAMAN, Airman 1/c, USAF 1954-58, served with the 12th Air Force, 21st Fighter Bomber Wing. After basic training at Lackland AFB, Texas and Electronics School, Scott AFB, Illinois, he was an electronics instructor at Scott AFB, Illinois.

Airman 1/c Carol P. Feaman

He was the forward air controller, Chambley AB, France with the 12th Air Force, 21st Fighter-Bomber Wing. He was discharged in New York and became an electrician and later a project manager.

Carol was born December 17, 1934 at Ellis Grove, Illinois, the son of Arnold and Aleda Ahrens Feaman.

CHARLES P. FEY, Chief Metal Smith Officer 3/c, was drafted into the Navy November 16, 1943 and went to Great Lakes Naval Training Center. He then served in Pearl Harbor, Guam, Carolina Islands and in the invasion of Iwo Jima and Okinawa in WWII.

Chief Metal Smith Off. Charles P. Fey

Charles was discharged January 3, 1946 and returned to Chester, Illinois to continue in the sheet metal business with his father, where he had worked before the war.

He was born in Chester, Illinois December 7, 1920 to Oscar and Lydia Wolter Fey. At the time of his death, January 14, 1986, he was a sheet metal instructor at Southern Illinois University in Carbondale, Illinois.

JAMES J. FEY, SS MB, 3/c Petty Officer, enlisted in WWII in 1943. Boot training was at Camp Hill, Faragut, Idaho; advanced training was in San Diego, California and Treasure Island. He served in the USS *Horace Wells*, USS *Wallowa, Bon Homme Richard* A.C., Headquarters Guam and other Pacific islands, also in Atlantic Theatre before discharged in 1946.

3/c Petty Off. James J. Fey

He was born in Chester, Illinois July 20, 1925. His parents were Edward and __ Bollman Fey. He retired from the Department of Corrections in Chester in 1985.

DANIEL F. FICKLES, Bugler, born September 13, 1839 and served in Company H.M., 7th Illinois Cavalry for three years during the Civil War. William P. Kellog was elected colonel when the 7th Cavalry was organized in September 1861. This regiment participated in many important engagements of the war. He mustered out October 15, 1864.

Daniel died January 4, 1881 and is buried in Kelly Cemetery in Evansville, Illinois.

JOHN WILLIAM FILE, Lieutenant, entered the U.S. Navy July 8, 1963, after completing ROTC at Notre Dame University. He served as communications officer aboard the USS *Independence*, in the Naval Security Group Activity in Todendorf, Germany and in the office of the staff civil engineer at Coronado Naval Amphibious Base. He was discharged from service July 25, 1968.

Lt. John W. File

John was born in Chester, Illinois July 16, 1941, the son of John A. and Helen M. Lamb File. At the time of his death in 1999, he was employed by Morrison and Foerester Law Associates in San Francisco.

LUCIEN ANDREW FILE, Lieutenant, served in the U.S. Navy during WWII serving in South Pacific Theatre, where he received four Battle Stars. He trained pilots at Vicuy Airport, Ferry Squadron One, delivering planes from factories to aircraft carriers, intelligence duties, personnel duties and operations officer with public relations rating. He served in USS *Onslow*, USS *Kenneth Whiting* and USS *Coos Bay*.

Lt. Lucien A. File

Awards received were the Navy Unit Citation, American Theater of Operation, Pacific Theater of Operation w/4 stars, Philippine Liberation w/star and Victory Medal.

Lucien is the son of John A. and Alice Potts File. He was born May 13, 1908 in Greenville, Illinois.

GRAYDON M. "FRENCHIE" FINK, Technical Sergeant, U.S. Army served with the 33rd Division, Company K, 130th Infantry Regiment during WWII and received the Silver Star for "resourcefulness and courageous conduct under intense enemy fire" during a battle in Luzon, Philippine Islands.

T/Sgt. Graydon M. Fink

He was recalled from the Reserves during the Korean War and served from January 1949 to March 1954. He was born May 8, 1922 in Fort Gage, Illinois, the son of Joyce and Bernice Louveau Fink.

JOHN J. FINK, Private First Class Medical Corpsman, was born March 28, 1919 in Ellis Grove, Illinois to Joyce and Bernice Louveau Fink. He was inducted into the Army Air Force February 25, 1943 at Scott Field and served in the 449th Bomb Group, 719th Bomb Squadron, 47th Wing of the 15th Army Air Force. He was first stationed at Grottagile, Italy, then saw action at Naples, Foggia, Rome, Arno, Northern France, Po Valley, Southern France, Normandy, Rhineland and Balkens European air combat offensives. He was discharged September 12, 1945.

Pfc. John J. Fink

Fink received the European-African-Middle Eastern Theatre Ribbon w/2 Silver Battle Stars, two Overseas Service Bars, Headquarters 719th Bomb Squadron 44 Distinguished Unit Badge w/Bronze Oak Leaf Cluster and Good Conduct Medal.

He returned home, owned grocery stores in Riley Lake and Ellis Grove, Illinois from 1941-84. He died March 11, 2000.

RICHARD D. FINK, Private First Class, U.S. Army 1951-53, served with

Pfc. Richard D. Fink

Battery A, 147th Field Artillery in the Korean War. He was born February 26, 1930, at Fort Gage, Illinois, the son of Joyce and Bernice Louveau Fink.

KENNETH OLIN FINLEY, U.S. Navy, WWII, served four years, primarily in the Hong Kong and Tai Pai areas aboard the USS *Salisbury*. He was born April 7, 1927 in Sparta, Illinois, the son of John Melville and Mary Ethel Steele Finley. He died March 10, 1998 in St. Louis.

EDWARD J. FISHER, Lance Corporal, served in the USMC from 1961-64. He was in Headquarters Fleet Marine Pacific, 29 Palms, California. Then a training center, also other bases in California.

L/Cpl Edward J. Fisher

He has been a practicing attorney in Chester, Illinois since 1971, and is senior partner in the firm of Fisher, Kerkhover and Welge. His parents are Edward J. Fisher Sr. and Vera Meyer Fisher.

WILLIAM E. FLANIGAN, Pharmacist Mate 2/C, was born December 19, 1923, the son of Robert and Ethel Jones Flanigan. He went into WWII service from Sparta, Illinois, in September 1942.

He was stationed at Great Lakes, Quantico, Virginia, Marine Barracks, 140th NCB, South Pacific FIC, Admiral Islands, Australia.

Ph M 2/c William E. Flanigan

William received the American Area Victory Medal, Asiatic-Pacific Ribbon and Good Conduct Medal. He was discharged in January 1946.

BILL FORTNER, First Sergeant, entered military service February 25, 1943, and received basic training with the 76th Infantry Battalion at Camp Roberts, California. He was then assigned to the 6th Infantry Division, Company C, 63rd Regiment, known as the "Sightseeing Sixth."

1st Sgt. Bill Fortner & son, Clay

After spending six months in Hawaii on beach defense, amphibious and jungle training, he was sent to New Guinea in January 1944 and landed in Milne Bay. The 6th Infantry Division spent one year there. Campaign of Maffin Bay included Toem and Lone Tree Hill, then onto Sansapor. He received a Bronze Star for action on Hill 265.

In January 1945, the 6th Division was shipped to the Philippines. January 9-31 they spent fighting what was called the Purple Heart Valley Campaign, including battles of Cabaruan Hill and Munoz. From combat in Bataan, we went on to break the Shimbu Line, protecting Manila.

February 20 through April 30, 1945, the 'Sightseeing Sixth' spent 112 days of continuous combat, which was a record for the Pacific Theater. Also saw action at Baguio and Central Luzon, and was fighting in Northern Luzon at Kiangan when the cease-fire stopped activity on August 15, 1945.

Discharged June 1947, he joined the 102nd Division at Fort Ord, California and in the spring of 1948 volunteered to escort dead soldiers home from Fort Sheridan. Escorted 66 soldiers home all over the U.S. by train. Served as a scout for the 63rd, then squad leader, and platoon sergeant while overseas, and after 40 years, five months, 27 days service, officially retired September 1, 1983.

He was born September 1, 1923, Flat River, Missouri, the son of Sam Henry and Ida Mirtle Mounce Fortner, he now resides near Sparta, Illinois.

ALAN "IZZY" FOSTER, E-4, to anyone who knows Alan, knows him as Izzy. Izzy was drafted August 14, 1969. He did his basic training at Fort Leonard Wood, Missouri. Then he did his AIT at Fort Ord, California. He was home for 28 days, then shipped to Nam.

E-4 Alan Foster

Arriving in that country with the 21st Cavalry Fire Base near the village of Song Mao, 40 miles west of Phan Rang. He went to Cambodia for 30 days in July, then back to Song Mao until September 1970. Then he was assigned to the 1/50th Mech. until December of 1970. He then joined a LRRP Team with the 1/10th Cavalry. They went out in four-man teams to seek out and evade the enemy and call in air strikes and be T extracted.

He came back to the States March 21, 1971 to Fort Lewis, Washington. Izzy was born in Sparta, Illinois December 3, 1949 to James and Allean (Lively) Foster.

To those that served and came back, welcome home!! To those that gave the ultimate sacrifice, you will never ever be forgotten!

JAMES M. FOSTER, Technical Sergeant, entered WWII March 14, 1942 and served with the 321st Service Squadron, 560th Service Squadron and 43rd Service Group.

T/Sgt James M. Foster

He left Camp Kilmer and arrived Casablanca in January 1943 and spent six months in North Africa. He was on Island of Sicily July 1943-September 1943, then to Salerno Beach, Italy until July 1944, from there to Corsica, France until April 1945, when they left for Bittle Born, Germany. The 321st was disbanded in May 1945, and was back in the States July 14, 1945.

James was born in Sparta, Illinois March 7, 1915, the son of Harry G. and Catherine France Foster.

WILLIAM FOWLER, Private, was from Camden District, South Carolina, which was later called York District, South Carolina. His service in the Revolutionary War was in Capt. John Chambers Company, in Colonel William Bratton's South Carolina Regiment. He served one year 1781-82.

Fowler was born November 18, 1764, in Mecklenburg County, North County. He was the son of Rev. James and Mary Stephenson Fowler. He was reared principally in York District, South Carolina and in 1811 left there for Livingston County Kentucky, where he lived until 1816, when he moved to Randolph County, Illinois, with his wife, Hannah Tindall, and five children. He died April 18, 1846, and is buried in Randolph County.

DEWAYNE L. FOX, Seaman 1/c, entered the Navy in WWII on April 28, 1941 and served as radio man SV V-6. He was discharged in 1945 from the U.S. Naval Hospital in Great Lakes, Illinois due to a problem with his knee.

Fox was born September 19, 1915, in Hillsboro, Illinois. His parents were Samuel and Taylor Fox.

HAROLD OLIVER FOX, Technician Fourth Grade, was in WWII in the 531st Quarter Master Supply (American Graves Command) from July 17, 1945 to May 14, 1947. He was stationed at Fontainebleau, France.

Fox was born at Elton, Illinois March 6, 1927, the son of Oliver M. and Edna Huff Fox. He married April 13, 1950, Doris M. Rust, and lived in Coulterville, Illinois. He worked for Fisher Body Plant in St. Louis. Fox died February 27, 2002.

ERWIN A. FRAGER, Private First Class, served in the Korean Conflict, in 101st Airborne Division, Japan Central Exchange from 1950-52.

He was reared in Chester, Illinois, the son of Morris J. and Kate S. Neuman Frager.

LEO CLYDE FRANKLIN, Painter 1/c, served in the U.S. Navy during WWII on USS *Castor Ksi*, taking supplies to other ships in Guadalcanal, Luzon and Leyte in the Philippines. He spent 38 months at sea, serving overseas bases with landing equipment and other supplies until February 15, 1945. He went into service November 10, 1941 and was discharged September 13, 1945.

Painter 1/c Leo C. Franklin

When he returned to the States he was in a bar in San Diego when a photographer came in and selected Franklin and two others to pose for advertisement for Milky Way candy bars and a Coca-Cola poster. Payment for this was getting his photo on a poster for Collier magazine, some candy bars and a bottle of hot coke. He still has the poster.

Franklin was born February 14, 1920 in Prairie du Rocher, Illinois to Harry and Agnes Braun Franklin.

ALVIN WILSON FRAZER, Seaman First Class, son of Harry and Susan Belle

Seaman 1/c Alvin W. Frazer

Cashion Frazer, was born at Rockwood, Illinois, October 3, 1925. He enlisted in the Navy September 24, 1943 and was assigned to 98th Special Naval Construction Battalion. He was discharged March 26, 1946.

Frazer died March 19, 1954 and is buried in Evergreen Cemetery in Chester, Illinois.

CLIFFORD FRAZER, Seaman First Class, was born March 1, 1925 in Rockwood, Illinois to Noah and Della Rice Frazer. He enlisted in the Navy at St. Louis, Missouri April 20, 1942.

Seaman 1/c Clifford Frazer

He served on nine known ships during his service and attended the Armed Guard Gunnery School. He was discharged October 4, 1945, as a seaman first class.

Clifford passed away in Flat River, Missouri April 12, 1986 leaving a wife and two daughters.

DAVID G. FRAZER, Sergeant E-5, U.S. Army, was born Aug. 7, 1929 in Chester, Illinois, the son of Noah and Della Rice Frazer. Enlisting July 1948, David served in Japan and Korea with Headquarters Company, 87th Infantry, 10th Infantry Division. He was wounded and received the Purple Heart.

Frazer was awarded the Army Occupation Service Medal, Korean Presidential Unit Citation, Good Conduct and Ko-

Sgt. E-5 David G. Frazer

rean Service Medal w/5 Bronze Stars. He was discharged in 1952.

He died October 10, 1997 in Percy, Illinois leaving his wife and four children.

ELLEN A. FRAZER, First Lieutenant, entered active duty as a nurse May 8, 1942, served in Northern France and Rhineland from October 9, 1943 until November 21, 1945 during WWII. She was discharged from Fort Des Moines, Iowa February 14, 1946.

Ellen received the WWII Victory Medal, Eastern-African-Middle Eastern Campaign Medal w/2 Bronze Stars and American Campaign Medal w/4 Overseas Bars.

She was born August 31, 1918 in Rockwood, Illinois, the daughter of Edward and Bertha Draves Frazer. She is now in a nursing home in Texas.

FRANK D. FRAZER, Private First Class, was with Company B, 24th Batt. Engineer Battalion in Germany from 1966-68, after enlisting and receiving training at Fort Leonard Wood, Missouri.

Pfc. Frank D. Frazer

He is the son of Harry A. and Wanda Hasemeyer Frazer of Chester, Illinois. He has worked on river construction for Luhr Brothers since discharge from the service.

HENRY S. FRAZER, Staff Sergeant, entered the Air Force May 15, 1944 at Fort Sheridan, Illinois. He served with the 117th AACS Squadron during WWII. He was discharged June 16, 1946 from Fort Leavenworth, Kansas.

He returned to the Belleville, Illinois area, later moved to Oklahoma. Frazer is the son of Ira and Grace G. Griffen Frazer. He was born in Rockwood, Illinois, November 29, 1921.

JAMISON FRAZER, Specialist 4, enlisted in the Army on June 4, 1991. He took basic training at Fort Polk, Louisiana. Then he went on to complete Airborne School at Fort Benning, Georgia.

Spec/4 Jamison Frazer

Frazer arrived to his unit in the fall of 1991 and 12 months later completed Air Assault School at Fort Campbell, Kentucky. Jamison was with Company B, 2nd Platoon, 4/325 82nd Airborne Division. He has been working at Menard Correctional Center in Chester, Illinois since 1996.

Jamison was born August 23, 1973, the son of Mike and Sherri A. Linton Frazer.

JOE T. FRAZER, attained the rank of wagoner with the 79th Field Artillery

Wagoner Joe T. Frazer

Wagon Supply Company of the Army Infantry. He enlisted in WWI at Jefferson Barracks, Missouri on May 11, 1917. He spent time at Fort Riley, Kansas. He was

Supply Wagon, Fort Riley.

discharged June 30, 1919. He was the son of Thomas and Mary Landis Frazer.

KENNETH C. FRAZER, Sergeant, entered the Army in April 1968. He took his basic training at Fort Leonard Wood, Missouri. He got to Vietnam September 7, 1968, as a medic, and was hit by a bomb two days later trying to help others wounded, neglecting himself.

Sgt. Kenneth C. Frazer

Medals he earned was a Bronze Star w/V Device for Heroism, Purple Heart for wounds received in action, Good Conduct Medal, National Defense Medal, Vietnam Service Ribbon, South Vietnamese Service Medal and the Airborne Insignia Aeromedical Insignia and the Marksmanship Badge (rifle).

Kenneth was 22 years, 11 months and 23 days when he was killed in action. His body was shipped home and his funeral held September 18, 1968. He is with his father now in Heaven.

MICHAEL W. FRAZER, Specialist 4, enlisted into the Army January 23, 1968. Mike took his basic training and AIT at Fort Leonard Wood, Missouri. He was shipped to join Company E, 2/505th Reconnaissance, 82nd Airborne Division, and 3rd Brigade in Vietnam in June 1968. Assignment with a very small reconnaissance group involved several daytime operations in addition to over 200 night ambushes in areas near Hue, Saigon, Nihau Tran and other Cambodian borders.

Spec/4 Michael W. Frazer

In January 1969 he was chosen and attached to Green Beret Special Forces at Nihau Tran for specialized training and missions earning a MACV Redondo uniform patch.

He was awarded six medals during his Vietnam tour including the Army Commendation Medal and Bronze Star Medal.

Mike was born May 19, 1948 in Littlefield, Texas to Alvin W. and Ruth N. Tiller Frazer.

TERRY W. FRAZER, Sergeant E-5, entered the military December 17, 1970, took his basic training at Fort Leonard Wood, Missouri. He went to Fort Polk, Louisiana for his AIT. Had his airborne training at Fort Benning, Georgia. Assigned to the 82nd Airborne Division at Fort Bragg, North Carolina. Then he completed Range Mountaineering School.

Sgt. E-5 Terry W. Frazer

While in Vietnam he was assigned with A Company, 2nd Battalion, 325th Infantry Brigade, and 82nd Airborne Division.

His awards included Airborne Insignia and Expert Infantryman's Badge. He was honorably discharged September 18, 1972.

Frazer is the son of Harry A. and Wanda Hasemeyer Frazer and was born in Ellis Grove, Illinois.

WALTER SIDNEY FRAZER, Technical Sergeant, entered the service April 6, 1943 and was assigned to Company F, 377th Infantry, and 95th Division during WWII. He was in Ardennes, Belgium, Rhineland, Germany and Central Europe. He served as platoon sergeant.

Frazer was awarded the Purple Heart, Silver Star, European-African-Middle Eastern Theatre Ribbon w/3 Bronze Stars, WWII Victory Medal and Combat Infantry Badge. He was discharged November 19, 1945 at Camp Custer, Michigan.

At the end of WWII he joined the Reserves and was recalled to active duty during the Korean War.

He was born in Rockwood, Illinois, January 6, 1925, the son of Ira and Grace G. Griffin Frazer. He now resides in Monahan, Texas.

WILLIAM D. FRAZER, Specialist 4, served with HHC 2/503rd Infantry, 173rd Airborne Brigade (Sep.) in Vietnam. He enlisted in the Army February 17, 1966 and had training at Fort Leonard Wood, Missouri, then advanced training at Fort Banning, Georgia for Jump School.

Spec-4 William D. Frazer

He was sent to Germany for six months and transferred to Vietnam, arriving there in February 1967 to serve 19 months with 173rd Airborne Brigade (Sep.). Frazer was discharged October 19, 1968.

His parents, Harry A. and Wanda M. Hasemeyer Frazer, live in Chester, Illinois.

CHARLES WAYNE FRICKE, Technician Fourth Grade, entered WWII service March 26, 1946 and served at Fort Sill, Oklahoma in Headquarters Battery, 18th Field Artillery attached to Instrument and Survey Company. He received the WWII Victory Medal.

Charles was born August 6, 1924 at Rockwood, Illinois, the son of Fred and Emma Bell Krug Fricke. He was discharged from Fort Sill, September 25, 1947.

He worked in construction work and farmed. He died September 24, 1984 at John Cochran Hospital in St. Louis. Charles is buried in Barnfield Cemetery on Pleasant Ridge near Rockwood.

JOHN C. FULFORD, Private First Class, was inducted into WWII October 27, 1942 and served with 858th CML Company where he drove 3/4 and 2-1/2 ton trucks, hauling personnel, demolitions, bombs, gasoline and other military supplies/equipment. He was discharged January 15, 1946.

John drove an ice and coal truck, farmed some and retired from Baldwin Power Plant as a teamster. He was born in Rockwood, July 8, 1921, the son of Jewett and Lottie Mansker Fulford. He died December 2, 1993 and is buried in Fulford-Springvale Cemetery near Rockwood, Illinois.

DALE L. FULTON, Lieutenant Colonel, USAF served February 1953 to September 1973. He was born in Tilden, Illinois, the son of William Vernon and Florence Nitzsche Fulton. Dale went through flight training in the Aviation Cadet Program.

Lt. Col. Dale L. Fulton

After earning his Wings, he flew fighter Aircraft in the Air Defense Command for 12 years. He then served in attaché, administrative and staff positions. He retired in 1973 with over 5,000 hours flying time and many awards and decorations.

WALTER F. DURHAM, Technical Sergeant, the son of Walter A. and Rose Jung Durham, of Sparta, Illinois, served in the Army during WWII from April 23, 1942 until January 2, 1946 with Company C, 770th Ry. Opn. Battalion.

PAUL ROBERT GAERTNER, Sergeant, was drafted into WWII at age 18, August 6, 1943 and served in Northern

Sgt. Paul R. Gaertner

Solomon and Luzon campaigns with the 145th Infantry. He was awarded two Bronze Stars. Gaertner was discharged January 31, 1946.

He worked at Con-Agra Inc., Chester, Illinois until his retirement. He was born April 30, 1925 at Evansville, Illinois and died July 15, 1999, with cancer. His parents were Lawrence and Susanna Hesse Gaertner Sr.

GREGORY P. GARDINER, Construction Mechanic, E-6, Construction Mechanic 1/c, entered the Navy after high school in August 1971. He went to boot camp at Great Lakes Naval Training Center, Illinois, then to Construction Mechanic School in Davisville, Rhode Island. He was shipped to Public Works Department Sid: Yahia Morrocco (U.S. Naval Air Station).

CM/1 Greg Gardiner

Greg returned to the States to "A" Company, A.C.B.II Little Creek, Virginia (Amphibious Construction Batt.). Then back to Supply Depot, Roosevelt Roads, Puerto Rico (U.S. Naval Station). Next to "A" Company, A.C.B.I Amphibious Construction Batt. He was then shipped to Naval Resale Activity, Adak, Alaska. Greg was discharged from Seattle, Washington in August 1991 after serving his country 20 years and four days.

He was born in Sparta, Illinois on February 25, 1952. His parents are Russell M. Gardiner and Ethel F. "Babe" Dobyns Gardiner Spitzmiller. After his military career he resides in California.

GERALDINE LANGWITH GARDNER, Sergeant, enlisted December 18, 1945 and was inducted January 9, 1945 in WWII, Army, 107th WAC Division. She served as company clerk, handled personnel records, reports for 400 WAC personnel, composed and typed correspondence and orders.

Sgt. Geraldine L. Gardner

She also served in Transportation Corps. She acted as first sergeant in absence of regular first sergeant. She was awarded the American Theatre, Victory and Good Conduct medals. She left the service May 13, 1946.

Geraldine was born in Sparta, Illinois on July 28, 1924, the daughter of Otis and Ruth Mann Langwith.

WILLARD GARDNER, AMM1/c (T), served in the U.S. Navy in WWII. He enlisted December 8, 1941, the day after Pearl Harbor was bombed. He had training at Naval Air Station, Corpus Christi, Texas, then to Guam. He served until January 7, 1946.

AMM 1/c Willard Gardner

Gardner was awarded the Asiatic-Pacific Ribbon, American Theatre Medal, Good Conduct Medal and Victory Medal.

He came home to work for Illinois Power Company for 41 years. He was the son of James W. and Gertie Harrell Gardner. Willard was born March 22, 1922 and died April 14, 2002.

ROBERT A. GEGGIE, Sergeant, served overseas 21 months in WWII. He was from Coulterville, Illinois, the son of Robert J. and Myrtle Carns Geggie. He entered service in the Marine Corps, November 7, 1942 and received basic training at San Diego. Attended Advanced Ordinance School in Norman, Oklahoma.

After training, he went to New Caledonia, off the coast of Australia, Espirito Santos, Brazil, New Hebrides Island, South Pacific, from there to Guadalcanal, where he joined MABs I-Ondago and Munda, and then to Mariana Islands. He was later stationed at Cherry Point, North Carolina; Boagfield, North Carolina; and Quantico, Virginia. He was discharged November 11, 1945 from Great Lakes Naval Station.

Robert has two sons who also served in the Marine Corps, one in Vietnam and the other in the Persian Gulf War.

JEAN BAPTISTE GENDRON, Private, was a soldier in the Revolutionary War from February 6 until March 13, 1779. He served with Captain Francis Charleville's Company of Kaskaskia Volunteers during George Rogers Clark capture of Vincennes or Fort Sackville. Kaskaskia was his hometown and Joseph Jacques and Marie Francoise Emond Gendron were his parents.

DONALD GENTSCH, Specialist 5, U.S. Army May 10, 1954-April 26, 1956, completed basic training at Camp Chaffee, Arkansas, then U.S. Army Ordnance School, Aberdeen Proving Grounds, Aberdeen, Maryland. He was assigned to the 256th Ordnance Company, Fort Riley, Kansas and 2nd Armor Davison, Baumholder, Germany.

Don was born in Chester on September 30, 1935, the son of William and Alma Bewie Gentsch.

LOUIS D. GERLACH, Private First Class, U.S. Army, was born October 13, 1930 in Chester, Illinois, the son of Albert and Lorene Modglin Gerlach. He served from April 1953 to April 1955 with the 115th Engineers in the States during the Korean Conflict. His basic training was at Fort Leonard Wood, Missouri,

Pfc. Louis D. Gerlach

then transferred to Fort Campbell, Kentucky.

RICHARD W. GERLACH, CMS E-9, served with the 1st Logistical Command in the Vietnam War. He enlisted October 15, 1958, in the Army and spent 27 years in various locations. From November 1968 to November 1969 he was stationed at Quinhon, Vietnam, then served four tours in Germany and one in Norway.

Stateside he was stationed in Missouri, Pennsylvania, twice in Virginia, Texas, Ohio and two times in California. He retired in Herlong, California on October 31, 1985 and moved to El Paso, Texas.

Richard was born in Chester, Illinois. His parents were Richard F. and Lena Weberling Gerlach.

DONALD GIBBS, Senior Master Sergeant, entered the Air Force in July 1966 and was discharged in 1973. He joined the Air Force Reserves in July 1973 in a dual role as a civilian military flight chief. While in Vietnam he served as a flight engineer on C-123 and C-47 aircraft.

SM/Sgt Donald Gibbs

Donald was born October 20, 1948 in Ware, Illinois to Jesse and Evelyn (VanDer) Hyden Gibbs. He served in Vietnam, Desert Storm and Enduring Freedom wars.

He will be leaving the U.S. Air Force in 2004 with over 38 years of service to his country.

JEFFREY D. GIBBS, E-4, U.S. Army, July 31, 1991-December 6, 1993, served with A Company, 864th Engineer Batt. in Somalia.

Jeff was born May 7, 1972 in Chester, Illinois, the son of Vincent and Marilyn Bodeker Gibbs.

Before enlisting he was a construction worker. After discharge he worked for Cerro Copper Products in Sauget, Illinois.

JESSE C. GIBBS, Private First Class, entered the Army in WWII in August 1940 and served with the 61st Coast Artillery, Anti-Aircraft Division. He was injured during an air raid at Keflavik, Iceland and was hospitalized for two years. He was discharged in October 1944 and returned to Chester, Illinois.

Pfc. Jesse C. Gibbs

Gibbs had a family of 10 children and worked at Menard Prison. He now resides at Marion Veterans Hospital. Jesse was born in Jonesboro, Illinois on July 5, 1920, the son of Arthur and Fannie Day Gibbs.

KEVIN LEE GILBERT, Petty Officer 2/c, enlisted in 1982 after high school. Kevin attended basic training at Orlando, Florida. Then he went to Aviation "A" School in Millington, Tennessee. He requested orders to an Anti-submarine Squadron (HSL 30) in Norfolk, Virginia, to be near his brother, Randy, currently

P.O. 2/c Kevin L. Gilbert

serving on the USS *Kid* (DDG-993). Kevin was discharged from active duty in 1988.

After active duty he returned to Illinois and attended college. Kevin joined the Reserves while in college in 1989 and continued to serve until 1994. He was with HS130, VP53 and NAFMISAWA.

Kevin was born in Chester, Illinois on September 1, 1964 to Walter E. and Ruby (Kirkover) Gilbert. He currently lives in the Chicago area with his wife, Denise, and their two sons.

RANDY E. GILBERT, Petty Officer 2/c, U.S. Navy March 1981-May 1986, was born in Chester, Illinois July 18, 1962, the son of Walter and Ruby Kirkover Gilbert.

P.O. 2/c Randy E. Gilbert

He served as electrician's mate aboard USS *Kidd*, GMD from February 1982-May 1986, making deployments, including operations in Grenada and Lebanon. He currently lives and works in Chester.

WALTER E. GILBERT, Sergeant, served in the 3505th Squadron of the U.S. Air Force during WWII. He entered service July 18, 1945 at Camp Shelby, Mississippi; boot camp at Sheppard Field, Texas; then transferred to Scott Field, Illinois for Radio School. He then worked in supply until discharged April 21, 1947.

Sgt. Walter E. Gilbert

Gilbert was born February 12, 1927, the son of O.M. and Mary Maupin Gilbert. He returned to Chester and worked in construction, then retired from Chester Water Department in 1989.

JAMES GILBREATH, a Revolutionary War Soldier, came to Illinois about the opening of the 19th century and settled at Kaskaskia, Illinois. He was an influential man in the history of early Randolph County.

As well as being a soldier, he was a land and slave owner, sheriff, county commissioner and a member of the House of Representatives. The house he built in 1772, at Kaskaskia, was the first capitol building for the state of Illinois.

He married in Pennsylvania and became the father of two sons, John R. and Barton. He came from Virginia where he served in the war. He died in Carlyle, Illinois, January 6, 1821 and was first buried in Kaskaskia, but later removed to Fort Gage when the current of the river washed away the old cemetery.

LOUIS H. GILSTER, Private, volunteered for service in the Civil War at age 17. He entered service in 1862 and served in Company H, Illinois Infantry, Army of Cumberland, then transferred to Company I, 22nd and 42nd Regiments of Illinois Infantry.

He took part in the battle at Stones River where 199 of 312 men were lost. He was in battles of Chickamauga, Mission Ridge, Chattanooga, Vicksburg, Shiloh Hill and New Orleans, then marched to aid Knoxville. After being wounded he was discharged and mustered out in 1864.

Louis returned to Chester, Illinois in 1865. He was the son of Henry Sr. and Dorothea Schrader Gilster.

ERIC P. GIRARD, AT-3, enlisted into the Navy on June 26, 1987 and was discharged on May 25, 1990. Following recruit training and Aviation Electronics School, he was assigned to the Special Projects Unit 2, NAS Barbers Point, Hawaii.

Eric was born October 20, 1965 in Clayton, Missouri. His mother is Delphine J. Koch. He is now employed as a field service engineer with Philips Medical Systems, headquartered in Best, Holland.

GARY D. GISCHER JR., E-5 (Sergeant), enlisted in the Army National Guard in 1989. He received basic training at Fort Leonard Wood, Missouri, then was assigned to 3/130th Infantry Unit, Marion, Illinois.

Sgt. E-5 Gary D. Gischer, Jr.

His duties were issuing equipment and vehicles and keeping records of all equipment in his job as supply clerk. He received advanced individual training at Fort Lee, Virginia before being discharged in 1995.

Gary was born in Chester, Illinois on September 25, 1969. He is the son of Gary and Linda Tindall Gischer.

LAWRENCE W. GOESSLING, Corporal, Technician Fifth Grade, entered service November 2, 1942 at Camp Grant, Illinois. He served in New Guinea, Luzon, Dutch East Indies, Japan and through South Pacific.

Cpl Lawrence W Goessling

He received two Bronze Stars, Asiatic Theatre Campaign Ribbon, three Overseas Bars, Victory Ribbon and ASR Sorce 59 Philippine Liberation Ribbon w/Bronze Star. He was discharged January 17, 1946.

Lawrence was born April 29, 1922 at Waterloo, Illinois. He died March 26, 2000 and is buried at St. Peter and Paul Cemetery in Waterloo.

LYLE NORMAN GORDON, born July 29, 1924 in Sparta, Illinois. He served in the U.S. Navy during WWII. He was inducted into service on January 22, 1942 with training at Great Lakes Naval Center. Gordon was discharged February 27, 1942.

He was the son of Paul and Lydia Gardiner Gordon. He was killed in car wreck May 19, 1948. Burial was in Caledonia Cemetery in Sparta.

STEPHEN E. GORDON, Sergeant First Class, enlisted April 25, 1986. Stephen took his basic training at Fort Dix, New Jersey from June 1986 to August 1986. Then he went to Fort Gordon, Georgia from June 1987 to September 1987 for advanced individual training.

Sgt. 1/c Stephen E. Gordon

He took an instructor training course at Illinois Military Academy in June 1989, after which Stephen went to Camp Ashland, Nebraska in August 1991 for a primary leadership development course. Then he went back to the Illinois Military Academy from November through December 1992 for basic non-commissioned officer course.

In June 1996 Stephen went back to Camp Ashland, Nebraska for an advanced non-commissioned officer course. He served with Company B, 133rd Signal Battalion. Stephen's service career ended on April 24, 2002. He is the son of Stan and Susan-Clinken-Beard-Gordon-Schram and s/son of Scot Schram.

TIMOTHY A. GRAFF, E-5, U.S. Army, August 1986-November 2000,

AT/3 Eric P. Girard

served with the military police. He completed basic training and AIT at Fort McClelland, Anniston, Alabama and served two deployments to Haiti and one to Bosnia.

He is presently employed by the Department of Energy, Albuquerque, New Mexico. He was born February 19, 1968, the son of Carol Winn Graff.

DONALD RAY GRAH, USAF, 1953-57, completed basic training at Parks AFB, California, then A&E School at Amarillo, Texas. He then was crew chief on a F-86-F and then crewed a 7-33 in Korea. Then Parks AFB for release of duty.

Donald R. Grah

He was born August 17, 1933 in Ellis Grove, Illinois, the son of Harlan and Opal Marie Bollinger Grah.

WILLIAM F. GRAH, Staff Sergeant, served in the Medics during WWII, in France and Germany. He enlisted in 1943 and was discharged in 1946. He returned home and continued farming and trucking, then worked for the Illinois Department of Transportation.

S/Sgt William F. Grah

Grah was born in Rockwood, Illinois, May 16, 1922, the son of Eugene and Regina Casten Grah. He died October 12, 1984.

MATTHEW A. GRAU, E-3, Lance Corporal, born March 20, 1980 in

L/Cpl Matthew A. Grau

Belleville, Illinois, to Norman and Thelma Schwenke Grau. He enlisted in the USMC September 9, 1998. He trained at MCRD San Diego and Camp Pendleton, California. He transferred to Camp Lejeune, North Carolina. A training accident caused him to leave service on May 15, 2000.

CHARLES ROY GRAY, Private, enlisted in the Army during WWI on February 24, 1918, at Chester, Illinois. He served as a cook and baker until discharged at Camp Grant, Illinois on July 29, 1919. His parents were Albert and Melissa Armstrong Gray.

GEORGE H. GRAY, Corporal, born at Rockwood, Illinois September 23, 1886 to Albert and Melissa Armstrong Gray. He served with Infantry, Company A, 309th Engineers in WWI from February 24, 1918 until discharged at Camp Grant, Illinois July 18, 1919.

He sailed from the United States July 11, 1918 and saw service in France until July 11, 1919.

George died February 21, 1962 and is buried in Ebenezer Cemetery near Rockwood, Illinois.

ROBERT W. GRAY, Sergeant, was inducted into WWII March 14, 1942 at Scott Field, Illinois. He served as a cook with Headquarters Detachment, 1908th SCU.

Gray received the American Campaign and Victory medals. He was discharged December 12, 1945 at Camp Cook, California.

He was born May 17, 1919 in Chester, Illinois, the son of Guy and Bertha Hindman Gray. He now lives in Chester.

RICHARD SAMUEL GRECCO, Chief Warrant Officer II, USMC April 1976-April 1996, enlisted in 1976 and served 20 years with the USMC Air Wing.

CWO/2 Richard S. Grecco

He served as a recruiter, earning "Recruiter of the Nation" in 1986.

Retiring from the Marine Corps, he now is employed by Chromoloy Aeronautics at Fort Walton, Florida. Richard was born January 26, 1956 at Scott AFB, Illinois, the son of Samuel J. and Norma Petry Grecco.

DELBERT L. GREEN, Private First Class, was born November 23, 1922 at Coulterville, Illinois. He was drafted into WWII in 1943 and served in the Army Air Force in Italy. Green was discharged in 1946.

Pfc. Delbert L. Green

Delbert died January 8, 1998. He was the son of Hugh and Eva Heinke Green.

FLOYD R. GREEN, Specialist 4, enlisted in June 1958 and took his basic training in Fort Leonard Wood, Missouri. Then he went to Fort Gordon, Georgia for AIT.

Spec/4 Floyd R. Green

After that he went to Fort Lewis, Washington and then to Germany until 1961. Floyd was with the 8th Army Division. He was in the Reserves until 1964.

Floyd was born February 28, 1940 in Coulterville, Illinois, the son of Hugh and Eva (Heinke) Green.

IVAN I. GREEN, Chief Warrant 2, enlisted in the Army in 1952. Ivan was stationed at Lawton, Oklahoma. Then he went to Seattle, Washington. From there he took a boat to Vietnam for his tour of duty. Ivan was with the HHB 41st Artillery Group.

CW2 Ivan I. Green

His family had moved back to Coulterville while he was stationed in Vietnam. Ivan had been in the military for 15 years. He was reported missing when his plane went down on April 8, 1969 and on August 8th the family was notified his body had been found.

Ivan was born in Coulterville, Illinois on April 26, 1935 to Eva (Heinke) and Hugh Green. Fort Sill, Oklahoma has a dining hall named in his honor. His body was brought home to Coulterville, Illinois. The family was proud and comforted when the flags were flown and the business places closed their doors in respect during the services. Ivan's interment, with full military honors, was in Memorial Gardens, Lawton, Ohio.

LAWRENCE E. GREEN, Chief Warrant 3, was with the 30th Infantry Division in the Battle of the Bulge during WWII. He was drafted July 4, 1944 and was a prisoner of war during the end of WWII. He served 12 months in Germany, 13 months in Korea and the remainder of his service time was in various locations. He retired from military service May 31, 1966.

Lawrence was born in Coulterville, Illinois on March 8, 1926, the son of Hugh and Eva Heinke Green.

RUSSELL GREEN, Airman 1/c, was born December 23, 1921 and spent his life in Rockwood, Illinois. He served in the Korean War.

Russell died June 8, 1973 and is buried in Buchanan Cemetery, Jackson County, Illinois.

VERNON H. GREEN, Corporal, served with Signal Corps, 8th Air Force during WWII. He was drafted in 1943 and did his tour of service in the United States. He was discharged in February 1946.

Cpl. Vernon H. Green

Vernon was born January 9, 1924, the son of Hugh and Eva Heinke Green.

BARRY J. GREER, IC-2, U.S. Navy, March 29, 1985-July 21, 1992, served aboard the USS *Wichita* AOR-1 and USS *Ainsworth* FF-1090. He completed basic training and BE/E and E.T. "A" schools at Great Lakes, Illinois; Nuclear Power School, Orlando, Florida; Naval Hospital, Oakland, California; then the USS *Wichita* out of Oakland, the USS *Ainsworth* out of Staten Island, New York. Greer was discharged from active duty in 1990. He was in the active Reserves until 1992.

Barry was born July 29, 1965 in Chester, Illinois, the son of Jimmie W. and Shirley Sebastian Greer. Currently he is an electrician living in Selden, Long Island, New York

BRUCE B. GREER, Seaman Apprentice III, U.S. Navy April 1, 1976-March 30, 1979, served with the Pacific Fleet aboard the USS *Kiska* AE-35. He completed basic training in Orlando, Florida and was assigned to the USS *Kiska*, becoming a hydraulic winch operator during UNRR (underway replenishment), transferring bombs and fuel. His homeport was Concord, California and overseas, Subic Bay, Philippine Islands.

SA-3 Bruce B. Greer

He was born in Chester February 9, 1957, the son of Jimmie W. and Shirley Sebastian Greer.

DAVID B. GREER, Private, U.S. Army, 1981-83, served with 502nd Engineers. He completed basic training at Fort Leonard Wood, Missouri, then Engineers Support training for the Airborne at Fort Campbell, Kentucky. He was discharged in 1983.

CW3 Lawrence Green

IC-2 Barry J. Greer

Pvt. David B. Greer

David was born October 19, 1962 in Chester, Illinois, the son of Jimmie W. and Shirley Sebastian Greer. He died September 12, 1991.

GERHARD WILBERT GREFE, Private First Class, was with the 222nd Quartermaster, 576th Air MAT, Squadron 13 in the Air Force during WWII, from February 16, 1945 until December 11, 1946.

Originally from Steeleville, Illinois, he is the son of Henry and Elfredia Trede Grefe. After four months of basic training he served 18 months on the island of Cebu, with the 13th Air Force.

LLOYD E. GRIGGS, Specialist 4, enlisted into the Army in 1965 and was with the U.S. Army Signal Corps. Lloyd served in Germany during the Vietnam War as a wire and lineman.

Sp/4 Lloyd E. Griggs

He was born September 16, 1945 in St. Louis, Missouri to Lloyd O. and __ Lang. Lloyd died November 6, 1985.

FREDERICK GROB, served in the Civil War as a blacksmith in Company B, 12th Regiment of the Missouri Infantry, for a term of three years. Frederick was severely wounded in the Battle of Vicksburg on May 22, 1863. He was hospitalized for six weeks in Memphis and returned to service in September 1863. He was honorably discharged September 4, 1864 from Jonesboro, Georgia.

Grob was born February 1, 1842 and died April 21, 1895. He is buried in the Grob family plot in Kelly Cemetery in Evansville, Illinois.

DENNIS E. GROSS, Builder 2/c, U.S. Navy Seabees, enlisted into the Navy September 25, 1968. Dennis served 14 months in Vietnam. He did construction in Da Nang, Chu Lai and Cam Rahn Bay.

Dennis was born in Chester, Illinois

Bld. S/B Dennis E. Gross

on October 15, 1948 to Lawrence and Helen (Bertholl) Gross.

HERMAN E. GROSS, Corporal, U.S. Army, active service 1954-56, served with the 820th Engineer Aviation Battalion. He completed basic training at Camp Chaffee, Arkansas and Fort Leonard Wood, Missouri. Job description: carpenter, assigned to Beale AFB, Marysville, California, then Camp Newenham, Alaska, distant early warning radar site, May 1955-December 1955 to lengthen and widen air strip.

Cpl. Herman E. Gross

Herman was born November 26, 1933 in Chester, Illinois, the son of Henry and Violet Cassoutt Gross. He died June 3, 1986.

LAWRENCE A. GROSS, Staff Sergeant, was stationed at Panama Canal for 30 months during WWII, then assigned to Fort Bliss, Texas as a gunnery instructor/mechanic.

S/Sgt. Lawrence A. Gross

He was born at Chester, Illinois, September 16, 1916. He went in the Army in October 1941 and was discharged in October 1945.

Lawrence is the son of Nicholas and Margaret Schoenberger Gross.

GERALD J. GROTT, Technician Fifth Grade, was born in Chester, Illinois October 3, 1921. He was inducted into the service on May 5, 1942 for service in WWII. Gerald was in the Air Cadets, out on eye problem, attended training with the 17th Airborne Division, qualified as paratrooper and gliderman.

T/5 Gerald J. Grott

He fought in Bastogne, Battle of the Bulge and on to Siegfried Line under General George Patton. He made only airborne landing in Germany under General Montgomery.

Gerald received the Purple Heart, Bronze Star for valor, Invasion Arrowhead, Paratrooper Badge and Gliderman Badge. He was discharged October 27, 1945.

He is the son of Jerome C. and Ursula M. Grott.

REYBURN JEROME GROTT, Master Sergeant, served in all three major conflicts: WWII, Korea and Vietnam, as an Air Force radio operator aboard aircraft, traveling around the world. He went into service in 1944 and was discharged in 1971.

M/Sgt. Reyburn J. Grott, (left, WWII and right, Korea)

Grott was born in Chester, Illinois in 1927, the son of Jerome and DeRousse Grott. He died December 25, 2000.

ALBERT A. GUEBERT, Sergeant First Class, U.S. Navy, WWII, was born in Percy, Illinois February 3, 1925, the son of Albert R. and Adela Hartman Guebert. He entered the Navy July 17, 1945, completed his basic

Seaman 1/c Albert A. Guebert

training at Great Lakes, Illinois, was transferred to U.S. Naval Repair Base at New Orleans, Louisiana, where he served as a clerk and remained until his discharge August 21, 1946.

ALBERT R. GUEBERT, Private, U.S. Army, WWI October 4, 1917-August 8, 1919, served with the 1st Battalion, 713th Guard Company, ASC.

Albert was born January 11, 1896 in Percy, Illinois, the son of August and Amanda Rathert Guebert,

DANIEL L. GUEBERT, Specialist 5, enlisted in the Army February 19, 1968 and served three years as a machinist specialist 44E20 with one-year tour of duty in Vietnam on November 17, 1968 serving with Army RA Ordnance, Company C, 123rd Maintenance Battalion, 1st Armored Davison.

Spec-5 Daniel L. Guebert

While in Vietnam he received the Vietnam Service w/4 Bronze Service Stars, National Defense Service Medal and the Republic of Vietnam Campaign Medal.

Daniel came back to the States on November 16, 1969 and was stationed at Fort Hood, Texas until he was discharged February 18, 1971. Then he served in the Reserves from February 18, 1971 until February 1, 1974 with the Control Group (REIN) USAAC, St. Louis, Missouri.

From left: Edwin A., Edwin F., Daniel L. Guebert

After his discharge Daniel returned to John Deere as a machinist, as well as developing his many skills in other areas and spending time with family and friends.

Daniel was born December 11, 1948 at Red Bud, Illinois, the son of Edwin F. and Nina M. Hanebutt Guebert. Daniel passed away December 10, 1995, at home and is buried at St. John's Lutheran Cemetery, Red Bud, Illinois.

EDWIN F. GUEBERT JR., Sergeant, enlisted in WWII on December 30, 1943 and served in Company C, 160th Infantry Regiment, Headquarters Division as a light machine gunner 604.

Sgt. Edwin F. Guebert Jr.

He was awarded the WWII Victory Medal, American Theatre Ribbon, Asiatic-Pacific Ribbon and Philippine Liberation Medal w/Overseas Bar. He was discharged April 5, 1946.

He re-enlisted March 29, 1949 and served as a corporal in the Korean War.

Edwin was born September 23, 1925 in Red Bud, Illinois, the son of Edwin H. and Anna Mueller Guebert. He died March 18, 1993.

EDWIN H. GUEBERT, Private, born in Red Bud, Illinois September 12, 1892, to Henry and Bertha Rosenburg Guebert, was called to serve in WWI. He entered service June 24, 1918 and served with Headquarters Company, 5th Regiment Field Artillery, at Camp Zachary Taylor, Kentucky until discharged December 17, 1918.

Pvt. Edwin H. Guebert Sr.

He followed the carpenter trade on his return home. Edwin died in December 1979.

ELVERA GUEBERT, Lieutenant Commander, of Red Bud, Illinois, served as a Navy nurse during both WWII and the Korean War. She was born September 30, 1920, the daughter of Albert C. and Marie (Mayme) Homrighausen Guebert.

She was within a month of graduation from Jewish Hospital School of Nursing when Pearl Harbor was attacked. After enlisting in the Navy at St. Louis, Missouri she was assigned to Reserves and sent to Great Lakes Naval Training Center. Procedure here was very different from hospital training she had received, and was often told to forget what had been learned in school and do things the Navy way.

At Great Lakes she was assigned to a hospital in Norman, Oklahoma that had about 1,000 patients, a good number of them psychiatric and only three nurses on duty at night. To make the most of a bad situation, Navy provided bicycles for nurses to ride to doorway of each ward, so as many patients could be seen per hour as possible.

She went on active duty March 23, 1943 and was sent to Pearl Harbor in 1945, lived in Quonset hut and assigned to two wards with 40 patients each. The nurses worked 12 hour shifts, every day for three months, with no days off, but not one nurse complained.

Elvera was at Pearl Harbor when war ended and very surprised when soldiers at Officer's Club, instead of partying, were sitting quietly, talking, watching celebrations going on in the States. Soldiers were simply relieved and thankful the war was over. She was discharged July 27, 1946 and returned to school for physical therapy training.

She was recalled for Korean War on November 10, 1950 and served until April 16, 1952. She was again recalled on July 3, 1952 and officially discharged June 29, 1953 in Philadelphia, Pennsylvania.

Returned to Red Bud, she worked at Deaconess Hospital, then as a physical therapist for 22 years at Litzsinger School for Handicapped in St. Louis, Missouri. She is now retired and lives in Red Bud, Illinois.

EUGENE T. GUEBERT, Sergeant, USMC, served from April 1959-September 1963, during the Cuban Crisis. He completed boot camp at San Diego, CA and served with the 1st Motor Transport, Camp Pendleton as truck driver for 5th Marines; attended Security Guard School in Henderson, Hall, Arlington, Virginia; additional security for President Kennedy, Paris, France to American Embassy, London, England; one and one-half years at Quantico, Virginia, motor transport.

Sgt. Eugene T. Guebert

He was born in Red Bud, Illinois on January 18, 1942, the son of Theodore Guebert and wife, nee Blumenschein. He retired after 34 years with Operating Engineers Local #520, Mitchell, Illinois.

OLIVER T. GUEBERT, Master Machinist Mate 3/c, entered WWII November 20, 1943 and served in the U.S. Navy on LST-1014, Mindoro, Leyte, Luzon, Palo in Philippines and Island of Okinawa, in invasions of South Pacific.

He received the Philippine Liberation Ribbon w/Bronze Star, WWII Victory Medal, American Campaign Medal, Asi-

MMM 1/c Oliver T. Guebert

atic-Pacific Medal w/3 Bronze Stars and Navy Occupation Service Medal w/ "Asia" Clasp. He was discharged April 3, 1946.

Oliver was born in Red Bud, Illinois on August 7, 1925, the son of Walter and Alma Ohla Guebert.

PAUL E. GURLEY, Private First Class, was a paratrooper with the 82nd Airborne during WWII. Service time was from 1942-46. He served in Ardennes, Rhineland and Central Europe.

Pfc. Paul E. Gurley

Paul was awarded the European Theatre Ribbon w/3 Bronze Battle Stars, Bronze Arrowhead, Purple Heart, Bronze Star and Belgium Fourragere.

He was born in Dongola, Illinois on March 5, 1924. His parents were Ralph and Betty Brust Gurley.

JOHN WESLEY GUYMON, Private, served in Captain William Short's Company, 31st Regiment of Illinois Volunteers from April 1, 1862 until September 1862. His hometown was Steels Mills (Steeleville), Illinois. He was the son of John and Mary "Polly" Wright Guymon.

Edward D. Kittoe, surgeon, General Hospital, Jackson, Tennessee, wrote "John Guymon had 'Struman's disease of the mesenteric glands producing chronic diarrhea which cannot be checked. The patient is much emaciated and edematous.'" With-

out the consultation of a trained medical person, it seems the patient was sent home to die. He was discharged on September 6, 1862 and died six weeks later on October 13, 1862.

The discharge gave no cause for probable death, but the family story handed down was that, "he was helping to build breastworks in the area of Nashville, Tennessee and a log rolled down crushing him, causing the injury which led to his death."

CLARENCE HABERMANN, Corporal, was in the Korean Conflict in the 5th Armored Division from December 1953 until December 1955. He received eight weeks basic training in the 81st Infantry Battalion, followed by eight weeks of artillery training in the 542nd Artillery Battalion, Company B.

The next two years were spent in 53rd Division Artillery as assistant to the Operations Officer of 5th Armored Division at Camp Chaffee, Arkansas.

Clarence was born in Steeleville, Illinois, the son of Albert and Lillie Liefer Habermann.

LAWRENCE JOHN HAGENE, SP3, served in the U.S. Army, 1954-56, with D Company, 45th Armored Infantry Batt. Division in Stateside duty. He was born

Spec 3 Lawrence J. Hagene

June 21, 1932 in Perry County, Illinois, the son of Jacob and Mary Mangin Hagene. He now lives in Sparta, Illinois.

HARVEY HALL, Sergeant, enlisted in Air Force in September 1948 and spent four years in military. Basic training was at Wichita Falls, Texas, then to Mt. Home AFB, Mt. Home, Idaho, next to Bolling AFB, Washington DC. He was then transferred to SAC Command Headquarters, Offutt AFB, Omaha, Nebraska. Sgt. Hall received an honorable discharge in Au-

Sgt. Harvey Hall

Pfc. Samuel L. Hall

Pvt. Archibald Hamilton III

gust 1952. Harvey was born March 12, 1929, the son of John Harvey and Carmen Corena Cross Hall.

MARVIN BRUCE HALL, Sergeant, served in the U.S. Marine Corps from October 10, 1955 to October 1961. He was born November 5, 1935 in Saline County, Illinois, the son of Noel and Pauline Watson Hall.

Sgt. Marvin B. Hall

Bruce enlisted at St. Louis, completed boot camp at San Diego, combat training at Camp Pendleton, California and amphibious combat training at Okinawa, Philippines, Iwo Jima, Japan and Thailand. He served with Weapons Company 3rd Battalion, 9th Regiment 3rd Division. Stationed at Cherry Point, North Carolina, he was assigned to Military Police as brig warden and intramural director. He was released to Reserves in 1960 and discharged in 1961.

After discharge he finished college, graduating from Lewis University, Lockport, Illinois, worked for Illinois Department of Corrections and retired as assistant warden of Operations, Menard, December 1988. He is married to Barbara Schulein Lake and resides in Chester.

SAMUEL LEE HALL, Private First Class, served active duty in the U.S. Army from November 13, 1950 to November 13, 1952, and in the Reserves, 1952-57. After basic training he trained as equipment mechanic, then was sent to Japan where they maintained equipment sent back from Korea. He was born September 16, 1928, Ellis Grove, Illinois, the son of Dennis and Rene McDonough Hall. He is currently retired and living in Ellis Grove.

WARREN D. HALL, Sergeant, entered WWII in June 1943 and served with the Marines in battles of Guam and Iwo Jima with Weapons Company, 3rd Marine Division in South Pacific, as machine gunner in Weapons Company, 3rd Marines.

Sgt. Warren D. Hall

Discharged in December 1945, he retired as inspector from Monsanto Company in 1985, and now resides in West County, St. Louis, Missouri. Warren was born January 15, 1925 in Nashville, Illinois. His parents were Rollie and Rose Pyle Hall.

ARCHIBALD HAMILTON III, Private, born April 27, 1818 in Liberty (Rockwood) Illinois, the son of Archibald and Susanna Bridges Hamilton. He served in the Civil War in Company K of the 5th Illinois Cavalry, from September 10, 1861 until October 31, 1864. He went to Camp Butler, near Springfield, Illinois, and from there to St. Louis and Pilot Knob, Missouri, where his company joined General Steele and marched through Arkansas to Pocahontas, having a skirmish before getting there.

After being in Helena for about a year, they joined the main Army at Vicksburg and from there went to Jackson, Mississippi. There they encountered and defeated General Johnston. After marching back to Vicksburg, and recruiting there, they went on a raid and captured the road from Jackson to Memphis.

Returning to Vicksburg on October 31, 1864, they were mustered out of service. Hamilton was captured and spent about six months as a prisoner, then was released and rejoined his unit at Helena. He died July 11, 1882, and is buried with his wife Rebecca Wells Hamilton in Reid Cemetery in Rockwood, Illinois.

ROGER R. HAMILTON entered the Korean War June 4, 1952 and served on aircraft carrier, USS *Bataan* for 19 months, operating in Yellow Sea off the coast of Korea, launching and landing aircraft. He spent four months at Agana, Guam at Naval Air Station and was discharged at Whibey Island, Washington, December 16, 1955. Roger was born in Sparta, Illinois on January 5, 1935, the son of William J. and Florence Reid Hamilton.

WILFORD "PAT" HAMILTON, Tech Sergeant, born in Marissa, Illinois on February 4, 1911, son of Albert and Laura Bartlett Hamilton. Inducted April 4, 1944 into Army, WWII and served in H&H Com-

T/Sgt. Wilford Hamilton

pany, 737th Ry Opr Battalion as a cook on Luzon, Philippines. His awards include the WWII Victory Medal, Overseas Bar, Good Conduct Medal and two ribbons with Bronze Stars. Pat was discharged April 13, 1946 and died January 15, 1984.

FREDERICK HAMMEL, Private, born in Missouri, January 8, 1865 and served in Civil War in Company A, 155th Regimental Illinois Infantry. He enlisted February 9, 1865 and was discharged September 4, 1865 at Murfreesboro, Tennessee. The son of J. George and Margaretha Blouth Hammel, who were both born in Germany. Frederick died May 18, 1866, and is buried Fairview Baptist Church, Sparta, Illinois.

MARVIN L. HAMMEL, Corporal, served in the U.S. Marine Corps from March 26, 1976 to March 26, 1982. He attended boot camp at San Diego, was assigned to 3rd Marine Division in Okinawa,

Cpl. Marvin L. Hammel

served BLt 2/9 in Korea—DMZ duty and transferred to 1st Marine Division, Camp Pendleton, California as instructor ITR, San Onafrey. "Marine Corps was the best experience of my life, everything I needed to know about life, I learned in Boot Camp."

OTIS L. HAMMEL, Corporal, served in the U.S. Army from August 1953 to May 1955 with H&S Company, 249th Engineer Battalion, during the Korean Conflict. Basic training was at Fort Leonard Wood, Missouri. After training, he served with Headquarter and Supply Company of 249th Engineer Battalion in Germany. He was born January 14, 1930 in Randolph County, Illinois, the son of Sam and Matilda Hammel.

DONALD DEAN HANEBUTT, BTG-3, was called to active duty on February 10, 1953 and took his training at Great Lakes, Illinois. Donald had two years of active duty and two years, one month and five days of inactive duty. He spent one year and four days on foreign soil.

BTG-3 Donald Hanebutt

He was recalled to active duty March 15, 1955, released from active duty and given an honorable discharge on March 15, 1957 from the U.S. Naval Station at Newport, Rhode Island.

Donald was born May 13, 1935 in Rising City, Nebraska, the son of Harry and Lottie (Stellhorn) Hanebutt. Donald died in 2001 and is buried in Jefferson Barracks Cemetery in St. Louis, Missouri.

ELROY HANEBUTT, Staff Sergeant, served as airplane and engine mechanic 747, during WWII, with 3rd Air Dep. Repr. Squadron at India depot. He began service November 9, 1942 and was discharged March 12, 1946, with American Theatre Ribbon, Asiatic-Pacific Theatre Ribbon, Good Conduct Medal, three Overseas Bars and Victory Ribbon. He was born in Evansville, Illinois, August 22, 1921, the son of Henry and Mary Kueker Hanebutt, and died July 7, 1990.

HENRY HANEBUTT, Private First Class, served in battles at Flanders, in Belgium and France with the 361 Infantry Company C during WWI. Many of his buddies lost their lives fighting from the trenches.

Pvt. 1/c Henry Hanebut

He received an honorable discharge and was awarded the Victory Medal w/ Battle Clasp, YPRES-LYS defensive sector. Entered service February 24, 1918 and was discharged May 23, 1919.

Born in Evansville, Illinois, November 20, 1893, he was the son of Louis and Mary Liefer Hanebutt. Henry died February 11, 1987.

RALPH L. HANEBUTT, Fireman 2/c, served aboard USS *Joyce* (DE-317) and USS *Marchand* (DE-249) in Coast Guard during WWII, from April 2, 1945 to May 15, 1946. Born in Evansville, Illinois, April 3, 1927, his parents are Louis H. and Clara Wolter Hanebutt.

WILLIAM HANEBUTT, served in WWI and trained at Fort Campbell, Kentucky. He received an honorable discharge

Cpl. Otis L. Hammel

S/Sgt. Elroy Hanebutt

William Hanebutt

and returned to work at Wagner Electric in St. Louis, Missouri. Born August 9, 1895, to Louis and Mary Liefer Hanebutt, he died January 10, 1971.

LENARD L. HANGER, Seaman 1/c, served in the U.S. Navy from December 7, 1950 to September 30, 1954. He attended boot camp at Great Lakes, Illinois and served aboard the USS *Oriskany* and CVA-34 during Korean War. He was born in

Seaman 1/c Lenard L. Hanger

Shirley, Missouri on October 3, 1931, the son of Lenard and Bessie Brewer Hanger. Now married with five children, he makes his home in Chester, Illinois.

LESLIE E. HAPPEL, Staff Sergeant, born April 10, 1924, in Randolph Company, the son of Richard and Edith Fairleigh Happel. He served with the Fifth Air Corps, during WWII. Missing in action at sea, June 11, 1944, he was declared dead February 13, 1946.

GERALD WILLIAM HARGIS, Lieutenant Colonel, served in the U.S. Army, in Vietnam from May 1966 to March 1967 with the U.S. Army Ordnance Group, Headquarters Saigon Support Command. After Vietnam he continued through Reserves as liaison officer to the U.S. Military Academy, West Point, retiring September 26, 1989. He was born July 16, 1938, Sparta, Illinois, the son of William Lester and Marjorie Ellen Neisler Hargis.

DAVID N. HARMON, Colonel, grew up in Randolph County, the youngest son of David L. and Margaret E. Dean Harmon. He attended Oak Grove Elementary and Chester High Schools, graduated June 9, 1941 from University of Illinois, and through the ROTC program, was commissioned 2nd lieutenant in the U.S. Army Reserves.

On June 26, 1941, he was ordered to report to the 2nd Armored Division, Fort Benning, Georgia for one year of active duty. He served seven months as platoon commander in Company H, 368th Armored Regiment. He entered pilot training, which he completed November 10, 1942, with the class of 42-J, then was transferred to Army Air Corps. Original orders were for the tour of duty not to exceed one year, the call to war on December 8, 1941, resulted in those orders being replaced calling for duty for an indefinite period of time.

After transferring to the newly created U.S. Army Air Force, he received promotion to colonel in June 1951 and served as operations officer and combat pilot in the 365th Fighter Group, 1943-44, flying 82 combat missions against Hitler's forces. He was assigned to U.S. Embassy, Cairo, Egypt, 1946-47 as Military Air Attaché.

In 1950, he flew 13 combat missions out of Japan, against North Korea Commander 522nd Fighter Squadron, 27th Fighter Wing, Special Air Attaché duty U.S. Embassy, Belgrade, Yugoslavia; Director of Materiel, 834th Air Division, Commander 366th Fighter Wing; Director of War Plans, Tactical Air Command; Director Operations & Plans, SIXATAF, NATO, Izmir, Turkey; Commander for Jet Pilot Operations and Training Wing; and Vice Commander 24th Special Operations Wing, U.S. Air Force Southern Command, Panama.

His awards include Legion of Merit, Commander, two Distinguished Flying Cross awards, 17 Air Medals, Air Force Commendation Medal, and 12 lesser awards, including the European and Korea Theater Ribbons w/stars, and Presidential Unit Citations. His career ended February 28, 1970, when he was honored with a Command Parade at Howard AFB, Panama.

JOHN L. HARMON, Master Sergeant, spent 20 years in the military. He enlisted in the U.S. Air Force in May 1951 and retired in October 1971. Those years spanned both the Korean and Vietnam Wars. He served in the 9th Strategic Reconnaissance Wing at Beale AFB, California; attended technical training at Tarleton State College in Stephenville, Texas; and served as an Air Force Recruiter in Roanoke, Virginia.

Other assignments took him to Guam, Arizona, Alaska, Germany and Okinawa. The majority of his career was assignments

M/Sgt. John L. Harmon

to intelligence collection organizations. His final assignment was with the SR-71 Program at Beale, AFB, California.

He was awarded the Meritorious Service Medal at his retirement ceremonies. His parents were Dean O. and Gertrude Tanner Harmon. His hometown was New Palestine, Illinois.

JOSEPH HARMON, Private, born November 1, 1787, to Michael and Catherine Ziegler Harmon. He served in Lieutenant Colonel Whiteside's Detachment of Illinois Militia during the War of 1812. Joseph died December 7, 1872 and is buried in New Palestine Cemetery, Randolph County, Illinois.

HAROLD HARMSEN, Sergeant First Class, served in the U.S. Army, from May 1952 to April 10, 1954. He served with the 89th Tank Battalion in Korea for 14

SFC Harold Harmsen

months, participating in "Punch Bowl" and "Iron Triangle." He was born July 4, 1931, the son of George and Grace Schilling Harmsen. He was a construction worker before military duty and an architectural inspector after discharge.

RONALD G. HARRIS, Lieutenant Colonel, born in Rockwood, Illinois, January 10, 1934, the son of Gertrude Harris. He enlisted in the U.S. Air Force in March 1954 and rose through the ranks to retire as a lieutenant colonel in January 1988. He graduated from Rockwood Elementary School in 1948, Gorham High School in 1952, and went on to attain a bachelor of science degree from Troy State University and a master of arts degree from Central Michigan University.

Lt. Col. Ronald G. Harris

Professional military schools include the Squadron Officer's School, Air Command College, and the Industrial College of the Armed Forces. He completed basic training at Lackland AFB, Texas and the airborne electronic countermeasures course at Keesler AFB, Mississippi. His initial operational assignment was to Ellsworth AFB, South Dakota, as an RB-35 Airborne EMC Specialist. After this assignment, he was assigned to Ramey AFB, Puerto Rico, Hunter AFB, Georgia and Lockbourne AFB, Ohio.

In 1959, he was accepted into Officer Candidate School, and received his commission in 1960. He then went on to navigator training at Harlingen AFB, Texas, combat crew training at Castle AFB, California, then returned to Ellsworth AFB, where he was assigned to the 28th Air Refueling Squadron as a KC-135 navigator. Later, he moved to Amarillo AFB, Texas and March AFB, California.

In 1970, Colonel Harris completed C-130-E conversion training, and was sent to Ching Chuan Kang AB, Taiwan. There he served as chief navigator of the Central Training Function. In 1974, he was assigned to the Pacific Airlift Center at Hickam AFB, Hawaii, as an air operations officer, and served as chief of the Exercise Plans Branch. His last assignment was to Little Rock AFB, Arkansas in 1978, where he took on the duties of flight commander and chief navigator of the 16th Tactical Airlift Training Squadron, from which position he retired, January 8, 1988.

A master navigator, Colonel Harris has more than 8,700 hours of flight time in the RB-36, EB-47, KC-135 and C-130 aircraft. He flew over 1,500 hours in combat and has more than 400 combat missions in Cambodia, Laos, and South Vietnam.

His military decorations include the Distinguished Flying Cross, Meritorious Service Medal w/2 Oak Leaf Clusters, Air Medal w/9 Oak Leaf Clusters, and the Air Force Commendation Medal w/Oak Leaf Cluster. He now resides in Little Rock, Arkansas, with his wife, the former Doris Johnson, of Rockwood, Illinois.

ORVILLE HARSTICK, Tech 5, served with Company A, 3rd Division, 30th Regiment during WWII. Basic training was at Fort McClellan, Alabama, and New Port News, Virginia, then to Cosa Blanco, Africa, Sicily, Naples and Salerno, Italy, where he was wounded February 24, 1944.

T/5 Orville Harstick

He was missing in action for one week in hiding, two ladies and a boy brought him food at night, until they were "taken." Finally he made his way back to his company, was taken to a field hospital, then to Percy Jones Hospital in Battlecreek Michigan. He entered service in April 1943 and was discharged in January 1946. His awards include the Purple Heart, Silver Star, Infantry Badge and European Theatre Medal.

Orville was born in Coulterville, Illinois, May 28, 1924, the son of Harry and Anna Illy Harstick.

DONALD HARTENBERGER, Sergeant, was born in Chester, Illinois, April 2, 1932, the son of Oscar and Laura Ebers Hartenberger. He enlisted in the Marine Corps October 2, 1950 and received his basic training in South Carolina.

He was then sent to Camp Lejeune and attached to the 6th Fleet. He spent the next six months in the Mediterranean Sea.

Sgt. Donald Hartenberger

After returning to the States, he was sent to Korea for eight months, then stationed at Camp Pendelton, California, and was discharged at Quantico, Virginia, October 2, 1953.

LLOYD H. HARTENBERGER, IC2 (E-5), was inducted into the Navy in May 1963. Homeport was Alameda Naval Air Station aboard the USS *Regulus*. Transferred to Port Chicago, California aboard the USS *Mauna Kea*.

1 C2 Lloyd Hartenberger

He served with the E Division while in Vietnam and was awarded the Armed Forces Expeditionary Medal and the Vietnam Service Medal. Discharged May 1967,

Lloyd was born in Chester, Illinois to Carl and Ada (Stellhorn) Hartenberger.

DALE J. HASEMEYER, Corporal, born at Fort Gage, Illinois, November 13, 1932, the son of Ed and Mable Pariset

Cpl. Dale Hasemeyer

Dale Hasemeyer on mountain top of eastern Korea, 1951-52

Hasemeyer. He enlisted in U.S. Marines January 29, 1951, and was sent to Paris Island, South Carolina for boot camp, then to Camp Pendelton, California for basic training.

Assigned to F-2-11, 1st Marine Division, he was sent to Korea on June 15, 1951 and earned three Battle Stars before leaving July 15, 1952. Served at Millington Naval Air Station after leaving Korea, until his discharge July 24, 1954. Dale earned the Good Conduct, National Defense, United Nations Service and Korean Service medals.

His brother, Ray Hasemeyer, was serving in the Army in Korea at the same time Dale was. Another brother, Courtland Hasemeyer, was serving in the U.S. Navy.

MILTON C. HAWKINS, Tech Sergeant, enlisted in U.S. Army Air Corps November 26, 1940 and was at Wheeler Field, Hawaii at time of Pearl Harbor attack with Pearl Harbor 15th Pursuit Group, 46 Squadron and 331st Squadron of 94th Bomb Group.

T/Sgt. Milton C. Hawkins

Crew Chief of P-36 airplane, he remained in Pacific three years, then returned to U.S. and completed training as flight engineer for B-17. He flew 28 missions with same flight crew in the European Theatre over Germany and rotated back to U.S. for discharge July 5, 1945.

Milton was born in Pinckneyville, Illinois November 15, 1921, the son of Evan and Clara Taylor Hawkins. He worked as electrician for coal mines and retired from Con Sol Company in 1986. He was a member of UMWA for 50 years.

DAVID EMMET "BLACKIE" HAWTHORNE, served in Marines during WWII. He was born in Blair, Illinois, January 17, 1915, the son of James C. and

David E. Hawthorne

"Josie" Blair Hawthorne, and died July 26, 2000, in Perryville, Missouri. After service he was employed by International Shoe Company, at various locations.

DAVID MCQUERY HAWTHORNE, born March 3, 1844 at Blair, Illinois, served in 30th Illinois Volunteer Regiment, Infantry Company C during Civil War. He was taken prisoner and spent time in Andersonville Prison in Georgia. After dis-

David McQuery Hawthorne

charge, he returned to his farm on Shawneetown Trail in rural Blair area, where he died October 26, 1929. He was one of the last Civil War survivors in Randolph County.

KYLE CRAIG HEINS, Corporal, enlisted in the Marines in July 1999 and took his boot camp at San Diego. Then he went to Camp Lejeune, North Carolina and from there he was deployed to Iraq, where he is at present with the 8th ESB Marines. Kyle is fighting in Operation Iraqi Freedom. He was born October 3, 1980, the

Cpl. Kyle C. Heins

son of Craig and Lisa Darnstaedt Heines, Sutton.

PAUL A. HEIRES, Staff Sergeant, served in 864th Bomb Squadron, 494th Bomb Group during WWII, from October 6, 1942 to November 8, 1945 as a radio operator gunner on a B-24 Liberator.

S/Sgt. Paul A. Heires

After Radio School at Scott Field, Gunnery School in Yuma, Arizona, he received phase training at Army Air Base Murock, California and was sent to South West Pacific as member of replacement bomber crew. At Kauai, Hawaii for one month, then to island of Anguar of the Paleau Islands, from there they bombed targets in Philippines. Base was then moved to Okinawa, and from there bombed islands of Japan.

Paul was born in Carroll, Iowa, June 15, 1922, the son of Walter and Rose Burch Heires.

CHARLES WILLIAM HEIZER, MM3/c, V-6, served in the Navy during WWII, aboard the USS *Bristol* (DD-453). He entered service September 13, 1942, and after training at Great Lakes Naval Training Center, was assigned to USS *Bristol*. On November 13, 1942 the *Bristol* engaged in the Invasion of North Africa. One month later, he had a 72 hour leave, due to ship being repaired.

He also participated in battles of Tu-

MM 3/c Charles William Heizer

nisia and Sicily. On September 13, 1943, the *Bristol* took part in the invasion of Salerno, Italy, where Charles was killed when the *Bristol* was torpedoed and sank off Cape Bouqaroun, Algeria.

Charles was born December 23, 1921, at Prairie du Rocher, Illinois, the son of William and Elizabeth Shea Heizer.

LEO J. HEIZER, Motor Machinists Mate 1/c, joined the U.S. Navy in WWII on July 10, 1943. He served in USS LCI (L) 945 and attended Diesel Service

Leo J. Heizer

Schools at Detroit, Michigan and Ames, Iowa. He was discharged March 21, 1946 and died September 28, 1991. Leo was born in Prairie du Rocher, Illinois on July 16, 1925, the son of William and Elizabeth G. Shea Heizer.

ROBERT L. HEIZER, Storekeeper 3/c, entered the Navy June 28, 1965 and

Storekeeper 3/c Robert L. Heizer

attended two Class A Service Schools while in the Navy. He served his country during the Vietnam Era and was discharged December 21, 1969. Robert was born July 13, 1947 in Red Bud, Illinois, the son of Leo J. and Rosalie A. (Heck) Heizer.

WILLIAM A. HEIZER, Specialist 4, served with the 2nd Infantry Division, 81st Army Band at Fort Campbell. William was

Sp/4 William A. Heizer

transferred overseas on March 10, 1970 to Korea. He served his country from June 12, 1969 to February 13, 1971, during the Vietnam Era. William was born in Red Bud, Illinois on September 19, 1949, the son of Leo J. and Rosalie A. (Heck) Heizer.

RUSSELL A. HELMERS, served in the U.S. Army during Korean and in the Air Force during Vietnam War. He was born February 8, 1929, to Harry and Gladyus Hathaway Helmers. Russell died February 6, 1996 and is buried in Paradise Cemetery near Steeleville, Illinois.

HERBERT L HERRELL, Corporal, was born November 11, 1929, son of Elmer and LeeElla Hendrix. He enlisted in Army in WWII in 1946. He served in Vienna,

Cpl. Herbert L. Herrell

Austria and one year in Germany as an MP with 796 Military Police Battalion. He was discharged in 1948 and spent 36 years working on railroad. One of his sons served in Vietnam and two grandsons served in Saudi Arabia.

JEFFREY M. HERRELL, E-5, enlisted in the U.S. Air Force in August 1988 and served in Desert Storm with 314 TAW, 314 OMS. Jeffrey was born in Red Bud,

Jeffrey M. Herrell

Illinois on August 15, 1970, the son of Steve and Donna Rinehart Herrell. Prior to enlisting, he served as an aircraft mechanic, servicing C-130E model aircraft at Little Rock AFB, Arkansas.

SETH ADAM HERRELL, E-4, serving in the U.S. Air Force from June 16, 1999 to the present. Seth was born in Chester, Illinois on February 18, 1981, the

E-4 Seth Adam Herrell

son of Steve and Donna Rinehart Herrell. He enlisted after high school and serves with the 22nd CES SQD in Operation Enduring Freedom. He was deployed four months to Masirah Island, Oman and is proud to serve his country.

STEVE L. HERRELL, Lance Corporal, enlisted in the U.S. Marine Corps in 1968 after graduating high school. He enlisted on the Buddy Plan, therefore, only having to stay in two years and they were supposed to be staying together the next two years (HA-HA). He did a tour in Vietnam from 1969-70 with the 1st Recon, 1st Marine Division.

Steve's father served before him, and

L/Cpl Steve L. Herrell

Steve's two sons served after him—all four served on foreign soil and all made it home. He thanks God for this great country, a free country. He has the greatest admiration and thanks for those who have served and those who are now serving so that our children and grandchildren are free. Maybe someday he can thank those who never made it home.

Steve was born July 6, 1949, the son of Herbert and Burnie (Wilson) Herrell.

HERBERT J. HERRING, General, enlisted in the U.S. Army at Jefferson Barracks, in 1939. He was stationed at Fort Benning, Georgia, in Headquarters Company, 2nd Battalion, 41st Armed Infantry Regiment, where he was promoted to sergeant. He attended Officers Candidate School, earned rank of 2nd lieutenant and served in WWII in England, where his regiment holed up in an old castle for a time until help arrived in the form of re-enforcement.

General Herbert J. Herring

He re-enlisted in 1943, and was sent to Germany and France. He was wounded and received the Purple Heart and the Distinguished Service Medal for the battle of Mulheim, near the Rhine River in Germany, 1944. His mother wrote, "he wears the Purple Heart, Oak Leaf Cluster, with five Battle Stars, Distinguished Service Medal, as well as the Infantry Badge and a bunch of those little candy striped badges, and won them all stringing along with General George S. Patton.

His service didn't end with WWII, he also served in the Korean War and before retirement was promoted to the rank of One Star General. Born in Rockwood, Illinois, April 3, 1921, he was the son of Walter and Eva B. Crittenden Herring. He now resides in the Veterans Home in Quincy, Illinois.

JAMES CHARLES HERRING, Seaman 2/c, born in Rockwood, Illinois on April 28, 1919, to Benjamin Clay and Edith Johnson Herring. He served in the U.S. Navy during WWII. After training at Great Lakes Naval Center, he was sent to San

Seaman 2/c James C. Herring

Diego, California and worked as a cook's helper until discharged at the end of the war. He returned to the International Shoe Company at Chester, Illinois, and later worked as a construction worker, until his death, January 25, 1974. James is buried in Union Cemetery, in Sparta, Illinois.

WILLIAM F. HERSCHBACH, Private, served in the U.S. Army, WWI, from June 24, 1918 to July 16, 1919, with Com-

Pvt. William F. Herschback

pany G, 22 Engineers, in France. He was born April 1, 1895, Chester, Illinois, the son of Charles H. and Sophie Schrader Herschbach. He died June 23, 1957 and is buried St. John Lutheran Cemetery in Chester.

BRIAN PAUL HERZOG, served in the U.S. Navy from July 17, 1997 to July 16, 2000. He was born in Chester, Illinois on May 14, 1979, the son of Paul A. and Carol F. Bievenue Herzog. While in the Navy,

Brian P. Herzog

he served in Air Detachment Wizards VAQ-133 at Whidby Island, where he performed maintenance on the EA6B Prowler. Brian also served in Ankara, Turkey in 1998. He was honorably discharged, July 16, 2000.

CRAIG R. HERZOG, A1/c, enlisted in the U.S. Air Force August 1, 2000 and is currently serving at Dover AFB, Delaware, where he repairs auto pilot flight

Airman 1/c Craig R. Herzog

control instrumentation and navigation systems on the C-5 Galaxy in support of Operation Enduring Freedom, following September 11, 2001. He was born May 14, 1979, Chester, Illinois, the son of Paul A. and Carol F. Bievenue Herzog.

JARRET O. HERZOG, Petty Officer 3/c, served in the U.S. Air Navy from October 10, 1994 to October 9, 1997. He was born in Chester, Illinois on January 2, 1976, the son of Paul A. and Carol F. Bievenue Herzog. Jarret served on board the USS *O'Bannon* (DD-987), a Spruance Class Destroyer homeported at Mayport, Florida. He served as a gas turbine engine tech during two Persian Gulf deployments as well as counter-drug operations through-

PO 3/c Jarret O. Herzog

out the Caribbean. Jarret was honorably discharged on October 9, 1997.

PAUL A. HERZOG, Lance Corporal, was drafted into the Marine Corps February 9, 1966. He served with the 5th 155 Gun Battery in Vietnam. He served in South Vietnam near the demilitarized zone in the Cam Lo and Quang Tri area.

L/Cpl. Paul A. Herzog

He was honorably discharged February 9, 1968 and returned to Prairie du Rocher and began farming. Paul was born December 10, 1946 in St. Louis, Missouri, the son of Thomas and Mary Detering Herzog.

THOMAS H. HERZOG, Chief Petty Officer, served in Navy Seabees during WWII. He enlisted April 26, 1942 and was a chief shipfitter throughout South Pacific Theatre, including Philippines.

C.P.O. Thomas H. Herzog

After receiving an honorable discharge October 17, 1945, he farmed in Randolph County until his death October 7, 1957. Thomas was born October 18, 1908, Ste. Genevieve, Missouri, the son of Henry and Barbara Wipfler Herzog.

CHARLES R. HIGGINS, E-4, enlisted in the U.S. Navy, January 27, 1959, in St. Louis. He had boot camp in San Diego, California until April 13, then was assigned to Hu-1, Imperial Beach, California until January 31, 1960.

E-4 Charles R. Higgins

He then began Staff Duty, COMNAVAIRPAC, San Diego, and transferred to AEW Barron Pac, Barbers Point, Hawaii. He was discharged at U.S. Naval Station, Treasure Island, San Francisco, California, January 16, 1963.

Charles was born in Carbondale, Illinois, March 2, 1940, the son of Raymond and Imogene Lipe Higgins, and graduated Chester, Illinois High School in 1958.

JEWELL H. HILLYARD, WAC, enlisted in the first WAC training camp at Fort DeMoines, Iowa on January 8, 1945. She was with Company 19, 3rd Regiment, serving during WWII. Jewell married Jack

WAC Jewell H. Hillyard

Armstrong from Tilden, Illinois in 1935. He died in a Japanese Prison camp during WWII. Jewell was born February 12, 1920 in Coulterville, Illinois, the daughter of Madison (M.M.) and Bertha A. (Riley) Hillyard. Jewell died January 21, 1987.

JOHN HINDMAN, Seaman 2/c, served his country in the U.S. Navy from December 14, 1917 until February 15, 1919. He was inducted at St. Louis, Missouri and discharged at Great Lakes, Illinois. John was born in Rockwood, Illinois, February 1, 1896, the son of James Harve and Fannie Shelby Hindman.

TERRY L. HIRTE, Specialist 4, entered the Army March 17, 1970. Terry completed his basic training at Fort Leonard Wood, Missouri and received his medical training at U.S. Army Training Center, Fort Sam Houston, Texas.

Spec-4 Terry L. Hirte

He served as medical specialist with the 1st Battalion, 25th Infantry Division "Tropical Lightning" stationed in Hawaii. While in Vietnam Terry served with 1st Battalion, 25th Infantry Division, Headquarters C. He was honorably discharged in 1972.

Returning home he worked for state of Illinois, Department of Mental Health & Human Services, for 33 years. Now retired he lives in Chester, Illinois. Terry was born May 19, 1950 in Red Bud, Illinois, the son of Charles and Lois (Mueller) Hirte.

ERNST HITZEMANN, served for a brief period in Civil War in 7th Cavalry, which was organized in 1861, and this regiment participated in many battles of the war. Ernst was born March 11, 1842, in Furstentum, Schaumburg-Lippe, Buckeburg, Germany to Friederich and Wilhelmine Hitzemann, he enlisted at age 22 to serve in the war. Ernst was discharged December 5, 1864 and returned to Randolph County.

ROBERT D. HOHGREFE, Corporal, born November 24, 1941, in Chester, Illinois, the son of Hugo and Margaret Zimmer Hohgrefe. He enlisted in the U.S. Marines in August 1959 and went through basic training at San Diego, California and Camp Matthews. He transferred to Cherry Point, North Carolina, where he served until his discharge in 1963. On returning to Chester, he drove a truck for Gilster-Mary Lee. Robert died in May 2002.

RALPH R. HOLCOMB, Tech Sergeant 4/c, born November 17, 1924, in Walsh, Illinois, the son of F.R. and Mary Jane Klee Holcomb. He served with 3rd Division, 7th Infantry Company K in WWII. After receiving training at Fort McClellan, Alabama, he served in the invasion of Casablanca, Africa, Sicily, Italy, Southern France, Germany, Austria and Belgium.

T/Sgt. Ralph R. Holcomb

He entered service in April 1943 and was discharged in December 1945. Medals received were European-African-Middle Eastern Theater Campaign Victory Ribbon, Bronze Service Arrowhead, four Overseas Service Bars, Bronze Star, French Arm Braid Croix de Guerre and the Belgium Croix de Guerre (Cross of War). He married Evelyn Schulze on June 7, 1947.

EUGENE LEE HOLLAWAY, Sergeant, served in the U.S. Marine Corps from August 1957 to May 1963. Eugene was born July 14, 1939, Akin, Illinois, the son of Dalton and Minnie Lee Hollaway. He completed boot camp and was sent to

Sgt. Eugene L. Hollaway

Okinawa and the Philippines then returned to 1st Recon Battalion in the States.

He transferred to HQMC for Embassy School, then was stationed in Phnom Penh, Cambodia and Hong Kong, BCC. He returned to the States with 6th Marines and was discharged at Camp Lejeune, North Carolina. He served with 1st, 2nd and 3rd Marine Divisions during his active duty. He is presently working for Gilster-Mary Lee as a truck driver.

GORDON V. HOLLEY, Private First Class, born July 28, 1919, Ava, Illinois to Newton and Lucy Gordon Holley. He was drafted into WWII, May 26, 1944, and served with Headquarters Battalion 2nd

Pfc. Gordon V. Holley

Marine Division in Okinawa and Ryukyu Islands. Gordon was discharged January 7, 1946 and returned to Chester. He worked as a painter, then for McDonald Douglas in St. Louis, from where he retired in 1984. He loved life and lived it to the fullest. Gordon died September 14, 2001, age of 82.

RICHARD D. HOLLEY, Lance Corporal, served in the U.S. Marines from March 1987 to February 1990. He was born in St. Ann, Missouri, January 26, 1968,

L/Cpl Richard D. Holley

the son of Roger and Connie Pautler Holley. Roger enlisted 1987, completed boot camp at MCRD San Diego, California, and attended Heavy Equipment Engineer School at Fort Leonard Wood, Missouri. His duty stations included Okinawa, Japan, Cherry Point, NC and other temporary duty stations.

RON T. HOLLEY, served in the U.S. Navy from 1975-79, re-enlisted and served 1982-98. He was born March 3, 1957 in Red Bud, Illinois, the son of Gordon V. and Rosanna Korando, Holley.

Ron T. Holley

He served four years at Long Beach, California, discharged and re-enlisted in 1982, serving out of Charleston, South Carolina on the *Mahan* (ODG-42), which went to the Gulf War. The *Mahan* was decommissioned in 1993. He was reassigned to Tinker AFB, Oklahoma, where he served as Navy Law Enforcement.

He retired, transferred to Fleet Reserve on May 1, 1998 and now resides in Chester, Illinois.

DALE HOLLOMAN, Colonel, born August 17, 1931, Chester, Illinois, son of Jesse M. "Mack" and Elisabeth Cushman Holloman. Dale entered the U.S. Army in 1952 and was initially assigned to the Army's 101st Airborne Division.

Col. Dale Holloman

He subsequently was re-assigned to Fort Benning, Georgia for Officers Candidate School Training. Graduating as a 2nd lieutenant, he was assigned to Fort Leonard Wood, Missouri as a company executive officer and instructor in small unit tactics.

Upon leaving active duty, he enrolled at the University of Illinois, graduating with a degree in mining (petroleum) engineering. He was employed by Texaco for more than 20 years in oil and gas well drilling and production. He subsequently joined Deminex U.S. Oil Company in Dallas, TX where he became the company's president and CEO. During this time, Colonel Holloman continued his military career on an active reserve status, holding numerous command and staff positions in Illinois, Oklahoma and Texas.

He retired after 32 years of military service while serving as Commander of the 4266th LOG Command in West Texas and Regional Military Emergence Coordinator, 5th Army Headquarters, Fort Sam Houston, Texas. He was inducted into the Army's OCS Hall of Fame at Fort Benning in 1987.

EZEKIEL BROWN HOLLOMAN, Private First Class, born June 29, 1886, in Mill Creek Precinct, near Chester, Illinois. He entered WWI at Waterloo, Iowa on June 1, 1917 and served in Jefferson Barracks from enlistment to June 8, 1918, then transferred to Personnel Office of 35th Infantry. On June 8, 1918, he was transferred to Headquarters Company, 35th Infantry before being transferred to Camp Dodge, Iowa for discharge February 1, 1919, with discharge pay of $30.38. Ezekiel L. Holloman was his father.

GEORGE H. HOLLOMAN Lieutenant Commander, born November 21, 1928, Chester, Illinois, son of Jesse M. "Mack" and Elisabeth Cushmann Holloman. George entered the U.S. Navy in 1946 under the Navy's pilot training enlistment program. He attended the University of Illinois as part of the program and was later commissioned an ensign after completing flight training at Pensacola, Florida.

Lt. Comm. George H. Holloman

He flew fighter aircraft during the Korean war and among other awards, was presented the Distinguished Flying Cross and Air Medal w/4 stars. During the early days of the Korean War, while flying the Navy's F9F Panther jet, he and his wingman were attacked by a Russian made MiG jet, which they managed to down in a five minute air battle. He had been shot down twice during the Korean War, each time managing to find his way back to UN held territory.

He served on the carriers *Valley Forge, Philippine Sea* and *Ranger*. Lieutenant Commander Holloman and the F8U-2 Crusader jet fighter he was flying were lost at sea while flying from the *Ranger* off the coast of Japan. He served in the Navy from July 1946 to September 19, 1961.

JOHN P. HOLLOMAN, Sergeant, born 1880 in Chester, Illinois, son of Ezekiel J. Holloman. He was inducted into military service for WWI at Leavenworth, Kansas on September 19, 1917 and assigned to Company H, 353rd Infantry. He had previously served in the U.S. Marine Corps.

He saw overseas service in Lucey Sector August 10 to September 11, 1918; St. Mihiel September 12-16, 1918; Enuezin Sector, September 17 to October 7, 1918; and Meuse Argonne, October 19 to November 11, 1918. He was commissioned Corporal October 2, 1917, sergeant on October 3, 1917 and promoted to mess sergeant on July 12, 1918. Qualified for sharpshooter May 5, 1919. He was discharged June 1, 1919 at Camp Funston Kansas.

WILBERT HOMAN, Staff Sergeant, served in the 185th Infantry Division of the U.S. Army, during WWII. He served from October 1944 until February 17, 1945 in the South Pacific, including South Philippines. Parents were Ernest and Frieda Fromeling Homan. Wilbert lives in the Chester, Illinois area, and is a life member of VFW Post 3553.

ROGER E. HOOD, Corporal, born January 18, 1920, entered WWII, October 10, 1940 and served in Army Infantry driving a half-track. He was in battles in Tunisia-Algeria-French-Morocco, Sicily, Normandy, Northern France, Ardennes, Rhineland and Central Europe. Discharged June 25, 1945, he received the American Defense Service Ribbon, European-African-Middle Eastern Theatre Ribbon w/Silver and three Bronze Battle Stars, five Overseas Service Bars and Good Conduct Medal.

ERVIN C. HOOPS, Sergeant, served in the U.S. Army Air Force in WWII and stationed at New Foundland AFB. He was born in Campbell-Hill, Illinois, August 20,

Sgt. Ervin C. Hoops

1920, the son of William and Matilda Kueker Hoops. He earned the Victory Medal, American Theatre Ribbon, two Overseas Service Bars and Good Conduct Medal. He was discharged in 1946 after four years service.

ALBERT HOPKINS, Gunner's Mate 2/c, enlisted in Navy April 20, 1942, traveled extensively carrying supplies to Italy, Russia, Casablanca, Jamaica, Cuba, Trinidad, Brazil, and Argentina. Ship was sunk in Atlantic by German Sub, and he spent three days in a life boat. He made 10 or more trips from New York to England.

GM 2/c Albert Hopkins

Discharged November 13, 1945, his awards include the Victory Medal, European-African Medal Asiatic-Pacific Ribbon and Good Conduct Medal. Albert was born in Buffalo Ridge, Virginia, the son of Albert and Rose Harbor Hopkins, June 27, 1922.

WALTER EUGENE HORNBERGER, Sergeant, born in Chester, Illinois, June 28, 1919, son of Walter Edwin and Iola Bell Durkee Hornberger. He was in WWII, 1942-46, with 247th Port Company, attached to 32nd Division. From Scott Field, Illinois, Camp Wolters, Texas, San Francisco, California, to New Guinea, Philippines and Australia. He was discharged at Jefferson Barracks, Missouri.

GERALD F. HORRELL, Staff Sergeant, was with 75th Headquarters, 145th Infantry, 37th Division, Company D, in Asiatic-Pacific Theatre during WWII. Inducted March 24, 1943, Jefferson Barracks, Missouri, he took his basic training at Fort Leonard Wood, Missouri, then to New Caledonia Island and from there to his first battle at Guadalcanal.

S/Sgt. Gerald F. Horrell

He made beachhead on Boganville and four months later the beachhead on Luzon. Their worse battle was when 87 troops went up Mt. Packawagon and only seven came down. The rest were killed or wounded. He was discharged December 21, 1945. Gerald was born August 6, 1918, Prairie du Rocher, Illinois, the son of Henry A. and Josephine M. Levery Horrell.

EMERSON TERRY HOWIE, SP4 (T) SEE 30, entered the Army December 15, 1965 and took his basic and AIT training at Fort Leonard Wood, Missouri. He was with the 11H20 Heavy Weapons Infantry.

Terry was shipped to Vietnam where he spent 10 months. While there he received the National Defense Service Medal, Combat Infantryman Badge (1st award), Vietnam Service Medal, Vietnam Campaign Medal and the Purple Heart. Terry received an honorable discharge September 22, 1967.

He was born Dec. 1, 1946 to William Emerson and Edith L. (Ledbetter) Howie. Terry and his wife Ann (Edwards) Howie live in Peoria, Illinois.

EVERETT D. HOWIE, Corporal, entered the Army on September 3, 1942 from Scott Field, Illinois. He reported for active duty September 17, 1942. Everett was with Company A, 583rd Signal Air Warning Battalion and served 11 months and 24 days in the States, two years one month and 27 days overseas. Everett served in the battles of Bismarck, Archipelago, New Guinea, Southern Philippines WDGO33.

Howie Brothers: From left, James, Everett and Herbert

The medals he earned included the American Theater Service Medal, Asiatic-Pacific Theater Service Medal, WWII Victory Medal and the Good Conduct Medal. Everett was honorably discharged November 8, 1945. He had blue eyes, brown hair, and was 5'11". Everett was born in Coulterville, Illinois October 6, 1908, the son of David and W.D. Adele (Rieckenberg) Howie. He died February 22, 1978 and is buried in the Caledonia Cemetery, Sparta, Illinois.

HAROLD T. HOWIE, Private First Class, was born in Ellis Grove, Illinois, the son of Eddie and Elsie Bendorf Howie. He served from February 1, 1951 to May 31, 1952 with H&S Company, 1st Battalion, 1st Marine Regiment, 1st Division in Korea, after his basic training. He served on both East and West sides of Korea during his tour, moving across the valley below Panmunjom.

Pfc. Harold T. Howie

HERBERT FERN HOWIE, Tech Sergeant, was drafted into the Army on March 7, 1941 and served with Company L, 185 Infantry. Herb had three months of infantry basic training, 10 months as a squad leader, and 31 months as a rifle non-commissioned officer.

T/Sgt. Herbert F. Howie

As a rifle non-commissioned officer, Herb's assignments were to train recruits in the use of infantry weapons and tactics; familiarize himself with standard operation procedure of infantry training; and keeping records of enlisted men's progress. He was responsible for enlisted men's care of weapons and equipment. He also taught the use of Garand rifle, Springfield rifle, pistol, light and heavy machine gun, mortars, bayonets, compass and map reading, and camouflage.

Herb was discharged November 5, 1945 from Camp Fannin, Texas. He was awarded the Expert Infantryman Badge, American Defense Service Medal, American Theater Campaign, Asiatic-Pacific Theater Campaign medals and the Good Conduct Medal. He spent four years and 16 days in the States and seven months and 13 days overseas.

Herb was born July 10, 1918 in Coulterville, Illinois, the son of David and Adele D. (Rieckenberg) Howie. Herb died

Spec 4 Emerson T. Howie

November 3, 1995 in Wyoming and is buried there.

JAMES WILLARD "WHIMPY" HOWIE, Private First Class, entered into the Army November 28, 1941. Whimpy's place of entry was East St. Louis, Illinois. He was with Headquarters Company, 2nd Battalion, 22nd Infantry.

Pfc. James W. Howie

Whimp was an Orderly 695 and fought in Northern France, Normandy, Rhineland Campaign. While there he earned the Combat Infantry Badge, Good Conduct Ribbon, Purple Heart, and three stars for wounds to the hip and back, received on Dec. 1, 1944 in Germany. Whimp, had two years, eight months and 18 days in the states and one year, one month and 10 days of foreign service. He was honorably discharged from Wakeman Convalescent Hospital, Camp Atterbury, Indiana on September 25, 1945.

Whimp was born February 8, 1915 in Perry County, Illinois, the son of David and W.D. Adele (Rickenberg) Howie. He died February 22, 1986 and is buried Baldwin, Illinois.

BERNIE L. HUBERT, Private First Class, took his basic training at Fort Leonard Wood, Missouri, then went to Fort Sam Houston, San Antonio, Texas for his medical training. Bernie was with the 53rd Medical Rescue Detachment. The rest of his duty he was a medic in a Rescue Helicopter Unit in Darmstadt, Germany. Bernie served during peacetime. He was born April 23, 1937 in Oakdale, Illinois, the son of Lawrence and Amelia (Walta) Hubert.

WILLARD M. HUEY, Major, spent time in Reserves, WWII, 1942, and Korean War. No overseas duty. Willard was born in Sparta, Illinois December 17, 1916, son of John and Jennie Huey. He owned Huey Oil Company from which he retired January 1, 1990. He died January 17, 1999.

JAMES HUGHES, Major, was in the War of 1812, in Captain William Boon's Company of Illinois Militia from March 6, until June 5, 1813. He was the son of Thomas and Martha Hughes, and survived the Indian attack near the falls of the Ohio River in the early 1780s that killed his father.

SYLVESTER J. HUNTER, Major, was born Prairie du Rocher, Illinois, April 13, 1918. He enlisted in U.S. Army Infantry in 1941 and was awarded the Distinguished Service Cross for extraordinary heroism in action during WWII.

Maj. Sylvester J. Hunter

On February 6, 1944, he led a platoon of 18 riflemen in assault up a rocky hill held by enemy near Cassino, Italy. They advanced in the face of machine gun and mortar fire until he and men reached a rock wall near top of hill. With eight remaining riflemen, they held this position for two days during six major attacks by the enemy until reinforcements arrived. An enemy bullet ripped the magazine of his submachine gun, knocking it from his hands. He picked up the gun, replaced the shattered magazine and continued firing, often at point blank range. He and his men estimated they killed or wounded about 50 German soldiers.

He participated in five battle campaigns in WWII, three battle campaigns in Korean War and received 23 decorations. He retired 1961 as major, died June 3, 1979, and is buried Fort Snelling National Cemetery, Minneapolis, Minnesota.

JAMES D. HUTCHISON, Sergeant, joined the U.S. Air Force February 23, 1955. He went to school for radio repairman at Scott AFB, Illinois. He spent time in France, England and in the States in

Sgt. James D. Hutchison

Texas, Illinois and Tennessee, getting out first part of Vietnam Conflict. He was discharged in July 1964. James was born March 21, 1936 in Talcott, West Virginia, the son of Burdett Watson and Mytle E. (Harvey) Hutchison.

JOHN W. IROSE, Sergeant, enlisted in U.S. Air Force after graduating from high school August 24, 1969 and was trained as heavy equipment operator. He served with 351st Civil Engineering Squadron in

Sgt. John W. Irose

Persian Gulf and Desert Storm. He was stationed in San Diego, California, with 800th Civil Engineering Squadron. He was discharged August 24, 1991. John was born in Chester, Illinois, September 11, 1969, the son of Leo and Jessie Irose. He now owns and operates a family cattle business.

JOSEPH L. IROSE, Corporal, served in the U.S. Army from December 28, 1954

Cpl. Joseph L. Irose

to December 27, 1956. He was born in Randolph County, Illinois January 9, 1930, son of Andrew and Mary Washichek Irose.

He was stationed at Dolan Barracks, Schwaebisch Hall, Germany, 50 miles north of Stuttgart. This was a heavy artillery outfit—8" Howitzers. This base was used by the Germans as a jet fighter plane base during the last stages of WWII, and he served there with Headquarters Battery, 291st FA Battalion.

HARRY MICHAEL JACKSON, EM3/c, born August 26, 1926, in Herrin, Illinois, inducted into U.S. Navy June 15, 1944, in Springfield, Illinois. After boot training at Great Lakes, Illinois, he had electrical training in St. Louis, Missouri, transferred "OGU" San Francisco, California.

Stationed aboard *Pennsylvania* in July 1945, until she left Puget Sound for Bikini Atoll Islands, then assigned to Naval Air Station, St. Louis. Discharged June 15, 1946. He attended Southern Illinois University, taught school, then worked at Menard Correctional Center, Chester, Illinois, in school administration for 25 years. He now lives in Ellis Grove, Illinois.

DANNY D. JAMES, Captain, retired from the U.S. Marine Corp, after serving from January 24, 1951 until August 30, 1976. This time included service in both the Korean Conflict and the Vietnam War. Boot camp was at Parris Island, South Carolina.

Capt. Danny D. James

He served in First, Second and Third Marine Divisions and was awarded Silver Star, Bronze Star, Navy Commendation and Purple Heart. He served as team commander of 2nd, 3rd, 5th, and 13th Counterintelligence teams. Commanded Marine Corps Counterintelligence School, 1969-70.

Born in Chester, Illinois, he was the son of Austin G. and Violet M. Dorway James.

STEPHEN ROBERT JAMES, Sergeant, served in the 3rd Division of U.S. Marines. He enlisted in 1963 while visiting his brother Danny, a U.S. Marine Recruiter, in Fargo, North Carolina. He went to boot camp in San Diego, California, served as a cook and did a tour of duty in Okinawa before his discharge in 1967. He died in 1971 in a house fire. His parents are Austin and Violet Dorway James.

ANDREW JANY, Staff Sergeant, entered service in WWII on February 25, 1943, with 84th Infantry Division, Company A, 333rd Regiment. Trained as a cook in Camp Roberts, California and saw action in Ardennes, Rhineland and Central Europe.

He was awarded three Overseas Bars, American Campaign Medal, European-African-Middle Eastern Theatre Ribbon w/ 3 Bronze Battle Stars, Good Conduct Medal and WWII Victory Medal. He was discharged January 18, 1946.

Andrew was born in Chester, Illinois, September 10, 1923, son of Roman and Stephanie Bert Jany. He returned from service to farm with his father. Andrew died July 10, 1982.

DELBERT LEE JANY, Specialist 4, served in the U.S. Army from March 6, 1958 to March 3, 1960. He was born in Chester, Illinois on July 1, 1935, son of

SP/4 Delbert L. Jany

Roman and Stephanie Bert Jany. After basic training at Fort Hood, Texas, he spent 15 months at Gelnkausen, Germany with Company D, 2nd Armored Rifle Battalion, 48th Infantry.

DONALD J. JANY, Corporal, of Chester, Illinois, served in Korea from June 1953 until April 1955, with the 196th Field

Cpl. Donald J. Jany

Artillery Battalion. He took basic training and Communication School at Fort Riley, Kansas.

Landed in Korea on December 23, 1953, and he was in charge of telephone, switchboard, radio and electricity, until he left the last part of April 1955, then was released from service May 17, 1955. His parents are Roman and Stephanie Bert Jany.

DOUGLAS R. JANY, E-3 Aviation Field, born May 16, 1967 in Chester, Illinois, son of Donald J. and Nedra Casetta Jany. He enlisted in the U.S. Navy in 1985 and was a member of ASF Team 3 as team

E-3 Douglas R. Jany

sniper and field medic. He deployed on three classified missions and was discharged June 30, 1989. He currently lives in California with wife and two sons.

MELVIN M. JANY, Specialist 4, entered the Army July 18, 1961 and went to

Spec/4 Melvin M. Jany

Fort Leonard Wood for eight weeks of basic training, then eight weeks Mechanic School, after which, Melvin was transferred to Orleans, France, until his discharge on June 21, 1963. He was with the 58th Ordnance Company during peace time. Melvin was born May 17, 1939, son of Roman and Stephanie (Bert) Jany.

GEORGE JANY, Private First Class, served in the U.S. Army from March 5, 1962 to January 5, 1964, with COM OPNS CO 5th SIG BN. He was born April 18, 1941 in Chester, Illinois, son of Roman and Stephanie Bert Jany.

HERMAN J. JANY, Radioman 2/c, served in WWII on U.S NTS, Farragut, Idaho for two months, LST-131, USS *Shawmut* (GM-11), AO-627, USS *Escatawra,* in and around the Philippines. He entered service October 20, 1943 and was discharged April 19, 1946. He received several medals and ribbons. Herman died June 14, 1992. He was born in Chester, Illinois, the son of Roman and Stephanie Bert Jany.

HERMAN MICHAEL JANY, Private First Class, from Fort Gage, Illinois, he served in WWII in the U.S. Army from May 1942 through April 1945. His parents were Frank W. and Mary Petrowske Jany. He was 28 years old when inducted and served as Armorer 511, Infantry, with Light Machine Gun Marksman qualification.

He was in the Normandy (D-Day) Campaign in France, where he was wounded in action, June 10, 1944. He was sent from a field hospital to London and to Army hospitals in the U.S. for rehabilitation until honorably discharged at Wakeman General Hospital at Camp Atterbury, Indiana on April 25, 1945. He received the Purple Heart, European-African-Middle Eastern Theater Ribbon, M-1 Rifle and Carbine Marksman Award and Good Conduct Ribbon.

KEVIN JANY, E-7, Chief Petty Officer, entered recruit training at Great Lakes Naval Training Center in October 1981. Reared in Chester, Illinois, he is the son of Donald and Nedra Casetta Jany. From Great Lakes, he went to Groton, Connecticut for submarine training, then to Dam Neck, Virginia for Guided Missile School.

He served on the USS *George C. Marshall* (SSBN-654) submarine from January 1983 until October 1986, when he returned to Dam Neck, Virginia and served as a naval guided missile instructor until April 1990. The next two years were spent aboard the USS *James Madison.*

Other assignments included Naval Recruiting Command, Pensacola, Florida; Navy Recruiting Station, Louisville, Kentucky; Atlantic Strategic Weapons Facility and Student Trident Training Facility, Kings Bay, Georgia until July 1996. He then served on the USS *Nebraska* (SSBN-739) (Blue) for three years. He was in both the Saudi Conflict and Persian Gulf War. Kevin retired from the Strategic Weapons Facility, Kings Bay, Georgia, July 19, 2002.

LAWRENCE R. JANY, Corporal, served in the U.S. Army from November 13, 1950 to August 13, 1952. He was born September 1, 1928, Chester, Illinois, son of Roman and Stephanie (Bert) Jany.

Cpl. Lawrence R. Jany

He was drafted while working for Caterpillar, Peoria, Illinois and served in Korea as a track mechanic. He served at Chosen Reservoir and Top of Old Baldy. He was discharged from Camp Carson, Colorado with the 5th Army Area, ERC Artillery, B Battery, 538th FA Battalion.

He is one of seven brothers who served their country in Armed Services. He worked road construction after discharge.

MARVIN JOHANNING, Corporal, was born in Waterloo, Illinois on February 3, 1931, son of Theodore and Anna Buettner Johanning. Inducted February 12, 1952, he attended Quartermaster Training in Virginia, and while there transferred to special assignment with SCARWAF to report to the 931st Engineer Headquarters in Korea. Their cargo plane landed on the banks of the Han River, August 14, 1952.

Cpl. Marvin Johanning

He reported to Headquarters Company which made the assignments to different locations. Thank God, he became permanent at Headquarters with a room on the 2nd level of an old Korean Hotel, which had been taken by their infantry. He was a private chauffeur for high ranking officers and at times an emergency night duty driver. He will always remember Korea, the 931st and the sign on the wall which read, "In God We Trust. Pray, Have Faith and Hope. There is no other way." He was discharged November 12, 1953.

CLAUDE B. JOHNSON, Sergeant, enlisted in Army Air Force June 19, 1943, for service in WWII. He served with 436th Bomb Squadron, 7th Bomb Group in China Offensive and Central Burma.

He was awarded the American Theater Ribbon, Asiatic-Pacific Theatre Ribbon w/2 Bronze Battle Stars, WWII Victory Medal and Distinguished Unit Badge w/Overseas Bar. Training included Air Cadet Training and Flexible Gunnery Training for his job of aerial gunner. He was discharged from Jefferson Barracks, Missouri on April 25, 1946.

Claude was born in Chester, Illinois, December 30, 1924.

EARNEST JOHNSON, Corporal, entered service April 11, 1917 at St. Louis, Missouri. He served at Fort Riley, Kansas

Earnest Johnson

in Company B of the 20th Infantry of the U.S. Army and was discharged at Camp Grant, Illinois, June 8, 1919.

Born in Rockwood, Illinois, April 25, 1898, to McKinsey and Minnie Cashion Johnson, he died January 22, 1973 and is buried in Ebenezer Cemetery near Rockwood.

GERALD MELVIN "RED" JOHNSON, Seaman 2/c, graduated from Chester High School in May and enlisted in Navy on October 25, 1942. Served on USS *Mannert L. Abele* as fire controlman. He was in sea battle at Okinawa, where 200 kamikaze's hit nine destroyers, one destroyer escort and several smaller craft, only USS *Abele* was lost. The ship sank in less than five minutes.

Seaman 2/c Gerald M. Johnson

A Japanese plane dropped bomb in midst of swimming survivors and six crewmen were killed and 73 reported missing. Gerald was one of the missing and declared killed in action, April 12, 1945. Memorial service was held at First Baptist Church in Chester, September 16, 1945. He received the Purple Heart posthumously.

Gerald was born at Modoc, Illinois on January 6, 1924, the son of Charles T. and Katherine L. Godier Johnson.

HERMAN CLYDE JOHNSON, Private, born at Rockwood, Illinois, February 27, 1896. His parents were McKinsey

Pvt. Herman C. Johnson

and Minnie Cashion Johnson. Inducted at Chester, Illinois on April 27, 1918, in WWI, he served in the 2nd Company, 159th Depot Brigade, 1st Tr. Battalion at Fort Riley, Kansas. Discharged at Camp Zachary Taylor, Kentucky on December 20, 1918. Herman died April 2, 1975 and is buried in Paradise Cemetery near Steeleville, Illinois.

HURD HUSBAND JOHNSON, born in Chester, Illinois on October 29, 1918 to Hurd and Jessie (Husband) Johnson. Hurd enlisted in the Army on March 21, 1941 at Fort McArthur, California. He departed for Italy on February 1, 1944 and returned August 22, 1945. He served there with the Army Air Corps as a sheet metal machinist. Staff Sergeant Hurd Johnson of 1103 Third Army Air Force Base Unit Squadron B was discharged at Scott Field Illinois on November 24, 1945.

Hurd H. Johnson

Hurd married Evelyn Spurgeon on November 16, 1946. They had two children, Jana and Richard. In civilian life he worked as a flight engineer for American Airlines for 30 years based out of Los Angeles, California, a career that took him from the era of prop planes to the modern jumbo jets. Hurd retired from American Airlines in 1982.

He spent his retirement pursuing many hobbies and interests including growing green house orchids, running marathons, traveling the nation by RV, climbing Mount Kilimanjaro in Africa, studying astronomy and spending time with his family. Hurd passed away on November 18, 2001 in Buena Park, California, following complications of a stroke.

JOEL C. JOHNSON, Private, enlisted at Chester, Illinois and served in Company A, 80th Illinois Infantry. Born March 25, 1843, in Randolph County, his parents were Bartholomew and Alice (Eliza) Darwin Johnson. After the war he returned to farming and died from tuberculous April 18, 1917. He is buried by his wife, Margaret Mansker Johnson, in the abandoned and almost destroyed Johnson Cemetery in Rockwood, Illinois precinct.

KERRY L. JOHNSON, Airman 1/c, entered Air Force April 6, 1976, graduated Air Force Police Academy, then served with 305th Air Refueling Wing as security policeman on alert aircraft at Grissom AFB, Bunker Hill, Indiana. He was discharged September 12, 1978. Born in Red Bud, Illinois, October 20, 1957, the son of William and Alma Jean Smith Johnson, he now lives in Rockwood and is an over-the-road truck driver for Gilster-Mary Lee.

WILLIAM LESTER JOHNSON, Specialist 4, was drafted into Army March 4, 1957 and served with 18th Field Artillery at Fort Sill, Oklahoma, attached to Motor Pool Strike Unit of the Infantry. Born

SP-4 William Lester Johnson

in Rockwood, Illinois, September 9, 1934, the son of Richard S. and Mollie Moss Johnson, he was discharged March 4, 1959, returned to Rockwood, and worked at International Shoe Company in Chester.

KEVIN G. JOKERST, E-5, USN, served August 12, 1984 to August 9, 1990. He was born May 21, 1966, Ste. Genevieve, MO, son of Ken and Wilma Staffen Jokerst.

E-5 Kevin G. Jokerst

Kevin served as a construction mechanic for the USN Seabees based in Gulf Port, Mississippi. He served in Pensacola, Florida, Guantanamo Bay, Cuba, Spain, Philippines and Guam. He was discharged in 1990.

FRANKLIN JONES, Private, was in 5th Company under Captain Charles Barrzhaf in the Civil War. He entered service November 13, 1961, in the Regiment of Veteran Reserve Corps Volunteers. He was discharged February 27, 1865 in Indianapolis, Indiana. He was from Modoc, Illinois, son of Cadwallader and Martha Ham Jones.

FRED JONES, Private, was born in Modoc, Illinois in 1896, son of Franklin and Ellen Webb Jones. He went into the Army in April 1915 and served as a steam

Pvt. Fred Jones

engineer, in the 52nd Headquarters 84th Division. He was discharged October 15, 1917, from Camp Taylor, Louisville, Kentucky.

LOWELL L. JONES, Sergeant, after induction in the Army, January 8, 1969, he received basic training at Fort Leonard Wood, Missouri. He was assigned to Company B, 1st Battalion, 18th Infantry, 1st Division and sent to Vietnam in June 1969.

He received the National Defense Service, Vietnam Service, Bronze Star, Combat Infantryman, Vietnam Campaign Medal w/60 Device, two Overseas Bars, Expert (M-14 and M-16), 1st C (Grenade) Marksman and the Purple Heart. He returned to U.S. in June 1970 and was discharged January 7, 1971.

Lowell was born in Modoc, Illinois, the son of Fred and Marjorie Campbell Jones.

ELMER A JOOST, Private First Class, of Percy, Illinois, was in WWII from 1945-47 with 393rd Engineer Construction Battalion. His basic training was at Fort Leonard Wood, Missouri and Fort Jackson, South Carolina. After having measles and spending time in hospital, he was sent to Fort Belvoir, Virginia. Parents were Herman and Emma Meyerhoffe Joost.

HENRY JOHN JUNG, Private, was drafted to serve in WWI on May 19, 1918, at Chester, Illinois. He spent his time in service at Camp Eagle Pass, El Paso, Texas, maintaining security of Mexican-Texas border. He was discharged January 15, 1919. Born in Walsh, Illinois, March 25, 1890, son of Henry and Margaret Muerer Jung, he died December 26, 1965, with burial in Ellis Grove, Illinois Cemetery.

LOREN BONIFACE JUNG, Tech 4, drafted April 5, 1945, received basic training Camp Fannin, Texas and spent the rest of his tour of duty as an Administrative NCO at Separation Center, Fort Bragg, North Carolina. He was discharged October 8, 1946. Loren was born at Ellis Grove, Illinois, December 10, 1926, the son of Henry John and Virginia Schulein Jung.

EDGAR F. JUNGE, Aviation Boatsman Mate 3/c, served in the U.S. Navy from December 5, 1950 to September 29, 1954. He was born November 5, 1929, Baldwin, Illinois, the son of Henry H. and __ Luebkemann Junge. Edgar went to Great Lakes, Illinois for his basic training, then served aboard ship (tours in Mediterranean Sea) used for aerial support for forces in that area, one of them where they removed Turkish troops from Korea at the Armistice. This took them around the world through both Panama and Suez canals.

HENRY G. JUNGE, Electrician's Mate 3/c, served in Navy, WWII, June 29, 1944, testing battery powered torpedoes. He was stationed at Solomon, Maryland, then Fort Lauderdale, Florida. He fired torpedoes at targets in the Atlantic Ocean for testing. Torpedoes were patterned from German torpedoes found in German submarines captured off the eastern area of Atlantic Ocean. Discharged July 5, 1946, he was the son of Henry H. and __ Luebkemann Junge.

VERNON J. JUNGE, Corporal T-5, served in WWII with 191st Tank Battalion. He landed in Africa after battle of Tunisia, then served all through Italy, France and Germany, in supply room repairing and issuing ammunition, guns, repairing tanks, and taking supplies to front lines. He entered service March 23, 1942 and was discharged September 24, 1945. Parents are Henry H. and __ Luebkemann Junge.

CLYDE JUNGEWAELTER, Private First Class, served in the U.S. Army during WW II, from December 28, 1943 until February 1, 1946. He saw duty in En-

Pvt. 1/c Clyde Jungewaelter

gland, France, Belgium and Germany. His parents were John Sr. and Sylvia Medcalf Jungewaelter. He came home to Chester, Illinois, to join his brother Earl in operating the Chester Bakery.

Sgt. Lowell L. Jones

From left: Vernon F. Junge, Edgar F. Junge and Henry G. Junge

JOHN JUNGEWAELTER, Private First Class, was in the U.S. Army from December 28, 1943 until February 1, 1946, during WWII. He was wounded in action in Italy. The son of John Sr. and Sylvia Medcalf Jungewaelter, he came home to Chester, Illinois and became the owner of the Grandview Hotel. He died November 9, 1998.

LEROY H. KARSTEN, Corporal, was in the Korean Conflict with Company D, 135th Engineer Battalion, 44th Infantry Division. He enlisted May 10, 1951 and after training and preparing at Camp Cooke, California, his division was called to active duty in November 1951 and sent to Korea as individual unit replacements. He returned to U.S. after truce was signed and was discharged. Leroy is the son of Harry G. and Hulda A. Fischer Karsten, of Steeleville, Illinois.

DONALD ALLEN KEETON, served in the U.S. Navy Active and Reserves from 1956-62. He served aboard the USS FDR. Donald was born February 17, 1939, Jackson County, Illinois and lived in Chester, Illinois.

VEARL LEE KEETON, SP-3, served in the U.S. Army from 1955-57, as a light vehicle driver. After discharge, he transferred to Reserves until January 13, 1963.

JACOB KELLER, born about 1841, joined the Sixth Missouri Infantry and served as a surgeon's assistant and then as a surgeon in the 83rd Indiana Infantry. He was wounded in the shoulder by a bayonet at the battle of Shiloh, was captured, then escaped and returned to his unit.

At the close of the conflict he continued advanced medical studies at the Missouri Medical College of St. Louis and then settled in Chester, Illinois and later moved to Steeleville, where he lived with his wife, Mary Glore of Shiloh Hill, Illinois. He died in Steeleville, Illinois May 21, 1887 and is buried in the Evergreen Cemetery in Chester, Illinois.

MELVIN LEE KELLER, Private, born May 6, 1922 in Cambria, Illinois. He entered service April 26, 1946, during WWII and served with Guard and Escort Detachment of 6200 Army Services Unit. Qualified as an M-1 Rifle Marksman, also served

Pvt. Melvin Keller

as a Military Police at Camp McQuaide, California, guarding disciplinary barracks. Received WWII Victory Medal and was discharged from Fort Ord, California on March 31, 1947. Melvin is the son of Claude M. and Lizzie Manis Keller. He died February 27, 1982.

DEWEY ROLAND KELLY, Sergeant, served in the U.S. Marines from February 8, 1951 to February 8, 1954. He participated in operations against the enemy

Sgt. Dewey R. Kelly

forces in Korea with the 1st Marine Division. His specialty was engineer equipment mechanics. He was born October 29, 1932, St. Louis, Missouri, the son of Stella Whitcher, and grew up in Chester, Illinois.

MARLAND R. KELLY, S1/c, of Sparta, Illinois, was inducted into service in WWII in 1945, and received boot training with Company 947 at Great Lakes Naval Training Station. Additional training was at Camp Parks, California, and from there he was shipped overseas. He served with Navy Seabees in the 53rd Battalion on Guam, 140th in Admiralty Islands and CB Det. 1153 in Japan. He was discharged in 1946. Parents are Clarien G. and Ethel Frazier Kelly.

ALBERT F. KEMPFER, Corporal, served in the U.S. Army from December

Cpl. Albert Kempfer

9, 1952 to November 22, 1954, then eight years in Reserves. He completed basic training in Camp Atterbury, Indiana, left for Germany in May 1952, and served 18 months as ammo truck driver. He was born July 29, 1932, Evansville, Illinois, the son of Roy and Minnie Keller Kempfer. He currently plays lead guitar with the "Country Gents" on weekends.

IVAN J. KEMPFER, Private First Class, served in the U.S. Army, 1951-53, then five years in the Reserves. He served with Battery B, 37 AAA Gun Battalion during Korean War. He was born September 20, 1929, Riley Lake, Illinois, the son of Vernon W. and Elva Sassanger Kempfer. He was discharged from Camp Carson, Colorado and earned the Army Occupation Medal.

PAUL E. KEMPFER, Sergeant, served in the U.S. Army from February 25, 1952 to February 24, 1955, then eight years in Reserves. He served with Headquarters

Sgt. Paul E. Kempfer

Battery, 11th Airborne Division Artillery. He was discharged from Fort Campbell, Kentucky and earned the National Defense Medal, Good Conduct and Paratrooper Badge. He was born January 17, 1932, Riley Lake, Illinois, the son of Vernon W. and Elva Sassanger Kempfer. He died in 1957 and is buried in Ellis Grove Cemetery.

VERNON C. KEMPFER, Boatswain's Mate 2/c, went into Navy September 13, 1943, and served on LST in Pacific during WWII. He was discharged December 31, 1945 and worked for Ameri-

BM 2/c Vernon C. Kempfer

can Steel, before relocating to Kansas in 1954, to work for Fairbanks Morse until retirement in 1982. Vernon was born in Roots, Illinois, June 13, 1920, the son of Vernon W. and Elva Sassanger Kempfer, he died April 15, 1992.

JOHN KENT, was inducted at Chester, Illinois, May 27, 1918, and attained the rank of Wagoner, in the Wagon Detachment 2 M Corps. He was discharged February 19, 1919, at Camp Shelby, Mississippi, with discharge pay of $32.45. Born in Rockwood, Illinois, October 2, 1891, he was the son of Thaddius and Johanna Johnson Kent. John died March 29, 1957 and is buried in Evergreen Cemetery in Chester, Illinois.

LOUIS JOSEPH KERKHOVER, Seaman 1/c, entered the U.S. Navy March 31, 1944, and received training at Great Lakes Naval Training Center. He then

SM 1/c Louis J. Kerkhover

transferred to Hawaii for additional training, then was sent to the Asiatic-Pacific, serving on Okinawa and Saipan with the 101st Navy Seabee's in the 39th Regiment Company A-3, during WWII. He was discharged January 9, 1946 and returned to Chester, Illinois. His parents were James T. and Amelia VanVooren Kerkhover. He died in Chester, Illinois, January 11, 2002.

FRANK PAUL KESSLER, Steward's Mate 3/c, was drafted late into WWII, leaving a wife and four small sons at home. He was inducted December 28, 1943 at Great Lakes Naval Training Center, then

Steward M3/c Frank P. Kessler

shipped to California for advance training. His permanent duty was aboard the USS *Kershaw*, on patrol around islands in the Pacific Ocean. He was discharged August 17, 1945. The son of John and Helen O'Sullivan Kessler, he was born October 10, 1909.

DENNIS KIEHNA, Operations Specialist 2/c Petty Officer, entered the service in June 1970. He served in Vietnam

OS 2/c Dennis Kiehna

on the aircraft carrier USS *Midway* (CVA-41) from March 1971 to March 1974, a total of 20 months in Vietnam. He operated surface and air search radar systems. The *Midway* became the first carrier to be home ported outside the USA. The homeport was Yokosuka, Japan in September 1973. His parents are Melvin and Nathalie (Des Rocher) Kiehna.

MELVIN L. KIEHNA, Electrician Mate 3/c, served in the U.S. Navy during WWII. He trained at Great Lakes, Illinois, Purdue University, Lafayette, Indiana, then shipped overseas to Caledonia Island, Hollandia, New Guinea and on to Manila Bay, Philippines to do shore duty. He entered service in 1943 and was discharged in 1946. Melvin was born in Percy, Illinois, son of Henry and Bessie Egbert Kiehna.

WILLIAM G. KIEHNA, Private, enlisted in WWI, July 17, 1918, and served

Pvt. William G. Kiehna

Camp Pike, AR. William is third from left.

until January 20, 1919. He was born in Jackson County, Illinois on October 5, 1885, the son of Heinrich August Wilhelm and Margaretha Mohr Kiehna. He served in Company 7, 163rd Depot Brigade, after enlisting at Grundy Center, Iowa (after spending the summer working on farms in that area). When discharged at Camp Dodge, Iowa, he was paid $60 and given a railway ticket to Pinckneyville, Illinois. He died April 24, 1946, and is buried in Steeleville, Illinois.

JIMMIE DEAN KILLION, Specialist 4, served in the Army from March 1982 to March 1985. He was born in Kodiak, Alaska, March 7, 1957, son of Lon and Geneva Eggemeyer Killion. He trained in Satellite Communication in a combat environment and served with Company A, 1st Signal Corps. He served in Kaiserslautern, Germany from November 1983 to March 1985 and was discharged from Fort Dix, New Jersey. He now resides in Thornton, Colorado and works in sales.

JAMES "ERNIE" KING, BM2/c, served in U.S. Navy in WWII with Task Force #58, South Pacific. Entered service October 2, 1942 and saw action against

BM 2/c James E. King

Japanese Fleet in East China Sea, Iwo Jima and Okinawa. He was in Tokyo Bay when treaty was signed. He was discharged April 26, 1946. Born October 1, 1925, Royalton, Illinois, the son of Noah and Martha Boyles King. Noah King served in WWI and his dress jacket is in the Sparta Museum.

JAMES E. KIPP, Corporal, served in the U.S. Army from 1948 to 1951. Jim began his tour in Army with the Infantry and was sent to Frankfort, Germany. There,

Cpl. James E. Kipp

Band with Kipp standing last in second row.

they discovered he played drums and he was transferred into Supply and the U.S. Army Band. They played for General MacArthur and other parades and occasions. He was later transferred to Salzburg, Austria, still with the Band. He was discharged September 27, 1951. He was born June 19, 1929 in Chester, the son of Victor and Beatrice Bean Kipp.

ALBERT EDWARD KIRK, Corporal, enlisted in U.S. Marine Corps February 8, 1943 and served with 4th Marine Division during Invasion of Saipan. He was wounded July 6, 1944 and died July 7 of those wounds. His remains were returned to Evergreen Cemetery, Chester, Illinois for burial on January 5, 1949.

Cpl. Albert E. Kirk

Prior to enlisting, he was employed at International Shoe Company in Chester and was the first factory employee to be a war casualty. Albert was born March 30, 1925, at Rockwood, Illinois, the son of John S. and Emma Sauerhage Kirk. His mother Emma Kirk Gretzmacher was awarded the Purple Heart posthumously for the service of her son.

KENNETH SMITH KIRK, Private, born in Rockwood, Illinois, February 18, 1894, the son of Stephen and Addaliza Mansker Kirk. He served in Company C, 24th Engineers, during WWI. Kenneth was killed in a car accident January 31, 1932 and buried in Mansker Cemetery near Rockwood, Illinois.

GEORGE LEE KIRKLAND, Specialist 4, born in Sparta, Illinois, September 27, 1945, son of Jesse and Geraldine

Sp-4 George Lee Kirkland

Apple Kirkland. He entered service January 6, 1964 and was sent to Vietnam and served with Battery C, 18th Artillery. He was discharged January 5, 1966.

BRUCE WAYNE KIRKPATRICK, Specialist 4, entered the military on August 14, 1969. His foreign service included USAR PAC, one year, two months, 14 days. Bruce was a 71B30 Clerk Typist, Republic of Vietnam from January 4, 1970 until March 17, 1971.

Sp-4 Bruce W. Kirkpatrick

He earned the National Defense Service Medal, Vietnam Service Medal, Vietnam Campaign Medal, Army Commendation Medal, and the Good Conduct Award. Bruce was honorably discharged March 18, 1971.

Bruce was born November 8, 1949 in Belleville, Illinois to Alberta James and Nettia Lou (Harris) Kirkpatrick. He died May 7, 1973.

HAROLD V. KIRKPATRICK, Airman 2/c, served in the U.S. Air Force from November 7, 1960 to September 7, 1962. He was born in Tilden, Illinois on May 21, 1942, the son of Bert and Nettie Lou Harris Kirkpatrick. Harold was stationed at Hamilton AFB, San Francisco, California,

A 2/c Harold V. Kirkpatrick

and operated a printing press while there. After discharge he married, has a son and a daughter, and is now enjoying retirement after 35 years with General Motors.

OSMOND J.G. KIRSCH, Corporal, of Red Bud, Illinois. He was born May 1895, served in the Army in WWI and was stationed in France. He became ill and died with pneumonia on February 3, 1919. He was brought back and buried at St. Peter's Cemetery, Red Bud, on October 18, 1920.

DONALD R. KLINGMANN, ET2, served in the U.S. Navy during the Korean War. He was born in Chester, Illinois on April 13, 1932, the son of Harry and Gladys Gnaegy Klingmann. He enlisted in the Navy in 1950 and served on the heavy

ET-2 Donald R. Klingmann

cruiser Los Angeles during three deployments to Korea as a radar electronics technician. After discharge in March 1954, he was employed as a field engineer for IBM Corporation until retiring in 1987. He resides at Lake Kincaid with his wife Marilyn.

OLIVER A KLOEPPER, Master Machinist Mate, 3/c Petty Officer, served aboard USS *Missoula* (APA-211) during WWII. He entered boot camp August 6, 1945 at Great Lakes Naval Center and was there when war ended.

MMM 3/c PO Oliver A. Kloepper

He was sent to Shoemaker, California, where on November 11, 1945, he boarded ship for Okinawa to bring troops home to Seattle, Washington. Later he went back to Okinawa and Japan for troops returning to Mors Island, California, where they began to decommission the ship. This was completed August 1, 1946 and he was discharged at St. Louis, Missouri on August 11, 1946.

Oliver was born in Red Bud, Illinois, July 24, 1927, the son of Albert and Olga Harms Kloepper.

ALBERT H. KLOTH, T/3, entered service in WWII on February 26, 1943 at Scott Field, Illinois and served in New Guinea driving kitchen truck with 166th Ordnance

T/3 Albert H. Kloth

Tire Company. Albert was discharged January 14, 1946, Jefferson Barracks, Missouri, the son of Herman and Bertha Eilers Kloth. He was born in Steeleville, Illinois.

CLARENCE KLOTH, Staff Sergeant, served in the Army during WWII in Company B, 52nd Signal Battalion. He was in four invasions in Southwest Pacific. He entered service May 13, 1941 and was dis-

S/Sgt. Clarence Kloth

charged August 16, 1945. The son of Henry and Emma Grefe Kloth, he was born in Walsh, Illinois on April 3, 1918. Clarence worked in a shoe factory until 1947 when he began farming. He died October 22, 1998.

GARY R. KLOTH, Petty Officer 2/c (ETR2), born August 29, 1950, in Red Bud, Illinois, son of Clarence and LaVerne Lorentz Kloth. He left the family farm and entered the Navy, May 18, 1970 and served as an electronics technician (radar), dur-

P/ Off. 1/c Gary R. Kloth

ing the Vietnam War. He saw no combat and was discharged May 17, 1977. Currently he is employed by Dynegy as a controls and instruments technician at the Baldwin Energy Complex.

GEORGE H. KLOTH, Private First Class, served in the U.S. Army from November 9, 1951 to October 16, 1953, during the Korean War. George worked the family farm before being drafted and became engaged to Ardell Eggemeyer the night before he left.

George H. Kloth

He was born September 23, 1928, Walsh, Illinois, the son of Otto and Violet Schultz Kloth. He retired from Spartan Printing, then owned Kloth Termite and Pest Control Service. George died March 9, 1997.

LAUREN O. KLOTH, Corporal, served with 297th Engineer Aviation Bat-

Cpl. Lauren O. Kloth

talion in Korean War. Basic training was at Fort Leonard Wood, Missouri from January 26 to August 1951. The battalion transferred to Fort Richardson, Anchorage, Alaska, detached to Aluetian Islands, then to Beal AFB, California. He was discharged January 26, 1953, Fort Leonard Wood, Missouri.

He was born in Sparta, Illinois on September 18, 1927, the son of Otto G. and Violet Schultz. He retired from McDonnel Douglas Aircraft after 38 years as an inspector and now lives in Columbia, Illinois.

RONALD D. KLOTH, Private First Class, served in the U.S. Army from June 2, 1953 to April 22, 1955, as heavy vehicle driver, Company C, 317th Engineer Battalion. He was born July 5, 1933, Schuline,

Pfc. Ronald D. Kloth

Illinois, the son of Otto and Violet Schultz Kloth. He farmed for 30 years, then worked for Carl Bannister Excavating Service.

TERRY LEE KLOTH, enlisted in the U.S. Air Force November 10, 1966 and served as weapons load crew chief at George AFB, California. During the Vietnam Era he served with the 476th Tactical Fighter Squadron. He was discharged from the Air Force September 1, 1970.

S/Sgt. Terry L. Kloth

Terry was born Nov. 16, 1947 in Red Bud, Illinois, the son of Clarence and (Lorenz) Kloth. He received a BS degree in mechanical engineering. Terry is currently married and working as senior facility engineer in oil and gas protection industry.

WILBUR KLOTH, served in both WWII and Korean Conflict. His service lasted 18-1/2 years throughout the world before being given a medical discharge due to a heart problem. His occupation was a mechanic.

DAVID JOHN KLUBA, SP3, served in the U.S. Army from May 26, 1954 to May 25, 1956. He was born July 22, 1935, son of Steven and Clara Probst Kluba. Dave was stationed at the Nike Base in Fort

Sp-3 David J. Kluba

Banks, Massachusetts, with 514th AAA Missile Battalion. He received the National Defense Service Medal and Good Conduct Medal.

THEODORE H. KNIGGE, Staff Sergeant, was born at Ruma, Illinois February 8, 1914, son of Louis and Minnie Junge Knigge. He entered WWII service on November 17, 1943 at Fort Sheridan, Illinois,

S/Sgt. Theodore H. Knigge

was assigned to Company A, 704th MP Battalion and sent to Camp Blanding, Florida, and Mississippi. He also served as supply sergeant. His awards include the American Campaign Medal, Good Conduct Medal and WWII Victory Medal. He was discharged December 5, 1945.

MERLE KNOPE, Private First Class, born June 18, 1922, Sparta, Illinois, to Louis and Mayme Schaffer Knope. He entered WWII, October 26, 1944, and served

Pvt. 1/c Merle Knope

in Company L, 25th Infantry Division. He was on Luzon Island in the Philippines, and later was driver for General Murray in Manila. He was discharged January 17, 1946, worked for Zeigler Coal Company for 38 years and now lives in Coulterville, Illinois.

JAMES D. KNOTT, Private First Class, served in the U.S. Army from July 14, 1948 to July 12, 1950. He was born in Chester, Illinois on October 16, 1928, the son of Dillon and Mae McKinney Knott. James

Pfc. James D. Knott

enlisted and after basic training he served as a clerk typist in Tokyo, Japan. Discharged, he worked in road building construction and retired as president of Johnson County Asphalt Company. He died December 17, 1995.

LELAND P. KOCH, Senior Chief (E-8), enlisted in the Coast Guard in 1953. Leland was discharged in 1976 after serving his country for 23 years. During his tenure, he served as an engineman aboard cutters, buoy tenders and ice breakers throughout the United States, Alaska, the Aleutian Islands and also the Arctic Zone. A long illness has required his residency at Saint Ann's Healthcare Center, Chester,

Chief E-8 Leland P. Koch

Pfc. Fred W. Koester

Cpl. Donald R. Kontz

Illinois. Leland was born April 3, 1935 in Steeleville, Illinois. He is the son of Alfred and Malinda (Castens) Koch.

EDWARD WILLIAM KOENING, Private, was drafted October 4, 1917, to serve in WWI. He was born May 31, 1893, the son of Edward and Eva Eliza Engelhardt Koening. He served with 345th Infantry Company in St. Mihiel, Meuse, Argonne, Aisne-Marne in France.

His training was at Camp Taylor, Louisville, Kentucky; Camp Pike, Little Rock, Arkansas; Camp Green, Charlotte, North Carolina; Camp Merrit, Tenafly, New Jersey, before sailing for France on May 22, 1918 on the ship *Fatherland* for a distance of 4,000 miles.

Arrived at Brest, France, May 31, and with 26,000 men attached to the 4th Infantry Division. he served with Ammunition Company G as Waggoner. His company was hit by enemy fire and some were wounded and many killed. They turned the horses loose and never saw them again.

After the war he was stationed at Greimersburg, Germany from December 18, 1918 until April 10, 1919. On July 15, 1919 he left France for U.S. aboard USS *Antigonne,* with 3,800 men. He was discharged from Chicago, Illinois on August 8, 1919. Edward died January 9, 1977.

HEINRICH KOENIG, a soldier in the Civil War, was born in Hannover Germany, came to this country and lived in Red Bud, Illinois. He fought in the war and died in a hospital in Decatur, Alabama, July 19, 1864, aged 21 years, 5 months and 17 days.

FRED W. KOESTER, Private First Class, served in WWII from July 6, 1942 until October 8, 1945. He was with Company C, 320th Engineers Battalion, 95th Infantry Division, and saw service in England, France and Germany.

He was awarded the Purple Heart as a result of being wounded in enemy action in the European Theater of Operations. He also received three Bronze Campaign Stars. The son of Fred and Mina Rowold Koester, he was from Ellis Grove, Illinois.

GLENN W. KOESTER, Third Class, joined the Navy October 7, 1963 and served in Vietnam as an air craft sheet metal mechanic. Glenn was discharged October 4, 1967. He was born April 28, 1945, the son of William and Ella (Hartmann) Koester.

PAUL KOESTER, Tech 5, of Ellis Grove, Illinois, was in Battery A, 331st AAA S/L Battalion in WWII. He entered service June 11, 1942, and served two years and nine months overseas in battles and campaigns in Tunisia, Algeria, French Morocco, Sicily and Rome.

T/5 Paul Koester

He received four Bronze Battle Stars, five Overseas Service Bars, the European-African-Middle Eastern Ribbons and the Good Conduct Medal. He was discharged June 12, 1945.

His parents were Fred C. and Mina Rowold Koester.

DONALD R. KONTZ, Corporal, served in the U.S. Army. He was born in Chester, Illinois, the son of Robert F. and Clara Runge Kontz. He joined the National Guard while a senior in high school and was called into the Army on February 15, 1952. In August he was sent to Germany and served with 14th Ordnance, MM Company DS. He was discharged January 29, 1954.

MICHAEL D. KONTZ, Specialist 4, served in the U.S. Army from November 18, 1976 to November 16, 1979. Mike enlisted and completed his basic training and 17 weeks of Automotive Repair School.

Sp4 Michal D. Kontz

He transferred to Germany for 12 months, then returned to Aberdeen, Maryland for 12 weeks of Advanced Automotive Repair School. He returned to Germany to finish his tour and was discharged November 11, 1979.

Michael was born May 31, 1956 in Chester, Illinois, the son of Donald R. and Marcella Hohgrefe Kontz.

ROBERT F. KONTZ, Private, enlisted in WWI on September 5, 1918, with Com-

Pvt. Robert F. Kontz

pany F, 1st Prov. Infantry Regiment. His tour of duty was short due to signing of the Armistice. He was discharged December 22, 1918. Robert was born July 20, 1895, in Marshal, Missouri, the son of Jacob and Melissa Holland Kontz.

FRED W. KORANDO, SM3/c, born at Raddle, Illinois, November 16, 1924, to Andy and Myrtle Wilson Korando and moved to Randolph County at age 2. He graduated from Chester High School and entered the U.S. Navy in WWII on November 9, 1943. Attended Signal School in Farragut, Idaho, then assigned to Armed Guard, Treasure Island.

SM 3/c Fred W. Korando

He sailed on merchant ships to several small islands in South Pacific and participated in Philippine Liberation.

Discharged March 30, 1946, he returned to Randolph County and retired from a lumber company in 1984, then moved to Jacob, Illinois.

GLENN R. KORANDO, Sergeant, served in the U.S. Marine Corps from August 31, 1954 to September 1, 1957. The son of Joseph and Philomena Bert Korando, he was born March 9, 1934, Randolph County, near Chester, Illinois.

Glenn went to San Diego, California for his boot camp, then to Camp Pendelton, California. He served with Headquarters Company, 2nd Battalion, 12th Regiment, 3rd Marine Division, FMF Okinawa, Japan Easy Battery, 1st Heavy Artillery Rockets, Battery FMF, 29 Palms, California. He was discharged September 2, 1957.

MICHAEL THOMAS KORANDO, Private First Class, was born October 2, 1922 at Raddle, Illinois, to Thomas and Ella Shields Korando. He entered WWII in April 1944 to serve with I Company, 2nd Marine Division and 3rd Battalion, 8th Marine Division.

Pfc. Michael T. Korando

He served in Pacific from August 14, 1944 until March 14, 1946, on Okinawa, Tinian, Saipan and Ryukyu Islands. He helped clean up Nagasaki after atomic bomb was dropped.

Michael came home, worked as auto body mechanic, and opened A&M Body Shop in October 1959 in Chester, Illinois.

MICHAEL T. KORANDO JR., Sergeant E-5, served his country from April 19, 1966 to April 1970. He belonged to the 1st Battalion, 4th Marine Regiment, 3rd Division and served in I Corps area.

Sgt. E-5 Michael T. Korando

He participated in seven campaigns against the North Vietnamese which included Dong Ha, Conti-en, Quang Tri, Hoi City, Cason. Michael was born May 20, 1948 in Randolph County, Illinois, the son of Michael and (Rodely) Korando.

PATRICK THOMAS KORANDO, Private First Class, was working at St. Louis

Pfc. Patrick T. Korando

Army Ordnance Depot May 11, 1944 when he enlisted in WWII to serve with U.S. Marine Corps. He was on Okinawa and Ryukyu Island.

His awards include the Rifle Marksman Medal and Good Conduct Medal. Discharged January 11, 1945, at Great Lakes, he was born January 14, 1918, in Modoc, Illinois, son of Thomas and Ella Shields Korando.

RAYMOND KORANDO, Tech 5, was inducted October 13, 1942 for WWII and served with Company C, 423rd Infantry as a tank driver in Normandy, northern France, Rhineland, Ardennes, and Central Europe.

Tec-5 Raymond Korando

His awards include Good Conduct Medal, Purple Heart w/Bronze Oak Leaf Cluster, European-African Middle Eastern Campaign Medal w/Silver Service Stars, WWII Victory Medal and WWII Honorable Service Lapel Button. He was discharged October 6, 1945.

Raymond was born June 9, 1922, Kaskaskia, Illinois, son of Charles and Rosa Shields Korando. He died June 29, 1980, near Jones Ridge, Illinois and is buried at Evergreen Cemetery in Ava, Illinois.

WILLIAM HENRY KRAFT, Machinist Mate, served in U.S. Navy in WWII, in South Pacific. On the Island of New Caledonia, he drove a PT boat help-

MM William H. Kraft

ing with rescue of wounded. His tour of service was from 1943-45. William was born February 12, 1910, to John Henry and Mary Caroline Meyer Kraft. He died July 15, 1980.

GUSTAV KRAUSE, born in Red Bud, Illinois, July 27, 1895, the son of Martin and Caroline Buse Krause. He trained at Camp Campbell, Kentucky. His job

Gustav Krause

was to feed and groom infantry work horses. His service ended after six months when the war ended and he received an honorable discharge. He returned home to a life of farming and died May 31, 1984.

VICTOR H. KRUSE, Private First Class, born in Evansville, Illinois, April 11, 1925, the son of Ernst and Minna Liefer Kruse. He entered military service December 5, 1950 and served with Company B, 1905 Engineers Aviation Batt. during the Korean Conflict.

Pfc. Victor H. Krause

He received basic training at Fort Leonard Wood, Missouri, then was sent to Camp Beale, California, where he served as a cook. He transferred to 297 H&S Company then to Fort Richardson, Alaska on temporary duty as a truck driver for supplies.

A farmer before service, he returned to the farm when discharged on December 7, 1952.

CHARLES ELLSWORTH KRUG, Private, served in Army as food service helper from January 3, 1957 until December 16, 1959 when he transferred to reserves, from which he was honorably discharged January 2, 1963. Born in Rockwood, Illinois, December 14, 1938, he is the son of Casper and Viola Moore Krug.

CHARLES A. KUEHNE, Sergeant First Class, served in Vietnam, in 1964-65 and again in 1968. He entered service

Sgt. 1/c Charles A. Kuehne

in August 1948 and was discharged in September 1968. Born June 6, 1931, in Raddle, Illinois, the son of Albert and Emma Childers Kuehne. He now resides in Chester, Illinois.

CLARENCE A. KUEKER, Private, entered WWII, April 26, 1944 at Camp Hood, Texas. He left for overseas with 104th Infantry on October 20, landed in

Pvt. Clarence A. Kueker

France November 5, and was killed in action November 20, 1944 at Benestroff, France. He was buried in Limey, France, November 25, 1944. His body was returned home and buried August 29, 1948 in Lutheran Cemetery, Evansville, Illinois. Born May 13, 1916, his parents were Martin and Frieda Behman Kueker.

DELBERT G. KUEKER, Corporal, inducted into Army February 6, 1952 to serve

Cpl. Delbert G. Kueker

in Korean War. He was sent to Camp Gordon for basic training, transferred to Germany and assigned to 29th Signal Construction Battalion.

Returned to States after 18 months and was discharged January 21, 1954. Delbert returned to work at McDonnel Douglas Aircraft and retired after 45 years. He was born in Ruma, Illinois, June 1, 1931, son of Edward and Frieda Kueker.

GREGORY D. KUEKER, Specialist 4, served in the U.S. Army from July 11, 1990 to December 11, 1992. He was born in Red Bud, Illinois October 31, 1972, the son of Donald and Eloise Becker Kueker. Gregory enlisted in the U.S. Army, graduated basic training with honors, and completed Patriot Missile training.

Sp-4 Gregory D. Kueker

After being stationed at the Army Post of Dexheim and Bitburg Air Bases, both in Germany, he was assigned to air bases in Saudi Arabia during Operation Determined Resolve. He received an honorable discharge on December 11, 1992.

He earned a bachelor of science degree in industrial technology from SIU Carbondale in May 1997 and is currently employed with Illinois Power Company in Belleville, Illinois as a design engineer. He is married to Leslie Segelken Kueker and they have three children: Elisabeth, Noah and Jacob.

JONATHAN ROBERT KUEKER, Specialist 4, served in the U.S. Army May 14, 1999 to May 13, 2001 and was re-activated January 2003. He was born in Carbondale, Illinois, May 24, 1980, the son of Robert Lee and Carol Ann Suhre Kueker.

Sp-4 Jonathan R. Kueker

He enlisted, trained in combat engineers, Fort Leonard Wood, Missouri, served six months in Bosnia and witnessed aftermath mass destruction from war. In January 2003, at SIUE studying criminal justice, he was recalled to active duty, 739th Engineer Unit, lst Army, Granite City Reserves, presently at Fort Leonard Wood training for War.

ROBERT LEE KUEKER, Specialist 4, served in the U.S. Army, June 16, 1966 to June 14, 1968. He was inducted into Army during Vietnam War, trained at Fort Leonard Wood, Missouri and served 13 months on DMZ 38th Parallel Patrol, Korea, a Forward Observer with live fire every night.

Sp-4 Robert L. Kueker

He returned to Fort Benning, Georgia, training with troops and serving at military funerals. He earned the National Defense Service Medal and Expert Rifle M-14.

Robert was born February 13, 1947, Red Bud, Illinois, the son of Archie Dean and Alice Marie Eggemeyer Kueker. He retired after 33 years with Egyptian Telephone Coop. Association and now has a catering business.

WILBERT F. KUEKER, Corporal, served in U.S. Army during WWII in Battery C, 602 AAA Gun Battalion from 1942 until November 20, 1945. He was sent to Germany and France and participated in Battle of the Bulge from December 1944

Cpl. Wilbert F. Kueker

to January 1945, where some 220,000 servicemen were killed. He received an honorable discharge from Fort Sheridan, Illinois on November 20, 1945. He is the son of Martin and Frieda Schenck Kueker of Evansville, Illinois.

JAMES J. LAFFERTY, Private, Sparta, Illinois, son of John Marshall and Julia Jordon Lafferty. He served in Civil War from February 1865 to September 1865 in Company F, 154th Regiment Illinois Infantry, which organized at Camp Butler, Illinois, February 21, 1865, under call of December 19, 1864 and deployed to Murfreesboro, Tennessee. Due to exposure of cold and rain, many men died from sickness.

On May 15 he arrived at Tullahoma, Tennessee, then to Nashville for guard and garrison duty. Many officers on courtmartial and military commissions. Post Commander, Colonel McLain F. Wood, died August 6, and regiment surgeon, Dr. Melvin W. Rush, died August 13. James returned to Springfield, Illinois and was discharged September 29, 1865.

JOHN W. LAFFERTY, Private, served in Civil War from May 1, 1864 until October 26, 1864 with Company K, 142nd Regiment, Illinois Infantry, organized at Freeport, Illinois, which mustered in June 18, 1864, Camp Butler, Illinois for 100 days. Moved to White's Station near Memphis, Tennessee and on June 26, he was assigned to guarding the Memphis-Charleston Railroad. He was mustered out of service at Chicago, Illinois, October 27, 1864. John was from Sparta, Illinois and

the son of John Marshall and Julia Jordan Lafferty.

DONALD MCCLELLAND LAHR, Seaman, received his boot camp training at San Diego, California and went to Electronics School at Treasure Island. He was in USS *Warwick* (AKA-89) and served in Supply Office and was duty manager of Enlisted Men's Club in Yokosuka, Japan. Donald was discharged in April 1953. Seaman Lahr was born in Chester, Illinois, the son of Alvin Elsworth and Pearl Catherine Ruppert Lahr.

DALE ALLAN LAMBERT, E-5, served in the U.S. Navy from 1980-96, as a boiler technician while aboard the USS *Fox,* USS *Blakely,* USS *Puget Sound,* USS *Preble,* and USS *Spartanburg County.* He

E-5 Dale Allen Lambert

served in the Gulf War in 1991. Dale was born November 6, 1955, Danville, Illinois, the son of Richard and Patricia Schumaker Lambert. He works at Sauget, Illinois, Steam Plant as lead operator.

FRANK C. LANDMANN, Staff Sergeant, served with Company L, 395th Army Infantry during WWII in France and Germany. He entered service on March 31, 1943 and was wounded August 20, 1944. He was wounded a second time on August 23, 1944, when shot in left upper chest, both while in France.

S/Sgt Frank C. Landmann

He was awarded the European-African-Middle Eastern Theatre Ribbon w/4 Bronze Stars, three Overseas Service Bars, Good Conduct Medal, Purple Heart, Bronze Oak Leaf Cluster and Silver Star. Staff Sergeant Landmann was discharged October 14, 1945.

Frank was born in Walsh, Illinois, son of Frank J. and Madeline Dickey Landmann.

LESLIE CHARLES LANG, Sergeant, inducted October 13, 1977 and served in U.S. Air Force, 352nd MSL Security Squadron (SAC). Discharged October 12, 1981 from Whitman AFB, Missouri, he stayed in Reserves until August 9, 1983. Leslie was born December 3, 1953 in Red Bud, Illinois, to William P. and Mary Josephine Yankey Lang. He died November 11, 2002.

DONALD F. LANGE, Metalsmith 2/c SV6, enlisted in the U.S. Navy in Atlanta, Georgia on August 6, 1943 and served in WWII as a metalsmith. He served in the Asiatic-Pacific, on the NTS

Metalsmith 2/c Donald F. Lange

San Diego, the ship repair unit and U.S. DeBase in San Diego, FDDIC, Tibouron, California and also in USS AVSD-4. He was the recipient of the Victory Medal for his service in the Pacific. Donald was born in St. Louis, Missouri on September 28, 1917, the son of Lorenz F. and Ester Pearson Lange, and died November 14, 1977.

STANLEY W. LANGREHR, SP5, served in the U.S. Army from January 23, 1968 to January 22, 1970. He was born in Red Bud, Illinois on March 23, 1948, son of Walter and Anita Liefer Langrehr. He was drafted after high school and served on Okinawa in a communication center. He now works at Baldwin Energy Complex-Dynegy.

WALTER LANGREHR, Tech 5, born August 14, 1918 in Evansville, Illinois. He served in WWII in Panama Canal Zone, basically on the Pacific side, with some time spent on Atlantic side, serving Army Transportation for military and civilian workers.

T-5 Walter Langrehr

His basic training was in Virginia, Shenango, Pennsylvania and New Orleans, Louisiana. He was discharged February 6, 1946.

Prior to war he worked at Curtiss Wright, St. Louis, Missouri and Columbus, Ohio, building Hell Divers. His parents were Charles and Caroline Hanebutt Langrehr.

JERRY R. LARAMORE, Specialist 4, served in the U.S. Army from 1965-67. He was born in Sparta, Illinois on November 12, 1946, son of Malcom and

Sp-4 Jerry R. Laramore

Juanita Mines Laramore. Jerry was drafted, served with C Battery, 2nd Missile Battalion, 562nd Artillery in Alaska as a long range radar operator. Discharged, he was in agriculture for 30 years and now works at Dodge/Chrysler dealer as sales consultant.

RONALD LARAMORE, Sergeant, served in the U.S. Army from January 8, 1962 to January 7, 1965. He enlisted and completed basic training at Fort Leonard Wood, artillery training at Fort Sill, Okla-

Sgt. Ronald Laramore

homa, Jump School at Fort Benning, Georgia, then assigned to Korea for 13 months.

Returned to Fort Hood, Texas until his release from service. Ronald worked at Spartan Printing 27 years, and for state of Illinois until retirement in 2002. He was born August 4, 1943, the son of Malcom and Juanita Mines Laramore.

WAYNE H. LARAMORE, Specialist 4, drafted into the U.S. Army June 18, 1970 and served with 1st Battalion, Infantry, 6th U.S. Army. He was a butcher at Dorf's Market, Tilden Illinois, before he was drafted. His tour was as a cook at Fort Carson, Colorado.

Sp-4 Wayne H. Laramore

Wayne received an early out on December 23, 1971 with an honorable discharge. Wayne served during the Vietnam Era. Born August 28, 1951, Red Bud, Illinois, his parents are Malcom and Juanita (Mines) Laramore.

MICHAEL D. LAURENT, Staff Sergeant, reported for active duty on November 13, 1969. Michael completed basic training at Lackland AFB, Texas and studied at Lowry AFB, Denver, Colorado, for technical training in aircraft weapons systems.

His first working assignment was at Tyndall, AFB Florida, where he worked on F-106 Interceptor aircraft. From Tyndall he was transferred overseas to Kunsan Air

Base in Korea, where he worked on F-4D aircraft. Michael stayed there for six months then was transferred to Osan Air Base in northern Korea for the remainder of his 13 months of overseas duty.

S/Sgt. Michael D. Laurent

From Korea he served his remaining time at Williams AFB, Arkansas as an F-5 aircraft weapons gun shop supervisor, with the 425th TAC Fighter Squadron. He was honorably discharged November 12, 1975. He served during the Vietnam War Era. His awards include the National Defense Service Medal, Air Force Medal 900-3, SAEMR 900-3, AFEM (Korea) Airman's Medal, SOGB-473, DAF dated 21 Jul 1971, AFGCM (13 Nov 1969-12 Nov 1972), AFM 900-3, AFLSA AFM 900-3 (November 1969-November 1973), AFOUA, SOGB-818, DAF dated 14 Nov 1973.

Michael was born October 20, 1950, Red Bud, Illinois, the son of Robert J. and Doris M. (Tockstein) Laurent Eggemeyer.

ROBERT J. LAURENT, Radarman 3/c, V6, enlisted in Navy February 19, 1944 and was sent to Farragut, Idaho for boot training. He boarded USS *Washington*, arrived at Pearl Harbor on May 10, 1944, transferred to USS *Wichita*, and assisted in operations at Saipan, Tinian and Guam. He was also involved in both Philippine sea battles and the conquest of Okinawa in March 1945.

Radarman 3/c Robert J. Laurent

Robert received the WWII Victory Medal, American Area Medal, Philippine Liberation w/2 stars and Asiatic-Pacific Medal w/4 stars. He was discharged April 19, 1946.

Robert was born March 21, 1926 in Prairie du Rocher, Illinois, son of Robert A. and Mabel Carr Laurent, and died August 29, 1986. His son Michael served in U.S. Air Force and grandson Chad Rickenberg is currently serving in the U.S. Navy.

JAMES LESLIE LAWDER, Sergeant, served in WWI from September 19, 1917, until July 23, 1919. He was inducted at Chester, Illinois and served in the Infantry Quartermaster Corps with the American Expeditionary Forces in France until July 23, 1919. He was discharged at Camp Grant, Illinois.

James was born November 21, 1894, in Rockwood, Illinois, the son of Henry and Annie Pinkerton Lawder. He died October 15, 1974 and is buried in Evergreen Cemetery in Chester, Illinois.

RAY AUSTIN LAWDER, born in Rockwood, Illinois the son of Samuel and Sarah Malone Lawder. He was inducted into service at St. Louis, Missouri on June 21, 1916, at age 20. He was commissioned Band Corporal November 18, 1918.

He served in the battles of St. Mihiel, September 11 to September 18, 1918; in the Argonne Meuse Offensive, September 25 to October 1, 1918; battle of Wesserling, June 21 to July 10, 1918; the Gerardmer Sector, August 14 to September 2, 1918; and Somme Aisen from October 10 to November 7, 1918. He was discharged from Camp Funston, Kansas on May 12, 1919.

EVERETT E. LEDBETTER, T/5, born at Sparta, Illinois, August 24, 1924, the son of Mr. and Mrs. (nee Saal) Lewis Ledbetter. He entered service in WWII, December 9, 1943, and was assigned to 302nd Field Artillery Battalion, 76th Infantry Division.

After taking basic training at Fort Sill, Oklahoma, he saw action at the Battle of the Bulge and in Germany. His job with the 76th Division was that of forward observer for artillery in radio communications. He was discharged May 23, 1945.

NORRIS BROWN LESSLEY, drafted into U.S. Navy in 1943, he served in WWII as a construction worker in the

Norris B. Lessley

Seabees in New Guinea. He was honorably discharged March 31, 1946, and returned to farming on family farm. Born in Sparta, Illinois on January 8, 1925, son of J. Vernon and Mabel Brown Lessley, he died March 1, 1999.

BONIFACE L. LEVERY, Sergeant, served in the U.S. Army from January 31, 1952 to October 30, 1953, with the 45th Infantry Division, 279th Regiment, Company M. He served in Korea and participated in Finger Ridge, Heartbreak Ridge, Anchor Hill, and Sandbag Castle battles.

Sgt. Boniface L. Levery

His awards include the Korean Service Medal, Combat Infantry Badge and United Nations Service Medal.

He was born June 7, 1931, Evansville, Illinois, the son of Lawrence and Olga Zipfel Levery. He worked as a commercial carpenter in St. Louis area and died December 24, 1979.

ROBERT LOREN LEWIS, Petty Officer 2/c, served aboard the USS *Strong* (DD-758) during the Korean War. He entered U.S. Navy in 1954 and served until 1957. Born in Poplar Bluff, Missouri, he is the son of Loren and __ Kearbey Lewis.

HERBERT E. LIEFER, Tech 4, born February 7, 1920, Campbell Hill, Illinois to Edward and Rosina Gielow Liefer. He served in WWII from February 1, 1945 to December 15, 1946, in the Harbor Craft Section of 4th Field Artillery Battery on Luzon in Philippine Islands.

MAUREEN K. CASETTA LIEFER, Lieutenant Commander, entered active duty in the U.S. Navy Nurse Corps, November 6, 1987, and was stationed at Camp Lejeune while on active duty. Following discharge on March 1, 1991, she entered the reserves and drilled at the Naval Reserve Centers in St. Louis and Cape Girardeau, Missouri.

Lt. Comm. Maureen K. Liefer

She is currently the health promotion director for the Naval Reserve Center in St. Louis. Born in Red Bud, Illinois, October 8, 1955, her parents are Walter F. and Marcella A. Lindner Rowold.

Maureen was called back into active duty to St. Louis Reserve Center on February 27, 2003, then on to Great Lakes, Illinois and is currently at Camp Lejeune, North Carolina.

DANIEL B. LIMBAUGH, Colonel, graduated from Chester High School in 1964, then graduated from West Point in 1968. Commissioned as second lieutenant out of West Point in June 1968 in the Field Artillery.

He graduated from Airborne and Ranger schools and served in artillery units at Fort Bragg, North Carolina and Central Highlands of Vietnam. While there he was with A Battery, 6/14 Field Artillery, Headquarters Battery, 1/92 Field Artillery and also at Schoffenburg, Germany.

The Army sent Dan to Law School in Tacoma, Washington from 1973-76. He entered the Army Judge Advocate General's Corps in 1976. JAG assignments included Fort Leonard Wood, Missouri; Charlottesville, Virginia; the Pentagon; Hawaii; West Point, New York; Fort Dix, New Jersey, then back to West Point. He finished at St. Louis, Missouri, where he retired in 1996 as a colonel.

His hometown is Chester, Illinois. Parents are Manley and Mary Jane (Heagler) Limbaugh.

FLOYD L. LINDERS, Tech 5, entered WWII at Scott Air Field, Illinois, December 15, 1942. He was a truck driver and served with 190 Port Company in Naples, Foggia, Rome-Arno, Italy, along the Mediterranean Sea, unloading war supplies from ships.

From left, back row: Floyd, Ralph and Clyde Linders. Front: Vernon Linders

Unloading D-Day Invasion supplies on January 22, 1944 on Anzio Beachhead, with no docks, the ship was left out at sea and material brought in with barges and amphibious craft. No lights were allowed due to being War Zone, and their ship was bombed and broke in two. They had to abandon ship in dark of night into sea and had to be rescued by barges.

He spent two years overseas and was discharged at Camp Grant, Illinois on November 25, 1945. His awards include four Overseas Service Bars, European-African-Middle Eastern Theater Ribbon w/2 Bronze Stars, Good Conduct Medal, Bronze Arrowhead Medal and WWII Victory Medal.

Born December 19, 1921, in Willisville, Illinois, son of Edward and Tillie Hecke Linders, his brothers are Ralph (born January 29, 1914), Vernon (born 1924) and Clyde (born August 14, 1919), all served in World War II.

JACKIE W. LINDSEY, Corporal, served in the U.S. Marine Corps. He was born December 28, 1934, Gasconade, Missouri, son of Clarence and Loretta Jett Lindsey.

Assigned to 221st Marine Fighter Squad at Lambert Field, St. Louis, Mis-

Cpl. Jackie W. Lindsey

souri; boot camp was at San Diego, California, then to 14 area, Camp Pendleton, California; TAD to Marine Corps Cold Weather Batt. in the high Sierra Mountains on Sonora Pass near Bridgeport, California, where he served as chief clerk in battalion headquarters. His MOS was 0131, Orders clerk. He was responsible for location of all personnel. This cold weather facility trained Marines for cold weather survival prior to going to war in Korea. Marines were transported from Camp Pendleton via Greyhound for two weeks training.

Summer duty was parades in areas surrounding Carson City and Reno, Nevada. Jack served as one of four mounted color guards, riding USMC horses. The Marine Corps had a baseball team that played in the Reno, Nevada industrial league, a semi-pro league. Jack played short-stop on the team for two summers, batting 420 the last year. Corporal Lindsey also served on weekends as Marine MP in Reno, Nevada. He was honorably discharged in 1955.

DANIEL BISHOP LING, Corporal, joined the Army February 29, 1864 during the Civil War and mustered in April 17, 1864 at Camp Butler, Illinois. He served with Company E, 30th Infantry, going through Tennessee, Alabama, and into Atlanta, Georgia.

Cpl. Daniel Bishop Ling

He joined the Grand Army under General Sherman and participated on the "March To The Sea." The regiment took part in the Grand Review, May 24, 1865 in Washington, DC. He was discharged at Camp Butler on July 27, 1865.

Daniel was born in January 1833, Monroe County, New York. He was a teacher and farmer. Daniel taught at Charter Oak School, 1872-73, and designed the current eight-sided building. He died January 27, 1876.

ROLLA CLENDENIN LING, Tech 5, Medical Aidman, was drafted in WWII on November 17, 1943. He was sent to Fort Lee, Virginia and worked as supply clerk. He was transferred to Fort Lewis, Washington and assigned to 316 General Hospital, where he had to take basic training a second time to qualify for medical work.

Rolla Ling

Rolla was sent to Philippines as part of Philippine Liberation and stayed there until end of war, then discharged October 23, 1945.

He was born March 21, 1907, Evansville, Illinois, son of William Sherman and Dora Belle Thompson Ling, and died October 2, 1979.

WALTER SIDNEY LING, Private, born in Evansville, Illinois, November 3, 1894, son of William S. and Dora Belle

Walter Ling

Thompson Ling. He entered service for WWI on February 24, 1918 with basic training at Camp Taylor, Kentucky. Assigned to Company D, 115th Infantry, 29th Division, he left for France June 6, 1918, and arrived on July 1. On October 8th he was in battle of Argonne Forest, where he received a severe leg wound, then spent time in hospitals in France and VA in Chicago.

After the war, the issue of government care and help for living veterans became quite a controversy. Veterans felt Regular Army, National Guard and Draftees, who had served side by side, all deserved the same treatment. They also felt the need to keep in contact with buddies they had served with. Experiences they had shared could not be easily forgotten. Unrest had spread to every Army group in France.

Word got to General J. Pershing in Paris and he sent word for the men to meet in Paris and form a committee to investigate these concerns. Seventeen men assembled and sent notices to officers of all branches of service, as well as Red Cross officials, of a caucus to be held March 15, 1919, in Paris and 460 men attended the meeting. Out of this caucus the American Legion was born. The first agreement was to have no rank or title among them, service to fellow vets would be main objective, and the organization would be nonsectarian. St. Louis was selected for first meeting site in the U.S.

Since Walter Ling had not yet been discharged and was in a VA hospital in Chicago, he was asked to represent the Illinois Division at the May 1919 meeting in St. Louis. He served as a liaison officer from the Illinois delegation at the next meeting at Minneapolis, Minnesota where the preamble, constitution and bylaws were adopted and the organization was set in motion.

After discharge on June 19, 1919, he returned to Evansville, Illinois, and helped organize Evansville Post 1172. Active in Boy Scouts, he was a rural mail carrier, 1927-54. Walter died September 11, 1978.

ROBERT SAMUEL LINK, Coxswain Mate, was inducted into WWII after graduation from Sparta High School. He first went to Great Lakes Naval Center, then to Landing Craft School at Coronado, California.

During his service, September 8, 1944 to June 22, 1946, he delivered supplies to

Coxswain Mate Robert S. Link

ships and assisted Camp Pendelton Marines with practice beach landings. Later he went to Hawaii and served on shore patrol.

He was born in Walsh, Illinois, April 11, 1926, son of Boniface and Grace Ragsdale Link, he married Doris Word Jackson in 1947, and they founded Link's Trucking Service. Robert died December 30, 2002.

CLAUDE LITTLE, Corporal, served in the U.S. Army, 1952-54, with B Battery, 816th Field Artillery Battalion. He served one year in the States, one year in Darmstadt, Germany. He earned the Na-

Cpl. Claude Little

tional Defense Medal, Army of Occupation Medal and Sharpshooter Badge-M-1. He was born January 22, 1932, the son of Delbert and Bertha Freemann Little.

RALPH WILLARD LIVELY, Gunners Mate 1/c, entered WWII in February 1942. He sailed overseas on an old WWI ship, the *Bernadeau*. He participated in invasion of Africa, then back to Orange, Texas, to wait for new destroyer, *Dyson*, to be completed, which he served on in islands of South Pacific, including Okinawa and Japan through remainder of war. He was discharged October 28, 1945.

Ralph was born in Sparta, Illinois, August 15, 1911 to Alonzo and Frances

GM 1/c Ralph W. Lively

E-5 Dale R. Lochhead

Leonard and Donald Lochhead

East Lively. He lived to be past 90 and died December 26, 2001.

WILLIAM J. LIVELY, Corporal, served in the U.S. Army from January 16, 1952 to October 15, 1953 and stayed in the Reserves until discharge in 1960. He was born Oct. 7, 1930, Sparta, Illinois, to Wm. A. and Anna Sitkoskie Lively.

While working on bridge crew, I.C.

Cpl. William J. Lively

Railroad, he was drafted and served with 3rd Ambulance Platoon, 27th Infantry Regiment, 25th Infantry Division in Korea on Heartbreak Ridge, Sandbag Castle and Iron Triangle.

After the war he returned to the I.C. Railroad and also worked for MO-PAC RR and NYC Railroad. He worked as railroad track foreman, 1958-79 at Peabody Coal Company and 1979-92 for Arch Mineral Coal Company. He married Nora Hood in 1955 and they have five children.

DALE R. LOCHHEAD, E-5, entered the Army December 14, 1971, and assigned to Company A, 560th Signal Battalion, 7th U.S. Army. He was in Vietnam with the Signal Corps but saw no action. The service he completed was not a bad tour, but at his age now, he is sure that he would not like to participate again.

When he returned home, after his discharge on November 15th, he worked with his brothers and father in the family service station. After that job, he worked as toll taker, Glisters, TG USA, then as counselor.

Dale was born in Chester, Illinois on July 13, 1940 to James H. and Hilda D. (Knigge) Lochhead.

DEAN L. LOCHHEAD, Corporal, served in the U.S. Army, 1950-53. He was born in Chester, Illinois on July 30, 1933, son of James H. and Hilda Knigge Lochhead. He enlisted, trained in Califor-

Cpl. Dean L. Lochhead

nia, then sent to Korea with Headquarters Company, 3rd Battalion, 5th Cavalry Regiment, 1st Cavalry Division. In 1951 he took part in "Operation Little Switch" and "Operation Big Switch." At the end when the armistice was signed, he came home and forgot about Korea."

DONALD JAMES LOCHHEAD, Motor Machinist Mate 3/c, served in Navy

MMM 3/c Donald J. Lochhead

during WWII from March 9, 1946 until November 28, 1947. He was in the USS *Bushnell,* stationed at Naval Air Facility, Attu, Alaska. Born in Chester, Illinois on February 26, 1928, son of James H. and Hilda Knigge Lochhead. After discharge he returned to Chester and operated Don's 66 Service Station until his death April 28, 1983.

LEONARD C. LOCHHEAD, Aviation Machinist 1/c, enlisted in Navy February 9, 1942 to serve in WWII. Stationed

AM 1/c Leonard C. Lochhead

near Pearl Harbor, he was discharged in 1945 and returned to Chester, Illinois. He made his living as auto mechanic. Son of James and Lizzie Lochhead, he died October 30, 1987, in Chester.

MELVIN LOCHHEAD, Sergeant, born March 19, 1914, to James F. and Lizzetta Pick Lochhead. He was drafted

Sgt. Melvin Lochhead

into WWII service in July 1943. He served in South Pacific and invasion of Leyte in Philippines, with return of General McArthur. Discharged in 1945, he returned to Chester, Illinois, and became a terrific artist (one of his paintings hangs in Chester Library).

VERNON CHESTER LOCHHEAD, Seaman 1/c, was inducted into the U.S. Navy during WWII in May 1944. He was sent to New Orleans, trained as a ship's gunner, then sent to Camp Wallace, Texas, and served in the camp fire department. He was discharged in February 1947 and returned to Chester, Illinois. Born August 6, 1918, in East St. Louis, Illinois, the son of David Albert and Nora Fey Lochhead, he died December 15, 1969.

JASON P. LOHMAN, Petty Officer, enlisted in the U.S. Navy on January 16, 2002. On March 22, 2002 he graduated from Navy Recruit training and was then assigned to advanced training at Sheppard AFB, Texas, where he graduated as Honor Graduate.

P.O. Jason P. Lohman

After successfully completing Construction Electrician A School, he was stationed at Gulf Port, Mississippi where he began his career as a Navy Seabee. He is with the 133 in Kuwait, in Operation Iraqi Freedom.

Jason was born November 29, 1982 in Chester, Illinois, son of Donald and Deborah (Brueggemann) Lohman.

DORIAN H. LOHRDINE, CM1/c, enlisted June 17, 1943 to serve in WWII with the 111th Seabee Operations Naval Construction Battalion, 25th Regiment, Company B, 3rd Platoon.

He participated in D-Day Invasion, Omaha Beach landing, Normandy, France. He crewed Rhino-Ferry landing craft in assault on Omaha Beach and was active

CM 1/c Dorian H. Lohrdine

in Seabee construction in Philippines and Hawaiian Islands. He was discharged November 20, 1945.

Born July 31, 1911, in Percy, Illinois, son of George Henry and Henrietta Priebe Lohrdine, he died November 9, 1976.

ROBERT JESSE LONG, Corporal, drafted January 3, 1952, he joined the U.S. Marine Corps instead of Army. Bob was with 2nd Amtrac Battalion, FMF Camp Lejeune, North Carolina and was in Korean War.

Cpl. Robert J. Long

He was a shoe worker before entering service, and after his discharge on January 3, 1960, he returned to the shoe factory. Later, he went to work for McDonnell Douglas, quit and went to work as a mechanic for Vernon Kisro, and in 1977 opened his own garage and gas station until 1998 when he retired.

Bob was born at home in Evansville, Illinois on September 2, 1930, the son of Charles and Vera (Wiley) Long.

SLYVESTER J. LORENZ, Corporal, born November 2, 1918, at Waterloo, Illinois, son of Hugo and Pauline Schneider Lorenz. He entered service February 27, 1942, and served in North Africa, Tunisia, Salerno and Cassano, Italy, with Company A, 141st Infantry, 36th Division during WWII. He was killed November 18, 1943, at Cassano, Italy. He had received

Cpl. Slyvester Lorentz

the Purple Heart for being wounded earlier. His remains were brought back in 1948 and buried at St. Peter's and Paul's Cemetery in Waterloo, Illinois.

FREDERICK D. MAASBERG, Private First Class, served in the U.S. Army November 1950 to September 1951 with the 6th Armored Division. Following basic training at Fort Chaffee, Arkansas and

Pfc. Frederick D. Maasberg

extended training at Fort Leonard Wood, Missouri, he departed for Korea, arriving April 21. He was killed in action on September 21, 1951. He was born July 30, 1928, Steeleville, Illinois, the son of August and Maggie Wine Maasberg.

VERNON F. MABE, Tech 5, served from June 19, 1941 until November 5, 1941 in the U.S. Army. He was recalled January 30, 1942 and served in Company B, 9th Armored Infantry Battalion, 3rd Armed

T/5 Vernon F. Mabe

Tank Division under General George S. Patton in Normandy, Northern France, Ardennes, Rhineland and Central Europe.

Vernon was in the Battle of the Bulge. His decorations include the American Defense Service Ribbon, European-African-Middle Eastern Theatre Ribbon, four Overseas Service Bars, one Service Stripe, Silver Battle Star and the Purple Heart for wounds received in action March 30, 1945.

Vernon was born July 16, 1912 in Washburn, Missouri, the son of Cicero Mabe. After discharge from WWII, he worked in construction work and was killed in car accident in 1967.

STANLEY MACIEISKI, Corporal, inducted November 27, 1941 during WWII and served in North Africa and Tunisia as a member of a tank crew.

Cpl. Stanley Macieiski

In a battle of Tunisia his tank was ambushed February 15, 1943, by forces led by General Rommel. The tank caught on fire and Stanley and a lieutenant stayed in tank until fellow soldiers were out. Then the lieutenant was killed and another shot hit Stanley in legs, causing him to lose both legs. He was taken prisoner and sent to Germany, later he was exchanged for a German prisoner in Spain.

Returning home Stan served as warden of Vienna Correctional Center and as mayor of Chester for eight years. He died December 15, 2001.

JOHN MACKE JR., Tech 5, was in Northern France, Rhineland and Central Europe in WWII. He entered service May 13, 1941, East St. Louis, Illinois and assigned to Battery B 132 AAA Gun Battalion.

He was rated first class gunner with MM rifle. Awards include the Good Conduct Medal, received COLTR AA 43, American Defense Ribbon, European-African-Middle Eastern Theater Ribbon w/

T/5 John Macke Jr.

3 Bronze Battle Stars, Asiatic-Pacific Theatre Ribbon, four Overseas Service Bars. After being overseas two years, four months and 10 days, he was discharged October 9, 1945, Fort Sheridan, Illinois.

John Jr. was born June 6, 1917, Ellis Grove, Illinois, son of John Sr. and Anna Marie Dehn Macke. He and his sister operated Macke General Store in Ellis Grove for many years. He is now a resident of St. Ann's Nursing Home in Chester, Illinois.

ARTHUR MAES, Mess Sergeant, born January 20, 1911, St. Louis, Missouri, son of Louis and Anna Postman Maes. He entered WWII April 27, 1944. Field artillery training was at Camp Roberts, California and jungle training in Gloster, Mississippi. He was then shipped to Barie and Naples, Italy, where he served as mess sergeant.

Mess Sgt. Arthur Maes

Arthur was discharged January 5, 1946, returned to Chester, Illinois and operated a restaurant. He later worked at Chester Mental Health for 15 years, retiring November 30, 1984. He resides in Chester.

MICHEAL MAGANY, Private, born 1837, Nashport, Ohio and served in 22nd Infantry, Company I, Illinois Volunteers in the Civil War. He mustered into service August 14, 1861, and served as a blacksmith for Headquarters. He was with General Sherian on the Atlantic Campaign, and was wounded in Murfreesboro, TN December 31, 1862. Before the war he lived in Sparta, Illinois and was married to Sarah Donald on May 9, 1861, in Pinckneyville, Illinois. He mustered out August 8, 1864.

DAN L. MAGERS, Chief Petty Officer, was born May 27, 1919, in Chester, Illinois, to Henry and Lucy Lohrding Magers. He entered the U.S. Navy in February 1938, and served in both WWII and the Korean Wars.

Chief P.O. Dan L. Magers

Duty assignments were in USS *Pierce,* USS *Tuscaloosa,* USS *Juneau,* USS LST-1190 and USS *Cavalier;* also served on U.S. Naval Station, Guantanamo Bay, Cuba; Naval Station, Norfolk, Virginia; and Recruit Training Command, San Diego, California.

During active service he received five Good Conduct Medals, American Defense Service, American Campaign, Asiatic-Pacific Campaign, WWII Victory, Navy Occupational Service, United Nations Service, National Defense Service and Korean Service Medals.

He was discharged February 1958, returned home and worked first as a meat cutter, then as a Security Therapist. Dan retired 18 years ago from Chester Mental Health.

JOHN PRESTON MANN, Lieutenant, enlisted at Camp Butler, Springfield, Illinois, September 5, 1861, to serve in Company K, 5th Illinois Cavalry in the Civil War.

Discharged, he returned to Rockwood, Illinois, was admitted to Illinois Bar and was a practicing attorney in Rockwood.

Born February 6, 1822, in Indiana, he died February 28, 1908 and is buried in Ebenezer Cemetery near Rockwood. He kept a journal during Civil War, which is now at Morris Library, Southern Illinois University, Carbondale, Illinois.

RICHARD J. MANN, Captain, was in Communications Service in the U.S. Air Force from April 21, 1970 until his discharge on April 30, 1974. His parents, Arthur C. and Ida A. Stumpe Mann, lived in Chester, Illinois. Richard now lives in Camarillo, CA.

ADAM MANSKER, EW2, entered the Navy in July 1995, received basic training at Great Lakes, Illinois, and advanced schooling for electronic warfare technician in Pensacola, Florida.

E-W2 Adam Mansker

He was assigned to the Destroyer USS *Hopper* (DDG-70), which was christened on January 6, 1996 at Bath, Maine and commissioned on September 6, at San Francisco, California. The USS *Hopper* was assigned to the Pacific Division of Fifth Fleet, stationed at Pearl Harbor, Hawaii. Adam was in the Persian Gulf War during hostilities there in 1998.

Born April 23, 1977, he is the son of Kirby and Carolyn Devall Mansker.

ARTHUR VERNON MANSKER, Private, enlisted in the Armed Service in the fall of 1942. He received his basic training at Camp Robinson, Arkansas with Company A, 62nd Training Battalion, graduating in February 1943.

Arthur Vernon Mansker

He was shipped to Europe where he saw action at Normandy in France and also in Germany with the U.S. Infantry. Among his medals were several Battle Stars and combat ribbons.

Born June 15, 1915, in Rockwood, Illinois, his parents were Noah Edward and Mary Louise Warren Mansker. He died March 6, 1980, at the Soldiers Home in Resil, Washington, and is buried in the cemetery there.

HENRY CLAY MANSKER, Private, was born in Rockwood, Illinois August 13, 1842. His parents were Samuel and Nancy Crawford Mansker. He served in the Civil War with Company K, 5th Illinois Cavalry from mid-1862 until April 11, 1863, when he was killed at Helena, Arkansas, when a gun held by another soldier discharged accidentally. His body was returned home and he is buried in the Mansker Cemetery, north of Rockwood, Illinois.

HERBERT LLOYD MANSKER, Private, served in the U.S. Army, during WWII. After basic training, he was sent to Florida, where he served almost a year

Pvt. Herbert Lloyd Mansker

then received a medical discharge. Born in Rockwood, Illinois, October 20, 1922, he was the son of Noah Edward and Mary Louise Warren Mansker.

HOWARD MANSKER, Staff Sergeant, entered service September 2, 1948, and was assigned to Edwards AFB, Muroc, California with Headquarters & Headquarters Squadron, 3076th Air Base Group. He was discharged September 1, 1955. The son of Bernard Cole and Iva Pearl Dunn Mansker, he was born in Sparta, Illinois, September 12, 1929.

IRA WARREN MANSKER, Machinist's Mate 3/c, was inducted into

MM3/c Ira (Jack) Mansker

the Navy, July 17, 1945, at Great Lakes Naval Training Center, then assigned to the 121st Naval Construction Battalion (CB's), CBRD, Camp Parks, California.

From there he was shipped to the Mariana Islands as a heavy equipment operator and built airstrips on Guam, Saipan and Tinian. He was discharged August 4, 1946.

Born in Rockwood, Illinois, July 28, 1926, he was the son of Noah Edward and Mary Louise Warren Mansker. He died January 7, 1999 and is buried in Ebenezer Cemetery near Rockwood.

JOSEPH HENRY MANSKER was too young to enter regular military service, so joined the U.S. Merchant Marines to do his part during WWII. He entered service December 24, 1944, just having turned 17 years of age. He served on the *R.J. Hanna* until April 16, 1945, delivering oil to military forces in many combat locations, then was assigned to the *F.H. Hillman*. He served aboard that ship until August 15, 1945, when he was officially discharged from active service.

Joseph H. Mansker

He received both the Atlantic War Zone and Mediterranean Middle East War Zone Medals. When he left the military, he found work with Standard Oil Company, delivering oil to ports around the world. He stayed 20 years in this job and became 2nd Officer of his ship.

Born December 11, 1927, in Rockwood, Illinois to Noah Edward and Mary Louise Warren Mansker, he died December 18, 1999 at the Veterans Center in Danville, Illinois. He is buried in Ebenezer Cemetery near Rockwood.

PAUL B. MANSKER, Private First Class, was drafted into service during WWII in May 1944. He was stationed in Germany with the 89th Infantry Division, attached to Patton's Army. He was discharged in December 1946. Born in Sparta, Illinois, March 3, 1920, the son of Bernard C. and Iva Pearl Dunn Mansker.

SAMUEL MANSKER, enlisted August 10, 1814 in the War of 1812 and served in both Captain Short's Company of Mounted Volunteers, and Captain Alexander's Illinois Militia until October 9, 1814, which was the usual 90 day enlistment, when he was honorably discharged at Camp Russell.

His pension application states, "He was stationed part of the time at Camp Russell and the balance of the time he was scouring the country after Indians." He has been granted a land warrant for this service.

Mansker was born near Louisville, Kentucky, December 16, 1795, the son of John and Margaret Robinson Mansker. He died January 9, 1885 and is buried in Mansker Family Cemetery near Rockwood, Illinois.

THADDEUS C. MANSKER, Corporal, lived at Rockwood, Illinois, moved to Missouri, and served with Company I, 47th Regiment of Missouri Infantry during the Civil War. Following is a story about him during the battle of Pilot Knob:

"After the Confederates had kept up a steady fire all day, about sunset everything got quiet. Thaddeus jumped upon the breastworks and immediately about a dozen shots were fired at him. He called the enemy a few 'hard' names, then scrambled down into the pit and fired a volley of shots back at them, then yelled loudly, 'I'll quit! I'll quit.'"

He enlisted in the Union Army September 6, 1864, lost an eye January 31, 1865 in Pulaski, Tennessee and was discharged March 29, 1865. He stayed in Missouri and taught school until his death October 10, 1912.

Born January 20, 1842, he was the son of Samuel and Elizabeth Bartley Mansker of Rockwood, Illinois. He is buried in Furr Cemetery near Marble Hill, Missouri.

ALBERT W. MANWARING, Private First Class, was born in Pulaski, Illinois on January 26, 1912, son of Raymond and Cazzie Sheets Manwaring. He served with the 1st Infantry Division in WWII as a firearms instructor at Camp Van Dorn, Mississippi. Discharged at end of war, he was a teacher at Sparta High School, principal at Steeleville and Chester High Schools and retired as math instructor from Belleville West High School. Albert died May 25, 1995.

RONALD S. MANWARING, Sergeant, entered service September 5, 1967, Fort Leonard Wood, Missouri and played on Army football team, U.S Military Academy at Fort Gordon, Georgia. He was sent to Korea as MP with United Nations Command. Stationed at Seoul, he again played on Army football team.

Sgt. Ronald S. Manwaring

Returned to Fort Leonard Wood and to Fort Gordon for advanced MP training and was assigned to 41st Military Police Detachment. He was on DMZ the day USS *Pueblo* crew was released by North Korea. He also served in Stutgart, Germany. Promoted to sergeant, he was discharged in June 1970.

Ronald was born in St. Louis, Missouri, the son of Albert and Ephemia McMurtrie Manwaring. Ronald retired as Murphysboro, Illinois Police Chief in July 2002.

RICHARD B.S. MARLEN, Private, served in the Civil War in Company H, 22nd Illinois Volunteer Infantry. He enlisted February 1, 1862. Born in Randolph County, Illinois in 1837, he was the son of William Riggs and Jane Gant Marlen. He died July 16, 1862, of disease at Farmington, Mississippi.

WILLIAM C. MARLEN, Private, enlisted August 1, 1862, in the 80th Illinois Volunteer Infantry, Company D, to do his part in the Civil War. Born in Randolph County in 1835, the son of William Riggs and Jane Gant Marlen, he was married at the time of his enlistment. He died January 4, 1863 in Gallatin, Tennessee of disease.

JOHN M. MARTIN, Private First Class, served in WWI with a Demobilization Detachment, from September 4, 1918 until May 15, 1919. He was born at Rockwood, Illinois to Thomas and Alice Richmond Martin. Inducted at Chester, Illinois, he was discharged at Camp Custer, Michigan. He spent his last years in the Illinois Veterans Home at Quincy, Illinois.

CHARLES E. MASSIE, Tech 5, inducted into WWII, February 26, 1944, schooled at Camp Davis, California; Camp Crowder, Missouri; and Plant Engineer School, Philadelphia, Pennsylvania.

T/5 Charles E. Massie

He went overseas in May and served in Paris, France with Signal Corps. He was discharged April 26, 1946. After discharge he returned to Sparta, Illinois and worked as a painter and paper hanger.

Charles was born in Jacksonville, Illinois September 25, 1912, the son of Charles and Anita Mullins.

BRUCE L. MATHIS, Specialist 4, was the last person drafted in Randolph County. Bruce was drafted on December 1, 1972 and discharged November 13, 1974. He took his boot camp at Fort Leonard Wood, Missouri, then went to Fort Benjamin Harrison, Indianapolis, Indiana for his advanced individual training.

Spec. 4 Bruce L. Mathis

Bruce served as a legal clerk at Fort Riley, Kansas, then given additional duties as mail clerk and duty driver. Bruce was a court reporter for 13 court-martials. He was with the 1/4 Cavalry, 1st Infantry Division.

Bruce was born On June 20, 1951 in Murphysboro, Illinois, the son of Clarence A. and Ramona (Steele) Mathis.

SCOTT E. MAYO, Petty Officer 3/c, enlisted in the Navy on October 18, 1992 and trained at Great Lakes Naval Station, Illinois. He was then assigned to the USS *Stetham* (DDG-63), a guided missile destroyer.

P.O. 3/c Scott E. Mayo

Scott finished his service in San Diego, California and was discharged from the Navy on May 17, 1997. Scott and his family reside in Pinckneyville, Illinois (Perry Company) where he is employed as an engineer for Illinois Central Railroad. He was born October 12, 1973 in Chester, Illinois.

DONALD RAY MCADAMS, E-4, Boiler Tech, joined the Navy April 1, 1966 and took his 11 weeks training at Great Lakes, Illinois. His first duty was aboard the USS *Harold J. Ellison* (DD-864) as a fireman in the boiler room. Homeport was at Norfolk, Virginia. He also served aboard USS *Rich* (DD-820), back to homeport. He traveled to 36 different countries around the world: Europe, Africa, Middle East, Far East, South America and many islands. He was discharged January 20, 1970.

He has many memories of classmates and friends: Charles Rader, Bruce Welge and Kenny Frazier, who gave their lives for us and their country. Teach your children about the cost of freedom and the men and women who served their country. Donald served during Vietnam, but not in war zone.

His parents are Jesse Daniel and Adeline (Baum) McAdams. He was born in Chester, Illinois on September 24, 1945.

PAUL HENRY MCCARTY, Tech 5, served from July 17, 1945, with the 9812th Tech Service Unit in New Mexico as a

T/5 Paul Henry McCarty

mechanical engineer aid. He was honorably discharged at Fort Bliss, Texas, February 20, 1946, and received the Victory Medal for his time in service. Born in Ellis Grove, Illinois, the son of Everett and Minnie Stipe McCarty.

HENRY MCCAULEY, Private First Class, was born in August 1892, Washington County, Illinois. He served in WWI

Pfc. Henry McCauley

during 1918-19, with Company E, 44th Infantry in Germany. Returned to work in a mine and farmed near Tilden, Illinois. He was the son of Hugh and Mary McCauley and died October 11, 1971.

NORAL A. MCCAULEY, Tech 5, born August 15, 1920, Washington County, Illinois, to Henry and __ Frieman McCauley. He served in WWII in Middle Eastern The-

T/5 Noral A. McCauley

atre with 150th Infantry, 656th TD. He enlisted in 1944 and was discharged in 1946. Worked for and later bought an implement company. He retired in 1992 and now lives in Coulterville, Illinois.

JOHN MCCLINTON, Private, born in Abbyville, South Carolina, the son of John and Elizabeth Anderson McClinton. He served in the War of 1812 from July 28, 1815 until November 3, 1815 in Captain Absolom Cox's Company of the Illinois Militia. His father came to Randolph County in 1802 and died in 1803 and is buried in Kelly Cemetery near Evansville, Illinois.

WILLIAM P. MCCLINTON, Private, born Perry County, Illinois, February 6, 1864, to John F. and Mary Orr McClinton. He entered the Civil War May 4, 1864, from Sparta, Illinois and assigned to 142nd Regiment, Company K. Illinois Volunteers. William was discharged October 26, 1864. He moved from Sparta to Kansas in 1882. His father, Samuel, was one of the early settlers of the county, coming here in 1804.

JAMES LEE MCCONKEY, Tech 4, born January 10, 1927, Rockwood, Illinois,

Pfc. James Lee McConkey

son of William R. and Florence Frazer McConkey. He was drafted into WWII May 2, 1945 and stationed in Anchorage, Alaska.

Discharged November 24, 1946, he returned home and worked as assistant manager 37 years for Metropolitan Life Insurance Company. James died June 27, 2001, Collinsville, Illinois. He was the grandson of James McConkey, a Civil War soldier of 1865.

JAMES WILLIAM MCCONKEY, Private, came to U.S. from Ireland in 1851. He enlisted in service for Civil War, February 15, 1865 and served with Company F, 154th Illinois Infantry, until May 23, 1865 when discharged.

He lived and farmed in Rockwood, Illinois until his death, November 20, 1924. James was born November 15, 1845, the son of Robert and Sarah McConkey, he is buried in Mt. Summit Cemetery near Rockwood.

CLIFFORD L. MCCORMICK, Staff Sergeant, entered the service October 4, 1964 and took his basic training and AIT at Lackland AFB, Texas. Nine months later he was sent to Travis AFB, California for 21 months there, then shipped to Vietnam with the 630 Combat Support Group (PACAF) for 12 months.

S/Sgt. Clifford L. McCormick

He returned to the States and finished his time at Keesler AFB Mississippi. Cliff was discharged October 1, 1968. He is the son of Herbert and Edith (Stewart) McCormick. His hometown is Rockwood, Illinois.

DALE E. MCCORMICK, E-4, enlisted into the Army in January 1967. He served in Germany with 7th Cavalry as a tank mechanic from March to December 1967. He was then shipped to the Republic of Vietnam as a mechanic and truck driver from December 1967 to August

E-4 Dale E. McCormick

1969. Dale served with the 34th Engineer Batt. and fought in the Tet Offensive 1968-69. Dale was born October 18, 1947, the son of Herb and Edith (Stewart) McCormick.

DONALD R. MCCORMICK, Specialist 3/c, served in the U.S. Army, January 30, 1955 to January 30, 1958. He was born October 23, 1937, Rockwood, Illinois, to

Spec-3/c Donald R. McCormick

Herbert and Edith Stewart McCormick. He served with I Company, 2nd Squadron, 87th Regiment, 10th Division. He spent four months in Fort Riley, Kansas, transferred to Aschaffenburg, Germany for 31 months, then to 2nd Armored Division in Worms, Germany

GERALD D. MCCORMICK, Corporal, served in the U.S. Army, 1953-56, with the 101st Airborne in Korea. He was born March 11, 1936 in Rockwood, Illi-

Cpl. Gerald D. McCormick

nois, son of Herbert and Edith Stewart McCormick.

HERBERT R. MCCORMICK, Sergeant, entered WWII December 4, 1942, and served in 988 Engineer TDWY Bridge Company. He died in service April 26,

Sgt. Herbert R. McCormick

1952 and is buried in Ebenezer Cemetery, near Rockwood, Illinois. Herbert was born February 12, 1912, son of Ross and Gettie Asbury McCormick.

JOHNATHAN F. MCCORMICK, Senior Airman, of Chester, Illinois, served in the Persian Gulf War and Bosnia Conflict with the 552nd Air Command Squadron, from April 1991 until March 1997. He is the son of Roger and Charlotte Robbins McCormick.

MICHAEL B. MCCORMICK, Lance Corporal, served in the U.S. Marine Corps from July 1993 to July 1997. He is from Chester, Illinois and the son of Cliff and Pam Jordan McCormick. Michael com-

L/Cpl Michael B. McCormick

pleted boot camp and was stationed at 29 Palms, California. He spent one year in Okinawa and had additional training there at Philippines, Guam, Okaido, Japan and Mt. Fuji. He was with Fox Company, 2nd Battalion, 7th Marines.

ROGER MCCORMICK, Specialist E-4, son of Herbert and Edith Stewart

McCormick, he served in "C" Battalion, 187th Division from 1966-68. In Vietnam he was attached to the 101st Airborne and the 4th Infantry Division before being transferred to "I" Corp Division in Korea as a machine gunner and scrapulator in radar division.

WILLIAM A. MCCREE, Private, son of Lowell and Marie Ashoff McCree, was born in Carterville, Illinois, September 7,

William McCree in Korea

1930. He served two years, 1952-54, with the 1st Marine Division in the Korean War.

JACK FLOYD MCDANIELS, Staff Sergeant, served his country from October 4, 1954 to April 30, 1976. Jack was with the 1st Infantry Division, B Battalion, 1/7 Artillery, 105 HQ W. He served five and a half years in the Coast Guard and 14 years and eight months in the Army.

S/Sgt. Jack F. McDaniels - Vietnam

Jack was in Germany, France, Japan, Hawaii and in Long Binh, Vietnam in 1967. From 1968-69 he served with the 1st Infantry Division at Canto in the Delta area. Jack was born July 6, 1937 in Sparta, Illinois, the s-son of Leonard Salger and Doris E. (Brelye) Salger.

ROY E. MCDANIEL, Sergeant, served in the U.S. Army, November 1941 to October 1945. He was born in 1915, Felt, Oklahoma, son of Charles C. and Carolyn Myers McDaniel. Sergeant McDaniel

Sgt. Roy E. McDaniels

served with the Army Medical Corps Air Evacuation in WWII, European Theatre, stationed in England and France.

Returning to the States, he married the former June Word, Sparta, Illinois. He graduated from the St. Louis College of Mortuary Science and has been a funeral director for 53 years. He has two children, Richard (Sparta, Illinois) and Vicki Hamer (Baldwin, Illinois).

WALDO D. MCDONALD, Staff Sergeant, enlisted August 9, 1942 at Peoria, Illinois, to serve in WWII. In April 1943, he was called to active duty and took his basic training at Camp Hood, Texas and Special Weapons School with Headquarters Company, 23rd Tank Destroyer Group (code name "Cigar Box).

He was at Omaha Beach (after D-Day) Ste. Mere-Eglise, Area 500 (an apple orchard) then to Paris, France. He went into Belgium, Red Ball Highway and was at Eupen during Battle of Bulge. From Belgium he went to Germany and was in Weimar when war ended. Waldo was involved in helping pass out rations at Buchenwald Concentration Camp and transporting the prisoners to other locations.

Involved in three major battles, he earned three Bronze Battle Stars. He was discharged December 23, 1945.

Born in Kaskaskia Island, Illinois, he is the son of William Perry and Laura Belle Voelker McDonald.

DONALD LEE MCDONOUGH, Private First Class, was employed in a steel mill when drafted in the U.S. Army on February 17, 1959. Donald completed basic training at Fort Leonard Wood, Missouri, followed by AIT at Fort Sill, Oklahoma. He was then sent to Fort Lewis, Washington, where he was assigned to the Signal Corps and spent the remainder of his time

Pfc. Donald L. McDonough

there. He was discharged February 16, 1961. Donald served his military time in the States during peacetime.

He was born in Chester, Illinois on August 25, 1936, the son of Joseph and Hester (Sipole) McDonough. Donald was employed at Menard Correctional Center until his death in September 1987.

JOSEPH BERNELL MCDONOUGH, Seaman 1/c, served aboard LST-941 during WWII. After training at Great Lakes, Virginia and Boston, he went to Cuba, Panama, Leyte in Philippines, New Guinea,

Seaman 1/c Joseph B. McDonough

Borneo Submarine Base then to Hiroshima, Japan. He entered service in June 1943 and was discharged in July 1946. Born in Ellis Grove, Illinois, February 6, 1926, he is the son of Joe and Hester Sipole McDonough.

JOSEPH NEAL MCDONOUGH, Specialist 4, was drafted into the Army on

Sp/4 Joseph Neal McDonough

March 19, 1969. Joe took his Basic and AIT at Fort Leonard Wood, Missouri. He was shipped to Vietnam with the HHC, 25th Infantry, America, from September 6, 1969 to October 20, 1970.

Joe attended Belleville Area College, 1972-74. He retired from Chester Mental Center November 30, 2002. Joe was born June 19, 1949 in Red Bud, Illinois, son of Jerald Peters and Viola (Pierce) McDonough.

LARRY S. MCDONOUGH, Private First Class, Larry was employed in a steel mill before he was drafted into the Army on March 3, 1964. He completed basic training at Fort Leonard Wood, Missouri, then went to Fort Sill, Oklahoma for AIT.

Pfc. Larry S. McDonough

Larry was stationed at Fort Lewis, Washington before being sent to Vietnam. He was with the 5th of the 27 Artillery, 105 Howitzer Battery. After arriving in Vietnam, Larry was assigned as a radio telephone operator for a forward observer for different artillery batteries. He was discharged from the Army February 28, 1966.

He retired from Chester Mental Health Center in 1999 after 30 years of service. Larry was born July 17, 1942 in Chester, Illinois, the son of Joseph and Hester (Sipole) McDonough.

SHANNON T. MCDONOUGH, Petty Officer 2/c, served in the U.S. Navy from February 22, 1994 to the present. He serves in Repair Division as naval nuclear components welder. He attended SIUE before enlisting in the Navy.

He completed his basic training at Great Lake, Illinois and graduated from Hull Technician "A" School, Philadelphia, Pennsylvania, followed by "C" School, (General Maintenance Welding School, High Pressure Pipe and Plate Welding School and Nuclear Components Welding School), San Diego, California. He was stationed at Naval Submarines Support Facility, Groton, Connecticut, 1995-98 as a naval nuclear components welder.

P.O. 2/c Shannon T. McDonough

In June 1998 he transferred to Norfolk, Virginia, aboard the USS *Enterprise* as a NNC Welder. He deployed to the Middle East in November 1998 and participated in Operation Desert Fox, December 16-20. He returned to Norfolk in April 1999. Deployed in April 2001, to the Middle East aboard the USS *Enterprise* and was involved in operation Enduring Freedom, October 7, 2001. He returned to Norfolk on November 10, 2001 and is currently in Norfolk, aboard the USS *Enterprise*.

Shannon was born October 10, 1972, Chester, Illinois, the son of Larry S. and Imogene Bierman McDonough.

ARMSTRONG MCGEE, Private, born in South Carolina about 1844 and died February 27, 1884 in Evansville, Illinois. He served in Company G of the 80th Illinois Infantry, organized in August 1862 at Centralia, Illinois and was mustered into service on August 25, 1862.

On September 4, they left for Louisville, Kentucky, as a part of the 33rd Brigade and assigned to the Tenth Division in General McCook's Corps. On October 1, they marched in pursuit of General Bragg and engaged in battle October 8, at Perryville, Missouri. The unit suffered a loss of 14 killed and 58 wounded.

On January 10, 1863, the unit was assigned to the 14th Army Corps, General J.J. Reynolds Division, making a brigade of 1500 men. On March 20 this brigade, with two pieces of artillery, repulsed John Morgan and 5,000 of the enemy. After meeting the enemy at Dug's Gap and Sand Mountain in the middle of April, two more were killed and 16 wounded. On May 4 the unit was taken prisoner by General Forrest and taken to Rome, Georgia, then sent to Atlanta, where the officers were sent to Libby Prison. The other men were eventually sent to Camp Chase, Ohio, and on July 23, were exchanged and sent to St. Louis.

On September 23, the unit started for the seat of war and reported to General Howard at Stephenson, Alabama in the 11th Army Corps, taking part in the battle of Mission Ridge. In 1864 they were with Sherman on his march to the sea and took part in the battle of Nashville on December 15th and 16th. On June 10, 1865, they were mustered out of service and received their final pay and discharge at Camp Butler, Illinois.

Armstrong McGee also had two brothers, George and Thomas, in the war. George was in the same company as Armstrong, and Thomas was killed in the war.

GLENNARD S. MCGEE, SP-5, served in the U.S. Army November 30, 1964 to November 29, 1966; and in the Army-Air Force Reserves, 1967-69. He was born in Chester, Illinois on June 11, 1943, son of George and Nellie Johnson McGee.

Sp-5 Glennard S. McGee

His basic training was at Fort Leonard Wood, Missouri, then assigned to Fort Sam Houston, Texas for medical-aid training, then to Frankfort, Germany. After Glennard was discharged, he joined the AFR at Scott Field and served weekends and summers.

WALTER G. MCGEE, E-3, USN, served in the U.S. Navy from November 1966 to December 1970. He was born in Chester, Illinois on September 5, 1947, son of George and Nellie Johnson McGee. He enlisted and completed basic training at Great Lakes, Illinois and had additional training at NAB Norfolk, Virginia.

He served aboard USS *Dubuque* (LPD-8) and working over side of ship in boatswain chair when the line broke and he fell to pier. He spent six months in Ports-

E-3 Walter G. McGee

mouth Naval Hospital, then six months light duty at Millington, Tennessee. He completed his tour in Bremerhaven, Germany.

BYRON H. MCGUIRE, Tech 5, was in Company C, Railway Operating Battalion during WWII. He worked on M&I Railroad before entering service January 11, 1944 and returned to work there after his discharge April 16, 1946. Born April 5, 1915, in Sparta, Illinois to Earl F. and Martha Schlimme McGuire, he died December 1, 1976.

FERN MCGUIRE, 2nd Lieutenant, Army Nurse, daughter of J.H. McGuire, a former Sheriff of Randolph County. She graduated from Washington University School of Nursing and served several years at Barnes Hospital, St. Louis, Missouri and with the Red Cross for three years before attending basic training at Camp Carson, Colorado. She was then assigned to Regional Hospital, Fort Leonard Wood, Missouri.

FREDRICK L. MCGUIRE, born in Sparta, Illinois on May 10, 1938, the son of William and Willadean Hendricks McGuire. In April, 1956, he volunteered for the U.S. Navy and was discharged in May 1976. He was a chief torpedoman and served on submarines: *Odox, Irex,*

Fredrick L. McGuire

Entemedor, Sirogo, Burfish, Hake and *Sea Robin.*

Before joining the Navy, he worked at Lochhead's Grocery and George Haier's Grocery in Chester. Following his service, he was employed by McDonald Douglas in Florida and for Lucent Technology also in Florida. He is now retired and lives in Chuluota, Florida.

HARRY B. MCGUIRE, Lieutenant, enlisted in the Army Air Force January 13, 1940. After basic training he served at Chanute Field, Rantoul, Illinois, graduated there as a sergeant and trained as a meteorologist. Soon after, he signed up as a cadet to be a pilot, dropping his sergeant rank, and started over as private at Maxwell Field, Alabama. The Air Force needed more navigators, so he graduated in September 1943 with Silver Wings and commission as navigator.

He left the U.S. early in January 1944 for North Africa, with less than 30 days flying time. Lieutenant McGuire was shot down over Italy on January 30, 1944, and lost.

WILLIAM EARL MCGUIRE, Master Chief-Systems Engineer, born February 22, 1934, in Sparta, Illinois, the son of William and Willadean Hendricks McGuire. In 1951 he volunteered for the U.S. Navy at the age of 17 and served for 20 years. He was discharged in 1971.

William Earl McGuire

He served aboard the destroyers: USS *Everett,* USS *Maddox,* USS *Parle,* USS *Cunningham,* USS *Rathburne,* and aboard submarines *Picuda* 382 and the *Blueback* 581.

Following his service, he worked as a civilian recreational director at the Patuxent Navy Base in Lexington Park, Maryland. He died March 5, 1998, in Daytona Beach, Florida.

WILLIAM J. MCGUIRE, Aviation Ordnanceman, was born January 12, 1914, in Sparta, Illinois, the son of Earl and Martha Schlimme McGuire. William volunteered for the U.S. Navy on April 26, 1944, served in WWII as an aviation ordinanceman and was discharged October 20, 1945.

William J. McGuire

Prior to enlisting, he was a salesman for Metropolitan Insurance and returned to that company following his discharge. He died January 5, 1984, in Dade City, Florida.

JERRY R. MCINTYRE, Specialist 4, entered service during Vietnam War August 11, 1966 and served with 34th Engineer Battalion until March 10, 1969. Basic training was at Fort Lewis, Washington and advanced individual training at Fort Leonard Wood, Missouri. He was assigned to Fort Hood, Texas until December 1967, then sent to Vietnam.

Spec-4 Jerry R. McIntyre

Jerry was born in Sparta, Illinois, December 30, 1946, son of Albert and Mildred Leadbetter McIntyre.

HUGH MCKELVY, Private, of the South Carolina Militia, served in the Reduction of Charleston, South Carolina. He received pay of four pounds, 15 shillings and eight pence for this service on April 19, 1785. This was accepted as Revolutionary War service.

He was born in 1765, bought land in Randolph County, Illinois in 1818. Hugh died in Randolph County in 1835 and is buried in Old Bethel Cemetery east of Sparta, Illinois. His parents were James and Margaret McKelvy. Hugh and his family are listed in the Prairie Pioneers of Illinois, Volume I.

CARL R. MCKENZIE, Seaman 1/c, enlisted in U.S. Navy, age 17, in June 1944 and trained at Great Lakes Naval Center and Camp Bradford, Virginia. He boarded LST-520 at New York City en route to South Pacific and finished his tour of duty in December 1945.

Seaman 1/c Carl R. McKenzie

Carl arrived in San Francisco in January 1946 on LST 1096. He was discharged at Great Lakes in March 1946. Carl is the son of R.H. and Grace Ratliff McKenzie.

LOREN D. MCKENZIE, Corporal, served in the U.S. Army from January 16, 1952 to January 15, 1954. He is the son of Robert H. McKenzie and Grace Ratliff McKenzie, Chester, Illinois.

Cpl. Loren D. McKenzie

Loren took his basic training at Camp Picket, Virginia, transferred to 9963D TS65 CO Valley Forge Army Hospital, Phoenixville, Pennsylvania for duty as a corpsman.

DWIGHT C. MCKINLEY, Staff Sergeant, entered the Navy for one year. Af-

Dwight C. McKinley - Navy

ter his discharge on August 6, 1950, Dwight entered the Air Force and served his three years after boot camp in Washington, DC, as a staff car driver for the Air Force. Dwight was discharged from the Air Force on September 5, 1953.

He was born November 3, 1930 to Ralph and Mary (Aitken) McKinley and died April 11, 2002.

LEE A. MCKINLEY, Fleet Air Wing 14, enlisted in the Navy in 1951 while still in High School. He went to San Diego, California for his boot camp, after which, he was shipped to Japan. Lee was discharged in 1955.

Air Wing Lee A. McKinley

He was born in Randolph County, Illinois to Ralph and Mary (Aitken) McKinley. Lee is a construction worker and lives in Tennessee.

ROY LYNN McKINLEY, Seaman 1/c, served in WWII from January 30, 1945

Seaman 1/c Roy L. McKinley

until July 2, 1946. He participated in Asiatic-Pacific Theater and worked in personnel office at Pearl Harbor one year.

He returned home and worked as carpenter for 40 years. Roy was born February 8, 1927, son of Ralph and Mary Aitken McKinley.

WILLIAM A. MCKINLEY, Sergeant, enlisted in WWII in 1944 while a junior in high school. He served with 5th Air Force, 39th Troop Carrier Squadron in Japan. He re-enlisted in 1945 and served until war was over in 1947.

Sgt. William A. McKinley

William was born April 2, 1925 in Randolph County, son of Ralph and Mary Aitken McKinley. He died February 6, 1989 and is buried in Tilden Cemetery.

HARRY W. MCLAUGHLIN, Private, born in Randolph County in 1890, the son of Sam W. and Elizabeth Dickey McLaughlin. He served in WWI from May 27, 1918, when he was inducted at Chester, Illinois, until June 9, 1919, when he was discharged. He served with the 151st Machine Gun Company and was later assigned to 36th Division, Company E of the 144th Infantry.

Pvt. Harry W. McLaughlin

He spent three months in Central Records Office in France after Armistice was signed. While in France he suffered the "terrible flu" and ended up in the hospital with a sheet pulled over him. He wasn't buried because he was "still warm." He survived this ordeal and was put on the last ship to return home.

Harry graduated from the Commercial Department of Sparta High School, and spent his life in banking and farming. He married and had three daughters. His death occurred April 9, 1941, as a result of pneumonia and before seeing his family reared. He is buried in a Coulterville, Illinois Cemetery.

MARVIN MCMICHAEL, Seaman 1/c, enlisted in Navy December 8, 1943 and served on USS *Sea Star* troop transport with combat duty in Japan, China, Pacific and Atlantic Oceans. He was discharged April 18, 1946.

Seaman 1/c Marvin McMichael

Marvin is the son of Hugh and Mary Krull McMichael, he was born at Sparta, Illinois on July 30, 1924 and died September 5, 1998.

MARVIN DALE MCMICHAEL, Private First Class, was drafted into the Army on May 10, 1966 and took his basic training at Fort Leonard Wood, Missouri. He went home for two weeks, before reporting to Fort Rucker, Alabama for AIT and helicopter mechanics. Marvin was with the 1/9 Cavalry Division and saw combat while in Vietnam. He was discharged in May 1968.

He retired from Department of Defense, Bi State Airport, 2002. Marvin was born May 2, 1947 in Red Bud, Illinois. He is the son of Marvin and Maxine (Petty) McMichael.

ROY LEE MCMICHAEL, Master Sergeant, served in the U.S. Air Force from June 25, 1973 to 1993. He was born in Red Bud, Illinois, March 3, 1952, the son

M/Sgt. Roy Lee McMichael

of Marvin and Maxine Petty McMichael. He enlisted, completed basic training and was stationed at Lackland AFB, Texas. He served overseas at Rhein Mein, Germany and Bitberg, Germany.

CHRISTOPHER A. MEISTER, Private First Class, enlisted in the Marines on August 13, 2002. Chris took his basic training at Marine Corps Recruiting Depot in San Diego, California. He took his Marine Corps Training at Camp Pendleton, California; artillery training at Fort Sill, Oklahoma, then he will be stationed in Kuwait. Chris is with the 3rd RTBN, Lima Company, Marine Battery 2-80 FA.

Pfc. Christopher A. Meister

He was born in Chester, Illinois on January 13, 1984, the son of Donald E. and Teresa A. (Miller) Meister.

DONALD WALTER MEIER, Staff Sergeant, served in Army Air Force, 3rd Tactical Control Group during WWII, on Island of Amchitka in the Aleutians. He entered service June 11, 1942, schooled

S/Sgt. Donald Walter Meier

for Radar Repairman 953, Athens, Georgia and Murphy, Florida.

He received American Theatre Ribbon, Asiatic-Pacific Theatre Ribbon, Good Conduct and Victory Medals. He was discharged November 8, 1945.

Donald was born in Walsh, Illinois on December 23, 1919, son of Edgar and Erna Donaldson Meier, and died October 29, 1991, St. Louis, Missouri.

ELMER PETE MEHRER, Seaman 1/c, C/S, served two tours in Pacific during WWII. He entered service April 14, 1943, was assigned to USS *Callaway* (PA-35), assault transport with 28 landing craft. He saw action Kwajalein, Atoll, in Marshall Islands; Emireu Island, St. Matthias Group; Saipan, Mariana Group; Palau, Caroline Islands; Leyte and Luzon, Philippine Islands; Iwo Jima and Okinawa. He made seven D-Day landings and took Army troops to Wakayama, Japan when Japan surrendered September 22, 1945.

Seaman 1/c Elmer Pete Mehrer

Awards received include the Navy Commendation, Presidential Unit Citation, American Campaign, Asiatic-Pacific, Navy Combat, Navy Occupation w/8 Battle Stars and Philippine Liberation Ribbon w/2 Battle Stars. He was discharged in November 1945.

Elmer was born in Chester, Illinois on April 26, 1926, son of Oscar and Stella Valleroy Mehrer.

Pfc. Marvin Dale McMichael

BURDELL G. MENKE, Corporal, was in WWII, serving in the 2nd Marine Division from March 1943 until his discharge in January 1946. After basic training in San Diego, California, he was sent to the South Pacific and served on the islands of Tarawa, Saipan and Tinian with an artillery division.

He participated in maneuvers on Okinawa in preparation for the invasion of Japan when the war ended. He was then sent to Nagasaki, Japan, for occupational duty until discharged.

Burdell was born in Sparta, Illinois, he is the son of Otto and Adeline Veath Menke.

ALBERT CHARLES MENNERICH,
Corporal, began WWII service October 31, 1941 and assigned to Battery B, 861st AAA A/W Battalion as anti-aircraft artillery weapons crewman. He was in campaigns, Ryukyus Islands and South Philippines.

Cpl. Albert Charles Mennerich

He was awarded two Bronze Stars for these campaigns and the Good Conduct Medal. He was discharged October 23, 1945.

Albert was born April 23, 1920, the son of William C. and Louisa Rall Mennerich.

VINCENT JAMES MENNERICH,
Private First Class, served in the U.S. Army from January 3, 1985 to December 18,

Pfc. Vincent James Mennerich

1987. Vincent served as a Lance Missile Crewman and also maintained and operated a five ton truck while stationed at Crailsheim, West Germany.

He was born August 3, 1962, son of Albert Charles and Helen Jany Mennerich.

WILLIAM MENNERICH was born
January 9, 1841 in Jurgenstorf, Kingdom of Hannover, Germany, the son of Franz John and Anna Catharina Goedeke Mennerich. He came to America in 1857 to join his parents who had arrived in Iowa in 1854.

William Mennerich

He and his brothers, Henry and Franz, enlisted in the Union Army at St. Louis, Missouri at the outbreak of the Civil War and served in the 2nd Missouri Infantry and Missouri 4th Cavalry, Company C. He fought in the Battle of Pea Ridge, Arkansas and on July 10, 1863, his entire unit was captured by Confederate soldiers at Union City, Tennessee.

William was imprisoned at Belle Isle, Virginia, released in February 1864, and returned to his regiment. He served as a bugler for his company and mustered out on October 24, 1864.

After his discharge, he settled at Waterloo, Illinois, and began farming. He married Elizabeth Horschmann. In 1883, he moved to Red Bud, Illinois. He was the father of 10 children: William C., Frank, Elizabeth, Margaretta, Wendell, Mary, Emma Gertrude, August and Mathilda. William Mennerich died October 8, 1932 in Red Bud, Illinois.

FREDERICK LUDWIG MEYER,
served in the U.S. Army in WWI for approximately one year, beginning June 24, 1918. Crossing the Atlantic, their ship pitched heavily in the rough seas. He survived on chocolate bars and dill pickles. He did not eat the mutton, which was spoiled and made the men sick.

Frederick Ludwig Meyer

Frederick arrived in France just after the armistice, and his unit combed the countryside for unexploded bombs. Returning to America, he became a farmer.

He was born February 13, 1896, Steeleville, Illinois. Frederick was the son of Heinrich and Mary Rabe Meyer.

HAROLD A. MEYER, served in the
U.S. Army, 1949-50. He was born October 10, 1925, Steeleville, Illinois, the son of Frederick Ludwig and Hulda Schaack Meyer. Harold had to quit high school to help on the family farm near the end of WWII, so his military service was deferred. However, he did join in January 1949.

Harold took his basic training at Camp Breckenridge, Kentucky, in the 101st Airborne, then to Conley AFB, Atlanta, Georgia for Mechanics School. Assigned to Fort Riley, Kansas in August 1949, he was an instructor in wheeled vehicle maintenance and repair.

Leaving the Army in January 1950, he continued in active reserves for the next six years.

RAYMOND FREDERICK MEYER,
Staff Sergeant, served in the U.S. Army from November 17, 1952 to August 27, 1954. He completed basic training at Fort Knox, Kentucky in the 3rd Armored Division. Assigned to South Korea with Company L, 17th Infantry Regiment, 7th Di-

S/Sgt. Raymond F. Meyer

vision as a Light Weapon Infantryman, May 21-June 22. A medical condition forced him to the hospital June 23-July 12, 1953.

He was re-assigned to Headquarters Company, IRD, 8057th AU as a general clerk from July 14-October 26, 1953. He then became a personnel administrative specialist until August 1, 1954.

He was discharged from Fort Sheridan, Illinois, August 27, 1954, returning to the family dairy and grain farm. He earned the Korean Service Ribbon, Bronze Star, United Nations Service Medal, Combat Infantry Badge, National Defense Service Medal and Korean Presidential Unit Citation.

Raymond was born March 29, 1932 in Steeleville, Illinois, the son of Frederick Ludwig and Hulda Schaack Meyer.

JOHN HENRY MILLER, Staff Sergeant E-6, enlisted December 12, 1971 and served until December 31, 1991, in 2nd Squadron 2nd Battalion Infantry in both

S/Sgt. E-6 John Henry Miller

Vietnam and Desert Storm. He was squadron leader and platoon leader and saw no actual combat. His last nine years he worked in Iruin Army Hospital, Fort Riley, Kansas, as NCO IC outpatient records. John was born May 15, 1952, his parents were Herman and Anna L. Rice Ralston Miller.

UDELL MILLER, Corporal, born and reared in Chester, Illinois, he entered military service shortly after Pearl Harbor. He was assigned to Pacific-Asiatic Theater with Army Air Force as an aerial gunner on B-17 Flying Fortress, flying combat missions throughout the Pacific during WWII. Late in the war his plane was shot down over Aleutian Islands by Japanese Zeros. He bailed out of aircraft, sustaining several wounds from shrapnel during the attack and spent several months at Tripler Army Hospital in Hawaii.

His awards include the Air Medal,

Cpl. Udell Miller

Army Air Force Good Conduct Medal, American Campaign Medal, Asiatic-Pacific Campaign Medal, WWII Victory Medal, U.S. Army, Combat Service, Overseas Service, Asiatic-Pacific Victory, and the Purple Heart.

Returning to Chester, he worked at Chester Mental Health Center and retired as a security therapy aide. Udell was born in Chester, Illinois on May 3, 1924, son of Walter and Nettie Mansker Miller. He died August 17, 2001 and is buried in St. Mary's Catholic Cemetery, Chester.

WILLIAM MILLER, Spanish American War Veteran, born December 21, 1872, the son of Jack and Ellen Miller of Sparta, Illinois. He died March 3, 1941, and is buried in Caledonia Cemetery.

EDGAR A. MISSELHORN, Sergeant, entered the Army December 9, 1952, and took basic training at Camp Atterbury, Indiana. After 10 days of R&R, he reported

Sgt. Edgar A. Misselhorn

to Fort Lewis, Washington, then was deployed to Korea, where he served in 7th Div. 13 ECB Dog Company. While in Korea he was chief carpenter. Born June 15, 1930, at Percy, Illinois, his parents were William and Hulda Ruback Misselhorn.

TIMOTHY L. MODGLIN, E-5 2/c, Petty Officer served in the Navy aboard the USS *Robert E. Peary* (FF-1073). He was inducted into service December 4, 1984 at Great Lakes Naval Station, and completed Operations Specialist "A" School. Timothy was in Pearl Harbor while serving aboard USS *Robert E. Peary.*

His awards include the Battle E Ribbon, Good Conduct Medal, Armed Forces Expeditionary Medal and Sea Service Ribbon. He completed West Pac with USS *Ranger* and USS *Missouri* as Battle Group Echo. He was discharged December 2, 1988.

Born February 7, 1964, in Red Bud, Illinois, he is the son of Myron and Arlene Albers Modglin.

ROBERT ANDREW MOFFAT, Private, entered WWI in April 1918 and served with Batt. F, 308th Field Artillery, 78th Div. until June 1919. He was born in Sparta, Illinois, to Robert E. and Henrietta Clyde Edwards Moffat on May 20, 1893. He died July 17, 1951 and was buried in Caledonia Cemetery in Sparta, Illinois.

ROBERT A. MOFFAT JR., Captain served in the Army Infantry during WWII. From Sparta, Illinois, he is the son of Robert A. and Dorothy Bertram Moffat. He served with Company H, 377 Infantry, 95th Div. in Europe, which was assigned to General Patton's 3rd Army.

The Division was awarded three Bronze Battle Stars, and he has a Bronze Star w/Oak Leaf Cluster and V, also the Combat Badge. He entered service in June 1942 and with active and reserve service he was discharged in April 1953.

LEONARD H. MOHR, Private First Class, served in WWI, as an automatic gun instructor in the States, then was sent to Europe and fought in battles in France and Belgium. His term of service was from April 1917 until April 29, 1919. Born in

Pfc. Leonard Mohr

Randolph County on December 5, 1895, he is the son of Henry and Anna Lisch Mohr.

VICTOR L. MOHR, Electrician 2/c, entered the U.S. Navy December 28, 1943 and attended Electrical School at Sampson, New York Naval Base. He was then assigned to duty on the USS *Ainsworth* and sent to the Island of Maui in the Pacific, then to Wake Island, where he worked in the electrical departments.

Elec. 2/c Victor L. Mohr

Born in Red Bud, Illinois, October 2, 1925, his parents were Leonard and Anna Brecht Mohr. He was discharged from WWII service on April 30, 1946.

DELBERT J. MOLL, Master Sergeant (E-7), born January 25, 1925 in Prairie du Rocher, Illinois. He served in WWII,

M/Sgt. Delbert J. Moll

1944-46, as merchant marine and was a paratrooper with 11th Airborne Division, SAC, TAC and MAC. He also served in Korea and retired with 23 years service. He had duty in England, France, Germany, Japan, China, Korea, Okinawa and USA. Delbert is the son of Theodore and __ Hunter Moll.

FERDINAND WILLIAM MOLL, FSMB3/c, began Naval training at Great Lakes, Illinois, April 26, 1945, in WWII, then went to San Francisco, and later served aboard USS *Washington*. He was

F.S.M.B. 3/c Ferdinand W. Moll

discharged May 17, 1946. Born in Randolph County, March 14, 1928, the son of William and Ella Mattingly Moll, he died August 9, 1977.

STEVEN WILLIAM MOLL, Corporal, was the only son of Ferd W. and June J. (Eggemeyer) Moll. He was born September 5, 1949 in Red Bud, Illinois and grew up in Chester/Evansville, Illinois. His service career began at Camp Pendleton, California on August 13, 1969. Steven belonged to Company B, 1st Batt., 1st Marine Division.

Cpl. Steven William Moll

Steven was sent to Vietnam February 29, 1970 and served as company supply person-getting food, mail and necessary equipment to the battle fields and camps. Under his leadership and without any casualties to his men, he fought in the hazardous Charlie Ridge Enemy territory

His military career ended abruptly on January 21, 1971. While serving his country in enemy controlled territory of Quang Nam Province in the Republic of Vietnam, Steven was in a helicopter which fell victim to the hazardous mountain terrain and crashed, killing all on board immediately. Steven was due to come home in approximately three weeks. Steven's family received letters telling of his heroic tales. His presence is greatly missed by all who knew him. Steven's hobbies included hunting and playing baseball.

GARRY R. MONRONEY, SPEC-5, enlisted in the National Guard for six years in April 1966. Garry had his basic training at Fort Jackson, South Carolina and

Spec 5 Garry R. Monroney

his last assignment was at Fort Dix, New Jersey. Garry was with Company B, 1140th Engineer Battalion. He was discharged in 1972. Garry was born in Red Bud, Illinois on March 1, 1945, the son of Gerald D. Glenna (Dregke) Monroney.

JEAN BAPTISTE MONTREUIL, Soldier and Guide, served with Lieutenant Colonel George Rogers Clark Expedition that went overland to capture Vincennes, a large populated stronghold that was essential to the British cause, but had only a small force defending it.

After taking Kaskaskia, Prairie du Rocher, St. Phippe and Cahokia, he regrouped his force in Kaskaskia and with 172 men and several French guides (among them, Jean Baptiste Montreuil) started for Vincennes. Lieutenant Governor Henry Hamilton of Detroit, surrendered without conflict. Clark was victorious in taking Vincennes for Virginia and the American Colonies. Montreuil served with Clark, 1778-79.

His father, Michael Sedilot dit Montreuil, was a native of parish Les Cedres Gov't Montreal, diocese of Quebec, and his mother was Marie-Josephe LaLonde. Jean Baptiste died April 11, 1766, at age of about 79 years.

ARMIN J. MONTROY, Yeoman First Class, served in the U.S. Navy from January 1951 to October 1954. The son of J.L. Montroy and Cecelia Moskop Montroy, he was born in Chester, Illinois on November 16, 1929.

After basic training at Great Lakes

YN 1/c Armin J. Montroy in foreground at Hong Kong

Naval Station, Yeoman Montroy served his entire time in Navy on the *Pickaway*, with additional training at the U.S. Navy Military Justice School at Newport, Rhode Island. He served as the engineering department yeoman, captain's yeoman and after schooling was a legal yeoman and military court reporter. He was in Japan, Korea, Guam, Philippines and China.

He is entitled to wear the National Defense, Korean Service, United Nations and China Service medals, along with the Good Conduct Medal.

DENIS R. MONTROY, Sergeant, entered the service August 31, 1964 and was discharged September 1, 1968. His service with the Marine Corps was with the Fleet Marine Force, 2nd Marine Division as a platoon sergeant. While serving in Vietnam they all grew up very fast serving our country.

Sgt. Denis R. Montroy

Denis was born November 19, 1945, son of Lawrence and Ethel (Hennrich) Montroy.

FRANCIS W. MONTROY, Corporal, served in the U.S. Marine Corps from January 1966 to January 1968. The son of Francis and Florence Sisson Montroy, he was born December 11, 1946 in Kankakee, Illinois. He served in Logistics with the 1st and 3rd Marines. The 13 months he spent in Vietnam is a memo-

Cpl. Francis W. Montroy

rable time of his life, and he's proud to have served.

HARRY E. MONTROY, enlisted in U.S. Army in 1948 to avoid being drafted. He served in WWII occupation of Japan. The Korean War started during his enlist-

Lt. Col. Harry E. Montroy

ment. He was commissioned in 1952 and remained active until 1970, when he retired. He served in both Korea and Vietnam, worked as a soldier, NCO and general staff officer during his service. Parents were Harry H. and Hazel Andrews Montroy of Evansville, Illinois.

SCOTT A. MONTROY, Sergeant, served in the U.S. Marine Corps from October 21, 1996 to October 20, 2000. He was born in Chester, Illinois, August 28, 1978, the son of James and Tammy Blum Montroy. Scott enlisted just after high school and was a squad leader in the In-

Sgt. Scott A. Montroy

fantry, G Company, 2nd Battalion, 6th Marines. He was deployed for temporary duty and training at Okinawa, Korea, Spain, Italy, Greece, Ukraine and Israel. He was discharged in 2000.

ARTHUR I. MOORE, Motor Machinist Mate enlisted in WWII on February 19, 1942, as apprentice seaman in U.S. Navy. He was in Amphibian Boat Pool on Noumea, New Caledonia Island, Amphibian Boat Pool #7, attended Landing Craft and Advanced Pilot Schools, and served aboard USS *Bottineau* (APA-235). He was discharged September 24, 1945.

Born December 28, 1919, son of Robert and Millia Inman Moore, he died January 4, 1986, and is buried at Pleasant Ridge Cemetery near Rockwood, Illinois.

DAYMON MOORE, Gunners Mate 3/c, served aboard USS LST-941, during WWII. He entered service April 23, 1943 and was discharged November 20, 1945. He was in Philippines during Japanese bombings, and his ship was the only one

GM 3/c Daymon Moore

saved during one raid. He went to Japan when war ended, then returned home to work in coal mines. Born in Jasper, Alabama, July 29, 1918, son of John and Elizabeth Laugton Moore, he died April 10, 2002.

GROVER LLOYD MOORE, Fireman 2/c, was born May 6, 1925, at Chester, Illinois, the son of Grover and Kate Williams Moore. He enlisted in the Navy April 26, 1944 and served during WWII until May 21, 1946. Training was at Great Lakes Naval Center. He served aboard USS *Phoenix* (CL-46) and USS *Tennessee* (BB-43). His awards include the Victory Medal, Asiatic-Pacific Campaign Medal w/4 stars, American Campaign Medal and Philippine Liberation Ribbon w/2 stars.

IRA MUREL MOORE, born October 14, 1918, in Rockwood, Illinois to William H. and Grace Martin Moore and served in U.S. Navy during WWII. Ira died July 9, 1977 and is buried Jefferson Barracks, Missouri.

IRA PORTER MOORE, Wagoner, was inducted into WWI at Chester, Illinois on June 24, 1918. He served in the Heavy Duty Division of the 10th Artillery Field Brigade and achieved the rank of Wagoner. He was discharged from service on January 26, 1919 at Camp Funston, Kansas. Moore was born in 1892 in Rockwood, Illinois to Harvey and Mary Henson Moore. He died September 15, 1950 and is buried in Barber Cemetery in Rockwood, Illinois.

LONNIE MOORE, BT2, served in the U.S. Navy from September 1959 to September 1963. He served during the Cuban Crisis, aboard the USS *Barry* (DD-933)

BT-2 Lonnie Moore

and the USS *Little Rock* (CLG-4), visited many ports and saw a lot of the world. He was born in Sparta, Illinois on March 15, 1941, the son of Damon and Leona Kohlhaas Moore.

OLIN E. MOORE, Corporal, was inducted May 19, 1918, at Chester, Illinois, at the age of 22 years and 5 months. He served as a member of the American Expeditionary Forces, in Causal Detachment 1441 Demobilization Group. His last assignment was with Company F 3rd Infantry before his discharge on September 22, 1919, at Camp Dodge, Iowa. Born in Rockwood, Illinois, his parents were Albert and Louvisa Payne Moore.

ROBERT I. MOORE, Tech 5, entered WWII service December 5, 1941, at Camp Wallace, Texas and assigned to Battery A, 540 Field Artillery Engineers, as a tractor driver in the European Theater from July 29, 1942 until discharge June 24, 1945. Medals received include American Defense Service Ribbon, European-African-Middle Eastern Theater Ribbon w/Bronze Battle Star, one Service Stripe and four Overseas Service Bars. Robert was discharged at Camp Grant, Illinois, October 11, 1945. Born in Chester, Illinois, May 1, 1919, he was the son of Grover and Kate Williams Moore.

RONALD MOORE, E-5, served in the U.S. Navy from May 1960 to March 1964. He was born in Sparta, Illinois on March 2, 1943, son of Damon and Leona

E-5 Ronald Moore

Kuhlhaas Moore. He served during the Cuban Crisis aboard the USS *Little Rock* (CLG-4) and made two Mediterranean cruises, four Caribbean cruises and visited many ports.

SIDNEY SMITH MOORE, Private, fought in Civil War with Company K, 4th Infantry of Tennessee Cavalry. He came to Randolph County in 1866, after war ended, and settled on land next to a Union soldier he had met during war. He married and reared a large family. His daughter married son of Union soldier. Born in Cumberland County, Kentucky on January 17, 1837, son of Wilson and Vashti Skipworth Moore, he died January 6, 1922 and is buried Pleasant Ridge Cemetery, near Rockwood, Illinois.

VINCE JAMES MOORE, Ship's Cook 3/c, born January 20, 1927, in Chester, Illinois, entered service in WWII on January 22, 1944 and served for one year and 10 months overseas in Navy. Training School was at Great Lakes, then to ATB Solomons, Maryland. He served in LCI(L)-977 and LST-848. Discharged February 19, 1946, he transferred to Naval Reserves and was relieved from active duty July 14, 1953.

VIRGIL E. MOORE, Private First Class, served with the U.S. Army in Korea from 1958 until discharge January 14, 1961. Born in Chester, Illinois, February 21, 1931, son of Grover and Kate Williams Moore, he died September 14, 1995 and is buried in Evergreen Cemetery in Chester.

WILLIAM MORRIS, Private, was in Captain William Ramsey's Company of Ohio Militia from October 11, 1813 until April 7, 1814, in the War of 1812. His hometown was Opossumden Prairie. He was the son of Samuel and Lucy Stevens Morris. Born in England, June 7, 1777, he died in Randolph County October 3, 1874 and is buried in Union Cemetery in Sparta, Illinois.

NORMAN J. MORRISON, Boatswains Mate 2/c, served in WWII from August 29, 1940 until discharge on August 12, 1946. A native of Sparta, Illinois, he is the son of Michael and Lillian Bradley Morrison.

BM 2/c Norman J. Morrison

He was stationed aboard the heavy cruiser USS *Indianapolis* when the Japanese attacked on December 7, 1941, but fortune favored them. They had departed Pearl Harbor with a detachment of Marines to relieve the garrison at Johnson Island, 400 miles southwest of Hawaii, so they missed the bombing. He served in the South Pacific and Aleutian Islands actions until December 1943, when the ship returned to Mare Island Naval yard for repairs.

He transferred to Oceanside, California, for training as a beachmaster in the Amphibious Forces, and from there went to England and France until V-E Day, then back to Oceanside Beachmaster School, where he was assigned to take a platoon through their training. Japan surrendered before training was finished, so they were assigned to the light cruiser, USS *Duluth*, where he finished the last year of his enlistment in the Philippine Islands, Japan, China and Southeast Asia.

RICHARD MORRISON "PING" BROWN,
Gunner's Mate 2/c, Petty Officer, born at Steeleville, Illinois on April 17, 1918, son of Richard Lee and Eva Morrison Brown. Enlisted in U.S. Navy February 9, 1942 for service in WWII and assigned to Little Creek Amphibious Base near Norfolk, Virginia as an instructor. Discharged in 1945, he returned to Chester, Illinois and became a partner in Standard Oil Service Station with his brother-in-law, Milton (Pete) Atchison, for many years.

CHARLES LONNIE "TERMITE" MORROW,
Lance Corporal E-3, joined the Marines October 1, 1957. His basic training was at Camp Lejeune, North Carolina. He was with Headquarters Company, Marine Corps Enhr. School, MCB, CLNC (2531-Field Radio Operator). Then he went to Camp Pendleton, California for ICT. From there he was shipped to Okinawa at Camp Sukiran in the central part of Okinawa. Lonnie served with the 9th Marines, 3rd Marine Division (Rein) FMF 2nd Battalion.

L/Cpl. Charles Lonnie Morrow

He received M-1 Rifle, Sharpshooter Badge, 45 Pistol, Marksman Badge and an honorable discharge on September 29, 1961 to the Marine Corps Reserves, Convenience of the Government, and discharged from them on September 30, 1963. He went back to work at McDonald Douglas in St. Louis, Missouri, after which he went to California where he worked at the airport. He retired in 2000 from the Randolph County Highway Department. Lonnie was born July 20, 1939 in Marissa, Illinois, the son of Samuel A. Sr. and Marie E. (Foertsch) Morrow.

JOHN WILLIAM MORROW,
Corporal, entered the Army January 20, 1942 and took his basic training at Camp Grant Illinois. John served with Tr. E Cavalry Reconnaissance Squadron. Being a Tank Gunner 1739 and SS W Rifle M1 was what he specialized in. John served his country mostly overseas, in Northern France, Rhineland and Central Europe.

John William Morrow

He spent a total of two years, 11 months and 13 days on foreign soil. While there he earned the American Theater Ribbon, European-African-Middle Eastern Theater Ribbon w/3 Bronze Battle Stars, five Overseas Service Bars, one Service Stripe, Good Conduct Medal and the Lapel Button. He was discharged October 4, 1945 from Fort Sheridan, Illinois. He served during WWII. John had blue eyes, brown hair, was 5'7" and 134 lbs. and 24 years old.

He was a farm hand in civilian life. John was born August 12, 1918 in Goodsprings, Alabama, son of William M. and Lula (Kirkland) Oglesby Morrow. John died May 1, 1960 in Sacramento, California and is buried in Cherokee Memorial Park Cemetery, Sacramento, California.

SAMUEL A. MORROW SR.,
Private, was inducted into the Army April 5, 1945. Sam took his basic training at Fort Sheridan, Illinois, then was assigned to the Headquarters Company, 11th Infantry, 2nd Battalion. He was a Cook 060.

Pvt. Samuel A. Morrow Sr.

Sam was discharged December 15, 1945, Separation Center, Camp Atterbury, Indiana. He received the WWII Victory Medal. Reason and authority for separation: Convenience of Government, AR 615-365 Red. of Army November 15, 1945.

Sam was born October 20, 1915 in Kellerman, Alabama to William and Lula (Kirkland) Morrow. He returned to coal mining after service and retired from there. Sam died November 17, 1993 and is buried at Caledonia Cemetery Sparta, Illinois.

SAMUEL A. MORROW JR.,
Lance Corporal, of Sparta, Illinois, enlisted in Marine Corps May 31, 1967 and spent two and a half years in Vietnam with 2nd Amphibian Tractor Battalion. He received the Navy-Marine Corps highest award for heroism when he saved six crew members that were stranded on a sinking amphibian tractor in their attempt to cross the Cau Viet River in Quang Tri Province, Vietnam.

L/Cpl. Samuel A. Morrow Jr.

On October 14, 1968, despite heavy seas, Morrow volunteered to ride a tracked landing vehicle to the men who were being swept out to sea. Clinging to the top of the landing vehicle, he rescued three men on the first trip, then again went into the turbulent sea and successfully rescued the remaining three Marines.

His main job was driving a vehicle troop transporter, that had a capacity for 26 men. Many times he got twice that many on board, when bringing dead soldiers back from the front line. He transported his fallen comrades back from where they were killed, driving alone mile after mile, with nothing but his own thoughts to keep him company.

On more than one occasion he volunteered to serve as "point man" for the main fighting force. This required him to be in front of the troops. He met, and won, four encounters with groups of enemy soldiers, and due to excellent marksmanship with his rifle and .45 pistol, he is one of the few surviving "point men."

Discharged February 2, 1970, he received, in addition to the Presidential Citation and Navy-Marine Corps Commendations, National Defense Medal, Purple Heart, Combat Action Ribbon, RVN Cross of Gallantry w/Palm and Frame, Vietnam Service Medal w/5 stars and Vietnam Campaign Medal w/device.

Born July 12, 1948 in Sparta, son of Samuel and Marie Foertsch Morrow, he now lives in Randolph County and works in construction work. *Written by Corporal Bill Sharette who served in Vietnam.*

CHARLES DAVID MUDD, SP4, Served in the U.S. Army from April 3, 1958 to March 31, 1960. He was born in Prairie du Rocher, Illinois on September 25, 1938,

Sp-4 Charles D. Mudd

son of Emory James and Anna E. Peyrot Mudd. He completed basic training at Fort Leonard Wood, Missouri and was assigned to Fort McClellan, Alabama and served a tour in Germany. Returning to the States, he was transferred to active Reserves to complete his six year obligation.

HAROLD FRANCIS MUDD, 2nd Lieutenant, served with the U.S. Army Air Corps during WWII as a pilot. He was born in Evansville, Illinois, June 3, 1920, to Alfred and Eolalia E. Simpson Mudd. He lost his life in an airplane accident in Lake County, California on August 13, 1945. His body was returned to Evansville, for burial on August 19, 1945.

LARRY MUDD, SPEC-5, Drafted into the Army September 26, 1966 and took eight weeks basic training, followed by eight weeks of AIT at Fort Leonard Wood, Missouri, then shipped to Vietnam in March 1967 with the 299th Engineer 20th Eng.

He came back to the States in July 1968 and was discharged September 25, 1968.

Spec-5 Larry Mudd

He is the son of Vernon and Leona (Naeger) Mudd and was born July 31, 1947 in Red Bud, Illinois. Returning home he worked for Pipe Fitters Local 562.

FRIEDRICH H. MUELLER, served in the U.S. Army Cavalry in WWI. He was born in Steeleville, Illinois on February 6, 1899, the son of Dietrich Friedrich and Anna Maria Ebers Mueller, and died November 2, 1960.

JOHN FREDRICH MUELLER came to America from Germany in 1860. The family settled near Bremen, Illinois, then moved to Texas County, Missouri. Loyalty to the Union caused his home to be destroyed, and he moved to St. Louis County, Missouri. At age 37 he enrolled on May 3, 1864 as a Militiaman in Company B, 13th Regiment of Missouri Militia. Born in Germany on February 5, 1827, son of Johann Freidrich and Ilsa Margreta Rajas Muller, he died July 4, 1908 in Steeleville, Illinois.

LOUIS MUELLER, served in the U.S. Army in WWI. He was born in Chester, Illinois, the son of Edward and Carolina

Louis Mueller

Mueller. Louis later had twin sons who served in WWII.

MELVIN MUELLER, Private First Class, served in the U.S. Army from Janu-

Pfc Melvin Mueller

ary 6, 1942 to October 29 1945, with AAF FW 328 ADrm. Sqd in India and Burma as a special vehicle operator, large transportation trucks, and maintained them. He drove through blackouts and over poor roads.

He earned Asiatic-Pacific Ribbon w/ 3 Bronze Stars, one Service Stripe, four Overseas Service Bars, Good Conduct and Distinguished Unit Badge.

Born a twin on July 4, 1920, he was the son of Louis and Emma (Bollmann) Mueller.

MILTON MUELLER, Corporal, served in the U.S. Army Air Corps in WWII in the Philippine Islands. He was born a

Cpl. Milton Mueller

twin in Chester, Illinois on July 4, 1920, son of Louis and Emma (Bollmann) Mueller.

RAYMOND C. MUELLER, Tech 5, served in the U.S. Army, April 5, 1945 to

T/5 Raymond C. Mueller

October 16, 1946. He was born in Chester, Illinois on December 8, 1926 to Henry O. and Josephine Bollmann Mueller. Ray was inducted and took basic training at Camp Fannin, Texas as a rifleman.

He was sent to Austria and served as a radio operator with Troop B, 24th Constabulary Sqd. and guarded river crossing on Danube River. Honorably discharged, he returned to Chester, married, and worked for Department of Corrections for 30 years before retiring.

ROBERT H. MUELLER, T/5, served in WWII with Company A, 313 Battalion Combat Engineers, 88th Blue Devil Division. He entered service February 27, 1946 in the Mediterranean Theater in

T/5 Robert H. Mueller

northern Italy, doing occupational duty which consisted of building Bailey Bridges and pontoon bridges and, also, guard duty. A native of Chester, Illinois, his parents are Henry O. and Josephine Bollman Mueller.

WALTER C. MUELLER, Tech 4, was inducted into WWII February 19, 1943 and served in Battery C, 142nd Antiaircraft Artillery Battalion in vital defense of first phase of German offensive of the Ardennes. They repelled aerial and parachutist attacks against vital communication links, and helped to convert the Ardennes Bulge into the Ardennes Bubble.

T/4 Walter C. Mueller

This battalion moved aggressively into zone of action through the Rhineland and Central Europe in defense of the Inde, Roer, Rhine and Weser Rivers, reinforcing field artillery units in addition to its normal AAA missions.

The 142nd destroyed 17% of all enemy planes within range of its guns, had 153 ground engagements, destroyed over 50 enemy tanks, caused the surrender of five towns, killed or captured over 1200 enemy personnel, while successfully defending all their equipment and personnel targeted by the enemy. For each aircraft destroyed only 127 rounds of 90mm ammunition was fired. From December 1944 to April 1945, they expended 7,000 rounds of 90mm ammunition, laid 500 miles of communications wire, sent and received more than 1,000 radio messages over their communications link. Communications were down only 1% of time during combat.

Mueller was discharged January 29, 1946 with American Campaign Medal, European-African-Middle Eastern Theater Ribbon w/3 Bronze Battle Stars, WWII Victory Medal w/2 Overseas Bars and Good Conduct Medal.

Born in Steeleville, Illinois, he is son of Fred H. and Frieda Hornbostel Mueller.

WILLIAM C. MUELLER, Private First Class, completed the 12-week basic military training at the Marine Corps Recruit Depot, San Diego, California in October 2002. In January Mueller completed the eight-week infantry training at Camp Pendleton, California.

Pfc. William C. Mueller

He was deployed to the Middle East January 31, 2003, William is with Operation Iraqi Freedom, Company B. 1st Battalion, 7th Marines.

He was born December 7, 1983, the son of Ralph B. and Susan (Bradley) Mueller.

JOHN MULHOLLAND, Private First Class, was born in Sparta, Illinois, son of J. Earl and Edna McKee Mulholland, and entered service in October 1946. V-J Day occurred two weeks before starting senior year of high school, and after graduation, he enlisted in Army and served in Occupation of Japan, assigned to 15th Quartermaster Troop, 1st Cavalry Division. Most interesting part of his service was what he was able to do in his free time.

Pfc. John Mulholland

He attended sports events in Olympic Stadium in Tokyo, swam in Olympic Pool in Yokohama, attended War Crimes Trials at Sugamo Prison, visited statue of Great Buddha at Kamakura and climbed Mount Fuji. He was discharged in January 1948.

His great-grandfather, Joseph Mulholland, served in Company C, 32nd Illinois Infantry during Civil War.

LEONARD LEE MULHOLLAND, SPEC-4, entered service in October 1963 and was discharged in 1965. Leonard was with the 1233rd Maintenance Battalion,

Spec-4 Leonard L. Mulholland

2nd Armored Division. He was stationed at Fort Hood, Texas and after returning home, he worked for World Color as a mechanic for 30 years. He lives in rural Coulterville, Illinois. He was born in Randolph, County, son of Joe and Pearl Hemphill-Mulholland.

TRAVIS C. MULHOLLAND, Quartermaster 1/c, was in U.S. Coast Guard during WWII and served in both Pacific and

Travis Mulholland

Mulhollands, New York, 1944. Travis, Loyd and Melvin.

European Theatres aboard USS *Calypso*. Inducted November 18, 1940 and discharged December 21, 1945. Travis was born September 16, 1919, son of Albert and Mayme Marshall Mulholland.

EARL BURDETTE NANCE, Staff Sergeant, enlisted in U.S. Army, December 6, 1944 and served as a paratrooper with 82nd and 101st Airborne Divisions in Luzon, Philippine Island Campaign in 1945, parachuting behind enemy forces, and in Japan and the Asiatic-Pacific Theatre during WWII.

Earl re-enlisted at Sendia, Japan and later served with occupational forces in Germany. He was discharged June 13, 1947, and worked for Caterpillar Tractor Co. in Peoria, Illinois.

Earl was born in Chester, Illinois, July 11, 1926, the son of Jesse and Effa Parker Nance, he died January 18, 1979, in Creve Coeur, Illinois.

FORREST B. NANCE, Radarman Tech 3, served in the Philippines, Sea of China and Sea of Japan patrols during the Korean War, in Navy (Air), which he entered after graduating from high school. He attended Radar School, then was sent to Far East to fly night patrol over the China and Japan Seas from a base in the Philippines. On August 7, 1952, his plane left Luzon, a propeller fell off the aging plane and it crashed into mountains on the north end of Luzon. There were no survivors.

Forrest was born June 25, 1931 at Chester, Illinois, son of Jesse B. and Effa Parker Nance. He was 21 years old at time of his death and left a wife and unborn daughter. He is buried in Evergreen Cemetery, Chester, Illinois.

RUSSELL PARKER NANCE, Staff Sergeant, enlisted in National Guard in May 1954. In 1952 he was called to active duty during the Korean War. His service was at Fort Leonard Wood, Missouri, Camp Cook, California and Fort Lewis, Washington.

Discharged in May 1954, he remained in the Tacoma, Washington. area, where he still lives after an accident caused him to be retired from job as Battalion Chief of the Tacoma City Fire Department.

He was born in Chester, Illinois on August 27, 1933, the son of Jesse and Effa Parker Nance.

GORDON STUMP NEISLER, served during WWII in the U.S. Army, 1941-45, serving first with the Infantry, then Military Police and finishing with the Medical Corps, primarily at Fort Ord, California.

He was born September 17, 1915 in Montgomery County, Illinois, the son of Edwin Burrell and Winifred Ethel Stump Neisler, and died August 11, 2002, Sparta, Illinois.

GWENETH JEANNE (BOLINO) NIEHAUS, E-3, served in the U.S. Air Force from August 1976 to November 1977. She was born in St. Louis, Missouri on February 16, 1952, daughter of Bert F. and Ruth V. Bourgeois Bolino. She served

E-3 Gweneth J. Niehaus

as an aerospace ground mechanic at Luke AFB, Phoenix Arizona where she was injured, honorably discharged, and now a disabled veteran. She served one year, two months and 16 days. She is currently employed by the U.S. Postal Service.

LEONARD ARTHUR NITZSCHE, Private First Class, was drafted, into the military in August 1969. Leonard took his basic training at Fort Leonard Wood, Missouri, AIT at Fort Ord, California, then shipped to Vietnam with Company B, 2nd Battalion, 3rd Infantry, 199th Light Infantry Brigade.

Pfc. Leonard A. Nitzsche

He was killed in action on April 8, 1970, 25 miles NE of Saigon Providence-Long Khanh. Leonard was a platoon leader on a reconnaissance mission.

Leonard was born January 28, 1950 in Red Bud, Illinois, son of C.S. "Bud" and Marjorie (Rockwell) Nitzsche.

HERBERT NORMAN, Private, enlisted in WWI at Cobden, Illinois, April 4, 1918. He served in Sahxse Division Quartermaster Corps until May 6, 1919. He was born at Creal Springs, Illinois, but spent his adult life in the Rockwood, Illinois area. Herbert is buried at Jefferson Barracks Cemetery in St. Louis, Missouri.

CASPAR NURNBERGER, served in Civil War in Company H, 49th Infantry

Casper Nurnberger

Division, which was formed in Monroe County, Illinois. His service was primarily in Kentucky and Tennessee. He mustered out of service at Alton, Illinois, November 22, 1865. He later was not able to do physical labor, and after much letter writing finally received a small pension.

DAN "DANNY" NURNBERGER, served in U.S. Navy during Korean Conflict. He enlisted October 12, 1952, and was sworn in at Soldiers Memorial in St. Louis, Missouri. Basic training was at San Diego, California and advanced training at Norman, Oklahoma and Millington, Tennessee.

Dan Nurnberger

Danny was sent to Treasure Island, California to be sent to Korea, but when truce was signed, he was re-assigned to Alameda Naval Air Station in San Francisco Bay until October 14, 1944, when was discharged.

HARRY NURNBERGER was drafted into service for WWII in 1943. At the time he was 36 years of age, with two children and a third on the way. His service was in the Navy aboard USS *Sherbourne* (APA-205). Primary duty was in charge of laundry, but in times of battle he was a "talker" in a gun turret. During his service he covered 65,000 miles of the Pacific, from the Aleutian Islands to the Philippines, from

Harry Nurnberger

San Francisco to the China Sea. His ship was in Tokyo Bay when Japan surrendered.

KENT NURNBERGER joined National Guard, Company B, 133rd Signal Battalion at Sparta, Illinois in October 1983. Basic training was at Fort McClellan, Gladson, Alabama and advanced training at Fort Gordon, Augusta, Georgia.

Kent Nurnberger

Transferred to El Cahoon, California from January 1999 to November 2001, then back to the Sparta unit. Kent was called for 30 days of flood duty in 1993 and served at Fountain Creek, Monroe County and greater Quincy, Illinois area. He resigned in 1996.

MYRON HARVEY O'BRIEN enlisted in Army in October 1945 at end of WWII, discharged in August 1947, and served in Reserves until 1954. He also served many years in Civil Air Patrol.

Myron H. O'Brien

Employed by Monsanto Company, Sauget, Illinois, for 30 years, Myron died November 23, 1996. He was born June 26, 1927, son of Harvey and __ Brayfield O'Brien.

WILLIAM J. ODLE, Fire Controlman 3/c, served in WWII in Coast Guard in Pacific area as Mark II rangefinder operator. He entered service July 2, 1942 and was discharged August 8, 1946. He saw action at Okinawa, received Asiatic-Pacific WWII Victory Medal, Good Conduct and China Service, Sharpshooter Rifle and Expert Pistol Medals.

He again entered service for Korean War, April 11, 1949, as corporal with 1st Division Cavalry, 7th Regiment, Mike Company 3rd Battalion as Infantry Squad Leader. He was in battle of Chosin Reservoir and was wounded at Cunahoin Reservoir on April 8, 1951.

Discharged October 1, 1953, his awards include the United Nations, National Defense, Korean Service w/3 Battle Stars, Good Conduct, Purple Heart and Combat Infantry Badge w/Rifle Bar. William was born December 3, 1924 and served 37 years as 14th District Quartermaster.

MELVIN H. OHLAU, Corporal, born in Steeleville, Illinois to Arnold and Alwine Meierhapp Ohlau on September 23, 1928. He enlisted November 13, 1950, and was sent to Fort Leonard Wood, Missouri for basic training, then sent to Camp Fuji, Japan, near Tokyo, from April 1951 until May 1952, when he went with the Signal Corps, 7th Division to Central Korea. Melvin was in Korea until October 1952. He was discharged at Camp Carson, Colorado on November 8, 1952.

Cpl. Melvin H. Ohlau

He married Betty Runge on March 10, 1951 and now resides in St. Louis, Missouri.

ROGER W. OHLAU, Sergeant, born July 21, 1931 in Chester, Illinois, son of Walter and Dorothy Fricke Ohlau. Roger enlisted in Illinois 44th Division National Guard on May 10, 1951. He was trained at Camp Cooke, California as part of Company D, 135th Engineers Battalion. He made corporal on August 1, 1951.

On December 10, 1952 he arrived in headquarters near Chunchon, Korea, just north of the 38th Parallel. There he joined the 1343rd Engineer Combat Battalion and

Sgt. Roger W. Ohlau

served as message center clerk. He made sergeant on April 4, 1953 and ended his military service on May 9, 1954.

Roger returned to Chester and married Betty Wucher. He worked as a carpenter and became a construction foreman for several construction companies. He died May 30, 1999.

DONALD O'REAR, Torpedoman 2/c, served in the Eastern Fleet of the U.S. Navy out of Norfolk, Virginia from July 1955 to July 1959. He served on the USS *New* (DDE-818) as part of Task Alda, Anti Submarine Warfare Unit, which consisted of six destroyers, one aircraft carrier, one submarine and a fuel supply ship. He served two tours overseas.

Returning from military service, he worked at McDonnell Douglas Aircraft and retired from the coal industry. Donald was born August 17, 1936 in Jasper, Alabama. His parents are Wiley S. and Hattie M. Smith O'Rear.

ALBERT J. OSER, Sergeant, inducted June 16, 1941, Fort Sheridan, Illinois and sent to Camp Polk, Louisiana, 83rd Reconnaissance, Company A, 7th Armored Division. Desert training was in California, followed by Fort Benning, Georgia and Radio School in South Carolina.

Sgt. Albert Oser

He sailed from Camp Shanks, New York on *Queen Mary* to Scotland, England; St. Lo, Chartres, Reims and Verdun in France; crossed Moselle and went into Holland. Albert was wounded near Weert and sent to hospital in England. He was next assigned to 542 Ordnance Company, then back to all places he had been.

European war ended when he was in Lubbecke, Germany. He had enough points to get out, but war in Japan was still going on. He got home in 1945.

HAROLD A. PAPENBERG, Corporal, born December 17, 1923 at Red Bud, Illinois, son of Oscar and Ella Luebkemann Papenberg. He was drafted into Army shortly after WWII in April 1946 and was

Cpl. Harold A. Papenberg

honorably discharged in April 1947. His tour of duty was in Philippine Islands with 3rd Platoon, Battery D-52AART Battalion. After discharge he worked as a salesman for Randolph Service Company. Harold died January 26, 1988.

SHIRLEY WARD PARKER, Private First Class, served as a rifle combat infantryman in WWII, in Normandy, Rhineland and Northern France. He entered service August 6, 1943 and was discharged December 12, 1945.

Pfc. Shirley Ward Parker

He earned the WWII Victory Medal w/3 Overseas Bars, European-African-Middle Eastern Ribbon w/3 Bronze Battle Stars, Good Conduct Medal and Purple Heart.

Shirley was born in Riley Lake, Illinois, May 14, 1909, son of John W. and Ada Ward Parker.

BEN R. PARRISH, Corporal, born in Chester, Illinois, October 17, 1930, son of George R. and Claudia Johnson Parrish. He enlisted in the Army, July 31, 1948 and assigned to the 12th Regiment, 1st Cavalry. The 12th disbanded two months later and he was assigned to 8th Army, 5th Ordnance and sent to Fukuoka, Japan.

He had been in Japan 18 months when the Korean War started on June 25, 1950. He was put aboard an LST and landed at Pusan in South Korea on July 1, 1950, where (after learning to drive and getting his license in Japan) he was given a truck driving job, in Transportation. He transported supplies and ammunition many times from one end of Korea to the other.

They were at Sinuiju, when Chinese troops came across the Yalu River and attacked them heavily. Due to extreme cold weather, their equipment was not in the best working condition and they were pursued for about three days (only 30 to 45 minutes behind them), blowing up bridges as they came.

When they reached Pyongyang, they were able to rest, before moving on to Seoul, where the tide of the attack turned in their favor. He spent 14 months in Korea, and nine of those months were considered combat time.

He received the Japanese Occupation Medal, American Defense Medal, Korean Service Medal w/5 Battle Stars, United Nations Medal, as well as the Good Conduct Medal. When they returned to Sasebo, Japan, they took their second hot shower in 14 months. The shower and clean sheets sure felt great after bathing in creeks and sleeping where ever they could for all those months.

Returning to the U.S., he was eventually sent to Fort Benning, Georgia, where he was discharged May 5, 1952.

ROGER DALE PARTINGTON, Captain, enlisted in the Marines on December 12, 1962, after attending Murray State and SIU-Carbondale Universities. Roger achieved the rank of 2nd lieutenant and was designated as a helicopter pilot in 1965. In 1967 Roger advanced to the rank of captain and served his first stint

Capt. Roger D. Partington

in Vietnam. He returned to Vietnam in 1969 for his second tour of duty.

During his times in Vietnam, Roger was awarded many citations (Air Medals and Gold Stars) for meritorious achievements in aerial flight during combat. On November 1, 1969, the helicopter Roger was commanding over the Bay of Pigs in Vietnam exploded and burned; his body was not recovered.

Roger was born December 12, 1940 in Sparta, Illinois, son of Gene and Leota (Colbert) Partington. Roger is survived by his wife, two sons, a daughter-in-law, two grandchildren, two brothers, a sister, and 21 nieces and nephews.

GILBERT PATTERSON, Seaman 1/c, of Sparta, Illinois, enlisted in Navy July 27, 1942, was honorably discharged December 14, 1945 and died just four years later on October 29, 1949. He is buried in Caledonia Cemetery in Sparta, Illinois. Gilbert was born July 2, 1922, in Sparta, next of kin listed on death certificate is Anna Patterson Wilson.

ANTHONY M. PAUTLER, Corporal, born November 2, 1930, Evansville, Illinois, son of Lawrence and Gertrude Young Pautler. He was drafted in U.S. Army January 16, 1952 and served in the 2nd Infantry Division in Korea, participating in "Heartbreak Ridge" and "Old Baldy" battles.

Cpl. Anthony Pautler

He was awarded the Korean Service Medal w/2 Bronze Service Stars, United Nations Service Medal and Combat Infantry Badge. He was honorably discharged October 15, 1953.

Returning home, his career was with the postal service. He died September 18, 1995.

BRIAN P. PAUTLER, Sergeant, served in the U.S. Air Force from June 30, 1981 to June 29, 1985, the son of Anthony M. and Margaret G. Heuman Pautler. He was born November 11, 1963. Brian served in the 513 FMS at RAF Mildenhall, USAFE and 4EMS at Seymour Johnson AFB, North Carolina.

Sgt. Brian J. Pautler

He received the Asiatic-Pacific Theater Ribbon, AF Good Conduct, AF Achievement, AF Longevity Service, AF Outstanding Unit Award and AF Overseas Long Tour Service Ribbon.

DANIEL JOSEPH PAUTLER, SP4, served in the U.S. Army from September 14, 1992 to June 15, 1995 and from June 20, 1999 to June 20, 2000 with the National Guard.

Spec/4 Daniel J. Pautler

He enlisted and served in Manneheim, Germany for two years as an armor crewman and the driver for the Company Commander's Humvee. He served one year in the National Guard as a communication technician. He is currently employed with General Motors as a warranty field adjuster

Daniel is from Evansville, Illinois and was born June 14, 1974, the son of Edward and Carla Pinter Pautler.

EDWARD B. PAUTLER, served in the U.S. Army in WWI from June 24, 1918 to December 13, 1918, with the 323 Guard of 1st Company. He was born in Randolph County November 19, 1894, died February 4, 1941, and is buried at St. Pius Cemetery, Walsh, Illinois.

EDWARD PHILIP PAUTLER, DT3, enlisted in the Navy in June 1960 and was discharged in May 1963. During his tour of duty, Ed attended U.S. Navy Dental Technician School and was with Company 200 during basic training.

D.T.-3 Edward Phillip Pautler

After graduation he was assigned to Main Navy, Washington, DC, where he attended the University of Virginia during his stay. He served in the Bay of Pigs (Kennedy Administration

Upon his discharge he attended Saint Louis University and University of Missouri, graduating with BS/BA degrees in 1968, after which he stayed in the dental field and is still a field sales consultant.

Ed was born in Evansville, Illinois on June 6, 1942 to Clyde W. and Anna Marie Pautler.

NORMAN A. PAUTLER, SP4, Headquarters Company, 1st SQD, 1st Cavalry, 1st Armored Division. He served in the U.S. Army from October 1960 to October 1962. After training at Fort Leonard Wood, Missouri he served remaining time at Fort Hood, Texas as a field communication specialist in the 1st Armor Tank Division. After completing active duty in 1962, he served four years in the inactive standby reserve. He was discharged in September 1966.

Spec.4 Norman Pautler

Returning home, he worked as a quality control inspector at McDonnell Douglas and retired from Boeing Company, St. Louis, Missouri after 42 years of service.

He is from Evansville, Illinois, the son of Lawrence and Gertrude Young Pautler. He is the father of two children, Kevin Pautler and Rhonda Pautler Fiechti, and the grandfather of Bryce Pautler, Brenda and Brittany Fiechtl. He and his wife Margie Walter Pautler now live in Red Bud, Illinois.

PAUL A. PAUTLER, Sergeant, served in the U.S. Army, 1953-55, as a wheel vehicle mechanic, Headquarters and Service Company, 682nd Engineer Battalion, Fort Benning, Georgia.

Sgt. Paul A. Pautler

Returning home, he worked at International Shoe Company, Evansville, continuing to farm. In 1993 he went to work for Gilster-MaryLee Corporation. He died August 18, 1999.

He was born October 12, 1932, Evansville, Illinois, the son of Ben and Marcella Gaertner Pautler.

ROBERT G. PAUTLER, Petty Officer 1/c, served in the U.S. Navy, March 1952 to February 1956. He was born June 16, 1933, Walsh, Illinois, son of Ezra and Bertha Stork Pautler. He served on the destroyer, *J.W. Thomason,* and made three

P.O. 1/c Robert G. Pautler

cruises to the Western Pacific before being discharged. At a later date he re-enlisted in Navy Reserves (Seabees) and attained the rank of chief petty officer before retiring.

ROSS L. PAUTLER, Staff Sergeant, entered service December 8, 1943, took basic training at Camp Blanding, Florida as combat infantryman. He served in campaigns and battles in Normandy, Northern France, Ardennes, Rhineland and Central Europe. He received many medals including Purple Heart.

S/Sgt Ross L. Pautler

Ross was born in Randolph County, December 9, 1917, son of Michael and Edna Ross Pautler, he died April 16, 1970.

ROY PAUTLER, SP4, served in the U.S. Army, January 7, 1964 to January 6, 1966. He completed basic training at Fort Leonard Wood, Missouri; Missile School at Fort Bliss (Logan Heights) TX; and Nike Hercules Missile Base, Shreveport, Louisiana. He was born in Evansville, Illinois on January 25, 1941, the son of Clyde and Anna Marie Parker Pautler.

CHARLES L. PAYNE, Private, born at Rockwood, Illinois, May 5, 1891, the son of Samuel and Emma Payne. He enlisted in the U.S. Marine Corps on May 11, 1917 at St. Louis, Missouri. He qualified as a sharpshooter May 22, 1918 and served in the Dominican Republic from June 14, 1917 until December 12, 1919. He was discharged at Philadelphia Naval Yard on December 23, 1919.

Charles died July 4, 1935 and is buried in Evergreen Cemetery in Chester, Illinois.

LEONARD A. PERZIA, staff sergeant, served 21 months in Asiatic-Pacific Theater as section leader of machine guns and seven man crews in northern Solomons and south Philippine Islands during WWII with 164th Infantry Americal Division. He went into service February 6, 1943 and was discharged February 1, 1946.

His awards are Asiatic-Pacific Campaign Ribbon, American Theatre Campaign Ribbon, three Overseas Bars, Victory Ribbon, Good Conduct, Philippine Liberation Medal w/Bronze Star

Leonard was born December 12, 1922, in Willisville, Illinois, son of Guy and Angeling Russo Perzia, and now makes his home in Randolph County.

WILLIAM J. PESTOR, Private, served in the U.S. Army, WWI. He was born January 21, 1890, near Wine Hill/Steeleville area, Illinois, the son of Henry Sr. and Caroline Messenbrink Pestor. He was a farmer and member of the Steeleville American Legion. He died March 24, 1976 and is buried in St. Peter Lutheran Cemetery, Wine Hill, where he was a member.

FRED J. PETERS, Chief Boatswain's Mate, enlisted in Navy Seabee's October 5, 1942. He served on Guam, Aleutian Islands and Asiatic-Pacific Theater with 301st Naval Construction Unit in WWII.

Chief BM Fred J. Peters

Discharged October 31, 1945, he returned to work at Commonwealth Steel in Granite City, Illinois. The son of William and Ruth Kempfer Peters, he was born February 3, 1911 and died March 28, 1975.

HARRY M. PETERS, Tech 4, served in Battery C, 10th Field Artillery and 27th Division New York National Guard, during WWII. He entered service March 31, 1943, trained at Camp Roberts, California, served at Hickam Air Strip, Hawaii, Ryukyus Islands, Saipan and Tinian in Mariana Islands, Okinawa, and in occupied forces at Wakamastu, Japan.

Memorable experience was meeting his brother, Fred J. Peters, on Saipan. He was discharged December 24, 1945, and his awards include three Bronze Stars.

Harry was born in Ellis Grove, Illinois on September 21, 1923, son of William H. and Ruth Kempfer.

DELMAR L. PETROWSKE, Private First Class, served in the U.S. Army from 1948-51. He was born April 5, 1930 in Chester, Illinois, son of Herman and Florence Singer Petrowske. PFC Petrowske served with Company C, 9th Infantry Regiment, 2nd Division in Korea and gave his life for his country. He was killed in action on February 11, 1951.

Pfc. Delmar L. Petrowske

DONALD R. PETROWSKE, Specialist 4, was drafted into the Army on August 14, 1969. He served 14 months in Vietnam, first as a medic, then as a radio/telephone operator. On March 18, 1971 he received an honorable discharge.

Donald worked for the city of Chester Gas Department and then for Peabody Coal Company for 21 years. Donald was born in Red Bud, Illinois on February 16, 1950. He was the son of Raymond and Dorothy (Bodeker) Petrowske and died August 31, 1995, as a result of lung cancer.

ELROY J. PETROWSKE, Specialist 4, was drafted in February 1968 for service in Vietnam. He served with Company B, 2nd Battalion, 1st Infantry Americal Division, as part of the jungle patrol in northern Vietnam.

He did see action and received an honorable discharge in June 1969. His awards include the Purple Heart and Commendation Medal.

Born in Chester, Illinois on June 15, 1948, son of Jesse and Mildred Alms Petrowske, he now works for U.S. Postal Service as a rural mail carrier at Rockwood, Illinois.

HERMAN A. PETROWSKE, Private, born February 11, 1896, at Rockwood, Illinois, son of Theophile and Magdalene Kloss Petrowske. He served in France with Company G, 22nd Engineers, 3rd Platoon in

Pvt. Herman A. Petrowske

WWI. Inducted June 24, 1918 at Chester, Illinois, he was discharged July 16, 1919, at Camp Grant, Illinois. Herman died July 20, 1977.

ROGER L. PETROWSKE, S2/c, served in the U.S Navy from January 23, 1946 to November 24, 1947. He was a Naval Armed Guard, U.S. Property Security, in Tsingtao, China from July 1946 to September 1947. Tsingtao was Headquarters for the 7th Fleet.

Roger was born in Chester, Illinois, February 16, 1928, son of Herman and Florence Singer Petrowske. He retired from Illinois Department of Corrections December 31, 1990.

THOMAS W. PHILLIPS, Aviation Radioman 2/c, enlisted in the U.S. Navy in 1943. He was sent to Radio and Radar School at U.S. Naval Technical Center, Memphis, Tennessee, then to aerial gunnery training at Purcell, Oklahoma. He served 19 months aboard the aircraft carrier USS *Antietam* (CV-36), flying in the SB2C Helldiver with Bomb Squadron 89 in the South Pacific.

A/Radioman 2/c Thomas W. Phillips

Thomas was born in Sparta, Illinois on December 25, 1925, to parents, Thomas W. and Mary Florence Weir Phillips. After his discharge in 1946, he spent 40 years at World Color Press in Sparta, Illinois and retired from there.

THOMAS W. PHILLIPS, Cook 6/c, born at Benton, Illinois, on October 17, 1891, son of Willis Allen and Amanda Webb Phillips. He served 1917-18 in Germany with Illinois Cook 6, Cook Company ASC in WWI. Thomas died May 28, 1958.

Spec. 4 Donald R. Petrowske

Seaman 2/c Roger L. Petrowske

Cook 6/c Thomas W. Phillips

JOSEPH E. PHOENIX, E-5, enlisted in the Army in March 2000. After 12 weeks infantry boot camp, he graduated with honors, then went to Fort Benning, Georgia. Joe received his airborne wings from there and graduated the Ranger Infantry Program. Then he was sent to Hunter Army Airfield in Georgia. In the fall of 2002 he went to Fort Stewart.

E-5 Joseph E. Phoenix

Joe is with the 3rd Infantry Division ACO 2/7 1st Platoon. Joe moved up in rank in two months and went to California for desert training. He became their team leader and gunner in a Bradley unit before deploying to Operation Iraqi Freedom.

Joe was born November 8, 1979 in Murphysboro, Illinois, the son of Michael and Rita (Bryant) Feaman.

JOHN WILLIAM PIERCE, Private First Class, enlisted into the Marines on June 27, 1956. He was with the H&S Company, 3rd Battalion, 1st Marine, 1st Marine Division (Reinforcements) Field Marine Force, Camp Pendleton, California. John was a 0341-Mortar Man.

He left the States and went to the Philippines, while there he got sick and was put on the Temporary Disability Retired list. John earned the Good Conduct award. He had brown hair, blue eyes, 6'1/4" and 178 lbs. John was discharged from Treasure Island, San Francisco, California on December 31, 1958.

He was born in Sparta, Illinois on February 10, 1937 to Roy E. and Rosa P. (Morrow) Pierce. John still lives in Sparta, Illinois.

RUFUS PIERCE, Tech-4, enlisted into the Army on October 26, 1940 from East Saint Louis, Illinois. Rufus was assigned with the 635 AAA AW Battalion. His military specialty was 345 Truck Driver-Light. Rufus qualified for the MG MM Rifle, MM Driver and Mechanic Bar with W Bar. He

T-4 Rufus Pierce

fought in the following Battles and Campaigns: Normandy, Northern France, Ardennes, Rhineland, Central Europe, and also in ground combat while in WWII.

Rufus spent one year, four months and one day in the States and three years, three months and 27 days overseas. He went overseas in February 1942 and returned June 7, 1945. He earned the American Service Ribbon, European-African-Middle Eastern Theater Ribbon w/Silver Battle Star and Bronze Battle Star. He also earned six Overseas Service Bars. He was honorably discharged June 23, 1945 from Fort Sheridan, Illinois. Rufus had brown hair, brown eyes and was 5'1" and 185 lbs.

Rufus was born in Jasper, Alabama on October 21, 1917, the son of James Thomas and Anna R. Honeycutt Pierce. He was a life member of VFW 2698 Sparta, Illinois. Rufus died in November 1993 and was buried in Jefferson Barracks National Cemetery.

WARREN DAVID PIERCE, Corporal, served in the Navy from August 1968 to November 1970 with the U.S. Navy Seabees. Dave spent two tours in Vietnam. His first tour was outside of Da Nang "Monkey Mountain." His second tour was at Dong Hoi on the DMZ. Dave was in charge of building a road through the jungle. Civilians hauled the six inch rock and they put asphalt on top. While in Vietnam Dave served with the MCB-5.

He joined the National Guard in August 1983 and retired in November 2002. Dave had 22 years of service and attained the rank sergeant first class.

He was born in Sparta, Illinois on February 3, 1949, son of Roy Sr. and Rose (Morrow) Pierce.

ROY D. PINKERTON, Corporal, served in the U.S. Army, WWI, from July 18, 1918 to September 9, 1919, Service Park Unit #531 MTC. He served AEF in France, November 1918 to August 1919, and was discharged from Camp Grant, Illinois.

He was born in Chester on August 7, 1893, son of Isaac and Harriet Gilchrist Pinkerton. He was a farmer, and after discharge, a mechanic and worked for Department of Corrections.

THEODORE T. PIRKLE, Navy Apprentice Seaman, born December 17, 1901, Hartwell, Indiana. He enlisted May 27, 1922 and served aboard the USS *Savanah*. Discharged May 26, 1926, he died in Sparta, Illinois November 2, 1938 and is buried at Caledonia Cemetery in Sparta.

KLONDIS R. PIRTLE, Sergeant, born June 13, 1906, Warren County, Arkansas, son of Henry Clay and Eliza Thornton Pirtle, served in the Army during WWII after being drafted in 1943 at age 37. He was stationed at Fort Hood, Texas and Fort Meade, Maryland. He worked in Army Post Office and helped train troops for D-Day Invasion.

Sgt. Klondis R. Pirtle

Discharged in 1945, he returned to Sparta, Illinois and worked at Lynn Furniture Company. Klondis died February 1, 1985.

JACK LEE PITTMAN, Sergeant, served in the U.S. Army from January 1952

Jack Lee Pittman

to December 1953 with 101st Airborne Division and 43rd Heavy Motor Co. After completing basic training at Camp Breckenridge, KY, he was sent to Augsburg, Germany.

After discharge he entered a training program with Brown Shoe Company and completed 40 years with the company, ending with Child Life Shoes and Munro Shoe Company. He was born February 12, 1931, the son of John Irvin and Roxie Tindall Pittman.

JOE POENITSKE, Private, was inducted into WWI, June 24, 1918, at Chester, Illinois, at the age of 23 years. He served with American Expeditionary Forces from October 27, 1918 until May 21, 1919, in the 95th Casualty Company and was discharged at Camp Grant, Illinois on May 30, 1919. Joe was born in March 1895 and died ca. 1967. His parents were Andrew and Josephine Shemonic Poenitske.

RICHARD A. PONISKE, Private First Class, served in WWII in Normandy, Northern France, Ardennes, Rhineland and Central Europe, with 5th Evacuation Hospital as a surgical technician. He was inducted May 27, 1943, entered active service June 10, 1943, at Camp Grant, Illinois and was discharged December 15, 1945.

Pfc. Richard A. Poniske

He received Good Conduct Medal, WWII Victory Medal, European-African-Middle Eastern Theater Ribbon w/Silver Battle Star and four Overseas Bars.

He was born February 16, 1925 in Chester, Illinois, son of Thomas and Anna M. Grott Poniske.

EDWARD H. POWLEY, Motor Machinist Mate 3/c, served in Navy during WWII. He was inducted in August 1944, sent to boot camp at Great Lakes, Illinois,

MMM 3/c Edward H. Powley

transferred to Little Creek, Virginia for training as mine sweeper engineer.

They picked up new mine sweeper at Mobile, Alabama, the USS *Murrelett* (AM-372), and after two month shakedown cruise out of Norfolk, Virginia, they sailed to San Pedro, California, by way of Panama Canal, and on to Hawaii. They island hopped through the Pacific to Sasebo, Japan, sweeping mines off the coast of Korea. He was discharged in June 1946.

Edward was born April 1, 1926, Pana, Illinois, son of A.E. and Nora Welten Powley, and now lives in Chester, Illinois.

JOHN C. PRESTON, Sergeant E-5, served in 1st Marine Air Wing, WER-17 in the Vietnam Era. He enlisted in December 1969 and served as heavy equipment operator (MOS 1340) with 1st MAW, WER-17 in Iwakuni, Japan. He had the honor of being Marine of the Month in August 1971.

After his discharge in December 1971, he returned to work at Illinois Power/Dynegy where he is currently employed. John was born in Washington DC on October 22, 1946, son of Scherer Preston and Wahneta Roehrkasse Preston.

JOHN D. PRICE, Sergeant E-5, entered the military in February 1970. John served with the 6th and 32nd Artillery. John served in Cam Rahn, Qui Nhon, Pleiku tri border. He served in a mobile heavy artillery battery on a 175mm Howitzer self-propelled with the 6/32 artillery "Proud Americans."

He was discharged in September 1971. John was born in Belleville, Illinois on July 21, 1949 to Howard and Beulah (Pflasterer) Price.

HARRY W. PRIESTLEY, Master Sergeant, was inducted into WWII February

M/Sgt. Harry W. Priestley

25, 1943. He participated in the battle of Normandy, and was stationed in Northern France, serving as a quartermaster with Headquarters Special Troops, 79th Infantry Division. He was discharged December 15, 1945.

Harry was born in Dardiff, Alabama on May 20, 1916, son of Harry and Emma Norman Priestley.

GEORGE DAVID PROSEK, Private, served in 326th Field Artillery, 84th Division in WWI. He was born November 2, 1895 in Chester, Illinois, son of Joseph

Pvt. George D. Prosek

and Francis Paulus Prosek. He died June 3, 1926 and was given a military funeral by American Legion. Burial was in St. Mary's Cemetery, Chester, Illinois.

GILBERT GEORGE PROSEK, Private First Class, enlisted November 15, 1942 in U.S. Marines and served in 1st

Pfc. Gilbert G. Prosek

Marine Division at Cape Gloucester, New Britain and Tarawa Islands in Pacific War Zone.

He made three charges against Japanese machine gun position so his company could advance. While providing cover from an exposed position for a member of his platoon, he lost his life by a Japanese sniper on January 3, 1944. He was awarded Purple Heart and Navy Cross.

Gilbert was born in Chester, Illinois October 1, 1921, the son of George D. and Theresa E. Grott Prosek. His mother received letters of condolences from General McArthur and T.C. Kinkaid, Commander of 7th Fleet.

DOROTHY R. (IVANOUK) RABE, enlisted in WWII March 9, 1943 at St. Louis, Missouri to serve in National Emergency. She was issued honorable discharge September 14, 1945 from M.B. Navy Yard, Washington, DC and received Honorable Service and Honorable Discharge buttons.

FREDERICK LUDWIG RABE, born in Hanover, Germany, June 22, 1833, son of Henry and Mary Fortmann Rabe, came to U.S. about 1857 to avoid training in German army.

Frederick L. Rabe

He enlisted in Union Army February 15, 1865 at Camp Butler, Illinois with 154th Illinois Infantry, Company F. He was sent to Louisville, Kentucky, then Murfreesboro and Tullahoma, Tennessee, and garrison duty in Nashville.

Discharged September 18, 1865, he returned to Randolph County. Service records show him a part of 154th Illinois Infantry, his tombstone bears 80th Illinois Infantry, Company D.

CHARLES WAYNE RADER, Lance Corporal, enlisted in the Marines July 21, 1963. Charles went to Vietnam and served with G Company, 2nd Battalion, 9th Marines. He fought in the Harvest Moon Battle.

L/Cpl Charles W. Rader

After serving 12 months and 20 days in Vietnam with only six days left overseas, he stepped on a land mine and gave his life for his country on March 3, 1966. He was two weeks short of his 21st birthday. Charles was born March 17, 1945 Red Bud, Illinois, son of George and Sylvia (Neihouse) Rader.

GEORGE EARL RADER, Corporal, enlisted in the Marines December 5, 1965. George served 13 months in Vietnam working in Motor Transport with the 2nd Battalion, 3rd Marine Division. He hauled ammo and other supplies from Da Nang to DMZ. He fought in Hill 55 Battle.

Cpl. George E. Rader

George was discharged in San Francisco January 4, 1968 and flew to Los Angeles for flight to St. Louis, Missouri. By chance, he met up with his brother Russell, who just got out of boot camp, and they both got to fly home on the same flight.

He was born April 24, 1946 to George and Sylvia (Neihouse) Rader in Red Bud, Illinois.

RUSSELL ALLEN RADER, Lance Corporal, enlisted in the Marine Corps August 22, 1967. Russell was discharged May 6, 1969. He graduated as honor man in boot camp and served 13 months on Okinawa for Supply Company, Supply Battalion, 3rd FSR, FMF, Vietnam.

L/Cpl. Russell A. Rader

Russ worked for the city of Chester, Illinois. for 28 years and retired as water superintendent in 2000. He was born in Redbud, Illinois on April 24, 1948, son of George and Sylvia (Neihouse) Rader.

JAKE B. RADER, Corporal, born September 5, 1923, Rockwood, Illinois to Jacob and Della Boyd Rader. He enlisted

Cpl. Jake B. Rader

in Army during WWII and worked in Chicago as construction foreman. Jake died in Chester, Illinois September 23, 1975.

PAUL ARTHUR RADER, Private, served in North Africa with 78th Smoke Generator Company during WWII. He entered service February 14, 1942 and was discharged October 20, 1943. Graduated wheel vehicle half-ton advance course as an auto mechanic.

Pvt. Paul A. Rader

He was born in Chester, Illinois in 1920, son of Jacob and Della Boyd Rader.

WILBUR EARL RADER, Tech Sergeant, enlisted in June 1942 in WWII and served with 315th Infantry, 79th Infantry Division, Company F. He was under General George S. Patton and fought in France from June 1944 until killed by machine gun fire while supervising a mortar attack at Chatenois in north eastern France, September 14, 1944.

T/Sgt. Wilbur E. Rader

Wilbur was born October 22, 1918, Cora City, Illinois, son of Jacob and Della Boyd Rader.

WILBUR PAUL RADER, Corporal, enlisted in the Marines in 1961 and served in a weapon platoon in Vietnam. Wilbur was an M-60 machine gunner. He was discharged in 1965. After returning home, he worked as a prison guard, a card dealer in Las Vegas, and a Bartender.

Cpl. Wilbur P. Rader

Wilbur was born April 4, 1943 in Chester, Illinois, son of George and Sylvia (Neihouse) Rader, and died June 19, 1996 from brain tumors.

KENNETH W. RAGLAND, Corporal E-4, entered the service in November 1965 and took basic training at Fort Leonard Wood, Missouri. He then went to Fort Campbell, Kentucky for his AIT, then sent to Vietnam. He served with the 3rd Army Division, 54th Battalion and 523 Company in Qui Nhon.

Kenny was honorably discharged in

Cpl. E-4 Kenneth W. Ragland

November 1967, then joined the Illinois National Guard for 13 years attaining rank of staff sergeant E-6. He was born November 5, 1946 in Red Bud, Illinois, son of Roy K. and Audrey (Kempfer) Ragland.

MASON C. RAGLAND, Gunnery Sergeant, served in WWII with 1st Marine Division. He enlisted in January 1939 and was in Iceland from July 1941 until March 1942; in Pacific War Zone from August 1942 to November 1945, Guadalcanal, Peleliu, Okinawa and other islands in the area.

G/Sgt. Mason C. Ragland

Discharged in November 1946, he worked for a transportation company in New Orleans until retirement. Mason was born January 5, 1918, West Frankfort, Illinois, son of Norman H. and Callie Crain Ragland, and died in 1989. One son was killed in action in Vietnam.

RON K. RAGLAND, Sergeant First Class, served in the U.S. Army from October 1966 to September 1969 and from November 1990 to December 1991. He enlisted in 1966 and served as a combat engineer in West Germany with Company C, 54th Engineer Battalion during Vietnam era.

He earned the National Defense Service Medal and Sharp Shooters M-14 Medal. He was discharged in 1969.

Ron returned to active duty in 1990

Spec-4 Ron K. Ragland

Sgt. 1/c Ron K. Ragland

as a Military Policeman for Desert Storm and served at Fort Riley, Kansas, Saudia Arabia and Kuwait as operations NCO and military police investigator in Southwest Asia. He later taught at NCO Academy at Fort Leonard Wood.

He retired with 20 years Reserve and active duty. He was born February 11, 1948, Chester, Illinois, the son of Roy and Audrey Kempfer Ragland.

ROY K. RAGLAND, Gunnery Sergeant, was in WWII with 4th Marine Division. He entered service November 26, 1940 with basic training at San Diego, California. He served in Iceland, July 1941 to March 1942 and in Pacific area, December 1943 to October 1945, Saipan, Tinian and Iwo Jima. He was discharged at Paris Island, South Carolina on November 26, 1946.

Roy was born July 18, 1920, son of Norman and Callie Crain Ragland.

G/Sgt. Roy K. Ragland

CLARENCE H. RAHLFS, Corporal, served in WWII from April 1945 until November 1946. He was born in Chester, Illinois,

Cpl. Clarence H. Rahlfs

son of Harry and Clara Gentsch Rahlfs.

HARRY A. RAHLFS, Private First Class, served with 517th Artillery, Missile Battalion (Nike-AJax) for the protection of Detroit and large cities during the cold war. Missile batteries were located around the cities for protection against enemy attacks. He went into service November 5, 1956 and was discharged November 4, 1958.

Pfc. Harry A. Rahlfs

Harry was born in Red Bud, Illinois on May 11, 1938, son of Harry H. and Clara Gentsch Rahlfs.

ORVILLE RAHN SR., Private, was in WWII with 34th Evacuation Hospital, 3rd Army. He entered service in September

Pvt. Orville Rahn Sr.

1942 and was discharged in December 1945. Active duty was in Normandy, northern France, Central Europe, Rhineland, Battle of the Bulge.

After his discharge he returned to farming and is now retired. The son of William and Freida Eggers Rahn, he was born at Ruma, Illinois on August 31, 1920.

ORVILLE RAHN JR., Specialist 5/c, served in the 87th Maintenance Battalion, from June 1965 until discharged in June 1968. He was born in Red Bud, Illinois, February 7, 1947, enlisted in the service after graduating from high school, and served in Germany.

Spec 5/c Orvile Rahn Jr.

His parents are Orville and Lena Mae Kirkley Rahn. Returning home he began work at Shell Oil Refinery in Wood River, Illinois, and is employed there today.

RAYMOND LUKE RALSTON, Sergeant, served in the U.S. Army in both WWII and Korea. He was a farmer prior to enlisting, and after his return he worked for the cities of Sparta and Chester.

The son of Luke and Bessie Darnell Ralston, he was born November 4, 1921, died July 22, 2002, and is buried in Evergreen Cemetery in Chester, Illinois.

WILLIAM RALSTON, Private, did service in Africa during WWII. He enlisted from Rockwood, Illinois in the early part

Pvt. William Ralston

of the war. His parents were George and Nellie Brown Ralston.

CHARLES D. RAMSEY, Corporal, served in the U.S. Marine Corps from June 1957 to June 1960. After boot camp in San Diego, California, he served as MP at Point Mugu for two and a half years. During this time, he served detached duty at other bases with the other services. His duties included serving in Color Guard, Military Funerals as well as his Military Police duty.

Cpl. Charles D. Ramsey

He was born in Chester, Illinois, December 20, 1938, son of Ben and Fleta Hathaway Ramsey.

DARREL L. RAMSEY, Sergeant, entered the military on July 21, 1963. He attended boot camp at San Diego, California and also served at Twentynine Palms Marine Corps Base, California in K Battery, 4th Battalion, 11th Marines, 1st Marine Division. He was then assigned to Marine Barrack, Naval Air Station, North Island, San Diego, California as a Military Policeman. Darrel was discharged from the Marines July 21, 1967. He never left the States during his service duty.

Sgt. Darrel L. Ramsey

Darrel born in Chester, Illinois, December 7, 1944, son of Ben and Fleta (Hathaway) Ramsey.

DONALD E. RAMSEY, Corporal, served in the U.S. Marine Corps from April

Cpl. Donald E. Ramsey

11, 1961 to April 9, 1965. He attended boot camp at San Diego, California, served with 1st Battalion, 7th Marines, and 2nd Battalion, 5th Marines. During the Cuban Crisis he was aboard ship out of San Diego, thru Panama Canal, stationed off Cuba with U.S. Naval Fleet. He also served NAS Iceland with 1st Marines.

He was born June 19, 1943, Chester, Illinois, son of Ben and Fleta Hathaway Ramsey.

WAYNE E. RAMSEY, Corporal, attended boot camp at San Diego, California, August 2, 1959. He trained at Camp Pendleton with A Company, 1st Battalion, 9th Marines, 1st Marine Division. Then he was transferred to Okinawa with A Company, 1st Battalion, 9th Marines, 3rd Marine Division. In 14 months he had served on seven ships, traveling to Hawaii, Japan, Korea, Okinawa, Philippine Islands and Hong Kong.

Cpl. Wayne E. Ramsey

Returning to the States he served with the 5th Marines Combat Engineers. He served in the Vietnam Era and Cuban Missile Crisis. Wayne was discharged from his duty on August 30, 1963.

He was born in Chester, Illinois on July 11, 1940, son of Ben and Fleta (Hathaway) Ramsey.

HEINRICH RATHER, enlisted in the Civil War, August 27, 1861, was captured October 15, 1863 and spent 18 months at Andersonville prison camp. After the war he married Friederike Heuer and they lived in Red Bud, Illinois. He died November 28, 1897, age 56 years, 11 months and 22 days.

RAYMOND C. RATZ, Staff Sergeant, received basic training at Camp Wolters, Texas, after entering the U.S. Army in 1942. He served with Company E 128th Infantry, 32nd Division, during WWII. After basic training, he was shipped to Fort George G. Meade, Maryland, then to Camp Stoneman, California, before being sent to Australia, Goodenough Island, New Guinea, Luzon, Leyte, and Camp Ascot in the Philippines.

S/Sgt. Raymond C. Ratz

He was awarded the Purple Heart after taking his platoon into the hills, where he received permanent injuries from a Japanese hand grenade, he also received an award for bravery in combat. The 32nd Division was known as the Famous Red Arrow Division. He was discharged from military service in November 1945.

Raymond was born in Red Bud, Illinois, son of A.J. and Ella Dinges Ratz.

LYMAN WADE RAY, Private, was in U.S. Army during WWII. He enlisted December 12, 1942 and was honorably discharged October 13, 1943 at Harrisburg, Pennsylvania. He was born in Ironton, Missouri, April 6, 1916, son of Bert and Nancy NcNew Ray, and died November 11, 1998. Burial was in Caldonia Cemetery in Sparta, Illinois.

ROBERT B. REED, Private First Class, was inducted into WWII, April 27, 1944, as a heavy machine gunner serving in north Apennines, Po Valley and Bologna, Italy. He was discharged December 11, 1946.

Robert was born in St. Mary's Missouri, November 12, 1917, son of Roger

Pfc. Robert B. Reed

S. and Barbara Brown Reed. He owned a gas station, car repair service, and trucking service after the war. He died December 28, 1999.

JAMES LEONARD REEDER, Chief Warrant Officer-4, born February 9, 1919, Grand Tower, Illinois, son of Raymond G. and Minnie G. Stone Reeder. He enlisted in U.S. Navy, July 10, 1939, served 30 years, including WWII, Korean and Vietnam Wars.

Prior to WWII he served in North Atlantic patrol against German submarines during the war in South Pacific. A Japanese torpedo hit his ship in compartment where he was sleeping. They filled hole with concrete and without power were towed 21 days across Pacific Ocean to Pearl Harbor. He remained in Navy after war and served on oil tankers, cargo ships, destroyers, repair and battleships, that took him completely around the world.

He became a Naval Recruiter at Louisville, Kentucky. He was stationed at naval stations throughout the U.S., then to Malta, England and Morocco, North Africa, retiring from last duty station at Orlando, Florida. On December 31, 1969 he returned to southern Illinois and was employed by Mental Health Center, Chester, Illinois and American Device Mfg. Company of Steeleville, Illinois. He lived on the farm he dearly loved in Rockwood, Illinois until his death, January 6, 1988.

DALLAS K. REES, Petty Officer 2/c, of Tilden, Illinois, was born December 29, 1939, the son of Harlan and Vera Vancil Rees. He was in the Navy during the Vietnam era, and also participated in the Cuban Missile Crisis while aboard ship. He entered service in March 1959 and visited several countries in Europe, Middle East, North and South Atlantic aboard the Destroyer USS *C.H. Roan* (DD-853). He

P.O. 2/c Dallas K. Rees

was discharged in March 1964 and lives in Sparta, Illinois.

ARTHUR CORNELIOUS "CONNIE" REID, joined the U.S. Navy, July 25, 1940, and made a career of military service. He rose through the ranks from apprentice seaman to retirement as chief gunner's mate, March 1, 1960. He spent 10 years in the Fleet Reserve, leaving the service May 1, 1970.

Arthur C. Reid

He received training then a Good Will Cruise in South Pacific during March 1941. He was assigned to heavy cruiser, USS *Chicago,* and stationed at Pearl Harbor, Hawaii, but was at sea December 7, 1941, at time of attack. He was in the battle of Savo, August 9, 1942, at Guadalcanal Island, aboard the *Chicago.* Arthur survived the sinking of the *Chicago* on January 30, 1943, off Rennel Island.

After the *Chicago* was sunk, he served on the following ships. USS *Sangamon,* USS *Eastland,* USS *Springfield,* USS *Shelton,* USS *Des Moines,* USS *George A. Johnson,* USS *Columbus,* USS *Saint Paul* and the USS *Uhlmann,* also at the Naval Ammunition Depot, Seal Beach, California and Naval Air Station, Hutchinson, Kansas.

He received the Purple Heart, for the battle of Savo, Asiatic-Pacific, American Defense, American Theatre, World War II Victory and the Good Conduct Medals.

Born October 4, 1915, Rockwood, Illinois, son of Harry DeRose and Cora E. Frazer Reid, "Connie" died April 19, 2001 and is buried in Ebenezer Cemetery near Rockwood.

HARRY GLENN REID, enlisted in the Navy, December 3, 1940, as apprentice seaman. After training at Great Lakes Naval Center, he was assigned to the heavy cruiser USS *Chicago,* and in March 1941 went on a "Goodwill Cruise" in the South Pacific. He was stationed at Pearl Harbor in December 1941, but was at sea on the 7th, during the Japanese attack that began WWII. He was on the USS *Chicago* in Guadalcanal, during the battle of Savo and survived the sinking of the *Chicago* on January 30, 1943, off the coast of Rennell Island, an island of the Solomons.

Harry Glenn Reid

Harry G. Reid (center), USS South Carolina

In March 1943, he was in subchaser training in Miami, Florida, and was assigned to the subchaser USS *South Carolina* (1002) in New Orleans, Louisiana. While in New Orleans, he was hospitalized off and on for six months due to infections in his finger, attributed to lifting depth charges. Other service included, U.S. Naval Ammo Depot, Crane, Indiana, shore patrol, Tower Hall, Chicago, Illinois.

In December 1945, he was at the Naval Receiving Station, Washington DC. The last part of his enlistment was spent living on USS LMS-535, USS LST-291 and USS LST-287, while de-commissioning ships on the St. John's River in Green Cove Springs, Florida. He rose from the rank of apprentice seaman to retire as gunner's mate 1/c on December 23, 1946, from Naval Air Technical Training Center, Memphis, Tennessee.

Harry was born in Rockwood, Illinois, May 21, 1917, son of Harry DeRose and Cora E. Frazer Reid.

JOSEPH DAVID REID, Carpenter's Mate 3/c, entered the U.S. Navy June 9, 1944. After training at Great Lakes he requested sea duty and was assigned to a submarine. His troop train was delayed en route to California by a train wreck in Colorado. The sub he was to serve on had sailed two days before he arrived. The Navy was forming a Seabee Battalion and assigned him to it, serving in New Guinea and Philippines. The sub that he was to have served on was lost with all hands.

Carpenters Mate 3/c Joseph D. Reid

Joe was discharged November 9, 1945, returned home, and worked for Missouri Pacific Railroad and state of Illinois. He died March 4, 1982. Joe was born in Samoth, Illinois, April 20, 1907, son of Caleb and Martha Bowman Reid.

FREDRICH W. REHMER, entered Civil War with 7th Illinois Cavalry, Company M on May 26, 1864. This company was mostly men from Red Bud, Illinois area.

Fredrich Rehmer

Under Sturgis when Forrest made his raid on Memphis, they fought on the Hernando road, losing several men, then advanced to Savannah, Clifton and Lawrenceburg in Tennessee. This unit helped to secure Nashville for the North at end of war.

Discharged November 4, 1865, at Nashville, Tennessee, he returned to Red Bud area to the occupation of farming. Fredrich died March 13, 1911.

JAMES D. REID, served in Company K, 5th Illinois Cavalry as a Soldier Orderly in the Civil War. He died in a camp near Vicksburg, Mississippi, September 21, 1863. He was born March 11, 1844 to Joseph and Margaret Ann Ryan Reid, and lived in Rockwood, Illinois at the time of his enlistment.

ALBERT REIMER, Private First Class, entered WWII, August 11, 1944 and served with Headquarters Company, 25th Infantry Division on Luzon in Philippines, driving a jeep in the 25th Infantry Motor Pool. Awarded Bronze Star, Good Conduct Medal and Silver Star, he was discharged January 10, 1946.

Pfc. Albert Reimer

Albert was born in Evansville, Illinois, April 8, 1920, son of Albert and Marie Heinke Reimer.

CHARLES ANDREW RES, Motor Machinist Mate 3/c, born Cora City, Illinois, September 6, 1909, son of Joseph and Etta Murden Res. He enlisted in Navy April 26, 1944 and served in Asiatic-Pacific, Funafuti and Russell Islands.

He received the American Victory Medal, American Theatre and Asiatic-Pacific Medal.

Charles was discharged January 26, 1946 and died November 27, 1993.

JOSEPH PAUL RHEINECKER, Corporal, was inducted into WWII February 25, 1943 at Peoria, Illinois, and entered active service March 4, 1943. He served with Aerial Engineer Division and attended Engineering School in Amarillo, Texas.

Qualified with SS Rifle and received Good Conduct Medal, America Theatre and Victory Ribbon. He was discharged February 16, 1946 at Jefferson Barracks, Missouri.

After discharge he worked at Monsanto for many years. Joe was born at Rockwood, Illinois, September 9, 1923, son of George W. and Bertha Clendenin Rheinecker, and died October 29, 2001. He is buried at Paradise Cemetery near Steeleville, Illinois.

GEORGE W. RHEINECKER SR., served in WWI in Company D, 102nd Machine Gun Battalion in France with the American Expeditionary Forces from October 2, 1918 to April 17, 1919. On May 22, 1918, he was inducted at Chester, Illinois, and was discharged at Camp Grant Illinois on April 28, 1919.

Born in Steeleville, Illinois on June 15, 1895, his parents were Joseph and Clara Bergfeld Rheinecker. He was a school teacher when he entered service. His death occurred August 8, 1971, with burial in Paradise Cemetery near Steeleville, Illinois.

CHAD A. RICKENBERG, E-6 Aviation Electronics Technician 1/c, enlisted in the Navy on August 24, 1993. He was stationed at the Aircraft Intermediate Maintenance Department (AIMD) Naval Air Station, Oceania, Virginia Beach, Virginia. Petty Officer Rickenberg spent his first tour repairing radar systems on the A-6 Intruder attack aircraft.

After re-enlisting for six years in 1997, he rotated to sea duty and, still based out of Oceania, deployed to the Mediterranean Sea on board the aircraft carrier USS

E-6 A/E 1/c Chad Rickenberg

George Washington (CVN-73). During his tour, he worked repairing reconnaissance cameras for the F-14 Tomcat air superiority fighter.

Six months after his return, he was again deployed on board USS *Enterprise* (CVN-65), during which he participated in Operation Desert Fox, which demonstrated to Iraq the consequences of violating international obligations. While on his deployment, he qualified as an air warfare specialist.

The third deployment during his sea tour was again on board the USS *George Washington* (CVN-73). During this tour, he qualified as a surface warfare specialist. In 2000, he rotated back to shore duty at AIMD Oceania, where he supervised the work center in which he was previously employed.

Currently, Petty Officer Rickenberg performs his duties as AIMD Production Control Supervisor, overseeing the entire production effort of his command. He has been awarded the Navy and Marine Corps Achievement Medal four times for outstanding initiative and exceptional performance. Chad was born in Chester, Illinois on January 6, 1975 to Morris and Linda (Laurent) Rickenberg.

DON RIDDLE, SPEC-4, BM/S, enlisted into the Army in February 1960. Don took his basic at Fort Leonard, Missouri, then went to Fort Bliss, Texas, Okinawa and Grand Island, New York. (These duty stations were either training for or duty assignments at Nike Missile Bases.)

He was discharged in early 1963 and joined the Navy in May 1963. Boot camp was at NRTC, Great Lakes, Illinois. Assigned to Headquarters, 13th Naval District, Seattle, Washington for duty with his brother, Harry Riddle. Then assigned to USS *Klondike* homeported in San Diego.

Discharged from active duty in Feb-

MMM 3/c Charles A. Res

Spec-4 Don Riddle

ruary 1966, he joined the Army National Guard for eight years in San Diego, California, serving during the Vietnam era.

He was born in Detroit, Michigan to Bob and Evelyn (Neely) Riddle.

HARRY RIDDLE, Dental Technician Senior Chief, served in the U.S. Navy from October 26, 1954 to January 16, 1976. He was born June 10, 1937, Rockwood, Illinois, son of Bob and Evelyn Neely Riddle.

Dental Tech Sr. Chief Harry Riddle

After basic training at Great Lakes Naval Station, Illinois, DTCS Riddle served aboard USS *Frontier* (AD-25), 1955; went to Dental Technician School, RTC, San Diego, California, 1955-56; Dental Clinic, Long Beach, California, 1956-59; Naval Station, Adak, Alaska, 1959; USS *Nereus* (AS-17), San Diego, California, 1960-61; USS *Iwo Jima* (LPH-2), Bremerton, Washington, 1961-62; San Diego, California Medical Administrative School, San Diego Naval Hospital, 1962-63; NAS Seattle, Washington, 1963-67; 17th Dental Company, 5th Marine Division, Camp Pendleton, California, 1967-68; 1st Dental Company, 1st Marine Division, Da Nang, Vietnam, 1969; Naval Air Station, LakeHurst, NJ; Naval Base Dental Clinic, Newport, Rhode Island, 1970 to retirement in 1976.

RICHARD KARRY "RICK" RIDDLE, Sergeant First Class, entered the military in December 1965. He served with the 17th

Sgt. 1/c Richard K. Riddle

and 44th Engineer Battalions. Rick took his basic training at Fort Leonard Wood, Missouri. Stateside he served at Fort Hood, Texas and Fort Knox, Kentucky. He had a three year tour of duty in Germany, three tours in Vietnam and a year tour in Korea. Duties while in Vietnam included building of a highway in the Da Nang area and transporting of supplies and heavy equipment.

Upon returning to the States after his final overseas tour of duty in Korea, he was once again based at Fort Leonard Wood, Missouri, where he was an instructor in heavy duty equipment. After 21 years of service he retired to southern Illinois in 1986. The purchase of a Ranger truck kept him moving across the United States until his health deteriorated due to cancer. Rick died in February 1998. He was born December 5, 1945 in Detroit, MI, the son of Jewell (Bob) and Evelyn (Neely) Riddle.

MARK C. RIESTER, Petty Officer 3/c, served in the U.S. Navy from March 1989 to March 1997. He was born October 25, 1956 in Belleville, Illinois, son of Jerry and Reta Radford Riester. He served aboard

P.O. 3/c Mark C. Riester

the USS *Saipan* (LHA-2) assault ship and participated in operations: Just Cause in Panama, 1989; Sharp Edge, in Monrovia Liberia, 1990; Gulf War, 1991-92; and Liberation of Kuwait. He is currently commander of DAV in Randolph County.

VIRGIL GALE RIGDON, Private, born August 20, 1914, at Tilden, Illinois, the son of George and Florence Hiller Rigdon. He enlisted in the U.S. Army, July 6, 1941, assigned to Company B, Quartermaster Training Regiment and honorably discharged October 17, 1941, at Camp Lee, Virginia, due to illness.

Pvt. Virgil G. Rigdon

A coal miner prior to enlisting, he returned to that profession and retired from Missouri Pacific Railroad. Virgil married Ruth Victoria Ralston on April 13, 1943. He died March 14, 2001 and is buried in Evergreen Cemetery, Chester, Illinois.

LESTER L. RINNE, Corporal, served in the U.S. Army, 1953-55. He was born July 14, 1933, son of Edwin and Elda

Cpl. Lester Rinne

Duensing Brammer Rinne. Les served his time in the Army at Fort Leonard Wood, Missouri. After he completed his basic training, he was in food service and a cook.

HEINRICH RITTER, a soldier in the Civil War, he was born in Rothheim Hessen, Darmstadt, Germany, and came to this country and lived in Horse Prairie, Illinois. He died in a prison camp in Florence, SC, on November 10, 1864, age 28 years, 1 month and 3 days old.

DONALD LEE ROBERT, SP1/c, was drafted into the military February 11, 1953, and served in the Korean War. Born Janu-

SP 1/c Donald L. Robert

ary 11, 1933, in Modoc, Illinois, his parents are Henry and Ethel K. Johnson Robert. Donald was in Pusan, Korea from August 1953 until December 1954, and was responsible for maintenance of the compound in downtown Pusan with the 8131st Army Transportation Unit Port Command C. The truce was signed while he was being shipped to Korea.

After returning from Korea, he served eight years in Reserves, was officially discharged March 11, 1961. Donald retired in 1994, when Inter-City factory closed in Red Bud.

ALBERT G. ROCKWELL, Private, born in Chester, Illinois in 1841, the son of Justus T. Sr. and Judith Cornelius Rockwell. He enlisted August 1, 1861 at Coulterville, Illinois to serve in the Civil War. He served in Company F, 10th Missouri Infantry, and died in Jefferson Barracks, St. Louis, Missouri on July 28, 1862 from typhoid fever. He never married and his mother, Judith (Rockwell) Ford, made application for his pension in 1890.

EPHRAIM ROCKWELL, Sergeant, served in the Civil War in Company D, 80th Illinois Volunteer Infantry. He enlisted August 1, 1862, at Camp Centralia, Randolph County, Illinois. His pension paperwork states he was present at the battle of Stone River, Murfreesboro, Tennessee on February 28, 1863, serving as 1st duty sergeant for his company.

Ephraim was also at Sand Mountain, Alabama in action referred to as Streight's Raid AKA Day's Gap, April 30, 1865, where he received a severe head injury when his saber was caught in the wheel of a caisson, causing him to strike his head against the corner of the wagon frame.

He was born May 13, 1832 in Chester, Illinois to Justus T. Sr. and Sallie Perkins Rockwell. He was married to Emma Marlen, September 4, 1856, and was listed as a carpenter at the time of his enlistment. He died December 12, 1912, in Randolph County.

JUSTUS T. ROCKWELL JR., Private, enlisted July 1, 1862 and served in Company H, 22nd Illinois Volunteer Infantry, until discharged January 31, 1865, at Independence, Missouri. He was wounded in action at Missionary Ridge, Tennessee on November 25, 1863.

Born 1835 in Randolph County to Justus T. Sr. and Sallie Perkins Rockwell, he died in Bollinger County, Missouri on January 4, 1902. He had married Martha J. Marshall on May 2, 1865, in Chester and was later married to Mrs. Sarah Cole in Bollinger County, Missouri in 1886.

ROBERT ROCKWELL, Private, enlisted August 25, 1862, in Company D of the 80th Illinois Volunteer Infantry at Camp Centralia, Randolph County, Illinois. Detached for heavy artillery duty August 11, 1863, he was in the battle of Stone Mountain, Murfreesboro, Tennessee and saw action at Marietta, Georgia, June 30, 1864, and at the siege of Atlanta, beginning July 31, 1864.

Discharged from service June 10, 1865, at Springfield, Illinois, he died February 17, 1919, in Yuma County, Colorado. He was born in Chester, Illinois, March 3, 1842 to Justus T. Sr. and Judith Cornelius Rockwell. He married Ozella Clore on November 26, 1870, at Chester.

RICHARD COLEMAN RODELY, was in U.S. Navy from June 1944 until 1945, during WWII. Stationed in South Carolina until he suffered rheumatic fever and was discharged due to illness. He

Richard C. Rodely

was born May 17, 1924, in Duquoin, Illinois, son of Bert and Marie Short Rodely.

THOMAS DALE RODELY, Corporal, served in the U.S. Marine Corps from June 1950 to September 1952. He was born January 26, 1932, in DuQuoin, Illinois and grew up in Chester, the son of Bert and

Cpl. Thomas D. Rodely

Marie Short Rodely. Tom loved the Marine Corps and hoped to make it his career, but while in Korea, he came down with rheumatic fever and was medically discharged.

DARYLE G. RODEWALD, SP4-MEDIC, entered the military in October 1967. Daryle took his basic training at Fort Bliss, Texas. After he finished his basic, he went to Fort Sam Houston, Texas for his AIT. Daryle took his jump training at Fort Benning, Georgia.

S/4 Medic Daryle Rodewald

He was deployed to Vietnam and while there, he was injured and sent to Vietnam Quin Trion Hospital. When he was able, he was sent to Camp Zama, Japan to recuperate and finished his tour there. Daryle was with the 173rd Airborne and was honorably discharged in October 1969. His parents are Omer H. and Ruth (Meyerhoff) Rodewald.

OMER H. RODEWALD, Staff Sergeant, son of Rudolph and Blanche Eggers Rodewald of Ava, Illinois, was assistant crew chief with 877th Pilot Transport Squadron during WWII. He enlisted February 13, 1942 and worked as airplane mechanic. Omer became ill and was hospitalized for four months. He was given a

Certified Medical Honorable Discharge on October 19, 1943 from Brooke General Hospital, Fort Sam Houston, Texas.

WILBERT H. RODEWALD, Tech 4, served in 3106th Ordnance Company, 606th Ordnance Battalion, during WWII in Naples, Foggia, Rome, and Arno, Italy. He entered service July 11, 1942 and was discharged December 2, 1945. Wilbert was born June 1, 1920, Ava, Illinois.

ARTHUR ROEHRKASSE, Corporal, born at Red Bud, Illinois, April 22, 1921, son of Hugo and Bertha Busse Roehrkasse. He entered WWII service in 1943 with basic training at Fort Knox and Fort Campbell, Kentucky, driving a tank in Company B, 27th Tank Battalion. He saw action in France, Austria and Germany.

Cpl. Arthur Roehrkasse

Arthur was missing in action for three weeks behind enemy lines in Germany until American Forces arrived. He helped to liberate death camps. After his discharge in 1945, he made Cutler, Illinois his home and worked as an accountant for coal mine. Arthur died December 17, 1998.

GENE ROGERS, A2/c, served in the U.S. Air Force from August 25, 1951 to August 24, 1955. He was born April 11, 1933, Charleston, Missouri and reared in Chester, Illinois, son of Irvin E. and Hattie Casey Rogers. Gene enlisted in the Air Force and after basic training was assigned to A&E School in Wichita Falls, TX. He spent the next several years at bases in Texas until assigned to the 5th Air Force in Osan, Korea for one year.

He was discharged in 1955, married and enrolled in college at SIU, where he earned BS and MS degrees and taught high school until retirement in 1992. He is now enjoying retirement very much.

A/2c Gene Rogers

GEORGE THERMAN ROGERS, Airman 1/c, born July 26, 1928 in Memphis, Tennessee, son of Irvin Earl and Hattie Casey Rogers. He enlisted in the Air Force in 1950 and served in Korean War in Strategic Air Command as a gunner on a B-36 bomber.

Discharged in 1954, he re-enlisted in 1956 and served until 1960. After discharge, he attended college, graduated with BA degree in education and taught elementary school in California. George died February 3, 2002.

HERMAN CHRISTIAN ROHLFING, Seaman 1/c, was born at Red Bud, Illinois, January 14, 1893, to Christian Heinrich (who was born November 19, 1849, Totenhausen, Minden Kreis, Germany) and Mary Anna Louise Linders Rohlfing (born November 20, 1854, Randolph County).

Herman entered WWI May 19, 1918 and served until September 1, 1919, making five round trips between New York City and Europe on the USS *Louisville* (originally the passenger liner SS *St. Louis*). The *Louisville* served as a troop transport and was reported to be the first non-combatant ship to be armed (one 5-inch gun, mounted forward) for travel through specified submarine-free lanes prior to entering WWI. He served as a fireman, feeding the boiler furnaces, and at times had the services of German POWs to help with this chore. Fortunately he spoke German.

He had to remain in service for about a year after Armistice of November 11, 1918 was signed, to return military troops from Europe to U.S. The USS *Louisville* caught fire and burned in 1920, while in port in New York City.

HOWARD WILLIAM ROHLFING, served with the U.S. Army during WWII. He was from Steeleville, Illinois and born March 21, 1911, the son of Henry Fredrick Sr. and Emma C. Breithaupt Rohlfing. He was involved in the invasion of Italy. No other information of his service record is known, other than he was discharged in 1945.

He married LaVerna Bruns and made his home in Percy, Illinois, working for International Shoe Company and American Device Company. He died November 2, 1977, and is buried with his wife in Paradise Cemetery near Steeleville, Illinois.

MARVIN W. ROHLFING, Sergeant, served 24 months in Panama during WWII, as Heavy Truck #931 Driver and also bus driver for Department of Transportation with Panama Canal Bus Company from July 29, 1943 until February 6, 1946, delivering personnel, rations and general warfare equipment (both day and night) over rough terrain, and he had to make many repairs on truck.

Sgt. Marvin W. Rohlfling

Awarded Good Conduct Medal, Rifle Marksman Medal, Lapel Button, entitled to wear American Theatre Campaign Ribbon, four Overseas Bars and Victory Ribbon. Born in Percy, Illinois, his parents are Henry F. and Frieda Luehr Rohlfing.

ROBERT ERNST ROHLFING, born July 5, 1933, Red Bud, Illinois, son of Herman Christian and Ida Josephine Deichmann Rohlfing. He was commissioned 2nd lieutenant, Quartermaster Corps, Army Reserve, out of ROTC at University of Illinois, June 20, 1954 and entered active duty August 28, 1954 at Fort Lee, Virginia. He was integrated into regular Army in 1963 with active duty until June 30, 1976, when discharged from Fort Dix, New Jersey.

Overseas duty stations include Bad Kissingen, Germany, Bupyong, Korea, Sattahip, Thailand, Saigon and Vietnam in combat area, and Mons, Belgium. From 1956-59 he served as a supply and service officer, without a specific combat role, on border between East and West Germany, near "Fulda Gap," which military planners expected to be the primary route should Communist forces invade.

Monthly alerts and periodic drives on back roads were conducted to the French border to allow them to learn the route by which to evacuate wives and children of local soldiers' to safety should war be threatened. Many visitors wanted the experience of having their picture taken at the fence separating the two nations. It was later learned that the fence and 35 feet of plowed ground on the west side of the fence were actually inside East Germany. This made those who posed for pictures at the fence international trespassers.

He spent the winter 1962-63 in Korea. The North China Sea froze for the second time in the 80-year history of the port of Inchon, which delayed docking of ships to resupply bulk heating fuel from Japan. Supply Point #50 was down to 5,000 gallons, this making it necessary to place kerosene heaters inside pre-fab refrigerators and light them periodically to keep them above freezing.

In Spring of 1971 he rode "shotgun" on Navy patrol boats on Mekong River, as protection for commercial barges hauling aviation fuels to Phnom Penh, Cambodia, for their small air force, when they and the capitol were surrounded by enemy forces during the incursion by South Vietnam.

He was in Pacific Theatre in 1973, and even though combat operations had ended OPEC's refusal to ship crude oil to U.S. entities threatened to severely curtail readiness of U.S. Forces and to require cuts in training and operations as well as having to reposition remaining inventories during the embargo. This was a stressful time for all involved.

His awards include the Legion of Merit, Bronze Star, Joint Services Commendation Medal, Army Commendation Medal w/3 Oak Leaf Clusters, National Defense Service Medal, Vietnam Service Medal, two Overseas Combat Service Bars, RVN Gallantry Cross w/Palm (unit award).

ROBERT L. ROHLFING, E-5, entered service in October 1965 and served in Vietnam from March 1966 to March 1967, with 329th Engineers. He was discharged in October 1968. Born in Red Bud, Illinois, April 9, 1947, his parents are Theodore and Bernice Schrieber Rohlfing.

ERVIN P. ROSCOW, Sergeant, served in the U.S. Air Force from 1962-66, He was born in Red Bud, Illinois, November

Sgt. Ervin P. Roscow

14, 1944, son of James and Thelma Roscow. After his discharge he married Ann Aubuchon, and they reside in Prairie du Rocher. He works for Dynegy MidwestGeneration as a Manager-Maintenance.

JAMES E. ROSCOW, son of Eldon and Sarah Roscow, was born in Red Bud, Illinois on November 28, 1919. He served in U.S. Army Air Corps during WWII, 1943-

James E. Roscow

44. Returning home he founded Roscow Roofing Company, which he owned and operated for 48 years. He died February 10, 1992.

JASON P. ROSCOW, enlisted in the U.S. Air Force, serving from 2001 to the present time as Senior Airman, Security

Jason P. Roscow

Services and currently stationed in Korea. He is the son of Ervin and Ann Roscow and was born in Belleville, Illinois on October 23, 1978.

JEFFREY M. ROSCOW, Specialist 4, U.S. Army, born January 4, 1971, Red Bud, Illinois, the son of Roger and Bonita Rosenberg Roscow. Jeffrey entered service on November 21, 1988, under the delayed entry program, and entered active duty after graduating high school August 3, 1989.

Spec-4 Jeffrey M. Roscow

He completed basic training at Fort Dix, New Jersey and AIT at Fort Monmouth, New Jersey, graduating as a 71M-Chaplain Assistant. He served most of his active duty with the 101st Airborne Division out of Fort Campbell, KY.

He is currently employed by the Illinois Secretary of State in the Sparta Facility.

MICHAEL P. ROSCOW, Sergeant, served in the U.S. Air Force from 1988-93. He was born in Red Bud, Illinois July 24, 1969, the son of Ervin and Ann Roscow.

Sgt. Michael P. Roscow

After his discharge, he married Jennifer Becker and they reside in Red Bud. He works as a private investment broker for Bank of America.

ROGER L. ROSCOW, Sergeant, served in the U.S. army from August 1966 to August 1969. He was born in Red Bud,

Sgt. Roger L. Roscow

Seaman 1/c Charles L. Rowney

Illinois, son of James and Thelma Hunter Roscow. Roger completed basic training at Fort Leonard Wood, Missouri and trained as heavy motor vehicle operator.

Stationed in Korea, early 1967, his time was extended because of the Pueblo Seizure. Late in 1968, he transferred to Germany. Roger now works for Randolph County, Maintenance Department, County Court House.

MARVIN ROSENBERG, Staff Sergeant, entered U.S. Army Air Corps January 20, 1942, at Camp Grant, Illinois. He trained as medic in Savannah, Georgia and Barksdale Field, Louisiana, he sailed on the Susan B. Anthony from New York with 17th Bomb Group, 432nd Bomb Squadron, landing 13 days later at Casablanca, Christmas Eve 1942.

S/Sgt. Marvin Rosenberg

The 432nd was in Tunisian Sicilian, Naples, Foggia, Rome, Arno, Southern and Northern France, Rhineland, and finally Zelmzee, Austria for R&R before returning stateside for discharge on October 7, 1945 from Fort Sheridan, Illinois.

Marvin was born December 8, 1916, Monroe County, Illinois, son of Henry C. and Effie Davis Rosenberg, he returned home and farmed for well over 50 years.

CHARLES LEE ROWNEY, Seaman 1/c, enlisted in U.S. Coast Guard, August 8, 1943 and served on *Hugh L. Scott*, making three trips around the world transporting men and supplies in WWII.

He left service in May 1946, and returned to a life of coal mining. Charles was born August 10, 1925, in Coulterville, Illinois, the son of Charles E. and Mayme Arnett Rowney.

HAROLD ROWOLD, Sergeant, served in the U.S. Army from December 8, 1948 to July 1954 with Company E, 38th Regiment, 2nd Infantry Division. He completing basic training at Camp Breckenridge, Kentucky, transferred to Fort Lewis, Washington, and on July 15, 1949, the 2nd Division shipped out to Korea. He participated in several battles at the Pusan perimeter and points north.

Sgt. Harold Rowold

Harold was born November 25, 1930, Murphysboro, Illinois, the son of August and __ Laramore Rowold.

JOHN DAVID ROWOLD, Sergeant, served in the U.S. Air Force from 1985-91 with 37th TAC Fighter Wing, Nellis AFB, Las Vegas, Nevada. After basic training at Lackland AFB, San Antonio, Texas, he took advanced technical training at Lowry AFB, Denver, Colorado.

While stationed at Nellis AFB, Nevada, he worked in aircraft maintenance on the F117A Stealth Fighter providing support during Operation Desert Storm.

John was born March 3, 1967, Belleville, Illinois, the son of Ken and Virginia Welge Rowold. He is currently working at Menard Correctional Center.

KEN ROWOLD, A1/c, served in the U.S. Air Force from 1956-60, with the 354th Tactical Fighter Wing Headquarters, Myrtle Beach AFB, South Carolina. Completing basic training at Lackland AFB, San Antonio, Texas, and advanced technical training at Sheppard AFB, Wichita Falls, Texas, Ken was stationed at Myrtle Beach AFB, South Carolina, where he served in the Wing Headquarters.

AM 1/c Ken Rowold

Returning home, he worked in the computer department of MO-Pac RR and then as administrator of Three Springs Lodge Nursing Home, Chester, Illinois.

WALTER F. ROWOLD, Motor Machinist Mate 2/c, joined the U.S. Navy and served with Naval Amphibious Forces in New Guinea. After boot training at Great Lakes and amphibious training at Norfolk, Virginia, he went to New Zealand, Australia then to the New Guinea war zone.

MMM 2/c Walter F. Rowold

He saw action at Lae, Fitchlaven, and New Britian Island in the Solomans. He entered service June 1, 1942, last duty being at Pearl Harbor before he was discharged October 23, 1945.

He was born October 14, 1918, at Red Bud, Illinois, the son of Conrad and

Emmeline Goetting Rowald, he says, "Join the Navy...see the world."

DALE WILLIAM ROY, Staff Sergeant, served in the U.S. Army, from July 30, 1968 to November 30, 1971. He was born July 24, 1950, the son of Aaron and Lucille Blow Roy. Dale served in the Infantry in Vietnam from December 22, 1969 to May 10, 1970 when he was wounded in action.

S/Sgt Dale W. Roy

He earned the National Defense Medal, Vietnam Service w/2 Bronze Stars, Marksman/M-14, Expert/M-16 and Purple Heart. He died June 21, 1979.

HOMER H. RUBACH, Private First Class, served in the U.S. Army from March 6, 1941 to August 22, 1945. He served with Company G, 160th Infantry, as a light mortar crewman in the Luzon Campaign and served on guard duty, "Coast Watchers" on the Islands of Hawaii from September 1942 to June 1943; Oahu, June 1943 to December 1943; Guadalcanal, December 1943 to April 1944; New Britain, April 1944 to December 1944; Luzon, December 1944 to January 29, 1945, when he was wounded in battle, then shipped to New Guinea.

Pfc. Homer H. Rubach

He earned the Asiatic-Pacific Campaign Medal, Philippine Liberation Ribbon w/Bronze Star, American Defense Service Medal, Good Conduct and Purple Heart.

He was born in Jackson County, Illinois on March 21, 1914, son of Herman and Emma Pinkerton Rubach.

LARENZ RUEBKE, Corporal, served in the U.S. Army from April 1952 to April 1955. He's the son of Fritz and Clara Hartmann Ruebke, living in Percy, Illinois, was drafted in 1952 to 5th Army and went to Fort Bliss, Texas. After four months in Texas, he was transferred to Fort Lewis, Washington on outpost duty, about 10 miles from Renton, Washington. He was discharged in 1955.

EARL J. RUNGE, Corporal, son of Henry F. and Ruth E. Hapke Runge of Chester, Illinois. He served in Company D, 135th Engineer Battalion, 44th Infantry Division after enlistment May 10, 1951, until discharge, May 9, 1954.

Cpl. Earl J. Runge

His division was called to active duty in November 1951. He trained and prepared at Camp Cooke, California, then the division was split up for replacement to locations throughout the world. He was sent to Fort Lewis, Washington in support position and discharged after truce was signed. Corporal Runge is now deceased.

LEONARD R. RUNGE, Private First Class, born December 6, 1929, in Chester, Illinois, the son of Roy F. and Velma Leonard Runge. He served in the Korean War, Spl. Training Regiment, 8th Infantry Division, Fort Jackson, South Carolina.

He was in service from April 5, 1951 until April 4, 1953, and while in service worked in NCO Club and later managed an Officers Club just before discharge.

Prior to entering service, he worked for Western Auto Store in Chester, and returned there after service. He attended SIU on GI Bill, and worked for GTE and Clauch Motors, retiring in 1996.

RICHARD L. "DICK" RUNGE, Corporal, was in military during the Korean Conflict. He took basic training at Fort Bliss, Texas, then was sent to Karlsruhe, Germany, where he spent seven months in Electronics School to become a radar repairman on the new M-33 antiaircraft. This radar was the "eyes" for the 90mm guns.

Cpl. Richard L. Runge

He served with Battery D, 552 Antiaircraft Battalion of the 7th Army from April 29, 1953 until April 14, 1955. After discharge, he spent 35 years with NCR as a repairman.

His military training helped him get his job with NCR. Dick was born in Chester, Illinois on May 14, 1933, the son of Roy F. and Velma Leonard Runge.

CLARENCE MARCUS RUROEDE, Corporal, served in the Army during the

Pfc. Leonard L. Runge

Cpl. Clarence M. Ruroede

Korean Conflict from November 23, 1951 until November 22, 1953 in Company B, 21st Engineer BR(C). After basic training at Fort Belvior, Virginia, he transferred to Fort Carson, Colorado, and Fort Laton, Washington, then to Ladd AFB, Alaska for five months.

After his tour in Alaska, Clarence returned to Fort Carson, and served as Company Clerk for one year, before his discharge. He received the Good Conduct Medal and National Defense Service Medal.

His hometown was Bremen, Illinois and his parents are Martin and Dora Hartmann Ruroede.

EDWARD ELMER RUROEDE, Corporal, received basic training at Camp Atterbury, Indiana, then eight weeks Military Police training at Fort Knox, Kentucky. He was in service from April 16, 1953 until March 23, 1955.

Cpl. Edward E. Ruroede

After training, he shipped from Camp Kilmer, New Jersey to Japan, and served as Military Police at the R&R center with the 701th MP Company at Camp Hokata, Kukora, Japan. Received the National Defense Service Medal.

Edward was from Bremen, Illinois, the son of Martin and Dora Hartmann Ruroede.

ERNEST CHARLES RUROEDE, Corporal, served his country in the U.S.

Cpl. Ernest C. Ruroede

Army during the Korean Conflict in the 297th Engineer Aviation Battalion. The son of Martin and Dora Hartmann Ruroede of Bremen, Illinois, he served from January 26, 1951 until January 26, 1953.

Basic training was received at Fort Leonard Wood, Missouri, then assigned to Elmendorf Air Strip in Alaska, then to Beale Air Base, Maryville, California. He served as Quarry Machine Operator at both bases.

He received the Good Conduct Medal and National Defense Medal. Ernest is a 48 year member of the American Legion.

KURT WAYNE RUSHING, Lance Corporal, born August 16, 1979, Rankin, Texas, the son of Kenneth and Melodie Mansker Rushing. He graduated from Chester, Illinois High School and attends University of Illinois, Springfield, Illinois Campus.

L/Cpl Kurt W. Rushing

He enlisted in the Marine Reserves in May 2002 and graduated boot camp at San Diego, California August 16, 2002, with H&S Company, 3rd Battalion, 24th Marines. Assigned to 3rd Battalion, 24th Marine Reservist Unit, Brighton, Missouri.

JOHN CAMERON RUSHING, Sergeant, entered military service September 16, 1996 with basic and advance training at Fort Sill, Oklahoma. Assigned to Fort

Sgt. John Cameron Rushing

Drum, New York, as number two man on M-119 Howitzer with 2nd Division of 15th Field Artillery Regiment. Stationed in Bosnia from June 1999 until May 2000 as base commander's driver.

In June 2000 he was promoted to sergeant and became gunner for 5th Howitzer Section, then went to Fort Jackson, South Carolina to reclassify as 63 Bravo Wheeled Mechanic and deployed to South Korea for year 2002 as shop foreman and motor sergeant with Gulf Company, 52nd Engineer Combat Heavy Unit.

He returned to Fort Carson, Colorado in mid-January 2003 and was deployed in April 2003 to Kuwait and Iraq in Operation Enduring Freedom.

John was born July 26, 1978, Jackson County, Illinois, son of Kenneth and Melodie Mansker Rushing of Rockwood, Illinois.

CHARLES WILLIAM "BILL" SAAK, HM3, served in the U.S. Navy, April 5, 1961 to April 4, 1965, with Marine Air Group 26, MCAS New River, Jacksonville, North Carolina as a corpsman. He served during the Cuban Blockade. He is the son of Wilbur M. and Edna G. Baughman Saak, born October 18, 1942 in St. Louis and grew up in Chester, IL.

JACOB SAAK, served in the Civil War from February 15, 1865 until September 18, 1865, in Company J, 154th Regiment of Illinois Infantry. Born in 1842, he died October 18, 1914 and is buried in Evergreen Cemetery in Chester, Illinois. He is the grandfather of Wilbert Saak of Chester.

ROBERT W. SAAK, 1st Lieutenant, attended ROTC at Louisiana State University for four years, then entered the Army on June 10, 1969. He was stationed in Germany with 1st Battalion, 63rd Armor, 1st Division, until June 10, 1971. He remained in Army Reserves five years after discharge from Regular Army. Born in Chester, Illinois, August 30, 1947, he is the son of Wilbur and Edna Baughman Saak.

WILBUR M. SAAK, Sergeant, entered service in WWII on November 11, 1943, and served in Company L, Battalion 142, 36th Division, in Rhineland, Germany, France, and Rome and Arno in Italy. Born September 23, 1919 in DuQuoin, Illinois,

Sgt. Wilbur M. Saak

his parents were William F. and Jennie C. Marlow Saak. He was discharged December 28, 1945, now resides in Chester, Illinois.

HUESTON SADDLER, Corporal, inducted into WWII November 20, 1942 and served with 589th Engineer Pontoon Bridge Company. He first trained as a rifleman with cavalry, reconnaissance car crewman, before being assigned to the 589th and served in Pacific Theatre for six months.

Cpl. Hueston Saddler

Discharged February 18, 1946, he returned home to southern Illinois, then moved his family to Wedron, Illinois, where he worked as a well driller for a sand company.

Born in Rockwood, Illinois, February 4, 1921, son of John E. and Lavilla Rader Saddler, he died February 10, 1991.

JOHN LARRY SADDLER, Private First Class, enlisted into the Army May 4,

Pfc. John Larry Saddler

1967. He received training in the Wheeled Vehicle Mechanics and the Artillery and Missile School. John received his orders on February 1, 1968 that he would be shipping out for Vietnam on March 11, 1968.

While on furlough, and before leaving the States, he was killed in an automobile accident on March 2, 1968. John was born April 28, 1947 in Chester, Illinois. John was the son of Hueston and Alberta (Neely) Saddler.

EDWIN GARY SALGER, Specialist 4, enlisted in the Army November 2, 1965. While in Vietnam, Gary was with the 34th Engineer Company, 20th Engineer Brigade

Sp/4 Edwin Gary Saddler

and served as a heavy equipment operator. He was there during the Tett Battle. Gary was discharged November 1, 1968. He was born in Red Bud, Illinois on July 11, 1947 the son of Edwin and Bernice (Stellhorn) Salger.

GLENN A. SALGER, Major, born May 1, 1942 to Paul H. and Leona Schoenbeck Salger. He enlisted in the Army in April 1964 and was commissioned as warrant officer and aviator from Helicopter Flight School in 1966.

Maj. Glenn A. Salger

He served with 1st Cavalry Division, 1st Aviation Brigade as aircraft maintenance officer and test pilot with two tours in Vietnam, 1967 and 1970, participating in Vietnam Counter Offensive I, II and IV.

Stationed in Germany four years and in Peru for six months. Commissioned 1st lieutenant in 1969 and retired as major in 1984. Glenn resides in Leesville, LA.

HARVEY P. SALGER, Lieutenant Colonel, son of Paul H. and Leona Schoenbeck Salger, was born in St. Louis, Missouri on November 11, 1938. Reared in Red Bud, Illinois, he attended Southern Illinois University at Carbondale and graduated with a BA degree in geography.

Lt. Col. Harvey P. Salger

He then entered the U.S. Air Force in June 1963 and completed pilot training at Vance AFB, Enid, Oklahoma. Harvey served with the 20th Tactical Air Support Squadron in the Vietnam War, where he flew 382 combat missions, receiving numerous decorations, including the Distinguished Flying Cross. He was in TET Offensive. Retired from Air Force in October 1984.

Harvey married Joan Green in Enid, Oklahoma and now resides in Grafton, Wisconsin.

HERBERT M. SALGER, Staff Sergeant, served with Company B, 323rd Infantry Regiment, 81st Division, during WWII. Entered service June 7, 1941 and was in action, Peleliu and Philippine battles. Stationed in Japan after the war, he was discharged December 7, 1945. Born in Steeleville, Illinois, his parents are William and Amanda Alms Salger.

BENJAMIN P. SAUER, SP, USA, MP, entered the Army on June 14, 1998. Benjamin's basic training and Military Police AIT was at Fort McClellan, Alabama. He also served Military Police duty including CID unit at Fort Polk, Louisiana.

He has spent time serving his country in the Armor Unit stationed at Fort Clayton in Panama, one year at Camp Walker in South Korea, and is currently

Sp. MP Benjamin P. Sauer

stationed at Fort Myer, Virginia, working at the Pentagon in Washington, DC, and due to get out in June 2003,

Benjamin was born May 6, 1980, the son of William F. and Bonnie M. (Roscow) Sauer. Benjamin is married to Lesley (Smith) Sauer and the family lives in Leander, Louisiana. They have two children, Page and Alexis, and are expecting a new baby in April.

WILLIAM "BILL" SAUER, served with the 173rd Airborne Unit with the U.S. Army in Vietnam from April 13, 1970 to February 11, 1971. Bill married Bonnie M. Roscow and they reside near Prairie du Rocher. They have four children: William J., Bradley T., Benjamin P. and Amanda R. Sauer.

WILLIAM "BILL" FRED SAUER, Sergeant, served in the U.S. Army March 19, 1969 to February 11, 1971. He was born February 12, 1949, son of Milton T. and Almaneda Becker Sauer, Red Bud, Illinois. Bill completed basic training at Fort Leonard Wood, Missouri and AIT at Fort

Sgt. William Fred Sauer

Ord, California. He also attended NCO School and Airborne Training at Fort Benning, Georgia. NCO On the Job Training was at Fort Polk, Louisiana.

JAMES WILLIAM SAUERHAGE, Corporal, served in Korean War, April

Cpl. James W. Sauerhage

1952 to June 1955, with the U.S. Marines. Wounded in service, he couldn't hold his job with the railroad when he returned home. The son of Louis and Alice Hefner Sauerhage, he was born June 28, 1931, in Chester, Illinois, died January 23, 2000 and is buried in Looney Springs Cemetery, Campbell Hill, Illinois.

EDITH FREDERICKA SCHAFFNER, Army Nurse, served in the U.S. Army Nurse Corps, with the American Expeditionary Forces during WWI. Born July 1, 1893 in Evansville, Illinois, the daughter of William H. and Mary Elizabeth Homan Schaffner.

Nurse Edith F. Schaffner

After graduating from Jewish Hospital Training School in St. Louis, Missouri, she joined the American Red Cross Nursing Service. She was called to active duty in July 1918 and was sent to Langres, France, where she was assigned to Base Hospital #53, treating the wounded and "gassed" soldiers from the front lines. She was discharged in July 1919.

HERBERT J. SCHAFFNER, Chief Petty Officer, was an electrician before enlisting in the U.S. Navy. He served in the Navy Seabees during WWII in New Guinea. Born November 3, 1900, he was the son of William and Mary E. Homan Schaffner. After discharge in 1945 he con-

Chief P.O. Herbert J. Schaffner

tinued as an electrician for Union Electric. He died July 9, 1979.

JAMES HOMAN SCHAFFNER, Corporal, served in the U.S. Army August 17, 1954 to August 4, 1956. He was born in Evansville, Illinois, August 3, 1935, son

Cpl. James Homan Schaffner

of William F. and Ethel Anita Thompson Schaffner. After basic training he was stationed in Germany with Company 47, Armed Infantry Batt. and worked in a QM Depot near Idar-Oberstein.

WILLIAM F. SCHAFFNER, SP-3, served in the U.S. Army May 19, 1955 to April 26, 1957. He was born in Evansville, Illinois, February 6, 1934, the son of Wil-

Spec/3 William F. Schaffner

liam F. and Ethel Anita Thompson Schaffner. After basic training, he attended Wheel Vehicle Mechanic School at Fort Leonard Wood, Missouri, then Track Vehicle Mechanic School at Fort Knox, Kentucky. He was transferred to A Battery, 27th AAA Battalion at Kapaun Barracks, located near Kaiserslautern, Germany.

PETER H. SCHERLE, Private First Class, served in the U.S. Army in WWI with Company I, 22nd Engineers from June 24, 1918 to July 18, 1919. He served in

Pfc. Peter H. Scherle

France where his unit maintained the narrow gauge railroad lines around Abainville, Dombasle and Tours, France. Discharged, he returned home to Evansville, Illinois.

BERTRAM IRWIN SCHIRMER, AFC, enlisted in U.S. Air Force in April 1949, completed his basic training at Lackland AFB, Texas, then assigned to Radio Operator's School, Biloxi, Mississippi, June 1949 to May 1950. Transferred in June 1950 to First Radio Squadron Security Service. From October 1951 to May 1952, AFC Schirmer was stationed in Korea. He was honorably discharged in November 1952.

AFC Bertram I. Schirmer

Schirmer Brothers - Korea. From left: Paul, Bertram and John.

Two of his brothers also served in Korea, Paul E. and John F. Schirmer. They are the sons of John W. and Caroline C. Sprengel Schirmer of Chester, Illinois.

JOHN W. SCHIRMER, Private First Class, served in the U.S. Army in WWI from June 24, 1918 to July 18, 1919. He served with Company I, 22nd Engineers in France, they maintained the narrow

Pfc. John W. Schirmer

gauge railroad lines around Abainville, Dombasle and Tours, France. He returned to America, was discharged and returned home to Chester, Illinois.

PAUL E. SCHIRMER, Staff Sergeant, served in the U.S. Air Force, June 9, 1949 to December 11, 1952. He attended Airborne Radio Mechanic School, Scott AFB, Illinois, then was sent to Korea, Sept. 30, 1950 to Feb. 25, 1952, with the 5th Air Force Comm. Group, 934th Signal Batallion. His tour took him from Teagu to Seoul and on to Pyongyang, the north Korea capitol and back to Seoul.

S/Sgt. Paul E. Schirmer

He returned to the States, Keesler AFB, Biloxi, Mississippi and was discharged December 11, 1952. He came home to Chester, Illinois.

FRED SCHMERBAUCH, Corporal, a member of 371st Engineers in WWII, was involved in one of the greatest engineering achievements of the war. They built

Cpl. Fred Schmerbauch

a bridge for railway trains and troops across the Rhine River in 10 days.

The 371st was brought to the front with all possible speed when the Roer line had been breached by German troops. Construction began under enemy fire, but the 371st didn't stop until the bridge was done and our troops could cross the Rhine to the Elbe River and beyond. Fred entered service in 1944 and served until 1945.

He was born November 25, 1924 in Kaskaskia, Illinois, the son of Louis and Charlotte Buatte Schmerbauch.

OTIS C. SCHMERBAUCH, Aviation Metalsmith 1/c, enlisted in the Navy December 17, 1941. He served with Squadron VC 72 aboard the U.S. *Kasaan Bay* aircraft carrier that performed 24/7 Antisubmarine Patrol with torpedo bombers and fighter planes.

AV. Metalsmith 1/c Otis C. Schmerbauch

Received training at Navy Pier, Chicago, Illinois and Norfolk, Virginia. He was then sent to Pearl Harbor and antisub patrol around New Hebrides, Guam, Saipan and from Seattle to San Diego. Discharged October 18, 1945, Alameda, California.

He was born October 14, 1913, at Kaskaskia, Illinois, the son of J. Louis and Charlotte Buatte Schmerbauch.

WILLIAM A. SCHMERBAUCH, First Sergeant, first served in Illinois Na-

1st Sgt. William A. Schmerbauch

Sgt. Schmerbauch receiving Bronze Star

tional Guard, January 11, 1937 to January 10, 1940, Company K, 130th Infantry. In WWII he served from March 5, 1941 until October 4, 1945 with Company K, 136th Infantry in Asiatic-Pacific Theatre, on New Guinea and Luzon Island.

Awarded two Bronze Stars for these campaigns, additional Bronze Star, four Overseas Bars, Philippine Liberation Ribbon w/Bronze Star, Good Conduct Medal and entitled to wear Asiatic-Pacific Theatre Ribbon.

Born November 18, 1916, Kaskaskia, Illinois, son of John Louis and Charlotte Buatte Schmerbauch, he died in Cairo, Illinois, February 26, 1978 and is buried in Mound City, Illinois National Cemetery.

EUGENE J. SCHMIDT, Chief Warrant Officer II, entered the Army in October 1961 and served as a fixed wing recon

Chief W.O. 2 Eugene J. Schmidt

pilot in Vietnam. He was with the 146th Aviation Company, U.S. Army. While there he was awarded the Air Medal w/33 Oak Leaf Clusters for flights over hostile territory. Gene also served in Korea, Thailand and Laos.

After military service in early 1968, he flew for and retired from United Airlines. After retiring he did volunteer work with Vietnamese immigrants.

Gene was born in Prairie du Rocher, Illinois November 9, 1940, the son of Oscar J. and Emma Mae Du Frenne Schmidt.

GEORGE SCHMIDT, born in Missouri, July 4, 1896 and served in WWI as a farrier in Headquarters Company, 87th Missouri Infantry. He lived in Rockwood, Illinois, until later years, then went to Illinois Veterans Home, Quincy, Illinois, where he died October 29, 1957 and is buried at the home in Sunset Cemetery.

EARL SCHMITZ, Sergeant, born Prairie du Rocher, November 25, 1915, son of George and Mary Schmitz. He entered WWII on April 29, 1941 and served in Ha-

Sgt. Earl Schmitz

waii with 627 Tank Destroyer DTN on extensive guard duty until discharge October 10, 1945.

ROBERT J. SCHMITZ, Platoon Sergeant, went into service in WWII on February 27, 1942 and had training at Fort Blanding, Florida, South Carolina and Camp Edward, Maine, then to Africa, where they had a lot of sand in equipment. He was with 141st Infantry, 36th Division, Company F as machine gunner. Participated in battles at Anzio, Rapido River, Monte Casio, during invasion of Italy, he was among the first troops into Rome.

About 90 miles north of Rome he was wounded in knee and sent to hospitals in Rome, Jefferson Barracks, Missouri, and discharged by way of Texas, Havana, Illinois and Chicago, Illinois on December 6, 1944. He was awarded the Purple Heart. Born near Prairie du Rocher, Illinois, September 14, 1915, the son of John and Helena Hoeft Schmitz.

JOHN A. SCHMOLL, Private, was born in Baldwin, Illinois, December 26, 1888, to John A. and Caroline Petzinger.

Pvt. John A. Schmoll

He served from June 24, 1918 until December 17, 1918, at Camp Zachary Taylor, Kentucky, during WWI. A farmer before he enlisted, upon returning home, he continued this occupation until his death, August 21, 1941.

LOUIS H. SCHMOLL, Private, the son of John A. and Caroline Petzinger Schmoll, was born in Baldwin, Illinois, December 5, 1890. He served in the Army during

Pvt. Louis H. Schmoll

WWI at Camp Zachary Taylor in Kentucky. A farmer before his enlistment, he spent his life farming. He died January 14, 1979.

FRIEDRICH SCHNEPEL, Private, son of Johann Cord Dietrich and Christine Luise Charlotte Berning Schnepel, born February 5, 1839 at Seelenfield, Germany. He enlisted in the Civil War May 15, 1864, in Red Bud, Illinois, and mustered in May 26, 1864 by Lieutenant Montgomery at Camp Butler, Illinois. He served until discharged at Nashville, Tennessee, November 4, 1865, by Captain Chickering.

He was a farmer prior to entering service. When he returned home, he was sickly, and died March 9, 1875 and is buried in St. John's Lutheran Cemetery in Red Bud, Illinois.

DEAN SCHNOEKER, E-3, enlisted in the U.S. Air Force February 10, 1977 and was discharged February 6, 1981. Dean completed his basic training at Lackland AFB. His next assigned duty was two years in Anchorage, Alaska in tele-communication.

E-3 Dean Schnoeker

He worked at Gilster Mary-Lee before entering service. Returning home Dean worked as a jailer in the Sheriff's Department. Dean was born in Red Bud, Illinois on October 17, 1959 son of Earl J. and __(Bollmann) Schnoeker.

DENNIS SCHNOEKER, Specialist 4, enlisted July 7, 1967 and was discharged April 17, 1969. Dennis took his basic and AIT in heavy equipment at Fort Leonard Wood, Missouri. He served a year in Vietnam at Long Binh, Bin Hoa USRV Headquarters as Operations Clerk. Dennis was with the 92nd Engineer Battalion while in Vietnam.

Sp-4 Dennis Schnoeker

Returning home, he worked as a truck driver, then as Therapy Aid II and as a transportation officer at Chester Mental Health Center. Dennis was born in Murphysboro, Illinois on November 15, 1947, son of Earl J. and __(Bollmann) Schnoeker.

DENNIS SCHNOEKER JR., BUS, enlisted in the service January 4, 1993 after graduating high school. He actively worked on construction projects in Cuba, Puerto Rico and Japan. He was with the NMCB5 Seabees during the Gulf War and was discharged January 3, 1998.

BUS Dennis Schnoeker

He has maintained a career as a carpenter in the surrounding area working for Barmac Construction. Dennis was born in Sparta, Illinois on March 26, 1974 to Dennis Earl and __ (Schutz) Schnoeker.

EARL J. SCHNOEKER, Sergeant, born September 7, 1920 in Chester, Illinois to Edmund and __ Sickmeyer Schnoeker. He served with Marines in WWII, in H Battery, 3rd Battalion, 10th Marines, 2nd Division, as Cannoneer with Artillery Battalion on Saipan, Tinian in Mariana Islands, and Tarrawa in Gilbert Islands.

Sgt. Earl J. Schnoeker

Earl was awarded Silver Star for bravery on Saipan. He entered service November 9, 1942 and was discharged December 13, 1945. He worked as chief of security at Chester Mental Health. Earl died December 23, 1996.

HARVEY W. SCHOBE, Private First Class, served in WWII with Headquarters Detachment as Supply Clerk 835 in Hawaii. He entered service January 10, 1945 and was discharged August 28, 1946. The son of Harvey and Mable Tatum Schobe, he was born November 11, 1926 in St. Louis County, Missouri.

WILBERT H. SCHOENBECK, Staff Sergeant, served in the U.S. Army from July 24, 1952 to July 24, 1954. He was born December 16, 1929 in Red Bud (Prairie), Illinois to Fred and Louise Nagel Schoenbeck. He was farming, had married Emma Wettig on September 24, 1950, when he was drafted into Army on July 24, 1952.

S/Sgt. Wilbert H. Schoenbeck

After eight weeks of basic training and six months Radio School, he remained in Camp Chaffee as instructor in various fields. He achieved the rank of staff sergeant and was discharged July 24, 1954.

He farmed full time at Prairie until retirement January 1, 1995. He now helps his son on the farm.

CLYDE EUGENE SCHOTT, E-6/CMI, entered the Navy in May 1941, the day after graduating from Sparta High School. He had won a football scholarship to Monmouth College, but instead of accepting it, he and his two buddies "Junior" Clarence Henderson and Robert Hein, decided to serve their country. His basic training was at Great Lakes, Illinois. During WWII, Clyde ended up on a hospital evacuation ship as a mechanic and was stationed at various locations though out the South Pacific.

E-6 Clyde Eugene Schott

The ship was a converted LST (Landing Ship Tank) designed to land on the beaches and retrieve wounded men, but it did not have special protected status under the Geneva Convention, as regular hospital ships did. As a result, the crew members were armed and often found themselves in the middle of battle.

Clyde left the regular Navy in 1947 and joined the Seabees, a reserve naval construction battalion. Later, Clyde was called for duty in Vietnam, where he was put in charge of heavy forklift equipment at the Da Nang base in 1969. After retiring from the Navy, Clyde worked as a heavy-duty mechanic in Casper, Wyoming.

He was born in Sparta, Illinois on June 15, 1924 the son of Alvin John Schott and Goldie Lilly (Howie) Schott. Clyde passed away January 27, 2003 and is buried in a Veteran's plot at Caledonia Cemetery, Sparta, Illinois.

CHARLIE T. SCOTT, Sergeant First Class, E-7, served in the U.S. Army July 27, 1950 to July 31, 1971 with the 3rd Infantry Division in Germany; the 5th Division in Korea, 1952 thru August 1953; in Vietnam, July 1967 thru February 1970; and the Tet Offensive in 1968.

He spent 12 of his 21 years in the Army, overseas, 48 months in combat, earning the Silver Star, Bronze Star and Army Commendation Medal.

He was born August 3, 1932 in Arkansas, the son of A.F. and Vergie Reves Scott. After retirement he worked at Menard Department of Corrections for over 20 years.

CLARENCE W. SCHRADER, Tech Sergeant, served in WWII from September 1942 until October 1945 in the Army Air Corps. He was a crew member aboard a B-24 bomber as a flight engineer and gunner and flew 30 combat missions over Europe.

He was awarded the Distinguished Flying Cross, Air Medal w/3 Oak Leaf Clusters, European Theater Ribbon w/2 Bronze Stars and the Air Member Badge (Wings).

A native of Percy, Illinois, he is the son of William H. and Clara Caupert Schrader.

ROGER A. SCHROEDER, Sergeant First Class, served in the U.S. Army from January 31, 1951 to January 30, 1954. He

Sgt 1/c Roger A. Schroeder

was born March 21, 1932 in Chester, Randolph County, Illinois, to Ludwig and Emma Hartenberger Schroeder. Roger served with H/S Company, 8th Combat Engineers, 1st Cavalry Division during the Korean conflict.

He spent two years and nine months in Korea and Japan, then returned to the U.S. to Camp Rucker, Alabama, Headquarters Company. Roger was discharged January 30, 1954. After the service he worked for World Color Press.

E. FRED SCHUCHERT, Corporal, enlisted in the 1st Missouri National Guard Infantry Regiment of St. Louis March 24, 1917. Later he served in St. Mihiel, Vanquvis Hill and Argonne Forest in France. He was wounded and gassed in the Argonne drive September 26, 1918, Company K, 3rd Battalion, 138th Division, and was in a hospital in France when Armistice was signed. Fred was discharged May 14, 1919.

Cpl. E. Fred Schuchert

Born in Chester, Illinois, December 12, 1892, son of John F. and Anna Schemmer Schuchert, he died in Chester, October 13, 1954

ELROY A. SCHULEIN, Staff Sergeant, inducted into WWII November 25, 1942, Jefferson Barracks, Missouri. Trained at Camp Claiborne, Louisiana and Camp Howze, Texas. He left the U.S. October

S/Sgt. Elroy A. Schulein

6, 1944 for Rhineland and Central Europe. Landed at Marseilles, France October 20, 1944 and engaged in fighting of Siegfried Line in Germany, with 409th Infantry Regiment, 103rd Division, 3rd Battalion, Company M.

They completed operations near Innsbruck, Austria, May 5, 1945. Awarded WWII Victory Ribbon, European-African-Middle Eastern Ribbon w/2 Bronze Stars, Good Conduct Ribbon and Combat Infantry Badge.

In 1949 he returned to Evansville area and began farming. Born at Evansville, Illinois, February 8, 1922, the son of Cletus and Mary Petry Schulein, he died May 16, 1982.

ROBERT C. SCHULEIN, Corporal, was drafted in May 1943 into WWII as one of seven brothers that served. His group, 11th Airborne Paratroops, were on a ship to invade Japan, when atomic bomb was dropped and Japan surrendered. Spent one year in Japan and was discharged in October 1945.

Cpl. Robert C. Schulein

Son of Cletus and Mary Petry Schulein, he was born in Evansville, Illinois, August 23, 1924. After service he worked in shoe factory, construction, owned and operated a school bus.

THOMAS H. SCHULEIN, Petty Officer 2/c, of Evansville, Illinois, was born January 17, 1936, to Cletus and Mary Petry

P.O. 2/c Thomas H. Schulein

Schulein. He entered the Navy, January 23, 1958 and attended boot camp training at San Diego, California, and from there went to Aviation School at Norman, Oklahoma.

After graduation he went to Kingsville, Texas, then to the Naval Air Station at Cubo Point, Philippine Islands, where his job was that of aircraft engine mechanic and flight engineer.

LESTER G. SCHULTE, Tech 5, served in Company B, 958th Army Air Corps during WWII. Working in Hammond, Indiana, prior to returning to Sparta, Illinois to enlist November 10, 1942. Discharged January 26, 1946, he returned home and

T/5 Lester G. Schulte

went into rock quarry business as owner/partner for 40 years in Chester. Born November 28, 1921, in Sparta, Illinois, son of August and Emma Gosejohann Schulte.

KENNETH LEE SCHULTZ, Lance Corporal, serving March 11, 2002 to

L/Cpl Kenneth L. Schultz

present time in the U.S. Marine Corps. He was born September 29, 1981, the son of Kenneth and Debbie Pierottie Schultz. Graduating high school, he chose the Marine Corps instead of college, completed boot camp at Parris Island, SC, then on to school at Fort Sill, Oklahoma. He specializes in the Artillery field and is currently at Camp Lejeune, NC, awaiting possible orders to Kuwait.

FRED P. SCHUPBACH, Master Sergeant, tried to volunteer three times in 1942 to serve in WWII. He was rejected due to being blind in one eye. He was then drafted January 7, 1943 for limited service, signing a forfeiting injury clause while in service.

On December 10, 1943, he left the U.S. with 742nd Squadron, 455, B-24 Bomb Group, and was sent to North Africa and Foggia, Italy. He was discharged September 2, 1945 at Fort Sheridan, Illinois.

He was born June 28, 1928, Denmark, Illinois, the son of Fred A. and Anna Porter Schupbach.

WILLIAM A. SCHUWERK SR., First Lieutenant, was an infantry officer with Patton's 3rd Army in 35th Division. He served from hedge rows of France through Belgium, crossing Rhine River into Germany until V-E Day. He was company

1/Lt. William A. Schuwerk Sr.

commander for most of this period. Born in St. Louis, Missouri to William H. and __ Crisler Schuwerk, on May 10, 1921. After D-Day, Battle of Bulge, he returned home at end of war in 1945.

WILLIAM H. SCHUWERK, served in Infantry during WWI. Born February 10, 1890, Evansville, Illinois, son of William M. and Hoffman Schuwerk, he died October 15, 1965.

BENJAMIN A. SEBASTIAN, son of Benjamin F. and Lilie A. Montroy

Pvt. Benjamin A. Sebastian

Sebastian, was born September 29, 1910, Cora City, Illinois. He enlisted in WWII, April 27, 1944, just two months after his stepson PFC Gilbert G. Prosek was killed in action on January 3, 1944. At Camp Hood, Texas he served as a rifle marksman with Company B, 147th Battalion. Given a medical discharge November 10, 1944, he died September 7, 1991.

CHARLES C. SEBASTIAN, Private First Class, served with Company G, 63rd Infantry, 6th Division on Luzon in Philippines and New Guinea Campaign during WWII. He went into service April 29, 1941, and was wounded in fighting on Luzon January 19, 1945 while defending a hill while comrade went for help. When found, he was wounded but still holding his rifle.

Pfc. Charles C. Sebastian

Discharged August 22, 1945, he received the Purple Heart and Bronze Star.

Son of Benjamin and Lillian Montroy Sebastian, he was born in Cora City, Illinois February 15, 1912 and died August 11, 1976.

HAROLD CARL SEEMAN, Private First Class (T), from Steeleville, Illinois, was in the Army during the Korean War. He served with the 94th Engineer Company, 3rd Armoured Division. He entered service March 31, 1953 and received basic training at Fort Knox, Kentucky, then

Pfc. Harold Carl Seeman

volunteered for the Far East Command and served one and a half years with the 94th Engineer Company at Hiyoshi, Honshu, and Yokohama, Japan.

He received the United Nations National Defense Service Medals and Korean Service Ribbon, before being discharged March 21, 1955.

His parents are Henry D. and Augusta Wolters Seemann. PFC Seeman has been an American Legion member for 40 years.

HENRY D. SEEMANN, Private, entered WWI June 24, 1918, at age 28, at Camp Taylor, Kentucky. He served in the Army as a private, Headquarters Company, 5th Regiment FARD. His service ended on December 17, 1918, when the war ended.

Pvt. Henry D. Seeman

He was born in Steman, Germany in 1890 and emigrated to the U.S. at age 5, and became a nationalized citizen. He lived in Steeleville, Illinois. His parents were Fredrich and Margareta Dreyer Seemann. He died 1958 and is buried at St. Mark's Cemetery, Steeleville, Illinois.

ARTHUR Q. SEYMOUR, Seaman 1/c, served in South Pacific during WWII on LST 598 from May 10, 1944 until January 30, 1946 when he was discharged. He returned to Fort Gage, Illinois, where he was born January 28, 1925, son of Arthur

Seaman 1/c Arthur Q. Seymour

H. and Millie Ennis Seymour. He died at age 28 in 1953 by drowning.

GERALD E. SEYMOUR, Navy Airman 1/c, served in the U.S. Navy November 16, 1950 to August 24, 1954 with Patrol Squadron 44, Naval Air Station, Norfolk, Virginia. After service he returned to Ellis Grove, Illinois where he still resides, is active in the community and the mayor for six years.

A/M 1/c Gerald E. Seymour

Known as "Splinter," he was born January 5, 1930, Fort Gage, Illinois, the son of Arthur H. and Millie Ennis Seymour.

DENNIS L. SHAW, Sergeant (T), served in the U.S. Army September 1966 to September 1968. After basic training at Fort Leonard Wood, Missouri he was assigned as a medical records specialist with Medical Detachment, 5th U.S. Army Hospital at Fort Benjamin Harrison, IN.

T/Sgt. Dennis Shaw

He was born in St. Louis, Missouri May 15, 1943, the son of Lynn H. and June McIntyre Shaw.

LYNN SHAW, Staff Sergeant, born May 6, 1920, Randolph County, Illinois, served in South Pacific with Medical Battalion during WWII, participating in island campaigns and occupation of Japan. He entered service in 1942 and was discharged in 1946.

The Shaw Brothers. Cpl. Kenneth "Shorty" Shaw, Cpl. Wayne Shaw, Staff Sgt. Lynn Shaw and Cpl. Stanley Shaw

He and three brothers, all sons of Alvin and Bertha Shaw of Coulterville, were all in service during WWII. Brothers: Corporal Kenneth Shaw was a paratrooper; Corporal Wayne Shaw was in New Guinea, Philippines and Japan; and Corporal Stanley Shaw served with the medical battalion in Europe and was wounded in action.

CHARLES C. SHEELER, Corporal, served in the U.S. Army from August 1952 to August 1954. He was born August 30, 1931, son of William C. and Margaret O'Neill Sheeler. Charles, "Bud" Sheeler entered the Army in August 1952, took basic training and signal training at Camp Gordon, Georgia. He was sent to Germany in January 1953, served with the 1st Signal Company, 1st Infantry Division as a telephone installer repairman.

Cpl. Charles C. Sheeler

He returned to the U.S. in August 1954 and was honorably discharged. He worked for A.O. Smith Company, Granite City, Illinois as a welder and quality control inspector. He also worked for the Randolph County Sheriff's Department, Spartan

Printing Company and is currently employed at Sparta WalMart.

FRANKLIN D. SHEELER, served in the U.S. Army from June 1955 to June 1958. He served with Headquarters Company, 507th Army Security Agency GP, completed basic training at Fort Leonard Wood, Missouri and specialty training at Fort Devens, Massachussets. He served two years in Heilbronn, Germany.

Franklin Sheeler

After his discharge he worked 35 years for World Color Press, Sparta, Illinois. He is the son of Wm. Curtis and Margaret O'Neill Sheeler, born November 8, 1936 in Coulterville, Illinois. He is married to former Leola Koester and has four children: Scott, Keith, Kristen and Kathleen.

THOMAS E. SHEELER, Sp-4, served in the U.S. Army, January 1962 to January 1964. He was born December 20, 1938, the son of William C. and Margaret O'Neill Sheeler. After basic training at Fort Leonard Wood, Missouri, he was sent to Fort Carson, Colorado and served there with Headquarters Company, 5th Division, as driver for Chief of Staff and was TAD for additional training at Fort Jackson, South Carolina and Fort Lewis, Washington.

Spec-4 Thomas Sheeler

He worked 30 years at Spartan Printing and retired from printing plant in Richmond, Virginia.

ELMER JAMES SHEMONIC, S1/c, served in the U.S. Army from May 9, 1951 to May 9, 1954, with Company D, 135th Engineers, Combat Batt., 44th Infantry Division, Illinois National Guard. Joining National Guard in May 1951, he took 10 weeks Wheel Vehicle Maintenance Training, Fort Riley, Kansas. Their National Guard unit, based in Chester, Illinois, was activated for duty in February 1952 and sent to Camp Cooke, California.

Sp. 1/c Elmer J. Shemonic

Sent to Korea in November 1952, he was assigned to 740th Ordnance Bat., 40th Infantry Division as senior wheel vehicle mechanic. Discharged September 25, 1958 at Camp Carson, Colorado, he returned to his local unit to finish enlistment.

Elmer was born October 19, 1930, Rockwood, Illinois, son of John II and Sadie Harmon Shemonic.

JOHN SHEMONIC, Private, entered Company E, 30th Regiment of the Illinois Infantry, August 2, 1861 at Camp Butler, Illinois. He was assigned to Brigadier General John A. McClernand's Brigade, under Brigadier General U.S. Grant. He fought in the battle of Belmont, Kentucky, and in the siege and taking of Fort Donelson, Tennessee. Went to Medan Station and from there moved with General Grant to Bruinsburg and on to Raymond, Mississippi.

John was in the battle of Champion

Pvt. John Shemonic

Mills, the siege of Vicksburg, then moved with General Sherman to Jackson, Nickajack Creek and on to the battle of Atlanta. He was discharged from service September 27, 1864. The son of Jacob and Mary ? Shemonic, he is buried in St. Mary's Catholic Cemetery in Chester, Illinois. His name is engraved on Company E of the 30th Regiment Plaque in the Illinois Memorial in Vicksburg, Mississippi Battlefield Park.

DONALD A. SICKMEYER, Airman 1/c, served in the U.S. Air Force from September 1948 to September 1952. The son of Adolph and Selma Vieregge Sickmeyer, Chester, Illinois. He completed his basic training at Sheppard AFB, Wichita, Texas and music training at Boling AFB, Washington, DC.

AM 1/c Donald A. Sickmeyer

He was transferred to Puerto Rico for six months, then de-activated to Panama Canal, Balboa Canal Zone. He was discharged in September 1952 at Alexandria, AFB in Louisiana.

After service he became a doctor of chiropractic medicine with a practice in Chester, Illinois. He continues his music, playing in the Chester Community Band.

EDWARD J. SIEMERS, First Sergeant, entered WWII March 7, 1941 and served on Luzon, South Philippines, Bismark Archipelago, New Britain around

1st Sgt. Edward J. Siemers

Solomon Islands. Landed on D-Day on Luzon, Panay and Negro in Philippines.

Served as first sergeant of Company M, 185th Infantry, 40th Division for three years. He was awarded the Bronze Star, Combat Infantry Badge and campaign ribbon. Discharged October 6, 1945.

Edward was born in Chester, Illinois, July 16, 1918, son of Ed and Leona Bockhorn Siemers.

DANIEL MARTIN HENRY SIMPSON, Sergeant, joined the University of Illinois ROTC program. Served with Army Security Agency, 1951-53; U.S. Army Chemical Corps, 1953-55; and U.S. Army Reserve 1956-61. He was born November 16, 1930, Evansville, Illinois, to Claude Henry and Nathalie Rosa Kennedy Simpson.

Sgt. Daniel M.H. Simpson

After ROTC, he joined the Army, November 3, 1953 with training at 5th Armored Division, Camp Chaffee, Arkansas and Chemical Corps School, Fort McClellan, Alabama. He served as the TI&E NCO in the 34th Chemical Company at Fort McClellan and was discharged on November 2, 1955 and assigned to U.S. Army Reserves, 1956-61.

Returned to University of Illinois in 1956, received a Ph.D. degree in soil chemistry and fertility in 1961. After 25 years with W.R. Grace, he retired as marketing manager of agricultural chemicals in 1990.

ORVILLE SIMPSON, Sergeant, of Evansville, Illinois, was killed in Germany March 21, 1945, during WWII at the age of 31 years, 6 months and 28 days. His body was brought home to Evansville and buried in St. Boniface Cemetery, November 5, 1948.

HARRY R. SINGER, Private First Class, entered WWII in January 1946 and served in 127th Constabulary. He was in Germany as a police, guarding German POWs; was in Nurnberg at war trials as they tried Goerring, a headman in Hitler's cabinet.

Born in E. Stroudsburg, Pennslyvania, son of Jeremiah and Alice Crowe Singer, he moved to Illinois when he married and lived in Randolph County until his death in 1998. Harry is buried in Paradise Cemetery, near Steeleville, Illinois.

MALDEN J. SIPOLE, Seaman 1/c, joined the Navy May 4, 1945, at St. Louis, Missouri. Served in SC+C TI-Sp-Ce1, Se-

Seaman 1/c Malden J. Sipole

attle, Washington, and USS *Yellowstone*, Boston, Massachusetts. Discharged August 10, 1946, he died August 24, 1990. Malden was born in Prairie du Rocher, Illinois on March 16, 1927, son of Emmett S. and Selma Hall Sipole.

PERCEL ELIAS SIPOLE, Seaman, served in the U.S. Navy from April 16, 1948 to March 31, 1952 aboard the USS *Navrecsta*, Seattle, Washington. He entered the Navy at St. Louis, assigned duty ComFltAct Navy #3923 and was awarded the Korean Service Medal, Navy Occupation w/Asian Clasp and United Nations Ribbon.

Seaman Percel E. Sipole

He was born August 2, 1929, Fort Gage, Illinois, the son of Emmett S. and Selma Hall Sipole. Percel is currently residing at St. Ann's Nursing Home, Chester, Illinois.

HEINRICH SIPPEL, a soldier in the Civil War, was born in Holstein, Kurhessen, Germany, came to America and lived in Round Prairie, near Red Bud, Illinois. He died at Andersonville, Georgia in the prison camp on October 6, 1864, age 25 years 1 month and 5 days old.

VICTOR EDWARD SLACK, Private First Class, served in the U.S. army 1950-52 with the 15th Infantry Regiment. He was wounded in Korea and received the Purple Heart. After his discharge July 31,

Pfc. Victor E. Slack

1952, he worked for the city of Chester and also the VFW Post 3553 of which he is a past commander. He was born in Palestine, Randolph County, the son of William and Clara Breithaupt Slack. He died December 16, 1998.

AUGUSTUS SMITH, Private, served with Company H of the 22nd Illinois Infantry during the Civil War. He joined the Army at Caseyville, Illinois, guarded the Memphis and Charleston Railroad, marched around Tennessee, Kentucky and Missouri fighting in various battles. He served from June 25, 1861 to July 7, 1864, mustered out in Springfield, Illinois.

He was born 1838, Mulhausen, Germany, the son of Ignatius and Theresa Smith. Augustus married Mary Dailey and had two daughters in the Evansville, Illinois area. He died April 23, 1868 and is buried in Kelly Cemetery, Evansville, Illinois.

EDWIN R. SMITH, Specialist 5, served in the U.S. Army from November 1959 to November 1962 with the 3rd Infantry Division, 41st Artillery in Bamberg, Germany.

He was born in Chester on July 9,

Spc-5 Edwin R. Smith

Spec-4 Norman A. Smith

1940, son of Renwick and Ella Phegley Smith. Edwin retired after 34 years with the state of Illinois.

JAMES A. SMITH, Private, born in Bremen, Illinois, the son of Francis and Agnes Adams Smith, served in Company L, 13th Cavalry Regiment in the Civil War from December 21, 1863 until October 4, 1865. His regiment was mostly in Arkansas and took part in the battles of Pea Ridge, Little Rock, Pine Bluff, Poison Springs, Arkadelphia and Spoonville. He received four injuries in the left side, during the fight at Poison Springs, and when under charge at Brownville, his horse fell with him and he fractured five ribs. He was sent to a convalescent camp and mustered out October 4, 1865.

JOSEPH SMITH, Private, born February 7, 1835, Mulhausen, Germany, son of Ignatius and Theresa Smith. He joined the Army February 21, 1865, at Camp Butler, Illinois and served with Company F, 154th Infantry. He was sent to Louisville, Kentucky, then to Nashville and Murfreesboro, Tennessee.

In March 1865, he was attached to 1st Brigade, to defend Nashville and the Chattanooga Railroad. On June 19, 1865, he mustered out at Nashville. Most of the regiment had been lost due to disease during service.

Joseph died December 25, 1903 and is buried in Old St. Boniface Cemetery, Evansville, Illinois.

NORMAN ANTHONY SMITH, SPC-4, entered the Army on December 15, 1965. Norman took basic training at Fort Leonard Wood, Missouri, then to Fort Sill, Oklahoma and trained on field artillery. In May 1966 he was sent to Vietnam and joined B Battery, 3rd, 18th Field Artillery, 1st Cavalry, operating an 8" self-propelled hawser.

Norman participated in "Operation Happy Valley" and others throughout South Vietnam. He was discharged December 14, 1967. Upon returning home he worked at Sparta News-Plaindealer, AFCO Furnace, Singer Furniture, Snyder Gen, Inter-City Products, Coulterville Equipment, and Hubbell-Weigmann.

He lives on and farms the family farm south of Walsh. He married June 28, 1969 to Janice Steele and is father to Lisa (Jeff Lake) and Perry (Jennifer Pollard) and grandfather to Bobbie and Blaise Lake. Norman was born March 14, 1946, son of Henry Salkeld and Eula (Gaertner) Smith.

PAUL SMITH, Corporal, served in Company D of the 22nd Illinois Infantry in Civil War. Paul is the son of Ignatius and Theresa Smith, Evansville, IL. Paul is buried in Kelly Cemetery, Evansville, Illinois.

POWELL SMITH, Corporal, was born February 28, 1844. Served in Company D, 80th Illinois Infantry. The 80th was organized in Centralia, Illinois by Colonial T.G. Allen in August 1862. On September 4 he was ordered to Louisville, Kentucky as part of the 33rd Brigade, 10th Division, under General Jackson and October 1, under General Buell. The unit marched in pursuit of General Bragg and engaged him in battle at Perryville, Missouri October 8, where they had a loss of 14 men killed, 58 wounded.

On January 10, 1863, he was assigned to 14th Army Corps, and on March 20, the brigade with 1,500 men and two pieces of artillery, met John Morgan and 5,000 enemy troops. After being mounted, he participated in battles of Dug's Gap and Sand Mountain. On May 3, the unit was forced to surrender to the superior troops of General Forest. Officers were sent to Libby Prison, and privates were sent to Camp Chase, Ohio, where on July 23, they were declared exchanged. On July 29, he went back to seat of war and later took part in battle of Mission Ridge. In 1864 he was with Sherman in his march to the sea.

Powell was mustered out of service, June 10, 1865, at Camp Butler, Illinois. He died November 27, 1927, and is buried in Kelly Cemetery Evansville, Illinois.

ROGER W. SMITH, Private First Class, served in the U.S. Army November 23, 1951 to November 11, 1953. Roger was born to Henry Salkeld and Juliana "Eula" Gaertner Smith, Walsh, Illinois. He served with Headquarters Company, 26th Infantry Regiment, 1st Division, he was trained as a field lineman.

Pfc. Roger W. Smith

After basic training, Company M, 11th Infantry Regiment, Indiantown Gap, Pennsylvania, he was stationed with occupational troops at Bamberg, Germany. He was discharged November 11, 1953, married June Heuman in 1954, and has five children and 10 grandchildren.

VIRGIL K. SMITH, Chief Petty Officer, enlisted in the Navy in 1942 and served as chief carpenter's mate on New Guinea until discharged October 31, 1945. A construction worker before enlisting, he returned home to work as construction foreman for Massman Construction until his death November 25, 1976.

Born March 6, 1911, he was reared

CPO Virgil K. Smith

in Rockwood, Illinois, son of George and Harriet Pinkerton Smith. Virgil is buried in Ebenezer Cemetery near Rockwood.

DARYL LESLIE SNODGRASS, Navy Radio Technician, served in Pacific Theater during WWII. He was discharged December 30, 1945. He died October 7, 1946 and is buried in Tilden, Illinois. Daryl was the son of Everett C. and Florence Morton Snodgrass.

EVERETT CLARENCE SNODGRASS, served in WWI in Europe with Battery F, 308th Field Artillery and was discharged May 27, 1919. The son of Martin L. and Mary Jane McIntyre Snodgrass, he died July 31, 1952, and is buried in Tilden, Illinois.

ISAAC EVERETT SNODGRASS, Sergeant, 30th Illinois Infantry, Company C, Veteran Volunteers, served in the Civil War, 1861-65, and was wounded at Vicksburg. He was the son of Archibald and Isabella Blair Snodgrass. He died November 11, 1902 and is buried at Union Cemetery in Sparta, Illinois.

JAMES A. SPIER, SP5, served in the U.S. Army from March 3, 1964 to March 2, 1966, at Fort Leonard Wood, Missouri as a heavy truck driver, then attached to

Sp/5 James A Spier

82nd Airborne and 101st Air Cavalry driving fuel trucks for the helicopters and other vehicles. He was assigned to Dominican Republic for four months in 1965. He was born in Red Bud, Illinois on August 8, 1942, son of Erhardt and Dorothy Eggerding Spier.

OSCAR W. SPRENGEL, Storekeeper 3/c, entered service in WWII in May 1945. He took basic training at Great Lakes Naval Center. Put USS *Nerevs* in commission on West Coast and relieved subtender

Storekeeper 3/c Oscar W. Sprengel

in Subic Bay, Japan. He blew up 32 subs before leaving Subic Bay. He transferred to Pearl Harbor to the USS *Fulton* for Atomic Bomb test and was discharged in October 1946. From Chester, Illinois, he is the son of Arthur and Hildegard Moll Sprengel.

NORBERT G. SPRINGER, Seaman 1/c, entered service in WWII on September 18, 1943. He had boot camp at Great Lakes Naval Center, Illinois, was stationed at USN Personnel Separation Center, Shoemaker, California and U.S. Naval Base, Treasure Island, California. He was discharged March 17, 1946. Son of Louis and Gertrude Good Springer, he was born at Oakville, Illinois on August 15, 1924 and now resides in Chester, Illinois.

LEWIS SPURGEON, Private, served in Company A, 155th Infantry, which was organized at Camp Butler, Illinois by Colonial Gustavus Smith. Mustered in February 28, 1865, nine hundred and four strong, went via Louisville and Nashville to Tullahoma, Tennessee, where they were divided into detachments of 20 to 30 men, and assigned to guard the Nashville and Chattanooga railroad, from Nashville to Duck River, a distance of 50 miles. Mustered out of service September 4, 1865, he was given final pay at Camp Butler. Private Spurgeon is buried in Kelly Cemetery, Evansville, Illinois.

PAUL C. STALLMAN, Corporal, served in WWII in U.S. Army Ordnance. Military training at David Rankin School of Automotive Mechanics, St. Louis, Missouri, then served two years in Motor Pool Division at Drew Field, in Tampa, Florida. He served five months in Asiatic-Pacific Theatre, Philippine Islands.

Discharged in February 1945, he is now a retired farmer living near Chester,

Cpl. Paul C. Stallman

Illinois. Born March 27, 1919, in Chester, his parents are Rudolph and Emilie Koopman Stallman.

PAUL EDWARD STALLMAN, Specialist 4/c, was the last person drafted by Randolph County Draft Board #185 on June 23, 1971. He served as a research physicist at the U.S. Army Cold Regions Research and Engineering Laboratory in Hanover, New Hampshire studying the strength of ice for the mobilization of Army units on frozen surfaces.

Spec. 4 Paul E. Stallman

Born December 28, 1947, in Chester, Illinois, he is the son of Paul C. and Henrietta Beck Stallman. Discharged from the Army Corps of Engineers, June 22, 1973, he is currently a math teacher and athletic director at Chester High School.

MURRAY STANLEY, Private, served in Company G, 152nd Infantry from May

Pvt. Murray Stanley

17, 1918 until March 5, 1919, when he was discharged desperately ill from the Army Hospital in Denver, Colorado. Born October 7, 1895, in Rockwood, Illinois to William and Cora Pait Stanley, he died September 3, 1919, and is buried in Barber Cemetery in Rockwood, Illinois.

CHARLES R. STEELE, Staff Sergeant, enlisted in Army February 16, 1945 and served in WWII with 770 RR Operation Battalion. He was discharged August 5, 1946. A railroad worker before enlisting, he served as a trainmaster in Korea. Returning home he worked as a trainmaster for the Gulf, Mobile and Ohio Railroad. Charles died September 5, 1999. His parents were Noah Luther and Hattie Benson Steele.

JOHN STEELE, Captain, was born in 1757 in England, the son of Captain Samuel Steele and Sarah Hunter Steele. He was a private in the Battle of Mt. Pleasant, Lord Dunsmore War, 1774 and served in the Revolutionary War April 4, 1777 as 2nd lieutenant. On May 26, 1778 he was transferred to 1st VA. Promoted to 1st lieutenant February 18, 1781 and taken prisoner at Charleston May 12, 1780. He was captain of independent company under immediate command of General George Washington. His father was also a captain in Revolutionary War. He and his sons were early founders of Steeleville, Illinois and named after them.

RICHARD T. STEFANI, Specialist 4, was drafted on August 13, 1970 and took his basic training at Fort Campbell, Kentucky. His advanced infantry training was at Fort Polk, Louisiana. While in Vietnam he served with the 4th Squadron, 12th Cavalry and fought in the Lom Som 719, MOS 11-Charlie, 81mm mortar.

He received the Army Commendation Medal for meritorious service against hostile forces while in Vietnam. He was discharged February 14, 1972.

Born on November 8, 1950 in St. Louis, Missouri, he is the son of Ernest and Dolores (Wittenbrink) Stefani.

MARTIN W. STEGMANN, Private, went in service in WWII, January 24, 1941, with Company L, 32nd Infantry, stationed at Fort Ord, California. The arches in both feet were broken while marching in train-

Pvt. Martin W. Stegman

ing. He spent a lot of time in infirmary and was given a medical discharge March 11, 1941. His parents were Herman and Alma Rubach Stegmann of Percy, Illinois.

CHARLES JOSEPH STEIBEL, SP-4, enlisted in the Army on September 28, 1965. Charles took his basic training at Fort Leonard Wood, Missouri. Then he went to Fort Eustis, Virginia for his AIT. On March 15, 1966 he left Fort Eustis for a year tour of duty in Vietnam. He was with 1098th Medical Battalion Company.

Spec. 4 Charles J. Steibel

When Charles returned to the States, he spent the rest of his time at Fort Eustis, Virginia. He was honorably discharged September 17, 1967. Parents are George and Wilmarth (Sis) (Dufrenne) Steibel.

COLIN J. STEIBEL, Specialist 4, enlisted into the Army in September 1990. Colin took his basic and completed his AIT heavy equipment mechanic training at Fort Dix, New Jersey. Then he was stationed for one year in Korea. Colin was with the 84th Engineer Battalion. His last duty station was Fort Lewis, WA. He was honorably discharged in June 1993. Colin was born in Red Bud, Illinois on September 9, 1972, son of Charles J. and Mary F. (Pautler) Steibel.

COREY J. STEIBEL, SP-4, entered the Army in October 1989. He took his basic and AIT training (heavy equipment mechanic training) at Fort Jackson, South Carolina. Then he was stationed in Korea for 15 months. His last tour of duty was at Fort Bragg, North Carolina. He was with the 362nd Engineer Battalion and received his honorable discharge in April 1992. He was born in Red Bud, Illinois on June 28, 1971. His parents are Charles J. and Mary F. (Pautler) Steibel.

CYNTHIA (STEIBEL) JORDAN, Specialist 4, enlisted into the Army in February 1987. After basic training at Fort Jackson, South Carolina, she went to AIT training as a medic at Fort Sam Houston, San Antonio, Texas. Then she spent the remainder of her service time stationed with the 269th Medical Detachment in Wertheim, West Germany.

She was discharged in July 1989. Cynthia was born April 21, 1969 in Red Bud, Illinois the daughter of Charles J. and Mary F. (Pautler) Steibel.

MICHELLE (STEIBEL) ZIMMER, Specialist 4, entered the Army on February 2, 1988, and completed basic training at Fort Jackson, South Carolina. Then she went to Fort Sam Houston, Texas for her AIT training as a medic.

Steibel Family: Front from left: Corey Steibel, Michelle Stiebel Zimmer and Colin Steibel. Back row: Cynthis Steibel Jordan and husband, Ken.

After her training she was stationed in Baumholder, West Germany with the 30th Field Hospital for the remainder of her service time. She was honorably discharged February 6, 1990.

Michelle was born in Red Bud, Illinois on April 9, 1970, the daughter of Charles J. and Mary F. (Pautler) Steibel. She still reside in Randolph County, Illinois.

LARRY D. STEINER, Specialist 5, was drafted into the Army in October 1967.

Spec. 5 Larry D. Steiner

Larry took his basic training at Fort Bliss, Texas. Then took his AIT at Fort Gordon, Georgia. He was sent to Vietnam in March 1968 where he served in the 3/22 Infantry, 25th Infantry Division, Company D near the Saigon area through July as a machine gunner. Larry received the Cross of Gallantry, after sustaining injuries in battle, he was transferred to the 25th Administration Company where he served until May 1969.

Upon returning home, he enrolled at SIU-C and received a BS degree in mechanical engineering. He worked for Peabody Coal Company as a maintenance supervisor and senior project engineer for 22 years and is currently employed at Chester Mental Health. Larry was born May 21, 1947 in Red Bud, Illinois, the second son of Julius and Edith (Hood) Steiner. He lives in Sparta, Illinois with his wife, Brenda, and has two children, Andrea (26) and Ryan (23), who is presently serving in the Illinois National Guard.

ALFRED A. STELLHORN, Corporal, served in the U.S. Army from January 15, 1952 to October 15, 1953. He was born in Evansville, Illinois, son of Edward and Elma Lucht Stellhorn on October 27, 1930. He was drafted in January 1952, completed 16 weeks of basic training in Hawaii, and transferred to Korea for 13 months as a truck driver for 38th Infantry Battalion and Tank Company. He returned to the States to Camp Crowder. After his discharge Alfred farmed on his father's dairy farm at Prairie, Illinois until retirement in 1995. He moved to Red Bud, Illinois in 2000.

CONRAD H. STELLHORN, Private First Class, was called to duty during WWII in November 1942. He received training at Fort McClellan, Alabama; Camp Philip, Kansas; Camp Campbell, Kentucky; and Fort Meade, Maryland before being sent overseas in June 1944.

Pvt. Conrad H. Stellhorn

Reported missing in action, July 29, 1944, he died August 29, 1944 in hospital in Rennes, France of wounds. Buried in cemetery in St. James, France. His body was returned to U.S. and buried at St. John Lutheran Cemetery in Baldwin, Illinois, August 1, 1948.

He was awarded Purple Heart, posthumously. Born April 19, 1913, his parents were Conrad and Wilhelmina Kloepper Stellhorn.

EDGAR H. STELLHORN, Corporal, served in the U.S. Army from June 3, 1954 to March 1956. He completed basic training at Camp Chaffee, Arkansas and Jump School at Fort Campbell, Kentucky. In May 1955 he transferred to Fort Benning, Georgia into 4th Infantry Division until his discharge.

He was born February 15, 1934, Evansville, IL, son of Oscar and Erna Harms Stellhorn.

GILBERT P. STELLHORN, Private First Class, served in the U.S. Army, 1953-55. He was born in Evansville, Illinois on October 17, 1932, son of Edward and Elma Lucht Stellhorn. He was drafted in 1953, completed basic training at Fort Sill, Oklahoma and served his tour in Arkansas and Texas.

Pfc. Gilbert P. Stellhorn

He was discharged in 1955, returned home and helped his father on dairy farm and drove a truck for Stamm Trucking and Rogers Redi-Mix. He was killed in an auto accident on July 18, 1964 on Prairie Oil Road.

GLENN R. STEWART, Corporal, served with 1st Army, 3rd Armored Division, 23rd Armored Engineer Battalion, under General Eisenhower in France and Germany. He entered service in September 1943, took training in Camp Abbott, Oregon and was shipped overseas to Liverpool, England in June 1944.

Cpl. Glenn R. Stewart

Glenn went into France on June 20, 1944, was in Battle of Bulge, and only 15 miles from Berlin when war ended. Awarded five Battle Stars and discharged in January 1946.

Glenn was born July 17, 1918, Cora City, Illinois, to Eugene S. and Anna Rodewald Stewart.

Cpl. Alfred A. Stellhorn

Cpl. Edgar H. Stellhorn

JAMES E. STEWART, Senior Master Sergeant, enlisted in August 26, 1965. James served in Air Rescue Service with the 122nd Fighter Wing and participated in Operation Splash Down. He served in Vietnam, Gulf War area, Philippines, Cambodia, China, and Japan.

M/Sgt. James E. Stewart

James is serving with the National Guard at present. James was born in Chester, Illinois. November 22, 1947, the son of James H. and Ruth Stewart.

JAMES H. STEWART, Staff Sergeant, entered WWII, October 8, 1940. He served with Company D, 7th Medical Battalion, 7th Infantry Division in battles in Attu, Aleutian Islands, Kwajalein, Marshall Islands, Leyte, Philippines, and Okinawa in the Ryukyu Islands. After retaking Attu from the Japanese, they moved to Schofield Barracks, Honolulu, Hawaii, then to Kwajalein in the Marshall Islands.

S/Sgt. James H. Stewart

Returning to Schofield Barracks, they next invaded Leyte, and on Easter Sunday morning in 1945, they went in on Okinawa. Shortly after that the point system was started and he was on his way home with a Purple Heart, but still alive.

Born in Cora, Illinois, November 10, 1919, he is the son of Eugene and Anna Rodewald Stewart. James now resides in Chester, Illinois, and is a loyal member of the VFW Post there.

MARVIN L. STEWART, Sergeant E-5, enlisted in the Army in February 1969. In July 1969 he was shipped to Vietnam for 15 months and stationed out of Hue, Phu Bia and Quang Tri Providence. Marvin was with the 82nd Light Infantry. Most of the time he was in and out of Fire Bases and the DMZ (demilitarized zone).

Marvin was discharged in September 1970. He was born December 16, 1948, in Sparta, Illinois, the son of Netter and Laura (Brenning) Stewart, and still lives in Sparta, Illinois.

ROY L. STEWART, Sergeant First Class, born October 31, 1920, in Cora, Illinois, the son of Eugene and Anna Rodewald Stewart. He made a career of the Armed Service, serving in WWII, Korea and Vietnam. He served in the Panama Canal during WWII and saw action in both the Korean and Vietnam Wars.

Sgt. 1/c Roy L. Stewart

A veteran of 30 years service, he received two Bronze Stars. Roy died at the Meadowbrook Manor, a nursing home in Columbus, Georgia, on October 6, 1993 and is buried in Parkhill Cemetery in Columbus.

BENJAMIN F. STIPE, Private, served with the Union Army in the Civil War. He was in Company I, 10th Illinois Infantry, which assisted General Grant near Columbus, Georgia; was in skirmish at Sikeston, Missouri; helped force General Marshall and 2500 men to surrender at New Madrid, Missouri; and was in General Sherman's attack at Mission Ridge.

His parents were John and Susanna H. Thurman Stipe. Benjamin died August 2, 1908 and is buried in New Palestine Cemetery, at Palestine IL.

BONIFACE G. STIRNAMAN, Private First Class, entered WWII July 21, 1943 and saw action in Northern France,

Pfc. Boniface G. Stirnaman

Ardennes, Rhineland and Central Europe, with Battery B, 136th AAA G Battalion (MBL).

He received two Overseas Service Bars, American Campaign Medal, European-African-Middle Eastern Ribbon w/ 4 Bronze Battle Stars, Good Conduct Medal and WWII Victory Medal. He was discharged December 15, 1945.

Born in Evansville, Illinois May 4 1920, to Clement and Emma Bessen Stirnaman, he returned home to work as grocery store owner, meat cutter and later as a correctional officer. Boniface died July 21, 1990.

COURTLAND E. STIRNAMAN, Tech 5, served in both WWII and Korea. Inducted in WWII April 27, 1944, he served as truck driver, Bridge Engineers 553rd and 167th in Rhineland and Central Europe. The 553rd bridged the Rhine River for General Montomery's 9th Army.

T/5 Courtland E. Stirnaman

He was discharged June 13, 1946. Entered Korean War on April 12, 1949 and served there with 114th QM Grave Registration National Cemetery, where men from 22 nations were buried until the bodies could be sent home. He was discharged October 31, 1952.

Courtland came home to work in fertilizer business and retired as a police officer in 1995. Born September 25, 1925, Creole House, Prairie du Rocher, Illinois, his parents are Archie and Mildred Longlois Stirnaman.

DELBERT R. STIRNAMAN, Specialist 4/c, served in the U.S. Army. He was born in Chester, Illinois on July 17, 1935, son of Nevlin and Irene McFaddin Stirnaman. He was drafted May 5, 1958 and discharged April 30, 1964.

Spec. 4/c Delbert R. Stirnaman

He completed basic training and Mechanical School at Fort Leonard Wood, Missouri, earning Expert in carbine and Marksman in rifle. He spent the next 13 months with 46th Transportation Company, Inchon, Korea, returning to Fort Leonard Wood as a combat engineer.

After discharge, he returned home to wife, Marcella, whom he married April 26, 1958, and worked for Cole Milling Company, later known as Con Agra, until retirement in 1994. He still resides in Chester.

EARL W. STIRNAMAN, Tech Sergeant, served in the U.S. Army, November 13, 1950 to November 19, 1957. He enlisted and served with the 3rd Infantry DET #3 5422 ASU-RB on the front lines in Korea as a radioman and later served as clerk.

T/Sgt. Earl W. Stirnaman

He was born June 11, 1928 in Prairie du Rocher, Illinois, son of Archie and Mildred Longlois Stirnaman. After his discharge he work as a meat cutter until retirement and died January 22, 2002 at age 73 years.

JAMES DOUGLAS STIRNAMAN, Private First Class, served in the U.S. Army June 20, 1957 to May 30, 1959. He was inducted into the Army at St. Louis, went to Armored Track Vehicle Mechanics School, Fort Sheridan, Illinois, then sent overseas for about 18 months.

Pfc. James Douglas Stirnaman

He was discharged May 30, 1959 with Good Conduct Medal, Expert Submachine Gun, Marksman (carbine), 1st Class Gunner (Rocket Launcher) and Mechanics Badge.

James was born December 21, 1934, Riley Lake, Illinois, the son of Roy and Bernice Davis Stirnaman. He died June 8, 1979.

WAYNE EDWARD STIRNAMAN, Sergeant Major, served in the U.S. Marine Corps from July 22, 1966 to October 1, 1996. He served in Vietnam December 1967 to August 1969 and Desert Shield-Desert Storm, August 1990 to March 1991.

Sgt. Maj. Wayne Edward Stirnaman

Served with the 9th Separate Bulk Fuel Company 5th Marine Division; Company C., 1st Batt., 25th Infantry, 5th Division; Company C, 1st Shore Party Batt., 1st Marine Division; Insp.-Instr. Staff, 4th Shore Party Batt. 4th Marine Division; H&S Company, 2nd Shore Party Batt. 2nd Marine Division; Instructor, Division Schools, 3rd Marine Division; 1st Recruit Training Batt. Marine Corps Recruit Depot; Landing Support Company Division Support Group, 1st Marine Division; Company B, Landing Support Batt., 3rd Marine Division; Company C, Landing Support Batt. 1st Marine Division; Beach and Port Company, Landing Support Batt. 1st Marine Division; Station Operation and Maintenance Squadron, Marine Corps Air Station, El Toro; VMFA 531, Marine Air Group 11, 3rd Marine Aircraft Wing; 3rd Recon Batt., 3rd Marine Division; H&S Company Headquarters Batt. Marine Corps Recruit Depot; 3rd Force Service Support Group.

Wayne's Parents are Courtland E. and Phyllis (Simpson) Stirnaman. He was born in Red Bud, Illinois on November 6, 1948.

GARY L. STORK, E-5, served in Tet Offensive of 1969, in Vietnam with C Company, 196th Infantry, American Division. Drafted into service June 1967, trained at Fort Polk, Louisiana and Fort Benning, Georgia, then assigned to Fort Jackson, South Carolina as a drill sergeant. He went to Vietnam in June 1968, and was discharged in June 1969. Born September 30, 1947 in Walsh, Illinois, son of Harold and Elizabeth Roche Stork.

GEORGE J. STORK, Corporal, served in the 5th Army Signal Corps from 1952-54, during the Korean Conflict. He received basic and communications training at Fort Gordon, Georgia, served at Crypto Center at Pentagon, and was assigned to temporary duty to the Eisenhower-Kruschev Summit Conference. Born in Walsh, Illinois, the son of Lawrence and Hazel Heinz Stork, his father, Lawrence, served in WWI, two brothers served in WWII, and his son served in National Guard during Desert Storm Era.

GERALD L. STORK, Corporal, born January 20, 1926, Walsh, Illinois, son of Lawrence and Hazel Heinz Stork. He en-

Cpl. Gerald L. Stork

tered WWII in 1945 with basic training at Camp Crowder, Missouri. He was in Motor Pool Staten Island, New York and Military Police, Hot Springs, Arkansas. Gerald was discharged in 1947.

LAWRENCE N. STORK, Private, son of Lawrence J. and Bertha Wesbecher

Pvt. Lawrence N. Stork

Stork, he was born in Walsh, Illinois on May 21, 1890 and served in WWI in 1918.

CHARLES DONALD STRAIGHT, Corporal, served in WWII, with 1st Marine Division on Okinawa and Ryukya Islands. He entered service May 26, 1944, and was sent to China after the war ended for several months. Discharged January 11, 1946, he came back to Chester, was father of 10 children, and worked as a dock truck manager for Gilster-Mary Lee Corp. Born June 14, 1920, Ellery, Illinois, son of Charles and Leta Mae Skinner Straight, he died August 17, 1966.

ROBERT C. STRAIGHT, Corporal, served in the U.S. Marine Corps from September 2, 1959 to September 4, 1963. He was born in Chester, Illinois March 10, 1941, son of Charles Donald and Dorothy Braun Straight. After boot camp, he served at Cherry Point MAS, North Carolina, TAD to Guantanamo Bay, "Bay of Pigs," Cuba for 90 days.

After his discharge, he married, sold

Cpl. Robert C. Straight

GM cars for 19 and a half years and worked at Chester Mental Health for 18 years. He died January 29, 2002 of lung cancer.

ALAN GEORGE STUMPE, served in the U.S. Air Force 1951-53. He was born in Chester January 18, 1933, son of Norbert G. and Martha Bauer Stumpe. Alan served in Greenland with the Air Police after basic training. Discharged, he worked for International Shoe Company, then as a custodian for the Chester High School District until retirement. He now resides in Chester.

DAVID STUMPE, Private, served in Company F, 154th Illinois Infantry in the Civil War. His brother, Henry Stumpe, also served in Company F of the 154th. They were from Chester, Illinois, the sons of Henry and Mary Pick Stumpe. David is buried in St. Mary's Cemetery in Chester, Illinois.

GEORGE H. STUMPE, Private, served in Company F, 154th Illinois Infantry in the Civil War. He was from Chester, Illinois and was the son of John D. and Marie G. Weber Stumpe. He died February 20, 1920 and is buried in St. Mary's Cemetery in Chester, Illinois.

JOHN H. STUMPE, Sergeant, served in the U.S. Army in the Motor Transport Corps in Repair Unit #399 in WWI. He had been a mechanic prior to his induction at Chester, Illinois, May 31, 1918.

Sgt. John H. Stumpe

He was born at Chester, Illinois to Rudolph and Josefeane Molly Stumpe and was 27 years of age at time of induction. He was commissioned to the rank of sergeant January 10, 1919 and was discharged March 20, 1919, with an excellent service record, no wounds and discharge pay of $108.13. John died in 1974.

NORBERT P. STUMPE, AFC, served in the U.S. Air Force from July 1, 1952 to July 1, 1956. After training in Biloxi, Mississippi he served as a radio and radar technician for two years in Fairbanks, Alaska. After his discharge, he attended SIU, taught school for 34 years and is now retired in Chester, Illinois. He was born May 26, 1934 in Chester, son of Norbert and Martha Bauer Stumpe.

PAUL E. STUMPF, Private E-2, born July 22, 1932, Columbia, Illinois and served in Infantry during Korean War. Trained at Indiantown Gap and was in battle of Pork Chop Hill in Korea.

Pvt. E-2 Paul E. Stumpf

Wounded July 6, 1953, he was hospitalized at Fitzsimmons Hospital in Denver. He entered service November 20, 1952 and was discharged July 31, 1954.

Paul returned to Red Bud, Illinois where he operated a shoe repair shop until his death January 9, 1983. His parents were Arnold and Elizabeth Reger Stumpf.

ROGER WILLIAM STUMPE, AFC, served in the U.S. Air Force 1948-52. He was born February 17, 1931, Chester, IL, son of Norbert G. and Martha Bauer Stumpe. He served in Kansas and England, in the meterologist unit.

After discharge, he married Dorothy Wilson, Bremen, Illinois, attended Shurtlef College, Alton, Illinois and graduated with degree in accounting. He worked for Olin Industries, Alton, Illinois. until his death in 1983.

BILLY F. SUHRE, Tech 5, served in WWII, 1944-46, and also a year in Korea. He was born September 21, 1921 at Riley Lake, Illinois, son of Earnest Hugo and Louise Catherine Brugert Suhre. He worked as a railroad signal repairman af-

Suhre Brothers. Billy, Charles and Vernon.

L/Cpl. Richard Joseph Suhre

ter military service. Billy died April 2, 1984 from cancer.

CHARLES H. SUHRE, Private, born April 19, 1918, Riley Lake, Illinois. He was inducted November 2, 1943 into WWII and participated in German and Western Europe Campaigns with Company A, 180th Infantry, Rifleman 745. He was on ship 15 days then to front lines in France and wounded October 15, 1944. His brother Vernon was hospitalized 12 days later in Naples, Italy.

Pvt. Charles H. Suhre

Charles received the Purple Heart, European-African-Middle Eastern and Good Conduct Medals. He was discharged April 2, 1945.

Later, he joined his brothers, Hugo and Vernon, operating Suhre Bros. Café, Ellis Grove, Illinois, before becoming a rural mail carrier for 18 years. He retired in 1985. His parents are Ernest Hugo and Louise Catherine Suhre.

RICHARD JOSEPH SUHRE, Lance Corporal, entered the U.S. Marine Corps Immediately after high school graduation on June 29, 1972. He was serving as company files clerk in the Headquarters platoon of his company. Richard was with Company D, 2nd Tank Battalion Force troops, Fleet Marine Force, Atlantic. He served in Vietnam.

On April 20, 1974, at U.S. Army Garrison, Camp Pickett, Virginia during company size training deployment, Richard was participating in training exercise and accidentally walked into the rear rotor blade of the U.S. Army helicopter he was preparing to board. Richard died while on active duty.

He was born August 22, 1954 at Red Bud, Illinois to Robert Lee and Violet R. (Jordan) Suhre. His mother and sister, Vicki, preceded him in death January 1965 (car accident) and his father died in November 1970 from cancer.

ROBERT LEE SUHRE, Corporal, served in the U.S. Army, from November 8, 1951 to November 7, 1953. After basic training, he received training in aircraft and engine mechanics and rotating wing mechanics at San Marcos AFB, Texas. He served with Company C, lst Special Troops Battalion and earned the National Defense Service Medal and Good Conduct.

He was born March 3, 1930, Fort Gage, Illinois, the son of Ernest Hugo and Louise Catherine Burgert Suhre. He died from cancer, November 21, 1970 while working as Kaskaskia State Park Custodian. His wife Violet and daughter Vicki preceded him in death, January 1965 in a car accident.

VERNON H. SUHRE, Staff Sergeant, was inducted into WWII February 6, 1942 and served in European Campaign with Infantry as mess sergeant. He participated in battle of Rhineland and was wounded in France October 27, 1944, just 12 days after his brother Charles was wounded.

Discharged July 4, 1945, he received the European-African-Middle Eastern Theater Ribbon, Bronze Battle Star, Good Conduct, Purple Heart and Silver Star.

Son of Ernest Hugo and Louise Catherine Burgret Suhre, he was born in Riley Lake, Illinois on January 7, 1916. After his discharge, Vernon and his brothers, Hugo and Charles, operated Suhre Brothers Cafe, Ellis Grove, Illinois.

PHILLIP SUMMERS, Specialist 5, son of Robert and Teresa Colvis Summers, was born April 10, 1944, in St. Louis, Missouri. He graduated St. Mary's Grade School in Chester, Illinois, and Chester High School in 1962. He enlisted in the Army, June 29, 1962, at Fort Knox, Kentucky, and received basic training at Fort Leonard Wood, Missouri, then was assigned to West Point, where he served until 1965.

SP-5 Phillip Summers

He re-enlisted for a second term of service and served in both France and Germany, until June 1967, when he was assigned to D Company, 14th Engineer Combat Battalion in Vietnam, as a construction machine operator. Phillip Paul Summers died December 1, 1967 in Vietnam as a result of wounds he received in an enemy ambush on the road approaching Bao Loc from the south. He is buried in St. Mary's Cemetery in Chester, Illinois.

LARRY G. SURMAN, E-4, enlisted in U.S. Marine Corps in December 1966. He served in Vietnam for two years as a radio operator with the 3rd Shore Party, 3rd Marine Division from September 1967 thru September 1969.

Larry is the son of Daniel and Marcella

E-4 Larry G. Surman

(Eggemeyer) Surman and Paul Schmerbauch. He was born September 17, 1947 in Murphysboro, Illinois. After his military discharge he worked for Chester Dairy.

HENRY C. SWINFERD, Private First Class, was born in Randolph County on February 11, 1908, son of Edwin and Marie Knigge Swinferd. He entered WWII service on January 19, 1943 and served in Battery B, 778th Field Artillery Battalion. He was a machine gunner on a four man crew manning 50 caliber machine guns in replacement forces. He spent four months overseas in Manila, Luzon and Japan as a heavy machine gunner and switchboard operator.

Pfc. Henry C. Swinferd

He was discharged from service November 12, 1945 and returned home to become the owner, operator of the Swinferd Paint and Wallpaper Store in Sparta, Illinois. He died in Sparta on December 10, 1975.

JOHN Q.C. TAGGART, Private, born July 14, 1888 in Chester, Illinois, entered WWI, May 28, 1918 at Pinckneyville, Illinois, to serve for the period of emergency. Served with Company H, 152nd Infantry Division. Received disability discharge December 5, 1918. Applied for pension May 1951, received a service connected award of $60 per month.

KENNETH SIDNEY TAGGART, Aviation Machinist Mate 3/c, enlisted in WWII November 17, 1943. Discharged February 26, 1946, awarded Victory Medal and American Area Campaign Medal. After training at Great Lakes, he had additional training at Norman, Oklahoma, and Memphis, Tennessee. Served on NTS Farragut, Idaho and CASU 53. Born February 4, 1925, son of John and Clara Jostes Taggart.

THURSTON T. TAGGART, Corporal, born May 23, 1918, Walsh, Illinois, was in WWII in 346th Field Artillery Battalion, 91st Infantry Division, in Rome-Arno, Po Valley and North Apennine Mountains in Italy, as a cannoneer, munitions officer, also supply and evacuation staff officer and artillery unit commander. Received European-African-Middle Eastern Campaign Medal w/3 Battle Stars, Bronze Star and WWII Victory Medal. Discharged from Fort Sill, Oklahoma, July 6, 1942.

JESSE L. TAYLOR, Sergeant First Class, U.S. Army, served 1980-2000 with Airborne Infantry Regiment. He served in Panama and the Persian Gulf, served with Delta Company, 4th Battalion, 325th Airborne Infantry Regiment 82nd Airborne Division.

Sgt. 1/c Jesse L. Taylor

He was born June 9, 1963 in Chester, Illinois, the son of George E. and Helen M. Gibbs Taylor. Retired, he now works for the Army as a junior ROTC instructor.

WARREN RANKIN TAYLOR, First Chief Engineer, served in WWII in Merchant Marine Oceangoing Service. Entered service December 7, 1941, was honorably discharged August 15, 1945. After discharge he worked on river barge lines, and McDonnel Douglas plant in St. Louis, Missouri.

On July 1, 1979, he joined Chevron Shipping Company as a Merchant Marine with U.S. Coast Guard. On October 11, 1988, he was made first chief engineer. Retired July 13, 1990. Decorations: Merchant Marine Emblem, Atlantic Zone Bar, Pacific War Zone Bar and Presidential Testimonial Letter.

Born November 5, 1925, son of Arthur and Grace Mizer Taylor. Lived in Rockwood, where his father was Presbyterian Minister for many years. He died December 10, 2002, near Swanwick, Illinois. Brother Roy Logan Taylor was killed in plane crash in Philippines during WWII.

JAMES H. THIERET, Sergeant, USMC, served March 18, 1952 to March 17, 1955. He was born March 2, 1933, Chester, Illinois, son of step-father, Ben Ramsey, and Fleta Hathaway Ramsey. He attended boot camp at San Diego, California, went to Korea as part of E Company, 2nd Battalion, 1st Marines, 1st Marine Division. He was involved in "Boulder City," one of the last major battles of the Korean War.

Sgt. James H. Thieret

Returning to the States, he was stationed at Cherry Point USMC Air Station, North Carolina. He was one of five brothers in U.S. Marine Corps from Chester—see RAMSEY.

HAROLD HERMAN THIES, Corporal, born July 10, 1929, in Chester, Illinois, served from March 8, 1951 until February 21, 1953, in post WWII occupation, with 804th Army Station Hospital in Germany. He received the Army Occupation Medal for his service.

Cpl. Harold H. Thies

The son of Sigmun and Clara Rubach Thies, he married Lillian Vallery and resides in Red Bud, Illinois.

SIGMUND H. THIES, Private First Class, born February 21, 1891, Steeleville, Illinois, entered WWI September 4, 1918 and served until January 28, 1919. Parents

Pvt. 1/c Sigmund H. Thies

MMM 3/c Clinton O. Thomas

were Henry C. and Dorothea Fuhrhop Thies. He died June 3, 1971.

CARL E. THOMAS, Master Sergeant, enlisted in the Army on June 22, 1942. Carl was with Company B, 634th Tank Destroyer Battalion. He entered from Jefferson Barracks, Missouri. Clinton was in the service for 30 years and served in WWII, Korea and Vietnam. The Battles he fought in included: Normandy GO 33WD 45, Northern France GO 33WD 45, Ardennes GO 33WD 45, Rhineland GO 22WD 45, Central Europe GO WD 45.

M/Sgt. Carl E. Thomas

His medals include the Silver Star Medal GO 153 HQ 1st Infantry Division, December 23, 1944; Good Conduct Medal GO 5 HQ 634 TD BN February 20, 1945; European-African-Middle Eastern Service Medal; and Lapel Button issued ASR score September 2, 1945. He was in Vietnam for two or three tours and received medals there.

Carl was born November 15, 1923 in Coulterville, Illinois to Albert D. and Lola A. (Hillyard) Thomas. Carl passed away September 28, 1988 in Arlington, Virginia and is buried there. He was married to Brunhilda Noke in Germany and had three daughters.

CLINTON O. "TOM" THOMAS, MOMM3/c, SV6, USNR, enlisted October 5, 1944 in the Navy, took his basic from NRS, Great Lakes, Illinois. Clinton served with the U.S. Navy in the South Pacific during WWII. While serving his country Tom served in the following vessels and stations: on a landing craft, then went to Pearl Harbor, Hawaii and from there headed to the Philippines to the island of Mindanao. After which, they sailed to northern Australia, picked up Australian military and carried them to the west coast of Borneo, Indonesia. They invaded Borneo and liberated that area; his ships were the LSTS Landing Ship Tanks, LCVM Landing Crafts.

He received an Honorable Service USNR discharge; emblems issued and ribbons include Victory, American Area, Asiatic-Pacific w/star and the Philippine Liberation. Later, as the war ended, he was stationed at Mariana and Marshall Islands while he waited to be shipped home.

After service he worked for the Ann Arbor and Grand Funk Railroad. He retired from Cornerstone Engineering in Clearwater, Florida. Clinton was born in Coulterville, Illinois on August 10, 1925 son of Albert Desper and Lola A. (Hillyard) Thomas. Clinton Thomas passed away February 12, 2002 at Durand, Michigan.

HOWARD LEROY THOMAS, Private First Class, entered the Army and served his country for eight years. Howard served during WWII with the 4061 AABU AC. Howard was shell shocked when a bomb was dropped during war, killing a buddy who was on a motorcycle with him.

Pfc. Howard Leroy Thomas

He worked in a gold mine in Lead, South Dakota. Howard worked on helping build the Mount Rushmore Memorial in South Dakota. He played the Sheriff in the play *"The Trial of Jack McCall"* for the killing of Wild Bill Hickock in Deadwood, South Dakota.

Howard was murdered January 21, 1970 by Mexican sheepherders. At the time of his death, he was working on the Alzada Pipeline in Alzadz, Montana. Howard is buried in Black Hills National Cemetery, Sturgis, South Dakota.

LESTER F. THURAU, Technician 5, served in the U.S. Army January 25, 1944 to April 11, 1946. After basic training at Fort Sheridan, Illinois, he served with Company C, 1636 Combat Engineers Battalion in the Pacific and European Theaters during WWII, earning the Victory Medal, Good Conduct, two Overseas Bars, American Theater, European-African-Middle East Theater Ribbon w/Bronze Star, Asiatic-Pacific Theatre Ribbon and Philippine Liberation Ribbon.

Tech-5 Lester F. Thurau

He was born December 26, 1912, in Ellis Grove, Illinois, the son of Emil and Lula Milligan Thurau. At home he worked as a print shop foreman. He died August 1, 1998.

BOBBY LEE TILLER, Chief Master Sergeant E-9, enlisted in the U.S. Air Force

CM/Sgt. Bobby Lee Tiller

January 14, 1955. Bobby served with 3rSSS and 917th Wing in Vietnam. Retired from the Air Force Reserves, March 23, 1994. He served as an aircraft mechanic, flight engineer maintenance control and maintenance superintendent.

He served five years active duty and 34 years in the Reserves. Employed as an Air Reserve Technician January 15, 1959 to retirement on October 4, 1990.

Bobby was born September 20, 1935 in Littlefield, Texas to Benjamin and Lydia (Watkins) Tiller.

CHARLES HAROLD TILLER, Staff Sergeant, served in the U.S. Army February 8, 1951 to February 8, 1954, served with 1st Cavalry Division, 8th Regiment, 3rd Battalion. After basic training at Camp Breckenridge, Kentucky, 101st Airborne Division was sent to Korea in June 1951 and assigned to 1st Cavalry Division.

S/Sgt. Charles Harold Tiller

He was in Korea until December 30, 1951, then sent to Hokkaido, Japan for nine months, then back to Korea for three months before returning to Japan. He participated in several offensive operations and a mock invasion, Wonsan Harbor, North Korea.

Charles was born June 13, 1932, Littlefield, Texas, the son of Benjamin Roy and Lydia Watkins Tiller.

HERSCHEL WARREN TILLER, Sergeant, served in the U.S. Army, 1948-51, with Company B, 65th Combat Engineer Battalion, 1948-50, in Alaska, and 1950-51 in Korea. He was born February 3, 1930, the son of Ben and Lydia Watkins Tiller. He is now retired and lives in Danville, Illinois.

JAMES LLOYD TILLER, entered service January 14, 1943 to serve in WWII. Basic was at San Antonio, Texas with additional training at Alexandria, Louisiana

James Lloyd Tiller

as part of ground crew in the Air Force. He spent one and a half years in England and was discharged September 22, 1945. James was born October 18, 1917 and died December 3, 1996.

WILLIAM ARCHIE TILLER, Private First Class, served in WWII in Company D, I Medical Battalion, 1st Infantry Division. He went in service April 23, 1942 and was discharged September 20, 1945. He was in Algerian-French-Moroccan-Tunisian-Sicilian Invasions, Normandy, Northern France, Ardennes, Rhineland, Central Europe.

Pfc. William Archie Tiller

William was born October 16, 1919, Calvin, Oklahoma, the son of B.R. and Lydia Watkins Tiller.

CHARLES O. TILTON, Platoon Sergeant, served with 8th Marines, 2nd Division during WWII on Guadalcanal and Tarawa, Saipan and Tinian Islands. He en-

Platoon Sgt. Charles O. Tilton

listed November 28, 1941, spent 33 months in South Pacific, was wounded four times and received the Purple Heart and Gold Star Medals.

Charles was born November 25, 1920, Carthage, Missouri, son of Claude and Estella Etter Tilton, and died May 13, 1990.

ISAAC C. TINDALL, Private 1/c, entered military service, April 1, 1957, from Red Bud, Illinois. Processed through Fort Leonard Wood, Missouri, then transferred to Fort Lewis, Washington for basic and advanced basic training.

Pvt. 1/c Isaac C. Tindall

He was attached to the 4th Army Division, and trained in Bravo Company of the 39th Infantry Division, then placed in the heavy weapons platoon of his company, with the rank of acting sergeant in command of an 81mm Mortar Squad. Received rating of private first class, then sent to NCO School to become a non-commissioned officer.

In January 1958, the company was sent to Anchorage, Alaska to test weapons under extreme cold temperatures, which at times reached 47 degrees below zero. After discharge on April 2, 1959, he returned to Red Bud, Illinois and his job at American Furnace Company as a machine operator.

Born in Rockwood, November 21, 1933, he is the son of James and Maggie Lorentz Tindall.

Sgt. Herschel W. Tiller

JAMES A. TINDALL, Private, of Rockwood, Illinois, he entered the Army, in 1947 and served until 1951. The first two years he was stationed at Fort Knox, Kentucky, then the recruiting officer told them if they would sign up for another two years for service in Alaska, they would "find a girl behind every tree," and Jim was one of those that signed on for the adventure and went to Adak, Alaska.

Pvt. James A. Tindall

Born in Rockwood, January 31, 1930, he was the son of James and Maggie Lorentz Tindall. James died August 2, 1997 and is buried in Mt. Summit Cemetery, near Rockwood.

JERRY D. TINDALL, Corporal, U.S. Army, born in Chester, Illinois April 11, 1931, son of Reggie and Kathryn Layne Tindall. Enlisted November 8, 1949 and went to Fort Riley, Kansas for basic training.

Cpl. Jerry D. Tindall

He was sent to Alaska spending one year at Fairbanks and one year at Anchorage. He returned to Camp Atterbury, Indiana and was discharged February 3, 1953.

Jerry married Genevieve Petrowske in 1953, and they have a son, daughter, grandchildren and great-grandchildren.

MARK A. TINDALL, Airman, born October 17, 1959, in Red Bud, Illinois, to Isaac and Lorna Stamm Tindall. He entered the Armed Service September 7,

Airman Mark A. Tindall

1977, during the Cold War period. He served with the 6950th Electronic Security Squadron, U.S. Air Force in Europe, as an intelligence analyst, was stationed in England and in Texas.

He was honorably discharged September 7, 1981. Later he earned a degree in electrical engineering and spent a decade in the semi-conductor industry. Currently he is self-employed doing Confederate research and living near Blanco, Texas.

WILLIAM TINDALL, Corporal, born August 14, 1895, Rockwood, Illinois to Charles and Elizabeth Holley Tindall. He served in France during WWI, with Company G, 22nd Engineers, 3rd Battalion. William died November 29, 1980 in Murphysboro, Illinois.

JESSE TOPE, served as a bugler in I Company 110th Regiment, Illinois Infantry in WWI. Born April 6, 1899, he died January 3, 1952 at Illinois Veterans Home, Quincey, Illinois and is buried in Sunset Cemetery at the home. He lived in Rockwood and reared a family there.

JOSEPH BARUTEL dit TOULOUSE, Patroit Soldier, joined Captain Francis Charleville's Company of Kaskaskia Volunteers, who joined George Rogers Clark. They left for Fort Sackville (Vincennes) through slush, with provisions and pack horses requisitioned from Kaskaskia. Buffalo was the meat for the first week. The second week provisions ran out. The third week they went hungry before meeting a group of hunters in canoes near the Wabash River. The hunters had a quarter side of buffalo meat. Broth from this meat enabled the soldiers to push on, cold and wet, until they came in sight of Fort Sackville.

Sitting on top of a small hill, surrounded by flood waters, Clark dared not rest because surprise was his main ally. He attacked the fort at night, and found it completely unprepared to fight. On the morning of February 25, 1770, the Americans took formal possession of the fort and named it "Patrick Henry."

Joseph was from Kaskaskia. His parents were Blaise Barutel dit Toulouse and Marie Ann Giar. He is buried near Kaskaskia, according to a list of Revolutionary War soldiers that are buried in Randolph County.

ROBERT J. "BOB" TRIEB, Sergeant, U.S. Army, born July 26, 1943 in Belleville, Illinois to Hugo and Georgianna Christophersen Trieb. Bob was drafted in

Sgt. Robert J. Trieb

March 1965 and served a tour of duty in Korea until December 1966, then transferred to Reserves until his discharge in March 1971. He has lived in Randolph County for 31 years and resides on a farm south of Tilden, Illinois.

LEROY R. TROST, Staff Sergeant, USAF, joined the service January 25, 1952, completed basic training in Texas, service schools in Biloxi, Mississippi and Albuquerque, New Mexico, then assigned as weapons tech to 99th Bomb Wing, Spokane, Washington.

On February 1, 1954, he reported for duty, 2nd AFDS, in RAF Station, Fairford, United Kingdom. He lived there with his wife until his discharge November 29, 1955.

He was born May 8, 1931, Waterloo, Illinois, the son of Walter and Alma Kraemer Trost.

LESLIE J. TROUE, Specialist 4, enlisted into the Army on December 15, 1965. Leslie went to Fort Leonard Wood, Missouri for his basic training. Then he went to Fort Gordon, Georgia for his advanced infantry training training. Leslie was shipped to Mannheim, Germany with the

Spec-4 Leslie J. Troue

28th Trans. Battalion. He coded and decoded messages. He was in Vietnam and received his discharge on December 15, 1967. Leslie's hometown is Steeleville, Illinois. He is the son of Herbert and Ethel (Meyerhoff) Troue.

DOUGLAS A. TUDOR, Private First Class, served in the U.S. Marines with the lst Medical AA Missile Batt. from 1956 until 1958. His entire enlistment was spent in California with boot camp in San Diego, combat training at Camp Pendleton

Pfc. Douglas A. Tudor

and balance of time at 29 Palms, California, from where he was discharged in 1958. He's the son of Maurice and Frieda Mansker Tudor of Rockwood, Illinois

PHILLIP L. TUDOR, Airman 2/c, born July 29, 1943, at Chester, Illinois, the son of Maurice and Frieda Mansker Tudor, served in the Air Force from 1961 until

A 2/c Phillip L. Tudor

1965. After leaving military service Phillip worked in both Iran and Saudi Arabia as an airplane mechanic. He now lives in Las Vegas, Nevada and works as a flight mechanic.

JOHANN "JOHN" UEBEL, Private, was born 1832 in Germany. A native of Bavaria, he applied and was granted citizenship, February 20, 1856, in Perry County, Missouri. He was living in St. Clair County, Illinois in 1860, in Perry County, Missouri in 1870, and 1880 found him in Cinque Homme, Perry County, Missouri.

He was living in Randolph County, Illinois in August 1888, at the time of his marriage to Mary A. Trout of Claryville, Missouri. In Chester, he was engaged in the butcher business and buying cattle. He died July 15, 1910 and is buried in Evergreen Cemetery in Chester, Illinois.

VERNON J. UFFELMAN, Staff Sergeant, joined the Army in 1942 and served with 70th Infantry Division in WWII. He fought against Germany's 6th SS Mountain Division in battles at Wingen, France, January 4-9, 1945, and Saarbruecken, Germany, February 26, 1945.

S/Sgt. Vernon J. Uffelman

He served as Sheriff of Randolph County, 1966-69; Superintendent, Chester Mental Health 1969-73; president, Chester Chamber of Commerce; president, Chester Boat Club; commander, American Legion Post 487; member of Forty-and-Eight, Veterans of Foreign Wars Post 3553, and 70th Infantry Division Association.

Vernon was part owner of Uffelman's Supermarket in Chester for 31 years. Born August 24, 1914 in Fort Gage, Illinois, son of Henry B. and Matilda Paperberg Uffelman. Vernon died September 13, 1984.

JOHN J. VALENTINE enlisted in 1918 in field of aviation and served in WWI. He was one of 10 children of John and Sophie Baer Valentine. He died April 7, 1941 in the Veterans Hospital, Excelsior Springs, had a military funeral.

ED VANCIL, Lieutenant, spent April 19 and 20, 1945, with 3rd Division of 148th Infantry Regiment in Philippine Islands on a mission to destroy Japanese defenses at Irisa, blocking road to Baguio, which involved crossing Irisan Gorge and taking hills C, D and E. By evening of 19, they had accomplished most of the mission, however they spotted Japanese across a road firing heavily at his men, until they threw a grenade and destroyed the heavy gun.

Lt. Ed Vancil & Varlan Vancil

On the 20th, he led his men on a successful sweep down the road to the Irisan Bridge, they encountered numerous Japanese, killing at least 50, setting a record for body count in combat in a single day not matched by any other rifle platoon in the Division. The cost to his platoon was one man killed and two wounded.

Ed was wounded near Baguio, but received no recognition for this combat action until sometime later when awarded the Silver Star for achievements of April 20, 1945.

FRANCE E. VANCIL, Major, served in Company I, 148th Infantry Regiment, 37th Division on Bougainville and Luzon

Maj. France E. Vancil

in Philippine Islands during WWII. Under his command, Vancil's company had the mission to destroy Japanese defenses at Irisan that blocked road to Baguio. The 3rd Platoon had the highest enemy body count by a 37th Division Rifle Platoon in a single day.

Awards included, Combat Infantryman Badge, Silver Star w/Oak Leaf Cluster, Bronze Star w/Oak Leaf Cluster, Army Commendation Medal w/Oak Leaf Cluster, Purple Heart w/Oak Leaf Cluster, American Defense Medal, American Campaign Medal, Asiatic-Pacific Campaign Medal, WWII Victory Medal, National Defense Medal, Philippine Liberation Ribbon, Philippine Independence Ribbon and Distinguished Unit Citation.

He later served in Korea. Retired from service after 20 plus years. He is the son of Willis E. (WWI Veteran) and Wilma Glenn Vancil.

VARLAN D. VANCIL, Staff Sergeant, was a squad leader in Company B, 129th Infantry Regiment, 37th Division during WWII. He saw service at Fiji, New Hebrides and Guadalcanal Islands. He was in assault landing on Bougainville, participated in annihilation of the infamous Japanese 6th Division, in extensive combat at Lingayen Gulf, Luzon, Clark Field, Manila, Baguio, Balete Pass, Cagayen Valley, Aparri in Philippine Campaign.

S/Sgt Varlan Vancil

Received Combat Infantryman Badge, Bronze Star w/2 Oak Leaf Clusters and V for Valor, Purple Heart w/Oak Leaf Cluster, American Defense Medal, American Theatre Medal, Asiatic-Pacific Medal w/ 2 Bronze Stars and Arrowhead, WWII Victory Medal, Philippine Liberation Medal, seven Overseas Service Bars. Later served in Korea with 23rd Regiment, 2nd Division as a 1st lieutenant. Varlan was the son of Willis E. (WWI Veteran) and Wilma Glenn Vancil.

ELVA "RED" VAN METER, Sergeant, entered WWII January 24, 1941 and served with Company C, CAS Battalion IARTC from July 7, 1942 until Septem-

Sgt. Elva Van Meter

ber 26, 1944 in Alaska and the Aleutian Islands. This was a most miserable place - so cold one could only work for 15 minutes at a time, then go inside to warm up. He was discharged July 12, 1945. Red was the son of Charlie and Minnie Tindall Van Meter of Rockwood, Illinois. He died February 24, 2003.

CARLIN RAY VANSANT, Private First Class, entered the service in March 1973. Ray took his basic training at Fort Ord, California and was discharged in June 1974 due to an ankle injury. Ray served in the Army during Peacetime.

Pfc. Carlin R. VanSant

Type of work after service was clerk, service station, and mechanical. Ray has had two, five bypass surgeries. He was born in Sparta, Illinois on March 21, 1941, the son of William Horace and Mozelle (Chism) VanSant. Ray and his wife live in Sandoval, Illinois.

CHARLES BOYNTON "CHUCK" VANSANT, E-4 (T), enlisted in the Army, Jan. 24, 1956 and took his basic training at Fort Leonard Wood, Missouri. He was a FA repairman. Chuck received a medal for Sharpshooter (Carbine). He attended Ordnance School at Aberdeen Proving Grounds, Maryland, May and June 1956. He served one year, one month and 25 days in peacetime at Korea.

E-4 Charles B. VanSant

After his discharge on Jan. 23, 1959, Charles joined the Army Reserves from Jan. 23, 1959 to Jan. 23, 1962. After discharge from service, Charles worked for Rauland Corporation, Chicago, Illinois from 1959-61; at Spartan Printing, Sparta, Illinois from 1961-82; state of South Dakota, Central Duplicating as printer, August 1984-May 1994. He was the first person to have Gastroeploeric bypass in Minneapolis VA Hospital in November 1995.

Charles was born November 13, 1938, Sparta, Illinois, son of William Horace and Mozelle (Chism) VanSant. He had six brothers, five of them Veterans. Charles is now enjoying retirement and lives with his wife in Reyno, Arkansas.

NADEAN N. THOMAS-VANSANT, Private, USMC, enlisted February 14, 1958 and went to the USMC Recruiting Depot, Paris Island, South Carolina. She spent six weeks in Naval Hospital in Beauport, South Carolina and after complications was honorably discharged May 4, 1958.

Pvt. NaDean N. VanSant

NaDean was an officer manager and dental assistant for Government Dental Clinic, Saint Louis, Missouri. She became an office manager for Jim Bloom Dental Office, Rapid City, South Dakota and Ellsworth AFB, South Dakota, then became a staff assistant for South Dakota Department of Social Services, Pierre, South Dakota.

NaDean was born in Coulterville, Illinois on January 13, 1940 to Albert D. and Lola A. (Hillyard) Thomas. She retired in June 1988 and her and Chuck live in Reyno, Arkansas.

THOMAS A. VANSANT, Corporal, enlisted in the Army and served during the Korean War Conflict. Tom was born Nov.

Cpl. Thomas A. VanSant

13, 1931 in Randolph County to William Horace and Mozelle (Chism) VanSant. He died August 29, 1978 and is buried in Jefferson Barracks National Cemetery, St. Louis, Missouri.

WILLIAM EUGENE "GENE" VANSANT, Private First Class, enlisted in the Army on November 12, 1952 and was discharged September 9, 1954. He served with the 89th Tank Battalion using 90mm guns.

Pfc. William E. VanSant

Returning home he married Louise Hartmann and they had two sons, Brian (deceased) and William Jr. William Jr. married Lisa King and has two daughters, Lauren and Kelly.

William Sr. was born June 2, 1929 in Randolph County, Illinois, the son of William Horace and Mozelle (Chism) VanSant. William E. VanSant died March 22, 1999 and is buried Caledonia Cemetery, Sparta, Illinois.

RICHARD G. VASQUEZ, Corporal, born March 19, 1918, St. Charles, Missouri, son of Peter and Rosalie Sills Vasquez. He entered the service February 13, 1942 during WWII and served with Company C, 22nd Armed Engineer Battalion in France and Hurtgen Forest in Germany.

Cpl. Richard G. Vasquez

Awards include Purple Heart for injuries received in Germany, two Bronze Stars, European-African-Middle Eastern Theatre Ribbon and Good Conduct Medal.

After his discharge June 7, 1945, he worked at Chester Mental Health Center. Richard died August 26, 2001.

MARVIN VICKERS, Private First Class, born June 7, 1931 in Chester, Illinois to William C. and Emma McKenzie Vickers. He was drafted into the Army in January 1952 and after basic training at Camp Pickett, Virginia, he went to Fort Sam Houston, Texas, then to Camp Carson, Colorado as a medic. He served in Japan and Korea during the Korean Conflict as a medic and a truck driver in Company A, 35th Regiment, 25th Division as a private first class. Marvin was discharged in January 1954.

MAURICE VICKERS, Specialist 4, born October 28, 1936 in Rockwood, Illinois to William C. and Emma McKenzie

Spec-4 Maurice Vickers

Vickers. He was drafted into the Army in 1960 and was stationed at Fort Bragg, NC where he was an SP4 in the Signal Corps during the Cuban Crisis.

He was discharged in 1962 and entered the Reserves from 1962-66. After his service, he returned to work at Granite City Steel. Maurice passed away January 18, 1971, leaving a wife and two children.

MELVIN D. VICKERS, US Army, born in Rockwood, Illinois, son of William C. and Emma E. McKenzie Vickers. He enlisted July 17, 1953 and completed basic training at Fort Leonard Wood, Missouri. He was assigned to 32nd MRV 6th Army, attached to Fort Lewis, Washington, then transferred to G-2, 5th Army, Chicago. Completed his enlistment in June 1955 and re-enlisted in February 1958 with one and a half years in Reserves as Administration 1st Sergeant in heavy construction engineers, Alton, Illinois.

Melvin D. Vickers

After completing basic training at Fort Ord, California he was assigned to the Nuclear Weapon Project, Sandia Base, Albuquerque, New Mexico, then transferred to Mercury, Nevada and completed his enlistment in February 1961.

Re-enlisted in June 1972 at Edwardsville, Illinois, completed basic training at Fort Leonard Wood, Missouri, and was assigned to Community Mental Health, Fort Gordon, Georgia as a therapist and consultant.

In May 1973 he transferred to Maunbeim, Germany as education coordinator and clinical director in Drug and Alcohol Program, then transferred to D&A School, Munich, Germany as instructor for two years.

He was then assigned as instructor at Academy of Health Science, Fort Sam Houston, Texas; transferred to Headquarters, U.S. Army, Europe as consultant for

D&A, three and a half years; Chief Administrator NCO for Civilian Support Agency, Heidelberg, Germany for one and a half years before medical retirement in September 1987.

MICHAEL VICKERS, SPC5, born June 25, 1950 in Chester, Illinois to William C. and Emma McKenzie Vickers. He enlisted in the Army in 1970 and went through training in Fort Leonard Wood and in New York. He was stationed at Fort Riley, Kansas in the 126th Med Company and was discharged in 1971. He then entered the Army Reserves from 1973-76 and served in Manhattan, Kansas. He was discharged as a SPC 5. His service was during peacetime.

JACK P. VINER, served six years active duty with Company C, 1st Bomb Group, 130th Infantry, 33rd Division and National Guard, beginning with enlistment in March 1957, and discharge in March 1963. He was stationed at Fort Jackson, South Carolina until transferring to Illinois National Guard.

Sgt. Jack P. Viner

He was born November 17, 1934, in East St. Louis, Illinois, the son of George and Gene Whitaker Viner. After service he worked 35 years as an electrician in Local 309 International Brotherhood of Electrical Workers. Married 44 years to the former Mary Schmoll.

ERNST B. VON BEY, Private First Class, born in St. Louis, Missouri on January 2, 1926, son of Ernst F. and Lyda J. Herr Von Bey. He entered service March 16, 1944, served in WWII and ETO operations in Germany with Company G, 97th Infantry, 387th Regiment. They landed at LeHavre, France March 26, 1945, crossed into Germany near the battered city of Hasselweiler.

On April 1, he was sent with a three boat convoy to capture a German for interrogation. He made it to German side unwounded, but was hit while laying on the ground, became a prisoner of war, liberated and flown to the U.S. After 13 months in O'Reilly General Hospital, Springfield, Missouri, he was discharged May 14, 1946.

CHARLES D. VUICHARD, Private First Class, joined the U.S. Marine Corps on March 26, 2000. Charles trained in San Diego, California and spent one year in Japan and three months in Australia.

Pfc. Charles D. Vuichard

He came back to the States and went to Camp Lejeune, North Carolina. Charles is now, March 2003, serving in Operation Iraqi Freedom.

Charles was born in Pinckneyville, Illinois on May 5, 1979, son of Charles R. and Betty (Church) Vuichard.

CHARLES D. VUICHARD, AFC, served in the U.S. Army, December 1948 to September 24, 1952, with the 39th Food Service Squadron and worked as a radio repairman.

AM 1/c Charles D. Vuichard

He was born October 21, 1930, Coulterville, IL, the son of Charles P. and Martha Hillyard Vuichard. He worked in the coal mines before service and after discharge, he ran a lumber yard for his father for five years, then back to the coal mines until retirement.

CHARLES F. VUICHARD, Private First Class, of Tilden, Illinois, entered WWII December 28, 1943 and served with 732nd Railway Operation Battalion, Fort Sam Houston, Texas. His awards include Good Conduct Medal and European Theater Ribbon.

Pfc. Charles F. Vuichard

He was discharged May 28, 1945, worked in coal mines, then bought a lumber yard, ran it until retirement at age 70. He died November 8, 1994.

Charles was born in Tilden, Illinois, April 11, 1907, son of George W. and Margaret Coppman Vuichard.

ERICH R. WAGNER, Private First Class, served in the U.S. Army, 1943-45, with 631st Military Intelligence. He attended basic training at Camp Lee, Virginia, was sent overseas and made the Normandy Landing at Omaha Beach.

Also participated in the Battle of the Bulge, Northern France, Ardennes, Rhineland, Central Europe.

He was born in Germany, September 11, 1911 and came to America as a teenager with parents, Ernst and Marie Springer Wagner. His father died, his mother returned to Germany and Erich stayed to be an American.

ROLAND L. WAGNER, USAF, served from January 23, 1953 to July 13, 1956. He was born January 4, 1934 in New Pales-

Roland L. Wagner

tine, Illinois, the son of Alva and Olinda Eggemeyer Wagner. After basic training at Lackland AFB, San Antonio, TX, he was transferred to Greenville AFB, Mississippi where he served as an aircraft engine maintenance helper with the 3508th FLM Squadron.

While at Greenville he was able to enjoy one of his favorite sports and played the left field position for the Greenville AFB 1955 Champion Softball Team.

He married Betty Mennerich in 1957 and they have a son Ronald and daughter Rhonda. Roland retired in 1999 after 15 years as the Chester Street Commissioner.

EDWARD F. WALDRON, Sergeant, a member of the Army Air Force in WWII and probably seen as much action as any Randolph County boy in service. He was inducted January 6, 1942, was a member of 309th Fighter Squadron (North Africa), 31st Fighter Group (15th Air Force) as a crew chief in a P-15 "Mustang" fighter group. He participated in the famous Dieppe raid on coast of France; a pilot in this group was the first American to shoot down a German plane. Participated in battles over France and most major battles in North Africa. Served with the first American fighter squadron in England and first to see action there.

Sgt. Edward F. Waldron

Cited for outstanding performance, the Mustang Group, engaged the enemy on April 21, 1944, after flying 550 miles in terrible weather conditions, fighting off 60 enemy fighters (which threatened a U.S. bomber formation) by destroying 16 planes and damaging numerous others. This enabled the 15th Air Force heavy bombers to complete a successful mission against important enemy installations in Ploesti-Bucharest, Rumania. Edward received European-African Eastern Bronze Stars for Algeria-French Morocco, Tunisia, Sicily, Naples Foggia, Rome Arno, Air Offensive Europe, Southern France, Northern France, North Apennines, Balkans and Germany.

Awards include the Blue and Gold Distinguished Unit Citation Ribbon, Distinguished Merit Badge w/Oak Leaf Cluster, and a Purple Heart for wounds received June 7, 1943 in Korba, Tunisia. He resided in Red Bud, Illinois and died December 16, 1998.

HAROLD S. WALDRON, T/4, born at Red Bud, Illinois, September 24, 1922, son of Edward J. and Elizabeth Mennarigh Waldron, entered service in WWII April 30, 1943. Had worked as a motion picture projectionist, was assigned to 4026 Signal Photo Battalion, 1st Operations Company with U.S. Signal Corps.

T/4 Harold S. Waldron

Served as instructor in projection, New York Army Signal Corps School. Spent 18 months in Southeast Asia, covering India-Burma. Was personal projectionist for Lord Mountbatton Supreme Allied Commander of SEAC. Was in Japan with Occupation Forces, discharged February 3, 1946, then worked 36 years as office manager for Caterpillar Inc.

ARDELL MERLE WALL, Corporal, served 1948-52 in the U.S. Army. He was born in Randolph County on June 20, 1931, son of Ardell J. and Edna Goudier Wall. He enlisted in 1948, served with WWII re-construction in Germany and Japan, then sent to Korea during that conflict. He was discharged in 1952 and worked at Chester Mental Health Center as a security therapist aide. He died March 16, 1996.

JERALD L. WALTER, E-3, of Walsh, Illinois, son of William and Ruth Schulein Walter, served in the Vietnam War, aboard the USS *Annapolis*. He enlisted in the Navy April 10, 1968 and was discharged December 14, 1973.

E-3 Jerald L. Walter

During his term of service he received the National Defense Service Medal and the Vietnam Service Medal (for two campaigns). Retired as a lieutenant from Menard Correctional Center, Chester, Illinois and now makes his home in Walsh with his wife and daughter.

CHARLES C. WARD, Machinist Mate 3/c, served in both WWII and Korea. In WWII he was the youngest man aboard an old and rusty Navy tanker that had not returned to States for years. New guys were assigned to it. He met his brother George on Okinawa, took him back to ship and gave him the first hot meal he had eaten in quite some time.

MM 3/c Charles C. Ward

Charles saw action on Iwo Jima and during the Korean War, he was aboard a transport ship.

Born March 6, 1927 at Wittenburg, Missouri, his parents were John J. and Edith Garris Ward. Charles retired from Menard Prison. He died December 9, 1997.

JOHN "JACK" WATSON, Corporal, entered service March 7, 1946, and served with 316th Bomb Wing, northern Luzon, Nickal Field, Philippines and Okinawa. He worked in message center, delivering classified information to all branches of service on Okinawa. He was discharged September 30, 1948.

John was born November 2, 1927, son

Cpl. John (Jack) Watson

of John H. and Florence Watson of Sparta, Illinois.

JOHN KYLE WATSON, E-4, USN, was born October 10, 1981, Murphysboro, IL, the son of Bill and Patti Martin Watson. Entered the service in September 1999 and

E-4 John Kyle Watson

is still serving. His home port is Gulf Port, Mississippi. He has been deployed to Okinawa, Harvey Point, North Carolina and Guam. He is with the NMCB Fearloss 74 Seabees and stationed in Kuwait during the Irag Crisis.

KORY WILLIAM WATSON, E-3, USN, serving from January 2002 to the present time. He was born April 14, 1983, Murphysboro, Illinois, the son of Bill and Patti Martin Watson. Kory enlisted in the

E-3 Kory W. Watson

service and completed basic training at Great Lakes, Illinois, followed by A School at Fort Leonard Wood, Missouri. His home port is Gulf Port, Mississippi. He has deployed to Guam and is now in Kuwait where he is with the NMCB Fearless 74 Seabees as an equipment operator.

WILLIAM H. WATSON, E-5, served in the U.S. Air Force January 1973 to January 1979. He was born August 17, 1953, Red Bud, Illinois, the son of Jack and Mary M. Cleland Watson. After basic training he went to Zaragosa, Spain, then to Warner Robbins, Georgia, followed by Norton AFB California. He then transferred to Zweibrucken, AFB, Germany - a Canadian Base.

ORVILLE WEAVER, Sergeant, was with the 513th Signal Company, 13th and 17th Airborne, during WWII. He entered service February 2, 1943 and saw action in Luxembourg at the Battle of the Bulge. He participated as a gliderman in an air assault

Sgt. Orville Weaver

across the Rhine River called Operation Varsity. A native of Steeleville, Illinois, he was discharged January 31, 1946. His parents are Edwin and Ella Dagner Weaver.

OTIS C. WEGENER, Sergeant, was drafted in the Army on December 4, 1950, and served in the Korean War. Stationed at Fort Leonard Wood, Missouri for six months, he was assigned to 1905th Aviation Engineers as a cook, then transferred to Camp Beale, California.

Sgt. Otis C. Wegener

On June 6, 1951, he married Bernadine Koester and they lived in Marysville, California until his discharge on December 4, 1952. The son of Henry and Minnie Hanebutt Wegener, he was born in Evansville, Illinois, July 12, 1928. He is retired from dairy farming.

RALPH W. WEHRENBERG, of Red Bud, Illinois, entered the Army in WWII, April 1943, and served with 96th Infantry Division. He participated in amphibious

Ralph W. Wehrenberg

landing on Leyte, October 20, 1944, when U.S. Forces returned to Philippines, and was in combat on Okinawa, May to August 1945, the last major battle in Pacific to end WWII. Awards include the Purple Heart and Bronze Stars.

JOHN E. WEIR, Corporal, born September 20, 1895 in Sparta, Illinois. He served with Company E, 3rd Infantry in

Cpl. John E. Weir

WWI. His parents were Joseph and Mary Temple Weir. He died in Texas October 26, 1918.

BRUCE L. WELGE, 1st Lieutenant, born January 5, 1945, son of William H. and Rudelle Fritze Welge of Chester, Illinois. He attended the Citadel in Charleston, from 1963-67, graduated as a 2nd lieutenant and was commissioned through the ROTC program.

He was then assigned to Fort Bragg,

North Carolina with the 82nd Airborne Division. During this time he completed ranger and airborne training. He entered active service in September 1968, and was injured in action soon after arriving in Vietnam. He returned to duty, but was killed in action January 26, 1969. At the time of his death, he was an airborne ranger 1st lieutenant with the 82nd Airborne.

During his time of service he received several combat medals, including the Purple Heart. Bruce is buried in Evergreen Cemetery, Chester, Illinois.

DONALD E. WELGE, 2nd Lieutenant, born in Chester, Illinois, the son of William H. and Rudelle Fritze Welge. He received a commission as second lieutenant through the ROTC program in August 1957 at LSU.

Entered Six Months Active Duty Six Year Reserve program in February 1958 and served on active duty until August 1958. He was assigned to Fort Eustis, Virginia, graduated basic officers training course and served as motor officer for medium truck company in 48th Truck Group there. While in reserves he attended several summer camps at Fort Eustis and Camp McCoy, Wisconsin.

EDGAR WELGE, Staff Sergeant, served in the U.S. Army, November 28, 1941 to May 24 1945, born February 13, 1916 in Welge, Illinois, son of Albert and Anna Hogrefe Welge. He served with the 127th Infantry Regiment, 32nd Red Arrow Division in WWII in the South Pacific, Philippine Defense, New Guinea and Papua Liberation.

S/Sgt. Edgar Welge

His citations include Asiatic-Pacific Theater, Philippine Liberation w/one Bronze Star, Distinguished Unit Badge, Good Conduct, American Defense Service ribbons and six Overseas Service Bars.

He was the postmaster at Welge Post Office for 30 years and owned the grocery store in Welge until his retirement. He lived in Chester, Illinois with his wife Elaine. He died May 7, 2000.

MICHAEL W. WELGE, 1st Lieutenant, born in Chester, Illinois, the son of William and Rudelle Fritze Welge. He entered service in 1962 and graduated as 2nd lieutenant Infantry, University of Illinois. Went to Infantry School at Fort Benning, Georgia and received an Expert Infantryman's Badge.

1st Lt. Michael W. Welge

Michael served in Europe after ranger training with Company C, 1st Battalion Group, 18th Infantry, 8th Infantry Division as a mechanized infantry company leader. He was executive officer and infantry company commander. Michael was discharged in 1964.

EDITH WELTEN, Corporal, born December 13, 1917 in Steeleville, Illinois, daughter of Louis and Alma Schnoeker Welten. She joined the WAAC's January

Cpl. Edith Welten

7, 1943, served in Des Moines, Iowa Training Center for the Women's Army Auxiliary Corps doing office work. Edith was discharged August 19, 1944. She died May 24, 1990, Decatur, Illinois.

DONALD A. WENTE, Staff Sergeant, served in the U.S. Air Force, 1951-56, completed basic training at Lackland AFB, Texas, then was stationed at Keesler AFB, Biloxi, Mississippi. He was born in Steeleville, Illinois, the son of Wm. C. and Ruth Elsey Wente, and died January 12, 1985.

GUIDO E. WENTE, Sergeant, served in the U.S. Army, WWI, from September 2, 1918 to April 21, 1919, with MTC Repair Unit #321. He was appointed corporal on February 1st and sergeant on March 18, 1919. He was discharged April 21 at Camp Zachary Taylor, Kentucky. He was born August 6, 1895, Steeleville, the son of William C. and Caroline Griese Wente. He died July 12, 1986 and is buried at St. John's Cemetery.

MERLE W. WENTE, Staff Sergeant, enlisted in the U.S. Army Air Corps in February 1943, at age 19. He served in WWII and Korean Wars in China and India, routing supplies to frontline troops with the 1340th Army Air Transport Command. He was also involved in fighter and bomber groups in China.

S/Sgt. Merle W. Wente

His awards include the Asiatic-Pacific Theatre Ribbon w/2 Battle Stars, Distinguished Unit Badge, WWII Victory Medal, Good Conduct Medal and four Overseas Service Bars. Discharged in December 1945 from WWII, he again served in the Korean War from May 1951 to June 1953.

Merle was born in Steeleville, Illinois on November 21, 1923, the son of William C. and Ruth Elsey Wente.

WILLIAM C. WENTE Jr., Sergeant, born in Steeleville, Illinois, son of William C. and Caroline Gray Wente. He enlisted June 24, 1918 and did service in WWI with the Quartermaster Corps. William was discharged on March 14, 1919. He was elected Sheriff of Randolph County in 1941, County Commissioner in 1946,

Sgt. William C. Wente

and served on the City Police force of Steeleville. William died June 1, 1963.

CYRIL "ZIP" WESBECKER, Private First Class, was drafted February 26, 1944, sent to Fort Sheridan, Illinois, then Camp Blanding, Florida for basic training. In August 1944, he left for overseas and landed near Naples, Italy. He was in Company C, 338th Infantry, General Clark's 5th Army in Rome-Arno and was in northern Italy when the war ended.

Pfc. Cyril Wesbecker

After his discharge on January 4, 1946, he worked as a concrete finisher in St. Louis. He was born May 11, 1916, Walsh, Illinois, son of Hilary and Frances Roth Wesbecker, he died January 2, 1974 and is buried in St. Pius Cemetery, Walsh, Illinois.

HAROLD WESBECHER, Corporal, the son of William L. and Leona Krull

Cpl. Harold Wesbecher

Wesbecher. Harold entered service June 19, 1952, and went to Camp Breckinridge, Kentucky for basic training. He was sent to Mt. Fuji, Japan, arriving there December 12, 1952, with the 24th MP Division. After six months, in July 1953, the 24th moved to Korea, and were there nine months. He arrived home June 2, 1954 and has farmed for the last 47 years in the Evansville area.

WILLIAM L. WESBECKER, Private, was inducted into WWI, June 24, 1918 and took his basic training at Camp Zachary

Pvt. William L. Wesbecker

Taylor, Kentucky. He was discharged from Battery C, 4th Regiment, Field Artillery Division, January 14, 1919.

ROGER G. WICKLEIN, E-4, entered the U.S. Army December 15, 1965, received training at Fort Leonard Wood, Missouri, advanced training at Fort Polk,

E-4 Roger G. Wicklein

Louisiana, then served in Vietnam with MACV Team 29 for one year as a member of advisory team. He was discharged from Fort Leonard Wood, Missouri, December 15, 1967. Roger was born in Evansville, Illinois, September 16, 1945, son of Glen and Linda Gietz Wicklein.

ALBERT LAWTON WILEY, enlisted August 15, 1917 to serve in WWI, in Centralia, Illinois, while visiting relatives in Salem. He trained at Camp Green, North

Funeral Procession of Albert Lawton Wiley

Carolina and was attached to Company B, 61st Infantry, 5th Division. Albert was killed in action at Argonne, France October 27, 1918. He was one of 10 men from Sparta area killed in WWI. His body was returned to the U.S. September 21, 1921 for burial. Albert was born in Sparta, Illinois, January 29, 1900 to parents Clement O. and Margaret J. Skinner Wiley.

JOHN ORVAL WILEY served in the U.S. Navy during WWII. He was born in Sparta, Illinois, September 10, 1920, son

John Orval Wiley

of William Fowler and Clara May Adams Wiley. He now lives in Allison Park, Pennsylvania.

WILBER ADAMS WILEY, Tech 5, served with the 209th Engineer Combat Battalion in Air Corps during WWII and

Tec/5 Wilbur A. Wiley

helped open Burma/India Road. Born in Sparta, April 17, 1922, son of William Fowler and Clara May Adams Wiley, he died in Sparta July 11, 1968.

WILLIAM WILEY, born February 17, 1843, Preston, Illinois, son of John and Mary "Polly" Little Wiley. He served in Company G, 18th Regiment Illinois Vol-

William Wiley

unteer Infantry during the Civil War. Contacting measles while in service, he was discharged September 9, 1863 and returned to Sparta, Illinois to farm. William died June 4, 1891.

DERRICK WILLIAMS, Corporal, served in the U.S. Marine Corps 1987-91 with I Battery, 3rd Battalion, 11th Marines, 1st Marine Division in Desert Shield/Storm. He served as an artillery cannoneer, went to the Persian Gulf in August 1990 and took part in the liberation of Kuwait International Airport.

Cpl. Derrick Williams, Desert Storm

He received the Combat Action Ribbon, National Defense Medal and two Sea Service Deployment Ribbons.

Derrick was born 1967, son of David and Rena Moore Williams. Although born in Pinckneyville he lived all his life in Sparta, Illinois. He's been in Local 309 IBEW for seven years and is glad he had the opportunity to fight for his country.

KENNETH F. WILLIAMS, Corporal, served in the U.S. Air Force 1949-56 as a rear gunner with the 149th White Bomber Group in Korea. After his discharge in 1956, he worked in the coal mines until retirement. He was born October 22, 1930, Sparta, Illinois, son of Westley and Anna Neighmeyer Williams.

EDMUND L. WILLIS, enlisted in the Army Air Corps in October 1942, and served until November 15, 1945. His duty was in communications on B-24s, at 10 different air bases in the U.S. during WWII. Edmund was born August 27, 1923 and resides in Percy, Illinois.

WOODROW "WOODY" WILLIS, Sergeant, took part in numerous battles in the European Theatre during WWII, with Patton's 3rd Armored Division. He was awarded the Purple Heart and Silver Star for his efforts in capturing 110 armed German soldiers. He served from 1942-46. Born in Madison, Illinois, son of Charles and Lulu Willis, he died March 13, 1986 and is buried at Evergreen Cemetery in Chester, Illinois.

JULIE (ROBERT) WILSEY, Captain, born December 21, 1969, in Red Bud, Illinois, the daughter of Jim and Rose Kessler Hutchison Robert. She graduated from West Point in May 1992 and began service with U.S. Army Corps of Engineers as a commissioned officer.

Capt. Julie (Robert) Wilsey

She was in U.S. Mission in Macedonia in 1995 and also served tours in Germany, Fort Leonard Wood, Missouri, Fort Belvoir, Virginia and Fort Bragg, North Carolina. She completed paratrooper and jumpmaster courses. Julie was discharged in December 1998.

GILBERT A. WILSON, Sergeant, served with Headquarters 32nd Division Artillery unit in WWII. Inducted December 6, 1944, at Chicago, Illinois, served as Message Center Chief 674, also qualified with M-1 MM Rifle as marksman. He saw service in Asiatic-Pacific Theater, for which he received a ribbon w/Bronze Battle Star, and was in the Philippine Liberation, for which he received a Philippine Liberation Medal w/Bronze Battle Star for the battle of Luzon Island. Gilbert was discharged August 4, 1946. He was born in Riley Lake, Illinois, April 4, 1921.

MELVIN WILSON, Sergeant, son of Albert and Alma Dierks Wilson, was born in Ellis Grove, Illinois on August 19, 1925. He entered the U.S. Armed service December 3, 1943 and took basic training at Camp

Sgt. Melvin Wilson

Blanding, Florida. From there to Camp Lee, Virginia, Indiantown Gap, Pennsylvania and Camp Kilmer, New Jersey. He boarded the *Queen Elizabeth* to Scotland, then another ship to Iceland and served as 36773199 Sergeant, SQ. H, 1386th AAF B U NAD ATC. Melvin was discharged April 6, 1946.

RALPH W. WILSON, Sergeant E-5, enlisted in the U.S. Army on January 23, 1960. Ralph served as a food service helper at Fort Leonard Wood, Missouri. Then he was sent to Camp McCoy, Wisconsin for two weeks active training. Ralph was with Company B, 3rd Battalion, 4th Infantry. He was honorably discharged December 15, 1965.

Sgt E/5 Ralph W. Wilson

Ralph came back home to the family farm after serving his country. He was born April 29, 1937 in Steeleville, Illinois (Bremen) son of Rudolph and (Beisner) Wilson.

DONALD ANTON WINGERTER SR., Private First Class, served in the U.S. Marine Corps from April 29, 1952 to March 26, 1954. He served in Korea for 11 months

Pfc. Donald A. Wingerter

and earned the National Defense Service Medal, Korean Service Medal w/star and United Nations Medal. He was from Steeleville, IL and the son of William and Mildred Dallas Wingerter. He died in 1989.

DONALD L. WINGERTER, Corporal, served in the U.S. Marine Corps from June 14, 1953 to July 30, 1955, with 4.2 Mortar Company, 4th Marine Regiment, 3rd Marine Division. He took basic training at San Diego MCRD, California and advanced training at Camp Pendleton. He was sent overseas, assigned to 4.2 Mortar Company and was in fire direction.

Cpl. Donald L. Wingerter

After discharge, he opened a business, Glass, Windows, Home Improvement, in Chester, Illinois. He was born July 30, 1935 in Chester, the son of Lenus and Eleanor Braun Wingerter.

JERRY DEAN WINGERTER, Airman 1/c, enlisted in the U.S. Airforce in September 1959, and served as an aircraft mechanic at McChord AFB, Tacoma, Washington with the 325th Organization Maintenance Squadron until September 1963.

He was employed by McDonnell Aircraft in St. Louis until September 1995

Air First Class Jerry Dean Wingerter

when he retired and moved back to the Rockwood area. He was born March 21, 1940 in Rockwood, Illinois to Joe and Iona (Tindall) Wingerter.

ROBERT C. WINGERTER, Sergeant, served in H&S Company Shore Party, 2nd Division, in Korean War from November 24, 1951 to November 3, 1953. Attended

Sgt. Robert C. Wingerter

boot camp and Communications School, San Diego, California, then to Camp Lejeune, North Carolina as wire man. Landing on the beach, he set up phone system, running wire on poles or trees. He was born in Chester, Illinois, July 10, 1931, son of Lenus and Eleanor Braun Wingerter.

RICHARD W. WITBART, Radioman 3/c, enlisted in WWII on December 6, 1944, and spent three months at Great Lakes Naval Training Center. He was sent to University of Wisconsin, Madison, Wiscon-

Radioman 3/c Richard W. Witbart

sin, in training for a radioman, then went to Mare Island, California, awaiting sea assignment. He was assigned to USS *Crosley* (DE-87). The following nine months were spent in Asiatic-Pacific, primarily in the Shanghai, China area, until his discharge on July 20, 1946. He was born in Welge, Illinois, the son of Albert and Anna D. Leaders Witbart.

LEE ANDREW WITTBRACHT, Private, enlisted at Parris Island, South Carolina on August 4, 1918 for service in WWI. He qualified as marksman September 18, 1918 and served in France, Belgium,

Pvt. Lee Andrew Wittbracht

Luxenbourg, was in march to Rhine River in Germany November 17, 1918 and Occupation of American Bulge Head, December 13, 1918 to July 8, 1919. He was discharged August 13, 1919, Quantico, Virginia. Lee was born in Steeleville, Illinois, September 18, 1896.

WARREN WITTBRACHT, Sergeant, enlisted in November 1942 and took basic training at Jefferson Barracks, Missouri. From there to Sioux Falls, South Dakota for Radio School, then to India. He was

Sgt. Warren Wittbracht

with the Air Transport Command and worked as a ground radio to aircraft, then made 15 round trips to China as a radio operator before being put in Air Traffic Control and ended up at Karachi, India. He lived in Steeleville, Illinois, the son of

Lee A. and Mona Fuhrhop Wittbracht. He was discharged in November 1945.

ANTHONY A. WITTENBRINK, Tech 5, served in 20th Infantry, 6th Division as a truck driver of light vehicles from date of induction, September 11, 1946 until discharge on May 31, 1947. He qualified as marksman with M-1 Rifle 158 and saw service in Occupation of Japan. He received the WWII Victory Medal and Army of Occupation Medal. Born December 4, 1923 in Evansville, Illinois, he was a construction machine operator prior to serving in Army.

DONALD RICHARD WITTENBRINK, MR1, served in the U.S. Navy from May 1, 1952 to January 11, 1956, as an aircraft mechanic, helper line service. He was born in Rockwood, Illinois January 25, 1935, the son of Fred H. and Eva Asbury Wittenbrink.

ELMER ROBERT WITTENBRINK, Motor Machinist Mate 3/c, enlisted in the U.S. Navy on January 19, 1944 for service in WWII. He served at NRS, St. Louis, Missouri; NTS Faragut, Idaho; NYSCH Dearborn, Michigan; Fleet Service School, San Diego, California; Landing Craft School, Comm, DET NS, Astoria, Oregon, and aboard the USS *Drew*.

Awards include the Victory Medal, American Area Medal, Asiatic-Pacific w/ star and Philippine Liberation Medal w/ star. Discharged from Personnel Separation Center, St. Louis, Missouri on February 15, 1946.

He was born in St. Louis, Missouri April 11, 1926.

FRED HARDING WITTENBRINK, Corporal, born August 6, 1920, Chester, Illinois, the son of Fred H. Sr. and Edith Carroll Wittenbrink. He entered WWII September 9, 1942, went from Scott Field to Florida, then to Kansas City, Missouri for Radio School, then returned to Florida and became a chauffeur. Assigned to guard a ship at San Francisco, he was then sent to Australia, and on to Fort Moresby, New Guinea, "over the hump" to a field with engineers constructing an airfield, with 710th Signal Battalion where they were bombed everyday.

He returned to the Philippines and was there when Japan surrendered. He went with the 583rd Signal Battalion from Manila to San Francisco, a 48 day trip, where all the girls came out to meet them when they docked. He was discharged November 30, 1945.

GEORGE EDWARD WITTENBRINK, Staff Sergeant, entered WWII February 2, 1942, and was killed in action July 5, 1944 on Corsica Island. He was with Army Air

S/sgt George E. Wittenbrink & John Byrne

Force 331st Combat Crew Detachment #22946. Born in Chester, Illinois, he was the son of Fred Henry and Eva Asbury Wittenbrink.

JOE W. WITTENBRINK, Staff Sergeant, served in A Battery, 580th AAA AW Battalion in WWII as auto mechanic. He also earned qualification with M1 MM Carbine. Entered service April 24, 1941, served in European-African-Middle Eastern Theatre and Asiatic-Pacific Theatre. Awards include Bronze Battle Star, two Overseas Bars, WWII Victory Medal and others. Discharged December 6, 1945, at Camp Grant, Illinois. He was born in Chicago, Illinois on November 19, 1917.

JOHN HENRY WITTENBRINK, Corporal, born in St. Louis, Missouri, January 7, 1930. He was inducted June 24, 1947

Cpl. John Wittenbrink

at Fort Sheridan, Illinois and served at Fort Lee, Virginia in 563rd Quartermaster Supply Depot. He was discharged at Fort Lee, Virginia on May 29, 1950.

VERNON O. WITTENBRINK, Staff Sergeant, served three years in U.S. Air Force, entering service July 23, 1947, at Sparta, Illinois. Attended Officers Candidate School and was assigned to Squadron TT, 3543rd AFBU, IDTRC, Lackland AFB, Texas until June 25, 1948 when he was discharged.

NICHOLAS W. WOLFF, Lance Corporal, enlisted in the U.S. Marine Corps on August 21, 1968 and was stationed at San Diego, California for boot training. Nick, took his advanced infantry training at Camp Pendleton, California. He served with Gulf Company, 2nd Batt., 4th Ma-

L/Cpl. Nicholas W. Wolff

rines, 3rd Marine Division. He was shipped to Vietnam where he served until his discharge September 24, 1969. He was born, the son of Omer and Gloria (Saak) Wolff, on July 26, 1948 in Murphysboro, Illinois.

OMER W. "TONY" WOLFF, Private First Class, served 1942-43 in WWII, in Camp McCoy, Wisconsin and Camp Carson, Colorado Springs, Colorado in

Pfc. Omer W. (Tony) Wolff

food preparation. Born in Evansville, Illinois, he was son of Leo N. and Eleanor Schittendecker Wolff.

REYNOLD J. WOLFF, Tech 5, served in WWII, December 1942 to December 1945, with Battery C, 230 Search Light Division. Looking back this all seems like fiction - all bad things he tried to blot out of his mind and remember only the good times. As they left San Francisco, the ship's captain, spoke over the loud speaker, "Take your last look at the Golden Gate Bridge." He was right, Reynold never did see it again.

They met a convoy and he had never seen so many ships! The first night out their ship had engine trouble, and next morning they were the only ship in sight and arrived at Honolulu two days late. He spent time on six islands. The three years he spent in the Army, he wouldn't want to go through again for anything.

SHANNON LEE WOLFF, Corporal, served in the U.S. Marine Corps October 1990 to March 1994. He was born in Chester, Illinois on May 23, 1972, son of Nicholas and Jacque Louvier Wolff. After enlistment Shannon was sent to MCRD,

Cpl. Shannon L. Wolff

San Diego, California for boot camp, followed by Logistics School, Norfolk, Virginia. He was transferred to Cherry Point, North Carolina, serving as an Embarkation NCO with a Harrier Squadron. He was discharged in March 1994.

JEROME JOSEPH WOLSHOCK, Fireman 3/c, born in Chester, Illinois, August 18, 1922. He enlisted in the U.S. Navy for service in WWII, September 4, 1942 and made the ultimate sacrifice for his country. He died on the USS *Worden* when it went down January 13, 1943, off Amchika Island in the Aleutians. His parents were Edward J. and Mamie Rahlfs Wolshock.

OLIVER H. WOLTER, Private First Class, served in the U.S. Army, January 13, 1949 to July 1, 1950. The day after his discharge from the Army he enlisted in the Air Force Reserves, serving from July 2, 1950 to July 1, 1953. He was born in Evansville, Illinois on February 17, 1925, son of Louis C. and Edna Goedelmann Wolter.

Pfc. Oliver H. Wolter

In the Army he completed basic training at Camp Breckenridge, Kentucky and served with the 25th Infantry Division, 35th Regiment, Company E. at Otsu, Japan. In the Air Force, he was called to active service in May 1951 and served with 92nd Motor Vehicle Squadron, 92nd ABO, FAFR, Fairchild, Washington. He was discharged in July 1953.

NORLYN R. WOLTERS, Corporal, enlisted in the National Guard, 44th Infantry Division, 135th Engineer Combat Battalion in February 1951. The 44th was activated several months later and he took engineer combat basic training at Fort Leonard Wood, Missouri, November 1951 to February 1953, with many of his fellow guardsmen, then took a troop train to Camp Cooke, California where they had additional combat engineering training.

From Camp Stoneman, California, they were shipped out to Korea and he was assigned to 10th Corps, 8th Army, Headquarters Company, 1343rd Engineer Combat Battalion, stationed about three miles behind the DMZ, 38th Parallel, and served there until the war ended in July 1953. He was discharged from Camp Carson, Colorado, September 23, 1953. Norlyn lived in Steeleville, Illinois, at time of his enlistment, the son of Elmer and Marie Bierman Wolters, and getting back home was one of the happiest days of his life!

RICHARD L. WOLTERS, Corporal, was a farmer until October 20, 1942, when he entered military service in WWII. He served with Troop F, 5th Cavalry in New Guinea and Admiralty Islands as a rifleman. On March 6, 1944 he was wounded in action on Admiralty Islands and received a Purple Heart. He was also awarded the Bronze Star, WWII Victory Medal and Asiatic-Pacific Theatre Ribbon. Richard received a disability discharge December 4, 1947 from Percy Jones Hospital, Battle Creek, Michigan. Born September 16, 1910, in Percy, Illinois, son of Louis and Anna Kothe Wolters, he died June 21, 1978.

HAROLD MERLE WOODS, Private, served in WWI, in Company 243 Prison War Escort, in both France and Germany. He was born in Rockwood, Illinois, April 26, 1893, to John Vance and Elveretta Mansker Woods. He was inducted at Chester, Illinois, May 27, 1918 and was discharged from service at Camp Dix, New Jersey on November 6, 1919. He died February 28, 1947, and is buried in Woods Family Cemetery near Rockwood, Illinois.

JOHN HARRISON WOODS, E-2, joined the U.S. Army October 3, 1952 with basic training at Fort Leonard Wood, Missouri, then attended STR 6th Armored Di-

Fireman 3/c Jerome J. Wolshock

Cpl. Norlyn R. Wolters

E-2 John H. Woods

vision School for Utility Repair. On July 3, 1953, he was given a Hardship Separation and transferred to Army Reserves for eight years. He was born February 4, 1932, Fort Gage, Illinois, the son of Cecil F. and Emma Sykes Woods. He died June 1, 1969.

CLYDE H. WOODSIDE, Seaman 1/c, joined the U.S. Navy April 22, 1943 to serve in WWII. His tour of duty was aboard USS *Pensacola* as a flagman, and he par-

Seaman 1/c Clyde H. Woodside

ticipated in the Battle of Saigon. After his discharge February 11, 1946, he worked for General Motors. Born October 26, 1924, the son of S. Harold and Anna M. Heinike Woodside, he died October 28, 1983.

IRL H. WOODSIDE, Sergeant, served in the U.S. Army November 30, 1949 to August 1952 as AF Artillery Specialist. He earned two Bronze Service Stars and the United Nations Service Medal. Returning home he worked for General Motors in St.

Sgt. Irl H. Woodside

Louis, Missouri, then transferred to New York where he was a foreman. He was born June 3, 1931, Perry County, Illinois, the son of S. Harold and Anna M. Heinike Woodside. He died June 10, 1992.

JOHN E. WOODSIDE, Corporal, served in the U.S. Army February 23, 1951 to February 6, 1953, in Kaiserslautern, Germany. With the Army Engineers he helped build bridges and make roads. He had

Cpl. John E. Woodside

worked for Gypsum Roofing Company before service and after service at General Motors, where he retired 30 years later at age 53. He was born April 2, 1929, Perry County, Illinois, the son of S. Harold and Anna M. Heinike Woodside.

ROLLAND DALE WOODSIDE, Spec 4, served in the U.S. Army, 1958-60, active duty and four years in the Reserves. He served with 4th Armored Division, B. Company, 4th Squadron in Germany as an engineer for 18 months, working on floating bridges. After his discharge

Spec-4 Rolland D. Woodside

he worked for General Motors until retirement. He was born February 7, 1940, Perry County, Illinois, the son of Harold and Anna Heinike Woodside.

WILLIAM CLYDE WOODSIDE, Seaman 1/c, served in the U.S. Navy September 10, 1980 to June 15, 1985. He

Seaman 1/c William C. Woodside

served aboard the USS *Puget Sound,* which was a repair ship. After his discharge, he worked as a diesel mechanic. He was born July 11, 1961, the son of Clyde H. and Loraine Schekel Woodside. He died October 25, 1999.

WILMER GENE WOODSIDE, Airman 2/c, served in the U.S. Air Force, 1955-59, in a flight testing center in California, duty in SC, a year in Iceland and a year

AM 2/c Wilmer G. Woodside

and a half in Alaska. After his discharge, he worked for General Motors until retirement. He was born October 18, 1937, Perry County, Illinois, the son of Samuel Harold and Anna M. Heinike Woodside.

JAMES H. WORD, Corporal, served in the U.S. Marine Corps, December 14, 1951 to December 2, 1953. He was born in Sparta, Illinois January 16, 1931, son of Carlos and Agnes Beveridge Word. Drafted into Marines, he completed boot camp at San Diego, California, transferred

Cpl. James Word

to El Toro Marine Air Station, driving a gas truck. During Korean War he served as a heavy duty truck driver in front line duties with the 110th Replacement Battalion, 1st Marine Division. He was discharged at Treasure Island, California. Returning home, he worked at World Color Press.

RAYMOND EARL WRIGHT, Corporal, served in the Korean War. He was born July 27, 1930, son of Edward and Mae Sutherland Wright, he died August 13, 1994 and is buried in Evergreen Cemetery in Chester, Illinois.

VERNON M. WUNDERLICH, Private First Class, served in the U.S. Army Infantry during WWII with Company E, 179th Infantry as a truck driver. He served in Rhineland, Central Europe and received the American Defense Service Ribbon, European-African-Middle Eastern Theater Ribbon w/2 Bronze Stars, Asiatic-Pacific Theater Ribbon w/5 Overseas Service Bars, Good Conduct Medal and Purple Heart.

Pfc. Vernon M. Wunderlich

He was wounded in Germany April 5, 1945, and was in GO 103 HQ 27th Evacuation Hospital 45. Born in Evansville, Illinois, February 22, 1914, son of John P. and Kate Klein Wunderlich. He was in the first draft from Randolph County and was inducted at East St. Louis, Illinois, January 23, 1941. He was discharged from Fort Sheridan, Illinois February 27, 1945. Vernon died December 6, 1994, at age 80.

HAROLD J. YANKEY, Private, served with Battery A, 797th AAA Auto Weapons. Inducted April 30, 1943, Peoria, Illinois and served until October 27, 1943 when discharged at Camp Haan, California due to disability. He qualified as marksman with M1 Rifle and Machine Gunner (606). Born June 14, 1924, in Rockwood, Illinois, son of Charles and Flora Holley Yankey, he died April 4, 1957 and is buried Evergreen Cemetery, Chester, Illinois.

JESSE C. YANKEY, Private, born July 5, 1919, Rockwood, Illinois, son of Charles and Flora Holley Yankey. He served in the infantry in WWII from 1944 until killed in action March 21, 1945. He was

Pfc. Jesse C. Yankey

in the battle of Luzon Island in the Philippines.

ROY LEE YANKEY, Tech 4, entered WWII, December 15, 1942 and served in Greenland (Artic Circle) with 194th Port Company as a winch operator, loading and unloading ships, and protecting base from

T-4 Roy Lee Yankey

enemy submarines. He was honorably discharged December 15, 1944 and went to work for Transworld Airlines. Roy died May 3, 2002. He was born in Rockwood, Illinois, March 7, 1922, son of Charles and Flora Holley Yankey.

SHIRLEY "PECK" YANKEY, Corporal, served in the U.S. Army, April 5, 1951 to March 20, 1953. He was born October 31, 1929, Rockwood, Illinois, the son of Charles and Flora Holley Yankey. He worked for McDonnell-Douglas and

Cpl. Shirley Yankey

Gilster MaryLee, he and wife, June (Mehrtens), had nine children.

WILLIAM GERALD YANKEY, Private First Class, was born in Rockwood, Illinois April 11, 1932, son of Carl and Flora Holley Yankey. He entered the U.S. Army, November 17, 1952 and served with Head-

Pfc. William G. Yankey

quarters Company 7888 in Occupation of Germany. He attended Food Service School from February until August 1953. He was discharged October 29, 1954, from Fort Sheridan, Illinois and received the National Defense Medal for overseas tour.

COLE R. YOUNG, Private First Class, serving in the U.S. Marine Corps, July 2002 to the present time. He is from Steeleville, Illinois and the son of Donald R. and Sue

Pfc. Cole R. Young

Gardner Young. He successfully completed boot camp at MCRD San Diego, California and infantry training at Camp Pendleton, California. He is currently deployed in the Middle East.

EDWIN J. ZIMMER, BT-1, a native of Baldwin, Illinois, son of Edwin F. and Emma A. Luebkemann Zimmer. He served in the U.S. Navy during the Korean War, from December 1950 until October 1954. From Great Lakes Naval Training Station, he was assigned to the USS *Siboney* (CVE-112), USS *Salerno Bay* (CVE-110) and the USS *Midway* (CV-41).

GERARD A. ZIMMER, Staff Sergeant, served in the U.S. Air Force November 17, 1983 to September 1, 1992 with 3345 Security Police Squadron. He enlisted and completed basic training, then entered the Air Force Security Police Academy. After police training he was assigned to the 7625 Security Police Squadron at the Air Force Academy as a patrolman.

In April 1988, he went to Belgium and was assigned to 485 SPS. In March 1989, returned to the States and was assigned to 3345 SPS at Chanute AFB, Illinois. Separated from Air Force on September 1, 1992. He was born October 16, 1962, the son of Ralph and Irene Duhigg Zimmer, Steeleville, IL.

JAMES A. ZIMMER, E-5, joined the Marines on February 4, 1991 and after completing basic training at Camp Pendleton, California, he went to MOS Electrical Equipment Repair Specialist training at Camp Lejeune, North Carolina. He was then stationed at Okayama, Japan. James was with the Marine Air Traffic Control Squadron 7. He finished the remainder of his tour at Yuma, Arizona until his discharge February 2, 1995. He was born in Red Bud, Illinois on November 26, 1970 to Carlisle and Joyce (Kreyer) Zimmer.

E-5 James A. Zimmer

RALPH R. ZIMMER, Master Sergeant, of Steeleville, Illinois, son of Richard and Meta Beisner Zimmer, served over 20 years in the Army Air Force, April 6, 1951 to June 1, 1971, a period that included both the Korean and Vietnam Wars. After basic training at Lackland AFB, Texas, he was assigned to the 1600th Air Traffic Squadron, Westover AFB, Maine, then to the 18th Maintenance and Supply Squadron in Korea.

After the Korean tour, he returned to Westover AFB, was then sent to McGuire AFB, New Jersey to the 1611th Air Traffic Wing. He served in Detachment 6 of the 1611th, at Idlewild Airport (JFK International Airport) New York, before being sent to Ankara, Turkey with Detachment 40 of the 5th Aerial Port Squadron. His next move was to the 62nd Air Terminal Squadron at McChord AFB, Washington, and from there to Thule AFB, Greenland with the 1628th Support Squadron, and to Lockbourne AFB, Ohio with the 1st Aerial Squadron.

While stationed in Ohio, he was sent to the Dominican Republic during the crisis of 1965. His next assignment was to Clark AB, Philippines, with the 604th Military Airlift Squadron, then with the 618th Military Airlift Squadron he was sent to Korat RTAFB, Thailand. His last assignment, before retiring, June 1, 1971, was with the 437th Aerial Port Squadron at Charleston AFB, South Carolina. He was awarded the Bronze Star, Air Force Commendation and the Air Force Achievement and Good Conduct Medals.

WILBERT F. ZIMMER, MOMM3, entered the U.S. Navy in June 1944 to serve in WWII. From boot camp, Great Lakes Naval Station, he was assigned to USS *Elkhart* (APA-80) for duty in Southwest Pacific. Wilbert is the son of Edwin F. and Emma A. Lueblemann Zimmer of Baldwin, Illinois.

MELVIN A. ZIMMERMAN, Corporal, served in the U.S. Army, May 12, 1953 to May 11, 1955. He was born August 7, 1927 in Percy, Illinois, the son of Gustav and Esther Alms Zimmerman. Melvin was drafted, completed basic training at Fort Bliss, TX, and was stationed at Camp Stewart, Georgia for the remainder of his service. He was discharged in May 1955.

Harry McLaughlin with Randolph County boys. Harry is second row, eighth from left.

Camp Pike, AR. William G. Kiehna on left, top row.

Grave of Harry McLaughlin in Randolph County, near Coulterville.

A heap of wrecked plance at Wheeler Field, Territoy of Hawaii, caused by Japanese bombings on 7 December 1941. (Official USAF photo #59995 A.C.)

Tanks on mountain in Korea.

GM Harry G. Reid with 5-inch Mark 37 model 6 gun, 6-mile ranage, 22 rounds per minute he operated on the USS Chicago.

Off the bombline, east coast of Korea, 1952. Heavy cruiser, Los Angeles coming alongside an AKA to replenish stores. Aircraft carrier Bonhomme Richard already on station. Part of Task Force 77

July 23, 1943, Egmont Key Island-This was "Home". From left: Stafford. Jack B. Pierce, Pat Venuti and H.C. Swinferd.

William Schmerbauch

 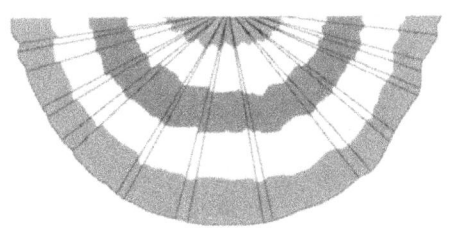 

A Salute to Those Killed In Action

The muffled drum's sad roll has beat,
The soldier's last tattoo;
No more on life's parade shall meet
The brave and fallen few.
On fame's eternal camping ground
Their silent tents are spread,
And glory guards with solemn round,
The bivouac of the dead.

Theodore O'Hara

★★ Revolutionary War ★★

By the rude bridge that arched the flood,
Their flag to April's breeze unfurled,
Here once the embattled farmers stood,
And fired the shot heard round the world.

Ralph Waldo Emerson

Hennrich M. Bollinger
Richard Smith

★★ Civil War ★★

Sadly, but not with upbraiding,
The generous deed was done;
In the storm of the years that are fading,
No braver battle was won;
Under the sod and the dew,
Waiting the judgement day;
Under the blossoms, the Blue;
Under the garlands, the Gray.

Francis M. Finch

Sgt. William Wesley Anderson	J.R. Strother Jones	Thomas McGee
Lt. Harvey Clendenin	Pvt. Henry Clay Mansker	James D. Reid
1st Sgt. George D. Eaton	Richard B.S. Marlen	Heinrich Ritter
Pvt. William Elsey	William C. Marlen	Albert Rockwell
Pvt. John Wesley Guymon	Armstrong McGee	Heinrich Sippel
Gabriel Jones		

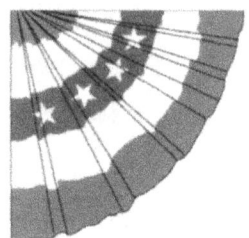
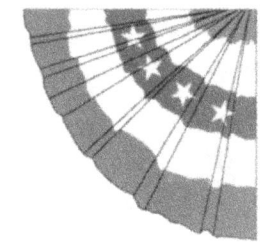

★★ WORLD WAR I ★★

Rest ye in peace, ye Flanders dead,
The fight that ye so bravely led
We've taken up, And we will keep
True faith with you who lie asleep
With each a cross to mark his bed,
In Flanders Fields.

R.W. Lillard

George Cheslick	William Dienfenbach
Alva Courier	Arnold Henderson
Rueben T. Cressy	John E. Weir

★★ WORLD WAR II ★★

They were defenders of the faith and guardians of the truth;
That you and I might live and love, they gladly gave their youth;
And we who set a day apart to honor them who sleep,
Should pledge ourselves to hold the faith they gave their lives to keep.

Edgar A. Guest

Aviation Radioman Harry J. Allison
1/Lt. Wilbur E. Acheson
2/Lt. Jerry (Jack) Atchison
2/Lt. Fred W. Ahlheim
Sgt. Dean W. Aitken
F.O. James H. Anderson
Sgt. Ernest M. Arnold
Sgt. Douglas W. Becker
2/Lt. Eugene Been
William Biesner
T/Sgt. Ward H. Blasius
Fred Borgard
Pvt. John Born
Seaman John R. Bowlin
Harrel D. Brandon
Pfc. Willard A. Burkhardt
Capt. James D. Butler
George Choate
Gordon Louis Cohen
Pfc. Alfred Dannenbrink
Seaman 1/c Orville C. Dayton
GM 2/c Edward Valentine Degenhart
S/Sgt. Kenneth J. Demick
S/Sgt. Ernest M. Deppe
Roy Deppe
Pfc. Wilbert H. Dettmer
Pvt. 1/c Clyde L. Eggemeyer

Pvt. Alvin H. Erdmann
T/Sgt. Robert H. Finley
S/Sgt. Leslie Happel
1/Lt. Clifford E. Heaton
Pfc. Charles Hill, Jr.
Pvt. Lester P. Holtz
T/Sgt. James M. Howie
Seaman 2/c Gerald M. Johnson
Henry Kasten
Cpl. Albert E. Kirk
Alfred Koehler
Walter Koopman
T/5 Floyd Kraft
Pvt. Alvin C. Kueker
Pvt. Clarence A. Kueker
Cpl. Sylvestor Lorentz
Pfc. John V. Loveland
Maurice Lynch
Pfc. Eddie Mabuce
Sgt. James Mathewson
Pfc. Myrl T. McDonald
2/Lt. Harry McGuire
S/Sgt. Clifford D. Miller
James Morgan
S/Sgt. Clement Mueth
Pfc. Raymond Nelson
2/Lt. Edgar W. Nevois

2/Lt. Burton W. Phegley
Pfc. Kurt H.H. Pohle
Pfc. Charles W. Porter
T/5 Vernon Powderly
Pfc. Gilbert George Prosek
T/Sgt. Wilber Earl Rader
Cpl. Edwin F. Richeson
Pfc. Edwin Roesemeier
T/Sgt. Ted R. Rutherford
Pfc. Arthur E. Secor
Pfc. Leonard Siemers
Sgt. Orville Simpson
Pfc. Conrad H. Stellhorn
Yeo. 1/c Frank A. Stepanek
Pfc. Clyde F. Sternberg
T/4 Fred F. Sunderman
George R. Taylor
Pfc. Charles J. Thimming
Airman Lyle A. Thompson
Albert Williams
Roger Williamson
S/Sgt. Norman B. Wilson
S/Sgt. George E. Wittenbrink
Fireman 3/c Jerome Joseph Wolshock
Pvt. Jesse C. Yankey
T/Sgt. Walter D. Yates

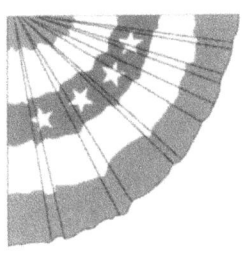 

★★ KOREAN WAR ★★

I have a rendezvous with Death,
At some disputed barricade
It may be he shall take my hand,
And lead me into his dark land,
It may be I shall pass him still,
On some scarred slope of battered hill,
And I to my pledged word am true,
I shall not fail that rendezvous.

Alan Seegar

Pfc. Harry Goetting
Lt. Comm. George H. Holloman
Pfc. Frederick Maasberg
Radarman T/3 Forrrest B. Nance
Pfc. Delmer Petrowske
Airman Armond L. Stewart
Pfc. Fred Voss

★★ VIETNAM WAR ★★

Their names are writ on every flower,
On every tree their sign is set
Birds are their word; by day and night
The very stones cry out our debt.
We will keep the faith! Our hands take up
The charge their dying hands let fall,
And in an everlasting peace
We offer this memorial.

Ada Jackson

Pfc. Frederick A. Allmeyer
Sgt. Robert J. Bowlin
M/Sgt. Roger Boyd
Pfc. Delbert P. Brockmeyer
Billy Ray Caby
Pfc. James Edward Cowell
Pfc. Terry Douglas
Sgt. Kenneth C. Frazer
WO Ivan I. Green
Eddie Huntley
Gary Koch

Michael McAdoo
Cpl. Steven W. Moll
Pfc. Leonard A. Nitzsche
Capt. Roger D. Partington
L/Cpl. Charles W. Rader
M/Sgt. Glenn Richardson
Eddie Simpson
L/Cpl. Richard Joseph Suhre
Spec/5 Phillip Paul Summers
Sgt. Alan D. Trucano
1/Lt. Bruce L. Welge

"TAPS"

No melody has had a more chilling or moving effect on those who have heard it than 'TAPS'. This song has affected millions of lives in various ways. It's a melody many have heard and none will every forget. Played by the military, it signals the end of each day. Played at a military funeral, it signifies the end of a soldier's life and a job well-done. The words are as follows:

> Day is done, gone the sun,
> From the hills, from the lake,
> From the sky.
> All is well, safely rest,
> God is nigh.
>
> Go to sleep, peaceful sleep,
> May the soldier or sailor,
> God keep.
> On the land or the deep,
> Safe in sleep.
>
> Fades the light; And afar
> Goeth day, And the stars
> Shineth bright.
> Fare thee well; Day has gone,
> Night is on.
>
> Thanks and praise, For our days,
> 'Neath the sun, 'Neath the stars,
> 'Neath the sky.
> As we go, this we know,
> God is nigh.

This song was first played by a lone bugler during the Civil War, from notes of music scribbled on a paper found in the uniform pocket of a dead Confederate soldier, who happened to be the son of Robert Ellicombe, a Captain in the Union Army.

The story goes, during a battle near Harrison's Landing in Virginia, a wounded soldier was heard groaning while lying on the battlefield. Although night had fallen, Captain Ellicombe decided he would attempt to get the soldier to the Union camp for the medical help he obviously needed.

Not knowing if the soldier was Union or Confederate, the brave Captain crawled, under gunfire, and reached the wounded soldier. He successfully pulled him inside the Union camp and in the light of a lantern the Captain found him to be a Confederate soldier, and saw the young soldier was now dead.

Looking more closely, by the dim light of the lantern, he looked upon the face of the soldier, and with shock and grief beyond words, he recognized the soldier as his own son.

The boy had been in the South studying music when the war began, and had never let his father know he had enlisted as a soldier in the Confederate Army.

The next morning, with a heavy heart, Captain Ellicombe asked his superior officers if he could give his son a full military burial. Because the son was considered an enemy, permission was denied. A full military service would have included an Army band. The Captain was told he would be allowed one musician to provide music for the burial of his son. The Captain chose a bugler.

He asked the bugler to play the series of musical notes he had found on the paper in the pocket of his son's uniform.

On that battlefield in Virginia, in a Union Army encampment, the first rendition of this haunting and now familiar melody, known as 'TAPS' was played by the lone bugler. It is now a regular part of military funerals, yet no matter how often one hears it played, a tear always comes to the eye.

Even though it has been well over 100 years since those few notes were first played, the melody has never failed to quicken the heart nor loose its chilling effect on those who hear it.

The History of the Service Flag

The Service Flag is an official banner authorized by the Department of Defense for display by families who have members serving in the Armed Forces during any period of war or hostilities the United States may be engaged in for the duration of such hostilities.

The history of the Service Flag is as patriotic and touching as the symbolism each star represents to the families that display them. The service flag (also known as "blue star banners" or "son in service flags") was designed and patented by World War I Army Captain Robert L. Queissner of the 5th Ohio Infantry, who had two sons serving on the front line. The flag quickly became the unofficial symbol of a child in service. President Wilson became part of its history when in 1918 he approved a suggestion made by the Women's Committee of the Council of National Defenses, that mothers who had lost a child serving in the war should wear a gold gilt star on the traditional black mourning arm band.

This led to a tradition to cover the blue star with a gold star on the Service Flag to indicate that the service member had died or been killed. The color of the stars is also symbolic in that the blue star represents hope and pride and the gold star represents sacrifice to the cause of liberty and freedom.

During World War II, the practice of displaying the service flag became much more widespread. In 1942, the Blue Star Mothers of America was founded as a veteran service organization and was part of a movement to provide care packages to military members serving overseas and also provide assistance to families who encountered hardships as a result of their son or husband serving during the war.

Virtually every home and organization displayed banners to indicate the number of members of the family or organization serving in the Armed Forces, and again, covered those blue stars with a gold star to represent each member that died. In 1960, Congress chartered the Blue Star Mothers of America as a veterans service organization and in 1966, the Department of Defense revised the specifications for the design, manufacture and display of the Service Flag.

The Department of Defense specifies that family members authorized to display the flag include the wife, husband, mother, father, stepfather, parent through adoption, foster parents who stand in loco parentis, children, stepchildren, children through adoption, brothers, sisters, half-brothers and half-sisters of a member of the Armed Forces of the United States.

The Service Flag may also be displayed by an organization to honor the members of that organization serving in the Armed Forces during a period of war or hostilities.

How to Display the Service Flag

The Service Flag is an indoor flag and should be flown facing out from the front window of the home or organization.

If the U.S. flag is also displayed with the Service Flag, the U.S. flag should be of equal or greater proportions and should take the place of honor above the Service Flag.

If a gold star is added to the Service Flag, it should take the position of honor and be placed over the blue star that is positioned closest to the staff.

The gold star should be smaller than the blue star to create a blue border surrounding the gold star.

SERVED OUR COUNTRY, TOO

The names listed here served in the military, however we were unable to obtain information of their service record. Some of the names are taken from cemetery records, others from newspapers and service memorials located in various towns. Rank and war served in are given if known. Even though we have used all material available to us, we know there are many names we have missed.

1/Lt Harry Adams, WWI
Pvt. John P. Adams, Civil War
Pvt. R.W. Adams, Civil War
Pvt. Roscoe Adkins, WWI
Dean Aiken
Pvt. John Henry Aitkens, WWI
John Robert Aitken
Pvt. Ralph Lynn Aitkin, WWI
Pvt. Charles Albert, WWI
Pvt. Elmer Alexander, WWI
Pvt. John R. Alexander, WWI
Pvt. William Alexander, WWI
Pvt. Lawrence J. Allard, WWI
Cpl. Aloysius M. Allen, WWI
Marine Pvt. Kenneth H. Allen
Pvt. John R. Allen, Civil War
Pvt. William McKinley Allen WWI
Pvt. Adolph H. Allmeyer, WWI
Horseshoer Martin H. Allwardt, WWI
Pvt. Edward Alms, WWI
Fred H. Alms, Korean War
Pvt. Henry F. Alms, WWI
Tiffany L. Alms, Peacetime
Pfc. William F. Alms, WWI
Cpl. Hollie Anderson, WWI
George Edward Andrews, WWII
Pvt. Joseph D. Antonale, WWI
Jack Armstrong
William J. Asbury, WWII
Seaman Dewey Austin, WWI
Cpl. Harry D. Bailey, WWI
Pvt. Obadiah Bailey, WWI
Pvt. John Baird, WWI
Pvt. Ernest E. Baker, WWI
William Baker
Dr. Joel C. Barber, Civil War
Albert M. Bardo, WWI
Pvt. Eli Henry Bardo, WWI
Pvt. D.P. Barker, WWI
Charles H. Barnes, WWI
John Barnfield Civil War
Seaman Joseph Barnes
Pvt. Andrew Barr, WWI
3M 3/c Sylvester Barth, WWII
Pvt. 1/c Charles F. Bartholemew, WWI
Harold Bartlett
Kenneth Bartlett
Sanner Bartlett
Trumpeter George Clark Bates, WWI
Joseph C. Bates Sr., WWI
Sgt. James Bates, WWI
Edward Bauer
Rupert Bauer
Pvt. Lawrence J. Baum, WWI
Pvt. Sam Baxter, WWI
Edward Earl Bayers, WWII
Pvt. Henry J. Bayers, WWI
Sgt. Lawrence Beare, WWI
Wagoner Walter Beare, WWI
Pvt. Charles Beattie, WWI
Pvt. Dewey T. Beattie, WWI

Everett Beattie, WWI
Dr. James C. Beattie, Spanish American War
John Beaty, 1812
Pvt. Lyman Beckett, WWI
C.F. Becker
Festus Becker
Walter Becker
Lt. E.M. Been, Civil War
Cpl. Francis E. Been
Pvt. William Been, Civil War
Edward W. Beisner, Spanish American War
Herman G. Beisner, WWI
James L. Bell
Opal E. Bell
Warren E. Bell
Pvt. 1/c George L. Belnap, Korean War
Pvt. Lewis Benson, WWI
Albert Bequette
Marine Pvt. Everett C. Bergman, WWI
Pvt. Ralph D. Bersche, WWI
Pvt. Ben J. Bert, WWI
Pvt. John Beveridge, WWI
Cpl. Henry Biddingsley WWI
Sgt. E.A. Bierbaum, WWI
Pvt. Albert Biethman, WWI
Cpl. Kenneth Biethman, Korean War
Pvt. Atley Bigby, WWI
Pvt. Harlan V. Bigby, WWI
Cook Shelton Billimock, WWI
Cook Cpl. Fred J. Binns, WWI
Cpl. Roland Birkner, Korean War
Sgt. Todd Birkner
Pvt. Laughlin Black, Civil War
A/Man Jeffrey Blair, Peacetime
Pvt. Robert T. Blair, WWI
Carl Bleem
Pvt. Joseph M. Bleem, WWI
Cpl. Leo Bleem, WWI
Pvt. Martin J. Bleem, WWI
Pfc. Perry W. Blow, WWI
Mechanic Herman H. Boeger, WWI
Ed Boester
John C. Bollman, WWI
Cpl. Clyde Bollinger, Korean War
Cpl. Willa A. Boman, WWI
Dr. D.S. Booth, WWI
Sgt. Fred Boston, WWI
Nurse Louise Botsai, WWI
Pvt. Paul A. Bourner, WWI
Cpl. William J. Bowman, Civil War
Pvt. David Boyd, WWI
Pvt. Robert M. Boyd, Civil War
Roy Lester Boyd
Pvt. William Boyd, Civil War
Sgt. Albert E. Boyer, WWI
Mechanic G. Boyer, WWI
Pvt. Otto J. Boyer, WWI
Cpl. Paul Boyington, WWI

Pvt. 1/c Harry Bradbury, WWI
T/Sgt. Edward E. Bradley, WWI
Capt. C.A. Bradshaw, Civil War
Army Reserve George Brandon, WWI
Cpl. Earl C. Brands, WWI
Air Service Pvt. Edward Brase, WWI
Pvt. Louis W. Brase, WWI
Pvt. Joseph Bratney, Civil War
David Braun
Albert W. Brazinski
Charles P. Brazinski
Jackson Bridgeman, Civil War
Pvt. Monroe Briggs, Civil War
Arthur W. Brinkman, WWI
Sgt. Bert Brinkman, WWI
Pvt. Walter Brinkman, WWI
Walter Broshears, WWI
David E. Brown, WWII
Pvt. Earnest Brown, WWI
Pvt. George W. Brown, WWI
Bugler Goldie Lee Brown
Sgt. 1/c James W. Brown, WWI
John I. Brown
Pvt. Moses A. Brown, WWI
Nickolas Brown, 1812
Flying Cadet Olin Brown, WWI
Sgt. Paul Brown, WWI
Cpl. Thomas Browning, WWI
Fireman 2/c Theo Brueggermann, WWI
Todd Brunkhorst
Sgt. 1/c Edgar Buch, Vietnam
Spec/5 Richard F. Buch, Vietnam
Horseshoer August C. Budde, WWI
SK-1 Vernon Budde, Korean War
Pvt. Frank A. Buehler, WWI
Pvt. Everett Bulliner, WWI
Howard Burdett
Pvt. W.H. Burgett, Civil War
Cpl. August Burmester, Korean War
QM 2/c Dale Burmester (USN 1975-79)
Sgt. Todd Burmester
Albert D. Burnett
Kenneth Burnett
Pvt. Frank Burns, Civil War
Sgt. 1/c Frederick Burns, WWII
Sgt. James G. Burns, Civil War
Blk. Smith Samuel G. Burns, 1812
Blk. Smith Stewart Burns, 1812
Walter I. Burt
Pfc. Arnold R. Burton, WWII
Cpl. Bennie Burton, WWI
H.C. Burton, Civil War
Clyde Dewey Bush, WWII
Ivan R. Bush, Korean War
Pvt. Calvin Buss, WWI
Pvt. Franklin Butler, Civil War
Pvt. James A. Butler
Pvt. John Lloyd Butler

Charles W. Byrd, WWI
Pvt. 1/c Fred B. Cairns, WWI
Pvt. Samuel Caldwell, WWI
Blk. Smith John G. Calvins, Civil War
Pvt. Hugh M. Campbell
Pvt. James G. Campbell, Civil War
Seaman Joe Campbell
Cpl. Arlo Cannon
Pvt. 1/c Samuel Carns, WWI
Pvt. 1/c Carl Carr, WWI
Austin V. Carter
Dewey Carter
Everett Carter
Cpl. Gomer Casey, WWI
Pvt. Joseph P. Cassoutt, WWI
Pvt. Henry W. Castens, WWI
Sgt. 1/c Michael A. Cavalier, Desert Storm
Joe Chambers, WWI
Thomas F. Chambers
William Chambers, 1812, Creek Indian
Russell E. Chandler
John W. Chappel
Raymond Chappel
Walter Chappel
William H. Cheek
Pvt. 1/c Fountain Childers, WWI
Pvt. 1/c Charles W. Childs
John Cima, WWI
Pvt. Jacob Cimmer, Civil War
E-2 Paula DeBenedetto Clarkson, Vietnam
Pvt. Julius Clayton, WWI
Pvt. Edward E. Cleiman, WWI
Nurse Flora Cleland, WWI
John M. Clemons
Pvt. John S. Clendenin, Civil War
Dr. Moses Walter Clendenin, Civil War
Pvt. Roy E. Cluster, WWI
Charles E. Cochran WWII
Pvt. J.T. Cochran, Civil War
Pvt. Gordon A. Cohen, WWI
Pvt. Sidney Cohen, WWI
Horseshoer Frank Cole, WWI
1/Lt. Margaret B. Coleman, WWII
Pvt. Albert B. Collier, WWI
Samuel Skinner Collins, Spanish American War
Pvt. John Colwell, Civil War
Alex Combs, WWI
S/Sgt. Charles Conner, WWII
Gilbert Conner
Christopher C. Conrad, Vietnam
Medic Frank L. Cook, Civil War
Pvt. Edward Cording, WWI
Pvt. H.P. Couch, Civil War
Pvt. Millington Couch, Revolutionary War
Pvt. Milton Couch, Civil War
Cpl. Robert G. Couch, Civil War
Pvt. 1/c Roy Couier, WWI

176

William Coulson
Pvt. Absaolm Cox, 1812
Cook Joseph Cox, WWI
Pvt. Marion Cox, Civil War
Pvt. Earnest Covington, WWI
Pvt. 1/c Anthony J. Coyle, WWI
James Cragen
Pvt. Elmer E. Craig, WWI
Pvt. Ralph Craig, WWI
Pvt. William C. Craig, Civil War
Andrew C. Crain, WWII
Cpl. Harry B. Crain, WWI
James H. Crawford, Civil War
Cpl. William J. Crawford, Civil War
Paul Crippen
Carl H. Crisler
Herschel D. Crisler
Silas Crisler, Civil War
Wayne Crisler
Pvt. Francis Crittenden, Civil War
David Cross, WWI
Archie C. Curtiss, Civil War
Pvt. Myren E. Cuthbertsen, WWI
Wagoner Edwin L. Dagner, WWI
Pvt. George E. Dahlhoff, WWI
Fireman Albert A. Danter, WWI
Pvt. 1/c Edmo C. Darl, WWI
Neely E. Davis
Noah Davis
Melvin Davison
Pvt. Solon R. Davison, WWI
Earnest Paul Dean, WWI
James Earl Dean, WWI
Chauffeur Robert Earnest Dean, WWI
Pvt. Roy A. Dean, WWI
David G. Deans
James K. Deans
RM 3/c Alfred H. Degener, WWI
Pvt. Harry Degener, WWI
Pvt. Herman L.C. Degener, WWI
Otto Demick
Saddler Clarence A. Dempsey, WWI
Cpl. Marshall Dennis, Civil War
Donald R. Deppe, WWII
James Ray Deppe, Vietnam
R. Dale Deppe, WWII
Samuel D. DesRocher, WWII
Pvt. John M. Dickey, Spanish American War
Lavoy Dickey
Pvt. Milton H. Dickey, WWI
Mechanic Sigmund C. Diefenback, WWI
Pvt. Otto C. Dierks, WWI
Pvt. Louis Dodge, Civil War
Pvt. 1/c Louis M. Donahue, WWI
Pvt. William T. Donahue, WWI
Pvt. 1/c Elsworth Donnie, WWI
Pvt. James Dorsey, WWI
Band Sgt. Alonzo E. Douglas, WWI
George Douglas
Cpl. William F. Dovenmuehle, WWI
James K. Dowen
Sgt. 1/c George W. Drake, WWI
Pvt. Richard Druin, Civil War

Cpl. Anthony Duchinsky, Korean War
Seaman Louis Duclos, WWI
Howard E. Dufour
Pvt. Jonh Dufour, WWI
Robert W. Dufour
Samuel Dufour
M.P. Leo DuFrenne (1970-72)
Cletus Dunker
Otto Dunker
Rudolph Dunker
Pvt. James A. Durham, Civil War
Pvt. 1/c Ben Edler, WWI
James W. Edwards
Richard P. Edwards, WWII
Pvt. 1/c Ben Eggers, WWI
Pvt. Fred T. Eggers, WWI
Cpl. Henry Eggers, WWI
Pvt. David P. Eggemeyer, WWI
Fritz Eggemeyer, Civil War
Phillip Eggemeyer, Civil War
Pvt. 1/c Robert M. Eiker, WWI
Wagoner Henry Fred Eilerman, WWI
Sgt. Mark Ellner, Vietnam
Benjamin L. Elmore
William Elms, Civil War
Edward R. Emerson, Civil War
Robert S. Emerson, Civil War
Marine Pvt. Ralph Oliver Ervin, WWI
Pvt. William W. Ervin, WWI
Mechanic Newel J. Euge, WWI
Pvt. Edward Evans, Civil War
S/Sgt. Arthur Everding, Reserves
Cpl. Brian Everding Marines (1980-84)
Spec/4 Curtis Everding (1967-69)
Pvt. 1/c Paul Everding, WWII
Pvt. 1/c Richard Everding, Korean War
Sgt. Steve Everding (1980-85)
M/Sgt. Jon C. Evers, Vietnam
Pvt. 1/c Dean M. Ewing, WWI
Pvt. William Fair, Civil War
Pvt. Fred Falkenheim, WWI
Pvt. 1/c Alvie Farmer, WWII
John Farnan, Civil War
Pvt. Alfred Eric Farrar, WWI
Pvt. 1/c Fred Daniel Faverty, WWI
Pvt. William Ferguson, WWI
Pvt. Otto Fey, WWI
Pvt. Edwin F. Fiene, WWI
Pvt. 1/c John T. Finley, WWI
Nurse Emilie M. Fischer, WWI
Pfc. John Fix
William M. Flannigan, WWII
T/Sgt. Ralph Flory, WWI
Lt. Col. Edward Foster, Civil War
Pvt. 1/c Morrison R. Foster, WWI
Pvt. 1/c Henry T. Fox, WWI
John Fox, WWI
Pvt. Rudolph Frambs, WWI
Edward Franklin
Robert Franklin
Pvt. 1/c Alex Frazier, WWI
Pvt. William H., Civil War
Arthur E. Frazer, Navy
Cpl. George J. Freeman, WWI
Pvt. Bolden French, WWI

Matthew French
Robert W. French
William A. French
Cpl. Edward P. Fuhrhop, WWI
Pvt.1/c Harry E. Fuhrhop, WWI
Earl Howard Fulford, WWII
Quartermaster Albert D. Fulton, WWII
Loyd Futter, WWI
Roy N. Futter, WWII
Pvt. Ora Gant, WWI
Seaman Ted Gardiner, WWI
Av. Machinist Charles E. Gardner, WWI
Sgt. DeWitt Garner, WWI
Pvt. Francis Garner, Civil War
Pvt. John H. Garner, WWI
William E. Garrett
Theodore Gartee
Pvt. Leslie Elmer Gates, WWI
J.C. Gault, 1812
Dr. H.L. Gault, Civil War
Sgt. Maj. John F. Gault, WWI
Pvt. Melville E. Gault, WWI
Pvt. Samuel Gault, Civil War
Pvt. Arch J. Gendron, WWI
Pvt. Dan Gendron, WWI
Sp. 4 Dwayne Gerlach, Vietnam
Raymond Gerlach
Pvt. Jefferson Gibbons, WWI
Col. Robert Gibson, WWI
Sgt. 1/c Vern Gibson, WWI
Stephen B. Gilbert
Pvt. Owen Gillan, Civil War
Pvt. Alvin R. Glascow, WWI
British Army John Glazebrook, WWI
Sgt. Ellihue G. Gleghorn, WWI
Pvt. Clendenin D. Glenn, WWI
Pvt. David E. Glenn, WWI
Pvt. Elias Glenn, Civil War
Pvt. Ira Glenn, WWI
Sgt. Benjamin Gnaegy, WWI
Pvt. Alfred Godier, WWI
Navy QM Fred William Goedecke, WWI
Pvt. Edward Goettin, WWI
Pvt. 1/c Virgil Goetting, Korean War
Pvt. William Goetting, WWI
Cpl. Fern W. Gordon, WWI
Pvt. Glenn W. Gordon, WWI
Seaman Richard Short Gordon, WWI
Pvt. Burnard Gorman, WWI
Elijah Gorsuch, 1812
Pvt. Oliver P. Gosnell, Civil War
Arthur C. Gottschammer
T/Sgt. Wilmer Graul, WWII
Harvey Dale Gray, Korean War
Sgt. J.L. Gray, Civil War
Robert Gray, WWII
Frank R. Graziani
James Graziani
Pvt. Martin L. Gremmels, WWI
Spec/5 Rich Griffin (1964-68)
Edward E. Griffiths, WWII
Pvt. Fred C. Grimm, WWI
Pvt. Fred Grobb
Pvt. Max Gross, WWI
Cpl. Sigmund Gross, WWI

Cook Oscar C. Grote, WWI
Pvt. Frank M. Grott, WWI
Sgt. Albert J. Guebert, Reserves
Sgt. Delmer L. Guebert (1956-64)
Emil E. Guebert, WWI
Spec. E-4 Harlan Guebert, Reserves
Pvt. Henry L. Guebert, WWI
Pvt. Guethley, WWI
Nolan Haberman, WWII
Nolan D. Haberman, Vietnam
Pvt. Richard Haberman, WWI
1/Lt. Logan Fred Hachman, WWI
Sgt. Peter Hachman, Civil War
Pvt. Ike Hager, WWI
Sgt. Othel Hahn WWI
Pvt. Eddie Haigler, WWI
Charles Bennie Hall, WWI
Pvt. Cooper Hall, Spanish American War
Tead Hall, WWI
Timothy Hall
Cpl. Walter Hall
Jack Hallock
James R. Hallock
William C. Hallock
Pvt. Patrick Halpin, WWI
Pvt. Charles F. Hamilton, WWI
Pvt. Charles Y. Hamilton, WWI
Pvt. Delbert L. Hamilton, WWI
Pvt. Elmer F. Hamilton, WWI
Pvt. John B. Hamilton, Civil War
Pvt. Clem F. Hamm, WWI
George W. Hammel
Navy Nicholas W. Hammel, WWI
Edwin Hanebutt
Pvt. Henry Hanebutt, WWI
Pvt. Louis Hanebutt, WWI
Pvt. James Hanson, Civil War
Thomas Hanson, WWII
Pvt. Roy P. Hapke, WWI
George Hardy, WWI
Edward Harding
Clarence S. Hargan
Lee H. Hargan
Osa W. Hargen
Richard E. Hargen
Anthony M. Harkins, WWII
Pvt. 1/c Homer N. Harmen, WWI
Pvt. Calvin Harmon, WWI
Pvt. Elijaha Harris, WWI
Pvt. Grover Harris, WWI
Pvt. Allen Harrison, WWI
Cook John E. Hartley, WWI
Pvt. Robert A. Hausman, WWI
Floyd Hayden, Vietnam
Inf. Man Hugh H. Haynes
John Hawk, Civil War
Pvt. Orno J. Hawk, Civil War
Pvt. Don L. Hayward, WWI
Gun Sgt. Lee S. Heberer, WWI
Emil Heck
George J. Heck, WWI
Leslie Heck
Spec. 5 Curtis Hecke, Vietnam
Pvt. Joseph Heckman Jr., WWI
Pvt. Earnest Leo Heinks, WWI
Pvt. 1/c John Heinks, WWI
E-5 Orville Heller (Navy 1974-79)
Pvt. Sigmund L. Helmers, WWI
Pvt. Carroll C. Henderson WWI

Mathew R. Henderson
John Hennrich
Orion Hennrich
Pvt. Fred Henrick, WWI
Pvt. 1/c Grover Henson, WWI
Pvt. Henry Henson, WWI
Pvt. Ralph Henson, WWI
Pvt. Edward Herberger, WWI
Albert H. Hermes, WWI
David L. Herring, Korean War
Pvt. Martin Herron, WWI
Pvt. Sigmund Herschback, WWI
Pvt. William Herschback, WWI
Otto Herzog
Henry Hesse, WWI
Pvt. William G. Hethington, WWI
Pvt. Louis C. Heuman, WWI
Pvt. Lloyd Hightower, WWI
Carl Hill Jr.
Charles Hill
Don R. Hill
Robert R. Hill
S/Sgt W. Clell Hill, WWII
Sgt. William J. Hill, Civil War
Alexander Hindman Jr., Civil War
Harold M. Hindman, WWII
Maj. James H. Hindman, Civil War
August Frederick C. Hirte, WWI
Delmaar Hirte
Emery Hirte
Harry Hirte
Robert Hirte
Sgt. William C. Hirte, WWI
William E. Hirte
Harry E. Hissong
S/Sgt. Lloyd Hissong, WWII
Lyle D. Hodge
George Hodgkiss, Spanish-American War
Cook Irving H. Hoening, WWI
Pvt. Eugene Hoffman, WWI
Pvt. Orville Hoffman, WWI
Robert L. Holden, Civil War
Pvt. Harold C. Holdoway, WWI
Benjamin K. Holeman
Edward C. Holeman
William Holeman
Alvin Hollgraze
Cpl. Roger E. Hood, WWII
Capt. Samuel Hood, Civil War
Louis Henry Hoops, Navy WWII
Robert E. Horrell, WWI
Edward E. Hottes
John D. Houghland
Pvt. John Houston, Civil War
Pvt. William T. Houston, WWI
Donald C. Howard, Korean War
Herbert A. Howard, WWII
John B. Howard, Vietnam
Merle E. Howard, WWII
Marine Pvt. John E. Hughs, WWI
Pvt. Joseph E. Hultz, WWI
Pvt. John Humphreys, Civil War
Sgt. Leonard Hunt, WWI
Pvt. Alexander Hunter, Civil War
Pvt. William Hunter, Civil War
Pvt. James F. Hunts, WWI
Milton E. Hurst
Noah N. Hurst
Pvt. 1/c Joseph E. Husband, WWI

Pvt. Daniel Daniel Hutchinson, WWI
Thomas Q. Hutchinson, Spanish American War
Pvt. Homer Hylton, WWI
Pvt. J.M. Hyndman, Civil War
Earl J. Ingram, WWII
Pvt. Andrew Irby, WWI
S/Sgt. Daniel S. Irwin, Gulf War
Edward Isom, WWI
George H. Isom, WWII
Elmer F. Jackson
Cpl. Henry O. Jacoby, WWI
Charles Jaimet
Kenneth R. Jaimet, Korean War
Homer L. Jamison
Clarence Jany
Cpl. Herbert Jay, WWI
Earl H. Jehling
Donald V. Jeremiah, WWII
Gerald Victor Jeremiah
Pvt. Charles E. Johnson, WWI
Pvt. George W. Johnson, Civil War
Pvt. Isaac F. Johnson, Civil War
John N. Johnson, Civil War
Pvt. Joel M. Johnson, Civil War
Cpl. Joseph Johnson, WWI
Lawrence Johnson
Loren Johnson
Philbert Johnson, WWI
Pvt. 1/c William A. Johnson, WWI
Charles Joiner
W.L. Joiner
Clyde Jones
Dale E. Jones
Helen W. Jones
Henry Jones
E-2 Jennifer L. Jones, Peacetime
Lewis H. Jones
Pvt. Louis Jones
E-5 HT2 Michael D. Jones, Peacetime
Capt. P.T. Jones, Civil War
Pvt. Thomas Jones WWI
Pvt. 1/c Albert F. Joost, WWI
Pvt. James B. Jordon
Pvt. Henry Joyce, WWI
E-4 Melvin Juelfs
E-4 Scott Juelfs, Reserves
Omar A. Juenger
Russel M. Juenger
Wilmer J. Juenger
Ben Jung
Pvt. Henry J. Jung, WWI
Pvt. 1/c Peter Jung, Civil War
Cpl. Louis Junge, WWI
Pvt. John M. Junger, WWI
E-4 Joseph Kadlec, Reserves
Elmer F. Kaesberg
Elmer L. Kaesberg
Cpl. Leonard Kaffenburger, WWI
Sgt. Henry L. Kahle, WWI
Jacob Kaiser
Pvt. John C. Kalk, WWI
Seaman Roland Kalbitz, WWI
Cpl. Russell F. Kamper, WWI
Carl E. Kane
Wilfred Karsten
Carpenter Herman Kattenbracker, WWI

Edwin Keiffer
? Keiffer (Tilden Cemetery)
Charles F. Keller, WWI
Joe Dean Keller
1/Sgt. Harold V. Kelley, WWI
Pvt. Edward B. Kelly, Civil War
Pvt. 1/c Ellsworth Kelly, WWI
Marine Pvt. Lafie F. Keller, WWI
John Kelmer
2/Lt. Francis A. Kennedy, WWI
Pvt. Robert Kessel, WWI
FF ABH2 Vernon Kessel Jr., Vietnam
Pvt. Englebert Ketterer, WWI
Herbert O. Keuker
Pvt. Conrad C. Kiefer, WWI
Pvt. Daniel F. Kieffer, WWI
Carl H. Killgrove
Clarence N. Killgrove
George L. Killgrove
Jake Killgrove, WWI
Sgt. Lyman Killgrove, WWI
Roy L. Killgrove
Elmer Ira King
Sgt. George E. King, WWI
Howard R. King
Miles B. King, Civil War
Pvt. 1/c Victor H.A. Kipp, WWI
Pvt. William Klein, WWI
John Klingle
Pvt. Earnest W. Kloepper, WWI
Sgt. Marvin Kloepper, WWII
Wagoner Oscar Kloepper, WWI
Wagoner Walter W. Kloepper, WWI
Harry Kmucha
William Kmucha
Arthur C. Knigge
Leo Knigge
James Knott, WWII
Pvt. Albert Louis Koch, WWI
Sgt. Delbert Koch, WWII Korean War
Airman E-3 John Koch, Peacetime
Pvt. John Kocher, WWI
Wagoner Edward Koeneman, WWI
1/Lt. Roy B. Koeneman, WWII
Cpl. Alvin Koester, Korean War
Spec/4 Dennis Koester (1970-76)
Pvt. 1/c Vernon Koester (1958-60)
Bernard Kohlber
Cpl. Fred Kohrs, WWI
Cpl. George H. Koopman, WWI
Pvt. Herman A. Knop, WWI
George Kowalski
Sgt. Leroy Kraig, WWI
Pvt. Henry Krull, WWI
Artillery Man Theodore Kruse, WWI
Pvt. John J. Krzebietke, WWI
Fritz Kueker, WWI
Harold Kueker
Cpl. Henry Kueker WWI
Pvt. Herman Kueker, WWI
Martin Kueker
Wilber Kueker
Wilbert Kueker
Nurse Otillie L. Kuhrtz, WWI
Robert D. Lacy
Pvt. J.W. Lafferty, Civil War
Horace LaFluer Jr., WWII

Cpl. Prentice LaFleur, WWI
Pvt. Pressley Lancaster, Civil War
Pvt. Edward Laird, Civil War
Pvt. M.F. Laird, Civil War
Pvt. Pressley Lancaster, Civil War
Spec/4 Richard Langrehr
Sgt. Ralph R. Larkin, WWI
Leo Lathum
Sgt. Sam Lato Sr., Vietnam
Lloyd Lauber
Pvt. William E. Lauber, WWI
Pvt. Henry Laufer Civil War
Pvt. George Laurent, WWI
Pvt. Welda H. Laurent, WWI
Harold M. Law
Ray F. Law
Band Cpl. Ray A. Lawder, WWI
Lt. C.C. Lawson, Civil War
Pvt. Robert B. Lawson, Civil War
Inf. Man John Leary, Civil War
Cpl. Edward Ledbetter, WWI
Howard Ledbetter, Navy, WWII
Pvt. Andy Lee, WWI
Pvt. Albert Lehnoff, WWI
Sgt. 1/c Robert P. Lehnherr, WWI
Pvt. John A. Leiner, Civil War
Pvt. Earl Eura Leming, WWI
Al Lemmerman
Muscian 3/c Henry C. Lemmerman, WWI
Herman Lemmerman
Pvt. Charles Lepere, WWI
Robert J. Lessley, WWI
Clestine Levery
Pvt. Charley H. Lewis, WWI
Clarence R. Lickiss
Loyd R. Lickiss, WWI
Cpl. Norbert Liefer, Korean War
Pvt. Walter L. Liefer, WWI
Pvt. George A. Lillman, WWI
Marine John F. Lillman, WWI
Sgt. 1/c Robert J. Lillman, WWI
Pvt. Henry T. Lilly, Civil War
Luther Lime, WWI
O.R. Ling, Civil War
Pvt. Arthur S. Linnertz, WWI
Pvt. William Lipscomb, WWI
Supply Sgt. William Lister, WWI
Gilbert S. Little
James L. Little
Pvt. 1/c Charles Lively, WWI
Pvt. L.B. Lively, Civil War
Pvt. Rowland T. Lively, WWI
William C. Lively, Civil War
Charles Lloyd
Delmer Dean Lodge
Pvt. Adolph L. Loesche, WWI
Pvt. Theodore Loesche WWI
Charles Long
James Lowe, Civil War
Gordon M. Lucy, WWII
Pvt. 1/c Emil Ludwig, WWI
Pvt. Jerome Ludwig, WWI
Spec./4 Larry Luebkemann (1965-71)
Dexter A. Lukes, Peacetime
Pvt. Joseph L. Lund, WWI
Cook Clemons Lusk, WWI
Pvt. Wilbur Lusk, WWI
Pvt. Joseph E. Lybarger, WWI

Samuel Lybarger, Civil War
Pvt. 1/c Isaac Lyghtle, WWI
Inf. Man John D. Lyle, Civil War
Pvt. Henry Lyle, Civil War
Georye R. Lyons
Leroy J. Lyons
Albert Mahan
Clifford J. Mahan
Delmar L. Mahan
Andrew G. Mahne, WWI
Hugh C. Malott
James A. Malott
John A. Mann, Civil War
Pvt. J.L. Mann, Civil War
Pvt. Roy Mannen, WWI
Henry F. Mansker
Inf. Man Jules Manuel, Civil War
Surgeon S.W. Marshall, Civil War
Pvt. Thomas H. Marlen, WWI
Pvt. John Martin, WWI
Pvt. John M. Martin, WWI
Pvt. 1/c Lynn Martin, WWI
Cpl. Sherman E. Martin, Korean War
John A. Massa
Sgt. Herman Massberg, WWI
Pvt. Thomas G. Massey, WWI
Pvt. Harry W. Mathews, WWI
Roland Mathews
Charles H. Mathis, Spanish American
Pvt. Charles R. Mathis, WWI
Jackie Alex Mathis, Korean War
Leo Mathis
Leonard R. Mathis, WWI
Raymond G. Mathis
Roy Mathis
Frank Matney, Civil War
Pvt. Pius G. Mattingly, WWI
Pvt. Charles Mauff, WWI
Duncan G. Maxwell
Pvt. 1/c William J. May, WWI
Pvt. Joseph G. Mayer, Spanish-American War
Pvt. Alexander McAllister, Civil War
Pvt. William R. McAtee, WWI
Pvt. 1/c Bert McBride, WWI
Pvt. 1/c Hamilton McBride, WWI
Pvt. 1/c Ernest J. McCarey, WWI
Noral McCauley
Robert R. McCauley
Pvt. Arthur McClane, WWI
Alfred McClinton, WWI
Leonard E. McClinton, WWI
Cpl. Joseph E. McClure, WWI
Pvt. David S. McConachie, WWI
T-5 Leland M. McConachie, WWII
A.A. McCormick, Civil War
Pvt. Floyd N. McCormick, WWI
Pvt. George Henry McCormick, WWI
John Lawrence McCuen, WWII
Pvt. Clyde Arthur McCulley, WWI
Pvt. J.M. McCullum, Civil War
Joseph W. McDaniel
Pvt. Clay H. McDill, Civil War
G/M 3/c Glen McDill, WWI
Pvt. A.J. McDonald, Civil War
Maj. G.B. McDonald, Civil War
Pvt. Verner T. McDonald, WWI

Pvt. Walter S. McDonald, WWI
James L. McDonough, Civil War
Solomon McDonough, Civil War
Pvt. Elihu McGuire, Civil War
Sgt. James F. McGuire, WWI
Cpl. Guey L. McGouyh, WWI
Pvt. Samuel McHenry, Civil War
Pvt. Daniel McIntyre, Civil War
Sgt. Edwin McKee, WWI
Mechanic Charles F. McKelvey, WWI
Cpl. Roscoe McKelvey, WWI
Waldo McKelvey, WWI
Pvt. Walter McKelvey, WWI
Pvt. Willard F. McKelvey, WWI
Pvt. Ralph W. McKinley, WWI
Seaman Andrew A. McMillian, WWI
Pvt. Archie McMillian, Civil War
Samuel McMillian, 1812
William F. McMillian, WWI
Pvt. William T. McMillian, Civil War
Pvt. James R. McQuater, WWI
Pvt. Joseph H. McQuater, WWI
Otis McQuater
Ray U. McQuater
Lt. John W. McMormack, Civil War
Pvt. Wayman Meeks, WWI
Pvt. William D. Meeder, WWI
Pvt. 1/c Elder Mehring, Korean War
Pvt. 1/c Robert Mehring, Korean War
Pvt. Edgar J. Meier, WWI
Pvt. Edwin M. Meier, WWI
Pvt. John Meissler, WWI
Pvt. Leander Mellier, WWI
August Melton
A. Menard, Civil War
Pvt. Walter E. Menke, WWI
Pvt. William J. Mennerich, WWI
Spec/4 Lee H. Mental
Pvt. Cyrus J. Metzler, Civil War
Pvt. Hugo Mevert, WWI
Pvt. Walter H. Mever, WWI
Pvt. William Mervert, WWI
Bob Meyer
1st/Sgt. Herbert Meyer, WWI
Pvt. Oscar W. Meyer, WWI
Cpl. William R. Meyer, WWI
Gem E. Meyerhoff, WWII
George Mileur
Charles W. Miller, Civil War
Clifford Miller, WWII
Edward W. Miller
George Miller
Howard W. Miller
Pvt. James A. Miller, Civil War
Sgt. Samuel B. Miller, Civil War
Pvt. James Milne, Civil War
Charles Mims
Pvt. 1/c Adolph L. Mines, WWI
Cpl. Fred Mines, WWI
Pvt. Emmet Minger, WWI
Pvt. August Misselhorn, WWI
Cpl. Charles Mitchell, WWI
Pvt. Roy F. Mitchell, WWI
Pvt. Edwin L. Moehrs, WWI
John Moll
Pvt. Matt Moll, WWI
Leroy H. Momberger, WWII
John P. Montroy, Civil War
Dwight L. Moody
Glen D. Moody

Arthur Moore, WWII
Clarence Moore, WWII
1/Lt. Isaac V. Moore, Civil War
Walter (Kelly) Moore, WWII
William Harvey Moore, Korean War
William L. Moore, Korean War
Pvt. Harry Morgan, WWI
Pvt. Jesse R. Morgan, WWI
Pvt. George H. Morris, Civil War
Pvt. 1/c John A. Morris, WWI
Paul E. Morris, WWII
Pvt. Frank S. Morrison, WWI
Pvt. Joseph Morrison, Civil War
Walter Morroson, WWI
Cpl. Martin R. Morrow, WWI
Sgt. William Morrow, WWI
Edward Motts
Harold Mudd
Cpl. Vernon Muench, Korean War
Wagoner Joseph Mulholland, WWI
1st/Lt. Lyle E. Mulholland, WWII
Wagoner Ralph P. Mulkey, WWI
Pvt. 1/c George A. Murer, WWI
Pvt. Everett J. Murphy, WWI
Russell Murphy
William Murphy, WWII
MM 2/c Earl Nagel, Navy
Fireman 1/c Robert Nagel, WWII
S/Sgt. Robert A. Neal, Korean War
Henry Nehrt, WWI
E 2/c Robert P. Neill, WWI
Pvt. 1/c Swanee Nelson, WWI
Keith Nesbit
Pvt. Leonard L. Nesbit, WWI
Sgt. John W. Neuling, WWI
Pvt. Walter H. Neuling, WWI
Morris Nilblock, WWII
Pvt. Henry G. Niemeyer, WWI
Everett Nitzsche
Leonard Nitzsche, Vietnam
Charles Nixon, WWI
Robert Nobles
Pvt. Herbert Norman, WWI
Pvt. Gustus Norton
Cpl. William F. Novack, WWI
Spec/4 Gary Nurnberger
Earl Nurnberger, WWII
Pvt. William Oates, Civil War
George Oliver
Pvt. Jasper Oliver, WWI
John W. Oliver
Lewis T. Oliver
Pvt. Walter E. Oliver, WWI
Pvt. William Arthur Oliver, WWI
Pvt. Virginio G. Orella, WWI
Sgt. Nelson Osborne, WWI
Pvt. Henry C. Otten, WWI
Michael Otten
Arthur Owens
Clifford Owens
Everett E. Owens
George Owens
Harold A. Owens
Pvt. John Owens, WWI
Richard C. Owens
Pvt. William Paine, Civil War
J.R. Pair, WWI
Pvt. Fred E. Palmer, WWI
Joe Parker
Lavern Parker

Pvt. George Partington, WWI
Gene Pasley
Pvt. Raymond Patterson, WWI
Pvt. Thomas J. Patterson, Civil War
Donald J. Patton, Korean War
Kenneth Patton
Wagoner Leslie W. Patton, WWI
Sherlan R. Paul
Anthony Pautler
Pvt. 1/c Edward B. Pautler, WWI
Paul Pautler
Ross Pautler
Victor Pautler
O. Dee Pearl, WWII
Pvt. Raymond Penn, WWI
Mess Att. Sanford C. Penny, WWI
Pvt. Claude B. Perryman, WWI
Wagoner Anton Petry
Phillip Pflasterer
Wendell Pflasterer
Pvt. Charles Phegley, WWI
Pvt. Joseph Phegley, WWI
Supply Sgt. John Raymond Phegley, WWI
Marine Pvt. William A. Phegley, WWI
Sgt. Benjamin Phelphs, Cold War
William Phillabaum
Pfc. Cecil R. Picket, WWI
S/Sgt. Brent Piel (1982-present)
Airman 3/c David Piel
Pvt. Edward Pierce, WWI
Sgt. 1/c Earl L. Pillars, WWI
Sgt. Prentiss Pillars, WWI
Pvt. 1/c Glenn I. Pinkerton, WWI
Pvt. Marshall S. Pinkerton, WWI
Marine Pvt. 1/c Alphonsus Piosik, WWI
EM/3 Theodore T. Pirkle, WWI
Thomas Poenitske
Virgil Popham
M/Sgt. William Powell, Vietnam-Korea
Pvt. William Powers, Civil War
Max Preslar
Walter Preslar
Myron Preston, Army College
Parley W. Price
Robert Harold Price, WWII
William Purcell
Pvt. Robert R. Pyles, WWI
Walter J. Quait, WWI
Jesse Radford
Fireman 3/c Albert Rahn, Navy–WWII
PN/3 Gerald Rahn, Navy
Harold Rahn
Clemon L. Rainey
Russell D. Ramsey
E-6 John H. Raney, WWII
Virgil R. Ranft
Pvt. Clarence A. Ratz, WWI
Seaman Roland Rauch, WWI
Pfc. William Floyd Ray, WWI
Pvt. Frank Rayborn, Civil War
Seaman 2/c Alfred Fred Rebbe, WWI
Edward N. Rednour
Pvt. Everett Rednour, WWI
Pvt. John A. Rednour, WWI

Nelson Rednour, WWI
Roscoe Rednour
Pvt. Clyde Burns Reed, WWI
Pvt. James P. Reed, WWI
William Ezra Reese
Sgt. Carl Rehmer, Reserves
Cpl. Garret M. Reid, Civil War
Pvt. James E. Reid, WWI
Pvt. Ralph O. Reid, WWI
Pvt. Charles Reinhardt, Civil War
Pvt. Fred K. Reinhardt, Civil War
Cpl. Phillip Reinhardt, Civil War
Pvt. Theodore Reinhardt, WWI
Louis Reisteck, WWII
Pvt. Henry A. Renne, WWI
Cletus Renner
Greyory Renner
Pvt. Herman Renner, WWI
Lester Renner
Hiram A. Rhodes, Civil War
Pvt. Otto C. Rhody, WWI
Pvt. 1/c Herbert Rickenberg, WWI
Pvt. 1/c William C. Ridgeway, WWI
Sgt. Joseph Riecan, WWII
Earl Rigdon
Marlan Rigdon
Seaman 2/c David L. Riggs, WWI
Peter Risban
Pvt. John T. Ritchie, WWI
Pvt. 1/c Cecil L. Robbins, WWI
Pvt. Harry Robbins WWI
Walter Yourtee Roberts, WWII
Clarence Robinson
Joe Robinson
Paul A. Robinson
Carl Lee Rody
Inf. Man H.S. Rogers, Civil War
E-5 Robert L. Rohlfing, Vietnam
Pvt. Henry S. Romay, WWI
James Rosan, WWI
Delmer Ross
Pvt. Edward S. Ross
Pvt. James Ross, Civil War
Pvt. Michael C. Rothmier, WWI
Albert C. Rothwell
Harold A. Rowald, Korean War
Cpl. John C. Rowlett, Spanish American War
Pvt. George Rucknagel, WWI
Sgt. 1/c John C. Rucknagel, WWI
Pvt. 1/c Theophile A. Rucknagel, WWI
Pvt. Herman Ruebke, WWI
Pvt. Charles E. Ruehmkorff, WWI
William E. Rumann
Pvt. Henry Runye, WWI Marine
Pvt. Ralph Edgar Ruppert, WWI
Cpl. Harold B. Russell, WWI
Homer R. Russell Jr., WWII
Nelson Russell
William Saake, Civil War
Pvt. August Salger
Sgt. Paul A. Salger, Korean War
Pvt. Fred Salger, WWI
E-4 Fred E. Salger, Reserves
Pvt. 1/c Norman Salger
Bugler Peter J. Sauer, WWI
Pvt. 1/c Theodore C. Sauer, WWI
Earnest L. Sauerhage, WWII

John Schaefer, Civil War
A.J. Schamahorn, Civil War
Wagoner Charles Scheffert, WWI
Pfc. Clyde Schellinger, WWI
Harold Scheltgen
Peter Scherle
Clarence Schilling
Cpl. Danny Schilling, Vietnam
Pvt. Herbert Schilling
Leo Schilling
Wilbur Schilling
Pvt. 1/c. John W. Schirmer, WWI
Cpl. Delmer Schleifer
S/Sgt, Glennard Schmidt
Pvt. Henry W. Schmidt, Civil War
Pvt. Otto Schmidt, WWI
Pvt. Arthur O. Schmierbach, WWI
Cpl. Rudolph Schmitz, WWI
Walter Schnepel, Coast Guard
Pvt. Lenard Schoenberger, WWI
Pvt. Leo Schoenberger, WWI
Nick Schoenberger
Pvt. 1/c Ava W. Schoeppel, WWI
Pvt. 1/c William Scholar, WWI
Engineer Frank J. Scholebo, WWI
Capt. Louis Scout, 1812
Pvt. Larry Schrader (1968-75)
S/Sgt. Fred Schramm, WWII
Pvt. Oliver Schrieber
Sgt. Clarence W. Schroeder, WWII
Pvt. Edward H. Schroeder, WWI
Sgt. QM Herman C. Schroeder, WWI
Sgt. Herman W. Schroeder, WWI
1/Lt. Medic Hugo C. Schroeder, WWI
Medic Pvt. Oscar C. Schroeder, WWI
Pvt. William H. Schroeder, WWI
Marine Pvt. Clarence Schuchert, WWI
Cpl. Earnest F. Schuchert, WWI
Pvt. Earl William Schuchert, WWI
Alfred Schuessler
Herman Schuline
Phar. Mate Walter J. Schuwerk, WWI
Pvt. Wendling Schwartz, WWI
John Schwarz
Sgt. George Schweizer, WWI
Pvt. Sam Scott, WWI
Sgt. 1/c LeRoy Seeman
John Sewell, WWI
Band Cpl. Everett C. Seymour, WWI
Cpl. Willis Shannon, Civil War
Pvt. William Shepart, Civil War
Pvt. Aaron Sheppard, Civil War
Seaman 1/c John Allen Short, WWI
Seaman Lawrence Siebold, WWI
Cpl. Emil Siegfried, WWI
Wayne Siegfried
Pvt. Fritz Siemers, WWI
Pvt. William Siemers, WWI
Joe L. Simms, WWI
S/Sgt Glenn Simpson, WWII
Cpl. Glenn U. Simpson, WWII
E-4 Michael Lee Simpson
Pvt. Thomas Simpson, WWI

Pvt. Roy A. Sisk, WWI
William Skelley, Civil War
Pvt. Henry W. Skidmore, WWI
Thomas Slanton
Pvt. Wiley Sloan, Civil War
Sgt. Maj. John R. Smiley, WWI
Pvt. Robert K. Smiley, WWI
Anthony D. Smith, WWII
Ben W. Smith
Charles J. Smith
T/Sgt. Francis Smith, WWII
George E. Smith
Pvt. Harry S. Smith, WWI
Sgt. Henry Smith, Civil War
Hollie E. Smith
Sgt. 1/c James Harry Smith, WWI
Pvt. Joseph Smith, Civil War
Pvt. Lee E. Smith, WWI
Leroy Clay Smith
Maurice E. Smith
Pvt. Thomas T. Smith, Spanish American War
Lewellyn Snider
William Snider
Pvt. Christopher Snyder, Civil War
Pascal A. Sparks Sr.
Pete Sparling, WWI
Volye Spence
1/Lt. William D. Spinney, WWII
Sgt. William J. Spinney, WWI
Sgt. Herman H. Spitz, WWI
Loyola Sprietler
Medic Pvt. Corbett H. Springs, WWI
Pvt. Matt Sproul, Civil War
Pvt. Charles St. Mary, WWI
Pvt. 1/c Edward F. Stallmann, WWI
Cpl. Leroy Stamm (1953-55)
Spec/5 Robert Stamm (1968-74)
Henry R. Stanton, WWI
Gary Lynn Steele, Vietnam
Pvt. Louis E. Steele, WWI
Pvt. Charles W. Steets, WWI
Pvt. 1/c Clifford Stellhorn (1956-58)
Medic Pvt. Floyd Stellhorn
Sgt. Marvin Stellhorn
S/Sgt. Wilbert W. Stellhorn, WWII
Capt. John J. Stepanek, WWII
Thomas G. Stephens
Nurse Elsie Stephenson, WWI
Nurse Mary Stephenson, WWI
Pvt. Alex Sternberg, WWI
Pvt. Harry Sternberg, WWI
Pvt. William M. Stevenson, WWI
Archie Stewart, Civil War
Armond L. Stewart, Korean War
Wagoner Charles M. Stewart, WWI
Pvt. Harry Stewart, WWI
Nurse Jane R. Stewart, Civil War
John Oscar Stewart, WWII
Pvt. Leander Stewart Civil War
Fireman 1/c Bertram J. Stille, WWI
Sgt. David L. Stine Sr., Vietnam
Leo Stirnamann
Cpl. James Stockwell, WWI
Pvt. Earl Stoffel, WWI
Pvt. George Stolle, WWI
Hilton F. Stone

Robert C. Stone
Pvt. 1/c Patrick Stones, WWI
Pvt. Henry C. Stotts, WWI
Cook Leo Stratman, WWI
Pvt. Edward H. Stumpe, WWI
Sgt. John H. Stumpe, WWI
Pvt. Homer D. Sturgeon, WWI
Sgt. Charlie St. James, WWI
Pvt. James A. St. James, WWI
Mathew Sullivan
Martin L. Svehla
Cpl. Ethis B. Swift, WWI
Stanley Syloski, WWII
MM 1/c Richard R. Tabiny, Korean War
Pvt. John G. Taylor, Civil War
Pvt. Peter A. Taylor, WWI
Walter E. Taylor
Robert Tepovich
Wilford W. Terry
Cook Jake Theobold, WWI
Pvt. 1/c John Theobold, WWI
Pvt. 1/c John CI Theobold, WWI
Pvt. 1/c William A. Theobold, WWI
Elmer Thies, WWII
Charles J. Thimming
Pfc. Adolph Tockstein, Civil War
Pvt. William Toulouse, Civil War
Pfc. Joseph C. Townsend, WWI
Pvt. Alex Thompson, WWI
Capt. James Thompson, Black Hawk
Pfc. Ralph Thompson, WWI
Richard J. Thompson
Pvt. R.H. Thompson, Civil War
Robert Thompson, War 1812
Seaman Terry Jay Thompson, WWI
William Thompson, Black Hawk
Robert Thummel
Steven Thurmel, Civil War
Pvt. Harry D. Tindall, WWI
Spec/4 Carl D. Todd, Vietnam
Jack Todd
Pfc. John R. Todd, WWI
S/Sgt. LeRoy R. Trost, Korean War
Pvt. Ed. Trumpfeller, WWI
Pvt. 1/c Willard Uffelmann, Korean War
Howard J. Ulrich
Susie E. Ulrich
William Underhill
Pfc. James E. Vallroy, WWI
Sgt. Willis E. Vancil, WWI
Nathan Vaughn, WWI
Boatswain Mate Irvin J. Vawter, WWI
Pvt. Ferd Veath, WWI
John Veath
Sgt. Robert E. Vermillion, WWI
Pvt. Murts Vernum, WWI
Pvt. Cyrus E. Vickery, Civil War
Sgt. Robert Voges
Pvt. James F. Waldron, WWI
Pvt. Alfred Walker, Civil War
Dewey Wall
Pvt. Eugene Wallace, WWI
M/Sgt. Elmer G. Wallach, WWII

Conrad G. Walter, WWI
Don Walter
Connie J. Ward, WWI
Pvt. Fredrick Warner, WWI
Pvt. Wilson Warner, Civil War
Pvt. Harvey Washington, WWI
Sgt. James Wasson, WWI
Arthur E. Waters
Francis L. Waters, Korean War
Pvt. James D. Watson, Civil War
George A. Watt
James W. Watt
Pvt. Henry P. Watt, WWI
Pvt. Phillip Watt, WWI
Pvt. 1/c Kenneth Weaver
Pfc. Glenn Weber, WWI
Clint Harold Webster, Korean War
Pvt. Albert Wehner, WWI
Dr. Thuro T. Weir, WWI
Lewis Welch, Civil War
Seaman 2/c Thomas E. Welsh, WWI
Musician Charles W. Wells, WWI
Virgil Welman
Pvt. Fred E. Welshans, WWI
Pvt. Nathan I. Welshans, WWI
Sgt. Herman H. Welton, WWI
Charles D. Welty
Clarence L. Welty

Pvt. Fred R. Wesbecker, WWI
Pvt. Ira F. Wesely, WWI
John W. Wheeler
Spec/4 Roland Wheland, Reserves
Albert White
Pvt. Joseph White, Civil War
Kenneth L. White, WWII
Robert L. White, WWII
Ronald White
Stanley White
Allen S. Whitehead, WWII
Pvt. Alonzo Whitney, Civil War
1/Lt. Alfred C. C. Wiebush, WWI
Pvt. Alonzo Wilcox, Civil War
Pfc. Dewey Wilfong, WWII
Cpl. James Wilfong, Korean War
Pfc. William Wilkening, WWI
Pvt. Karl H. Wilkinson, WWI
Carl A. Williams
Pvt. Edward Williams, Civil War
Avn. Mech. Frank L. Williams, WWI
John A. Williams
Raymond Williams
Marine Pvt. Thomas Williams, WWI
Pfc. Gilbert Williamson, WWI
Pvt. Lacy R. Williamson, WWI
A/A Comm. Edmund L. Willis, WWII

Harold E. Willis
Pvt. J.W. Willis, Civil War
William John Willis
Pvt. Alexander Wilson, Civil War
Pvt. Bert Wilson, WWI
Pfc. Frank Wilson, WWI
Pvt. George E. Wilson, WWI
Recruit Guy S. Wilson, WWI
Jack R. Wilson
James F. Wilson, WWI
Pvt. James F. Wilson, WWI
Pvt. John D. Wilson, WWI
John Edwin Wilson, WWI
Cpl. J. Merle Wilson, Korean War
Kenneth M. Wilson
Norman Wilson
Wilber A. Wilson
Cpl. Arlen Windelman
Walter Wine
Seaman Leroy Wingerter, WWII
Airman Russell Wingerter
Pvt. Don Winkleman
Gunner 3/c Edwin T. Winter, WWII
Pvt. Arthur Winterbottom, WWI
Donald Witbrach, WWII
Pvt. Albin Wittenbrink, WWI
Pvt. Julius Wittembrink, WWI
Roy Wittmer

Ohmer Wolff
Pvt. Pleasant Wolfington, Civil War
Pvt. Antony Wolshock, WWI
Sgt. Edward J. Wolshock, WWI
Pvt. Horace M. Wood, WWI
John L. Woods, Civil War
Lt. Col. William Woods (1942-1972)
Pvt. Gus W. Woodside, WWI
Pvt. Medic Miller F. Woodside, WWI
Cpl. James Word, Korean War
Cpl. Murray Wright, WWI
Sgt. Posie Wright, WWI
Ralph G. Wright, WWI
Pfc. John Wylie, WWI
Pvt. Ralph Wylie, WWI
Albert G. Yearman
Pfc. Calvin K. Young, WWI
Pvt. James Young Jr., Civil War
Pvt. James Young Sr., Civil War
Pfc. Edward Paul Zeiner, WWI
Maj. Chaplin Fred S. Zeller, WWI
Pfc. Albin E. Zipfel, WWI
Alphonse Zipfel
Dennis Zipfel
Herman P. Zweigert, WWII

Revolutionary War Veterans Buried In Randolph County

Bazelle Allere
Joseph Allere, born Virginia
Joseph Anderson, died near Nine Mile
Michael Antere, buried near Kaskaskia
Jean Baptiste Barbau Sr., b. 1722, d. 1820
Eziekial Barber, b. April 12, d. 1806, m. Elizabeth Goddard, buried Ephriam Bilderback farm
Zebediah Barker, Minute Man and Orderly Sgt.
Antoine Bienvenue Sr., buried near Kaskaskia
Daniel (David) Blouin, b. ca. 1740, d. Feb. 23, 1782, buried near Kaskaskia
Robert Bratney, b. Ireland, d. 1832, buried near Kaskaskia
John Brown, d. May 6, 1832, buried Fairview
Benjamin Byrum, b. PA, d. after 1781, wife Mary ?, buried Kaskaskia
Francis Charleville, buried near Kaskaskia
Jean Baptiste Charleville, buried near Kaskaskia

John Clendenin, b. 1759/60 VA, d. 1836, buried Clendenin Cem., Chester
Mellington Couch
Henry Crutcher, Quartermaster
James Curry, lived near Nine Mile
Jerome Danis, died near Kaskaskia
Joseph Danis, died near Kaskaskia
Michael Danis, died near Kaskaskia
John Dodge, b. CT, d. before 1800, buried near Kaskaskia
John Doyle, buried near Kaskaskia
Capt. John Edgar, b. ca. 1733 Ireland, d. Dec. 1830, buried near Kaskaskia
William Fowler, b. SC, d. Randolph County
James Gilbraith, buried Kaskaskia, moved to Ft. Gage
Michael Godin, lived at Kaskaskia
Paul Harrelson, b. SC, wife Mary
John Hilterbrand, near Nine Mile
David Hix, near Nine Mile
David Hoar,
Capt. Nicholas Janis
Antoine Lavigne, buried near Kaskaskia

Lawson, John
John Lively, b. probably SC 1826, buried Central
John McDill, b. 1748/49, buried Old Bethel, d. Mar. 1824
Hugh McKelvey, b. 1762 Ireland, d. Mar. 13, 1835, buried Old Bethel
Charles McNabb, b. Maryland, d. Feb. 1, 1822
Haydon Mills, buried near Nine Mile
John Montgomery, had a water mill 4 miles from Kaskaskia
Charles Moore,
Daniel Murray, d. Aug. 5, 1820
David Pagen, b. 1745, d. Jan. 16, 1815 near Nine Mile, 1st wife Elizabeth Farrel, 2nd wife Mrs. Mary Carter Harman
James Pillars, b. ca. 1760, VA, d. 1833/34
Richard Pillars
Rawleigh Ralls, b. ca. 1762 VA, d. May 6, 1828, buried near Red Bud, wife Mary Hansbury
Joseph Richards, buried near Kaskaskia

John Roberts
Robert Seybok
William Sharp, b. 1762 MD, died after 1860
Elijah Smith
Henry Smith, near Kaskaskia
George Stamm, b. MD(?), d. Kaskaskia
Capt. John Steele, b. 1737, VA, d. Sept. 11, 1820
Jacob Stopplebean, b. NY, d. 1845, buried Hull Cem.
John Stufflebean, d. Jan. 16, 1844, wife Elsie
Levi Teel, near Nine Mile Cr.
Archibald Thompson, b. Sept. 3, 1760 Abbeville, SC, d. Sept. 5, 1833, buried Preston Cem.
Joseph Toulouse, buried near Kaskaskia
Alexander Whitaker, near Kaskaskia
Robert Whitehead, near Kaskaskia
Samuel C. Woodside, b. 1737 SC, d. July 22, 1819, wife Jannet

Roy B. Koeneman, 1942-1946

Fred Koester

Paul Koester

Dean Langin

Edward H. Lemburg

Charles Lybarger

McCormick Family

Herbert McCormick, served more than 20 Years.

Donald McCormick, 1957-59. Son of Herbert McCormick

Jerry McCormick, 1957-59. Son of Herbert McCormick

Clifford L. McCormick, 1964-1968. Son of Herbert McCormick

Dale McCormick. 1966-69. Son of Herbert McCormick

Roger McCormick, 1966-68. Son of Herbert McCormick

Michael Bradley McCormick, 1993-97. Son of Clifford McCormick

Johnathan McCormick, 1991-1997. Son of Roger McCormick

Clifford Andrews, 1984-1990. Son of Sue McCormick Andrews

Jo Lynn Andrews, 1989-92. Daughter of Sue McCormick Andrews.

Maurice Tippett, 1959-62. Husband of Peggy McCormick

Douglas Tudor, 1956-58. Husband of Patsy McCormick.

Harley Henson, 1957-59.

Husband of Wanda McCormick

picture unavailable

Old Glory

This famous name was coined by Captain Stephen Driver a shipmaster of Salem, Massachusetts in 1831. As he was leaving on one of his many voyages aboard the brig CHARLES DOGGETT – and this one would climax with the rescue of the mutineers of the BOUNTY – some friends presented him with a beautiful flag of 24 stars. As the banner opened to the ocean breeze for the first time he exclaimed "Old Glory!" He retired to Nashville in 1837, taking his treasured flag from his sea days with him. By the time the Civil War erupted, most everyone in and around Nashville recognized Captain Driver's "Old Glory."

When Tennessee seceded from the Union, Rebels were determined to destroy his flag, but repeated searches revealed no trace of the hated banner.

Then on February 25, 1862, Union forces captured Nashville and raised the American flag over the Capitol. It was a rather small ensign and immediately folks began asking Captain Driver if "Old Glory" still existed. Happy to have soldiers with him this time, Captain Driver went home and began ripping at the seams of his bedcover. As the stitches holding the quilt-top to the batting unraveled, the onlookers peered inside and saw the 24-starred original "Old Glory!"

Captain Driver gently gathered up the flag and returned with the soldiers to the capitol. Although he was 60 years old, the Captain climbed up to the tower to replace the smaller banner with his beloved flag. The Sixth Ohio Regiment cheered and saluted – and later adopted the nickname "Old Glory" as their own, telling and re-telling the story of Captain Driver's devotion to the flag we honor yet today.

Captain Driver's grave is located in the old Nashville City Cemetery and is one of three (3) places authorized by act of Congress where the Flag of the United States may be flown 24 hours a day.

I have so far been unable to determine where "Old Glory" resides today. A caption above a faded black and white picture in the book, The Stars and the Stripes, says only that "Old Glory" may no longer be opened to be photographed, and no color photograph is available.

Visible in the photo in the lower right corner of the canton is an appliqued anchor, Captain Driver's very personal note. "Old Glory" is the most illustrious of a number of flags – both Northern and Confederate – reputed to have been similarly hidden, then later revealed as times changed.

A Witness at NUREMBERG

Fifty-eight years ago, it fell to a Lutheran Army Chaplain, Henry F. Gerecke to offer spiritual counsel to 15 high-Nazi war criminals and walk with 10 of them to the gallows. Though visiting jailed men was nothing new to the pastor-he had spent the bulk of his pre-war career ministering to inmates in stateside prisons, nothing in his past had prepared him for this.

His orders had come in the fall of 1945. Chaplain (Capt) Henry F. Gerecke serving in Munich at the 98th General Hospital Unit, was to report to the 685th Internal Security Detachment, which was overseeing the major war-crimes trials at the Nuremberg Palace of Justice.

The Army had chosen Gerecke for three reasons: He spoke German, he had extensive experience in prison ministry and he was a Lutheran. (Fifteen of the 21 Nazis on trial identified themselves as "Protestant.") Assisting him would be Chaplain Sixtus O'Conner, a priest in his early 40s who would see to the spiritual needs of the six Roman Catholics in the dock.

Gerecke had no shortage of grounds for finding his assignment distasteful. He hadn't seen his wife in two-and-a-half years, two of his sons had suffered severely as a result of the war, one at the Battle of the Bulge. He had spent 15 melancholy months in English hospitals, sitting at the bedsides of frontline wounded and dying, and he had visited the Dachau extermination camp, where his hand, touching a wall had been smeared with human blood seeping through.

But as there was plenty to be disgusted about with these Nazis, there was also plenty to be intimidated about, too. "How can I," Gerecke asked himself, "a humble pastor, a Missouri farm boy, make any impression on these disciples of Adolf Hitler?. How can I approach them? How can I summon the true Christian spirit that this mission demands of a chaplain?" He prepared himself by praying, "harder than I ever had in my life" that he could "somehow learn to hate the sin but love the sinner." Then he set to work.

On his first round of visits, the man in the cell jumped to his feet, clicked his heels and bowed. Then thrusting out his hand, he said, "I am Hermann Goering. I heard you were coming. Will you please come in and spend some time with me?" Later, leaving Goering's cell, he thought that Goering had been too amiable, too receptive, too slick. His suspicion was confirmed when he overheard Goering telling Rudolf Hess in the exercise yard that, "things might go better" for them if they appeared repentant, attended chapel, and feigned an interest in what the chaplain had to say. Gerecke visited with Wilhelm Keitel, whom he found immersed in a book. "What are you reading?" the chaplain asked. "My Bible."

Briefly taken aback, Gerecke stood silent.

"I have carried this Bible through both wars," Keitel continued, "and in between. I know from this book that God can love a sinner like me." "Another phony!" thought Gerecke. But as the visit went on, the more sincere he thought Keitel might be. The prisoner said he was grateful "that the nation (the United States) that would very likely put me to death, thinks enough of my eternal welfare to provide me with spiritual guidance." Toward the end of the visit, Keital, after reading aloud some Scripture, knelt at his cot and prayed at length for God's mercy and forgiveness. Then he and Gerecke spoke the Lord's Prayer together.

The chaplain proceeded to complete his initial round of visits with the other Protestant defendants. Some received him eagerly, others coolly. Only two, Rudolf Hess and Alfred Rosenberg, told him they would have no use for his company, or his chapel services.

But the other 13, almost from the start, came to chapel regularly (though Goering made it clear that he came only to escape his cell for a while). At one point, Albert Speer, the most outspokenly remorseful prisoner (and who, in fact, had plotted to kill Hitler in April 1945), asked what arrangements might be made for those desiring it, to receive Holy Communion. Gerecke began holding classes for Speer, Hans Fritsche and Baldur von Schirach. When he deemed them ready, he communed them according to the rites of the Lutheran Church.

In time, four other prisoners, Keitel, Joachim von Ribbentrop, Fritz Sauckel and Erich Raeder, after taking similar classes with Gerecke, partook of communion, too.

Over the months, Gerecke would come to believe that most of his 15-member "congregation" (as well as most of Father O'Conner's Catholic group) had come to their moral senses and were, to varying degrees, contrite. Walther Funk, even after weeks of conversations with Gerecke, steadfastly refused to admit to any guilt. The Chaplain bluntly reminded him that as head of the Reichsbank, Funk had cheerfully accepted for deposit a vaultful of gold—gold taken from the teeth of Jews put to death in the so-called "baths" of Auschwitz.

But most of the others – Keitel von Ribbentrop and Karl Doenitz among them – owned up to their gross sinfulness. One Sunday morning, while still on his knees after receiving communion, Keitel looked up at Gerecke, with tearstained eyes and said: "You have helped me more than you know. May Christ stand by me all the way. I shall need Him so much." The International Military Tribunal concluded the trials in the summer of 1946. The proceedings had lasted 10 months. Now the judges went into secret sessions for several weeks to decide the verdicts.

These were days of high tension for the 21 prisoners—and for Gerecke and O'Conner. The chaplains petitioned the court to let the prisoner's families come visit their husbands and fathers. "Let them come before the verdicts are read," said the chief justice. When they came, they were kept separate from the prisoners by screens, they were not allowed to touch. Sometimes Gerecke would more or less babysit a couple's children in his office so that the spouses, though always closely guarded, could have a few moments of relative privacy.

Gerecke was present in the courtroom on Sept. 30, 1946, the day the verdicts were read. As far as he could tell, none of the defendants-even those condemned to death-betrayed his emotions, save for a lowered head.

For reasons of security, chapel services were now suspended. Prisoners not sentenced to die were moved to an upstairs tier of cells. The 11 doomed men were given one last chance to see their wives.

These final two weeks brought feverish activity to the cells, with some of the condemned men requesting four or five visits a day. Sauckel, frozen with fear, appeared to Gerecke to be cracking up. Keitel poured over his Bible, searching for verses that spoke of redemption through Christ. Von Ribbentrop asked for, and received, a final private communion in his cell.

On October 15, the last day, the tension was terrific. The Chaplains went from cell to cell, again and again, spending a few minutes with each man.

The executions were scheduled for 1:00 a.m. At about 8:30 p.m., Gerecke stopped by Goering's cell. The chaplain tried, for the last time, to witness the faith to him, but Goering waved him off. Two hours later, a guard came running from Goering's cell. "Goering's having some kind of a spell!" he cried. Goering had managed, no one ever learned how, to come by a potassium-cyanide capsule. He was dead in minutes. In cheating the hangman, he joined Heinrich Himmler, Paul Goebbels, and the Fuehrer himself in a rogue's gallery of high-Nazi suicides.

At midnight, the 10 remaining men were offered a final meal. Few ate. Only an occasional outburst of sobbing broke the silence throughout the cellblock. Finally, at 1:00 a.m., von Ribbentrop's name was called. Gerecke prayed with von Ribbentrop in his cell then walked with him and guards to the gallows. Asked if he had last words, he said, "I place all my confidence in the Lamb who made atonement for my sins, may God have mercy on my soul." Turning to Gerecke, he added, "I'll see you again." The black hood was then pulled over his face, the noose adjusted around his neck and he dropped through the trapdoor.

Keitel's last words also included sentiments directed at Gerecke. "I thank you and those who sent you, with all my heart."

The last of Gerecke's group to die was Rosenberg, who had always refused the chaplain's assistance. When asked if he would like a prayer, Rosenberg smiled at Gerecke and said, "No, thank you." The last of all to die was Julius Streicher, who defiantly gave the Nazi salute, "Heil Hitler!" as he climbed the gallows' steps. When the trapdoor opened beneath him, he cried out his wife's name.

In 1950, on July 9, Chaplain Henry F. Gerecke came to Chester, Illinois to serve as assistant pastor of St. John Lutheran Church and as Chaplain of Menard Correctional Center and Chester Mental Health Facility. On Oct. 11, 1961, while pulling into his parking space at the Menard Correctional Center, he suffered a massive heart attack. Somehow, he managed to drive himself home, whereupon his wife took him to the hospital. He died 20 minutes later. He is buried in St. John Lutheran Cemetery, Chester, Illinois. Much beloved by the inmates at Menard Correctional Center, they collected and bought a lighted cross in his memory which now shines from the top of St. John Lutheran School, Chester, Illinois.

Articles From the *Chester Herald Tribune* paper
May 16, 1918

More Men For The Army

The following is a tentative list of the young men who will be called into the army during the week beginning May 25. Changes may be made in the list. Individual notices will be sent by the Local Board to each man called as soon as a definite date has been fixed for the contingent's departure.

Henry J. Jung	Alfred McClinton	Ralph L. Aitken	William P. Hunter	Engelbert Ketterer
Walter H. Becker	Emmet L. Chamberlain	Grover C. Felt	James L. Aitken	Alexander Wehrheim
Thomas A. Jacoby	DeWitt Gardner	Theodore C. Sauer	Homer Kroemer	Fred H. Wood
George E. Course	Nathan McCormick	Ralph V. Diskey	Theodore H. Loesche	Shelly F. Calvert
Fred Henrice	Fred Schultz	James Panford	William H. Schuwerk	Max M. Siegfried
Archie Winning	Henry L. Lohrhers	Joseph W. Tomek	Roy J. Devine	Lawrence J. Allard
Cyrus E. Course	Henry Swyear	Samuel Coils Jr.	George Cheslick	Murray A. Stanley
Ralph L. Mudd	George W. Stolle	William H. Mueller	Roscoe E. Adkins	Fred W. Gordon
Walter S. Brinkman	James L. McDonough	John L. Schmidt	Ralph P. Hoy	
Charles W. Wells	Fred E. Welshans	Ellisworth Kelly	Georye E. Dahlhoff	ALTERNATES
Robert T. Blair	Mathew C. Reid	Anton Petry	William. H. Brueggeman	Harold M. Wood
Arthur Linders	Martin Gremmels	George W. Rheinecker	Robert J. Lillimann	James A. Waldron
Olin E. Moore	Louis C. Diefenbach	Charles H. Niehaus	Charles R. Russell	Arthur Brinkman
Clois L. Steele	J. E. Weir	P.E. Wilson	Henry F. Saxenmeyer	James A. Ryan
Fred Godier	William Hetheriny	John Butler	Harry W. McLaughlin	Edwin Salger
Paul G. Brown	Alfred O. Levery	Dan Gendron	Oscar C.F. Schroeder	Rufus Ethington
Georye J. Rucknagel	Henry C, Stants	James F. Hults	Clarence Throop	George M. Newton
Charles P. Moskon	Charles H. Statis			

Making More Soldiers

Last Thursday afternoon, six more boys went from this county to join Uncle Sam's big army which is destined to put the kibosh on the Kaiser sooner or later. And it seems that nobody in this country, except an ignoramus who doesn't understand the situation, or one who is at heart a Kaiser lover, wants the war to end while the Kaiser can still do destruction. The six boys who went from the county Friday morning were: Ettes B. Swift, who closed his newspaper plant at Willisville to enter the ranks, August J. Huegle, Eddie Gendron, Dean M. Ewing, Noah Ducles and Clyde Schellinger. Gendron was only a substitute when he came to Chester, from his home near Prairie du Rocher last week. So sure was he that he was going with the contingent that he disposed of all his property and bid his family farewell. When he arrived here he found that all of the regular drafted men in the contingent were present, and then he was disappointed. He insisted on going to Camp Thomas, Kentucky. None of the regular draftees were willing to give up his place, but finally Henry J. Jung consented to give way to Gendron. He said he could make himself useful at the store in Walsh where he had been working until the next call.

No exercises accompanied the induction. The boys were given a splendid supper at the Grand View hotel, and later they were taken to a picture show and thus entertained for the evening. They departed for East St. Louis on the early morning Cotton Belt train.

Chairman Hylton expects a new registration which will include all those young men who have reached the age of 21 years since the last registration was made, and in it the age of registrants may be raised up to 45 years.

It seems the government's purpose is to raise an army of 5,000,000 men as quickly as possible and get them trained.

FROM A SOLDIER IN FRANCE

Homer Hylton, son of Walker L. Hylton, Chairman of the Local Board of this county, is serving in the mechanical division of the army. He arrived in France in March, and the following letter to his father is dated April 4.

Rain in the morning, followed by sunshine and more rain, which preceded more rain and more sunshine. Such describes the weather that has been for the past five or six days. France is noted for her rainy seasons, but so much rain is not welcomed by the soldiers.

Last Sunday, being Easter, I surprised myself by attending a French church. A YMCA secretary conducted the service and I understand there will be services every Sunday. Of course, I will avail myself of the opportunity to attend often.

Refugees driven from town and countryside near the battle front arrived here Sunday to be taken care of. They are women and their children and old men, and they are quartered in this market place. They seem to bear their misfortune bravely, but to see the condition they are in, and there are thousands more just like them, is a convincing argument that Germany should be defeated. The women of France are heroines as the men are heroes.

This morning about five hundred Chinese bound for somewhere, coming from Indo-China, stopped in this camp to get breakfast. To us they were curiosities, and on the other hand I suppose we were curiosities to them.

They gladly accepted cigarettes and chewing tobacco, and I think there must have been several sick Chinamen after they swallowed their first chew. It seems several regarded candy as souvenirs. A ban has been placed on the selling of candy, cakes and pies in the French stores. I suppose that now, when Monsieur calls on Mademoiselle he takes along a bag of figs or English walnuts. There seems to be plenty of fruits and nuts of that sort in France, and the selling of them is a means of livelihood for many of the French, since the arrival of the spendthrift Americans.

Background of Wars In This Publication

From the time Randolph County was designated a county by Gov. Arthur St. Clair, on October 5, 1795, it has given its fair share of men and women to serve their country in each and every war.

The familiar story of the ride of Paul Revere from Boston to Lexington, April 18, 1775, heralded the beginning of the Revolutionary War, and was the prelude to many conflicts yet to come. This first conflict, a revolt by the Thirteen Colonies against British rule, was officially begun on the common at Lexington, Massachusetts, when the first volley of shots whistled through the air killing or wounding 16 of the patriots assembled. This setback did not deter the patriots though, and they re-assembled at Concord Bridge, stood their ground, and from there fired the "shot heard round the world."

Less than a year later, on July 4, 1776, the signing of the Declaration of Independence was the decisive break with Britain. However the fighting and unrest continued until 1783, when The Treaty of Paris was signed and the new country had gained full independence.

Early settlers who came to this area were men who had fought in the "American War of Independence." Those who came carved out farms from the forests, made homes, and raised families from what was later to become Randolph County. They are buried in family plots and cemeteries throughout the county.

By 1812 another conflict between the U.S. and Britain was taking place. The main source of friction was Britain's maritime policy of intercepting U.S. merchant ships and the treatment of U.S. sailors aboard those ships. Also, additional problems along the border between the U.S. and Canada led President James Madison in 1811 to impose a non-trade policy against Britain, contributing to the unrest and eventual attempt by U.S. forces to invade Canada. The invasion failed because the U.S. was not prepared for a war. In September 1813, a victory on Lake Erie by Stephen Decatur, enabled U.S. forces led by William Henry Harrison, to force British troops back across the Canadian border. Then in 1814, the British imposed a naval blockade, captured Washington, D.C., and burned the White House.

Shortly after this the war came to a stalemate. John Quincy Adams and Henry Clay began negotiations with Britain that resulted in the Treaty of Ghant, December 24, 1814. The war officially ended in 1815, after Andrew Jackson's victory at New Orleans.

As we read through the pages of this book, we find that many men from Randolph County shouldered arms and went to serve in the War of 1812.

The next major conflict was the Spanish-American War, which lasted only ten weeks, April to July 1898. This short war was fought in the Caribbean and Pacific between Spain and the U.S. It began when Spain sank the battleship Maine at Havana, Cuba. It only took a short period of time for the superior U.S. Navy to destroy Spanish fleets in both Cuba and the Philippines. Meanwhile Theodore Roosevelt's Rough Riders defeated Spanish forces at San Juan Hill. At the surrender Spain ceded Guam, Wake Island, Puerto and the Philippine Islands to the U.S. for $20 million dollars, Cuba gained independence, and the war ended Spain's political ambitions to gain footholds or power in the Americas.

In researching and reading the histories submitted for this book, it was found that approximately 13 men from Randolph County offered their services during this conflict when their country needed them. It is certain there are more Spanish-American War veterans who served from Randolph County for whom we do not have a record.

The Civil War, one of the most heart-rending of all wars was fought within our own country, with brother against brother and friend against friend.

The election of President Abraham Lincoln in 1860 was a virtual guarantee that southern states would withdraw from the Union. Ten of them did, as early as 1861, and formed the Confederate States of America. The general cause was the issue of slavery. However, the South felt they were being given little, if any respect or voice in political matters by the Northern states, and this created divisions within their ranks that simply could not be ignored or worked out. Another factor that played a large role in dividing opinions of the Northern and Southern portions of the country, were the many books that had been published in the years preceding the war.

The popularity of the books being published depended on the animosity the authors kept writing about between the two sections of the country. The manners, customs, and beliefs of one section were constantly held up to the ridicule and scorn of the people of the other section. The North believed the South indulged in inhumane practices by using slavery, and the South had the opinion that the Northerners were cold-blooded and arrogant. The minds of both Northerners and Southerners were being prejudiced by these publications. After a time many ambitious men from the South were ready to destroy the Union, while many scheming and greedy men in the North wanted to punish the South in order to accomplish their own selfish purposes.

The war began on April 12, 1861, when Confederate forces attacked Fort Sumter, South Carolina. President Lincoln issued a call for 75,000 volunteers, a short time later he called 500,000 additional troops, and in 1863 he ordered a draft for another 200,000 men. In 1864, the President called for 300,000 more men to replace those who had served their enlistment or had been killed or wounded. The Unionists had greater economic resources and the Confederates had strong convictions and outstanding generals, such as Robert E. Lee and Stonewall Jackson, so the war dragged on and took its toll on both sides, until it ended with Lee's surrender at Appomattox on Palm Sunday, April 9, 1865. General Ulysses S. Grant and General Robert E. Lee met at the courthouse and agreed on the terms of surrender for the Army of the South. After four years of bloodshed, destruction and sorrow, the Civil War was finally over. The South was economically ruined by the war, and the policies of reconstruction that were put into place strained relations between North and South for more than an entire century. Almost every family in Randolph County had a family member who served in the Civil War, many didn't come home.

The next major war in which young men from Randolph County participated was World War I, which started in Europe in July and August of 1914. This war had been brewing for many years due to rivalries between Austria, Hungary and Germany, also known as the big powers or central powers; the problems dated back as far as the 1870s. The policies they had pursued against Serbia had gotten out of control. Austria invaded Serbia on July 28, followed by Germany declaring war on Russia August 1, and on France August 3 – the war was underway. Anti-German feelings were strong because of Germany's invasion of Belgium. Even though the invaders were checked at the Marne, the Western Front settled into an attempt to grind down and wear out the enemy, with heavy casualties on both sides, but advancing very little.

At first Americans paid very little attention to this war on another continent, but within a short time they began to take sides and support their Allies, Britain and France. When a German submarine sank the British liner Lusitania in the summer of 1915, resentment toward Germany increased. By July of that year, the U.S. and Germany were on the verge of war, a situation that grew worse after Germany continued submarine warfare and after the revelation of Germany's plan to involve Mexico in a war with the U.S. By April 1917, President Wilson decided all avenues for peace had been exhausted, and asked Congress to declare war on Germany and her Allies. The War Department then asked Congress to pass a proposal "to draft all males between the ages of 18 and 25." Many people were extremely opposed to compulsory military service, however they realized if the invading nations were to be stopped, it would require a much larger military force than America had at her disposal. The U.S. entered World War I with a lot of zeal and enthusiasm. Slogans put out by Wilson's administration led the American people to believe this was a great crusade to save the world from barbarism and militarism. This was the "war to end all wars" and would make the world "safe for democracy." Never before had the American people been more moved by patriotism.

The year of 1918 opened with attacks in Picardy and Flanders by the Germans. They believed they could swiftly and successfully defeat the Allies in this area, but each time they breached a defensive line, Allied forces quickly responded and filled the breach. The Germans fell short of their anticipated victory.

On July 18, 1918, the Allies made a decisive move which resulted in their driving the Germans to retreat from Marne. On September 26, under command of General John J. Pershing, the American Army went into battle between the Argonne and the Meuse. Many soldiers from Randolph County participated in the fighting in this sector. In two days U.S. troops had captured 8,000 prisoners and more than 100 pieces of artillery. From September 28 to the end of October, the Germans had given up 20,000 prisoners, 1,000 trench mortars and about 6,150 machine guns. The tide had turned and fighting was coming to an end.

A Naval blockade of Germany caused severe food shortages and helped to end the war. On November 11, with threats of U.S. and France launching a major attack in Lorraine, the Germans surrendered in open country to save themselves from complete destruction. An armistice was agreed to and peace treaties were signed at Versailles in 1919. The war was over. An estimated 26 million people had died, approximately 20 million were wounded, nine million became war orphans, five million became widows and 10 million were refugees. The number killed was twice as many as all who had died in major wars fought between 1790 and 1913. The cost of the war would have provided every family in England, France, Germany, Russia, the U.S., Canada and Australia with a $2,500 house on a one acre lot that cost $500, and money for $1,000 worth of furniture. It would also have provided a $10,000,000 university for each of the countries and a $1,000 bonus for all 125,000 teachers and nurses in these countries, and still had enough left over to purchase every piece of property and all the wealth in Belgium and France at a fair market price.

Of the many men who served from Randolph County, in the research we conducted for this book, we found only a short list who had lost their lives in World War I.

The greatest war in history began September 1, 1939, at dawn, with the invasion of Poland by Germany. The world reeled with the speed and power of this attack, which was Hitler's first step to conquer the world.

Twenty five years earlier, in August 1914, Kaiser Wilhelm of Germany, headed a global conflict that virtually engulfed the free world, known as World War I. At the end of this war, the Treaty of Versaillies imposed very severe restrictions on the future military rebuilding of Germany. The Allies did not want to risk another war of this magnitude. It is more than likely that as years passed the German government chafed at these terms, and the seeds sown after World War I grew and became the basis for World War II. On the first day of the invasion approximately 1,400 German planes systemically destroyed Polish airfields, wiping out the entire Polish Air Force of 450 planes. Then German tanks led two large German armies into Poland. In the Polish attack, the Germans had introduced a new type of warfare using tanks and airplanes. Polish soldiers, mounted on horses, went down in massive numbers. Fighting a war from horseback had now ended. Poland's allies, France and England, were unprepared for war and could do little to help them.

Poland suffered another devastating blow when on September 17, Russia invaded them from the east as a result of a secret plan Stalin had made with Hitler. Poland fought back as best she could from her last stand in Warsaw, but on September 27, could hold out no longer, and Warsaw fell. Twenty two million of her people and 150,000 square miles of her territory, which included most of the mines and factories, were now taken over by Germany. The other 13 million people, along with all Poland's oil resources, were given to Russia. Hitler's pact with Stalin gave him the freedom to turn west and continue his conquest of Europe. By the summer of 1941 he had achieved his goal and had conquered most of Western Europe.

The newfound friendship with Stalin was coming to an end. Throughout early 1941, Hitler had been secretly preparing to invade Russia, and on June 22, he turned and invaded his one time ally by sending in 150 German divisions and 2,700 airplanes to begin the attack. Both President Franklin Roosevelt and Britain's Winston Churchill had warned Stalin this was going to happen, but he did not believe Hitler would turn on him, since his troops had helped Germany secure the Eastern front.

Hitler also planned to have control of Bulgaria and Yugoslavia by March of 1941. Hungary and Romania, the other two states that made up the Balkan states, were already in the Axis camp. On April 18, Hitler achieved this goal, Yugoslavia surrendered. Athens was the next to fall on April 27.

British forces had retreated to the southern beaches of Greece, hiding out by day and destroying equipment by night. They waited for the rescue craft that finally arrived on the last day of April. The force of 57,000 was down to 43,000, they had fallen back while fighting fierce rear guard actions. Half of the men were taken back to Greece and the others to the Island of Crete. Germany was operating well on plan. Crete was her next target. On May 20, the airborne attack was carried out, and by June 1, Britain surrendered the Island of Crete.

On June 10, 1940, Italy had declared war on France and Great Britain, and on June 22, France signed an armistice dictated by the Germans, which ended fighting in France. After France fell the Italian Navy was in complete control of the Mediterranean.

By December 2, 1941, the German army arrived in the suburbs of Moscow.

They had come through snow, fog and rain and the temperature stood at zero. Not equipped to face the cold Russian winter, the soldiers were suffering. Weapons froze, food froze, and tanks and trucks had to be started every few hours to keep them from freezing. Rations were low and the soldiers ate everything they could to stay alive, they even killed horses for food. Russian soldiers, on the other hand, were used to the extreme cold and held off the freezing Germans until a huge reserve unit of troops and tanks came up from the rear and drove the Germans back two hundred miles. Germany suffered 800,000 casualties. Russia launched a counter-attack on that same day, December 6, 1941. The next day Japan bombed Pearl Harbor and on December 8, the U.S. and Britain declared war on Japan. On December 11, Germany and Italy declared war on the United States. and Japan invaded the Philippines on December 22. Wake Island fell to Japan on December 23,. That was the end of the first two and a half years of World War II. Now the U.S. was fighting on two fronts, Europe and Asia.

As the U.S. Congress declared war on Japan after December 7, there was no discussion and only one vote of nay. All over the country recruiting offices were jammed with young men volunteering to fight. Some slept in hallways while they waited for physical exams and induction.

By the beginning of 1942, Japan occupied Manila. MacArthur's troops had to fall back to Bataan. German submarines were torpedoing U.S. tankers off the East Coast, and the Allied fleet was badly beaten by the Japanese in the Battle of Java Sea. On April 9, Bataan fell to the Japanese. Disaster to U.S forces was increasing. On a second attempt, Japan had captured Guam on December 23, 1941. They landed in Thailand, Singapore, took Hong Kong, sank the British battleship, Prince of Wales and the carrier Repulse. These heavy blows left the Japanese navy in control of the Pacific.

American forces retreated to Corregidor after the fall of Bataan, but Corregidor fell to Japan only a short time later, on May 6, 1942.

In mid-April American spirits were lifted when planes from the aircraft carrier Hornet bombed Tokyo. Flying 668 miles from the Hornet, 16 B-25 Mitchells dropped their bombs on the unsuspecting capitol. Pilots were trained to take off from the carrier, but could not land on the short deck, so they flew on to China or crashed in the ocean off the China coast. Eight members of these crews were captured and three were executed.

After six months of lightening triumphs, Japan became anxious and over-confident, and decided to capture outposts closer to America, perhaps even Australia. In May 1942, two large invasion forces set out for New Guinea and the Solomon Islands. The group headed for New Guinea was forced to turn back when planes from the U.S. carriers Lexington and Yorktown, sank one of the Japanese carriers. The next day Japanese pilots found the Americans and from May 4-8 they engaged in the Battle of Coral Sea. The Japanese were turned back, but the Lexington was lost.

The Battle of Midway, June 4-6, began when the Japanese Admiral got in a hurry to destroy the American Pacific Fleet. He hoped to do this before 1943, because he knew the American industrial machine would produce war material at a rapid rate with which Japan could not cope.

The Admiral collected a fleet of 162 ships and divided them into a large and a small convoy. He started the small one toward the Aleutian Islands, and left the larger one at Midway. He hoped to use the smaller one as a decoy to draw American ships away from Midway. Then Midway could be taken at his own will. The Americans didn't take the bait. With their 76 ships against Japan's 162, they fought a savage battle. Hoping to catch the Japanese carriers refueling, when they would be the most vulnerable, U.S. planes were launched. All 15 bombers from the Hornet were shot down, 10 out of 14 from the Enterprise were lost, the Yorktown lost all her planes but four. It looked like an American disaster, and seemed Japan had won the battle, but revenge of Pearl Harbor was on the minds of the commanders and crews. Thirty-seven dive bombers from both carriers found the enemy and by the end of the battle Japan had one large carrier left. Forty planes launched by the Japanese had been shot down, but those planes had scored three hits on the Yorktown. Still wallowing in the water overnight, a submarine torpedo sent her to the bottom the next day, yet for the first time in history, the Japanese navy had been beaten, they had lost the entire fast fleet, the Emperor's big guns of the war! From the Battle of Midway on, Japan was on the defensive. America took the war to them. The next major battle of the Pacific was Guadalcanal. Marines landed on August 7, and on December 15, the battle ended with an American victory.

The odor of decay was all over Guadalcanal. Rain either fell in torrents or the sun was unbearably hot. The men were either drenched or scorched. They were always hungry, the battles going on in the air and sea around them kept supply ships from providing the supplies they needed. At the beginning the battle seemed to be favoring the Americans, however it soon turned the other way. When Japan heard of the landings, Admiral Mikawa led a Japanese force of ships down the 'Slot', a watery strip of water running between the Solomon Islands. A fleet of Japanese ships came down the 'Slot' and slipped past the American outpost ships. Savo, a round island rising from the harbor mouth, shadowed the Japanese fleet until about two o'clock in the dark morning of August 9, when an American destroyer spotted strange ships entering the harbor and gave the alarm. In the light of flares, dropped by Japanese planes, the American ships were bombed and struck with torpedoes. Five ships were sunk and the Chicago was damaged. The victory from this battle was that the Japanese fleet fled during the night without sinking the transport ships. When the Marines looked out over the bay in the morning, they found it empty. Most of our fleet was on the bottom of the bay. They gave it the name of Iron Bottom Bay. In history this battle is called the Battle of Savo Island.

Meanwhile on the Western front, Germany launched a massive attack on Stalingrad and British and American troops were landing in North Africa. The year of 1942 had come to an end but heavy combat continued.

By the first of 1943, Germany had begun to withdraw from Stalingrad, and Russia announced the 17 month siege of Leningrad had been lifted. After a stormy meeting on July 25, the King of Italy accepted Mussolini's resignation and immediately placed him under arrest and sent him to the island of Ponza. Now the way was clear to talk peace with the Allies. On September 3, the new dictator signed a secret armistice with the Allies, this same day Allies stormed Sicily and Italy. German officials convinced Hitler that Italy could be saved from the Allies by putting defensive lines across the peninsula. Germans would fight and fall back from line to line and make the "Allies buy every yard with blood." Then Hitler had Mussolini rescued from his captors. The 5th Army landed at Salerno, on September 9, 1943, with their mission to secure the port of Naples. After many bloody and disheartening days of fighting, the 5th Army held out until bombers flying in from bases in Sicily and North Africa came to their rescue. Indeed every foot of ground was bought with American and British blood. Next, the Allied forces landed on Italy's West Coast in 1944 and the battle of Anzio began.

In the Central Pacific Americans also made landings at the Atolls. Some of the worst fighting in U.S. military history was fought during the advance through the Central Pacific. Japan had turned this string of islands into heavily armed ocean forts. An atoll is a ring of coral islets surrounding a lagoon. Not all the islets of the ring had to be fortified for the group to become effective. The larger one could hold an airfield from which planes could attack troop and supply ships, would be the major fortress. Getting control of this chain of atolls was tremendously important. Heavy fighting took place February 1 on the Kwajalein atoll. Marines landed, and shot for shot and foot by foot, Kwajalein was taken in four days. At Eniwetok, another islet in the chain, on February 17, U.S. battleships sailed inside the lagoon, but the Japanese took their toll on the U.S. Marines with mines and bullets. One Marine wrote, "many Marines had to die, but we finally killed them all."

During the months of June and July, the invasion of France began under General Eisenhower. Americans broke through the German line in Normandy, Germans surrendered Paris on August 25. Allies took Brussels and Antwerp in Belgium and crossed the German border. The U.S. began new attacks on the Siegfried Line and Germany counter-attacked - this started the Battle of the Bulge. After a bloody battle, the Germans were stopped and the Bulge became an American victory.

Fighting in the Pacific was still going hot and heavy. U.S. troops landed on Saipan, Guam and Tinian, then defeated the Japanese in the Battle of the Philippine Sea. American troops returned to the Philippines, landing at Leyte on October 20, 1944, then by October 26 had destroyed the remainder of the Japanese navy in the Battle of Leyte Gulf. The year 1944 had ended with a possible end to the war in sight.

Early January 1945, Americans invade Luzon, in Northern Philippines, and entered Manila. With an end in sight, Stalin, Roosevelt and Churchill met at Yalta, in what became known as the Yalta Conference. There they agreed that the states of Eastern Europe would be behind the Iron Curtain of communism, dictated by Russia. This was very unfair to the Polish people. After the invasion by Germany, Russia had urged the patriots of the Polish Underground to rise up against the Germans. They did just that, fighting hand-to-hand combat in the streets of their cities. The U.S. and Britian urged Russia to come to their aid but Stalin had other plans for the Poles. He knew that some who had fought in the Underground movement were anti-communist and would eventually rise up against the communist government he intended to put in place in Poland. He believed if the Germans killed them during conflicts, it would save him a great deal of trouble later on. The Polish people received no help and were enslaved under communism by the country they had helped to secure from the Germans. Politics between the countries wasn't what was best for those who had suffered so much.

Shortly after the Yalta Conference, Americans landed on Iwo Jima to fight the bloodiest and most well-known battle in Marine history, but on March 26, the U.S. flag was raised over the island. Okinawa was the last ground battle of the war and was the largest amphibious assault of all time. There were 183,000 men in the attack force and 1,300 of our largest ships. Thousands of Japanese suicide bombers and their pilots were ready by April 1, 1945, to fight what was to become the last major battle. Their ground commanders were ordered to dig in and fight to delay American troops so supporting ships would be exposed to suicide bombers as long as possible.

The first day of the assault the U.S. had virtually no opposition. They moved forward until they reached the south end of the island where the Japanese had built their "cross island" defense. This battle was fought in mud and extreme heat by the Marines on the ground and the exhausted sailors and pilots aboard the support ships, and after 83 days the Island of Okinawa fell to the Americans on June 22, 1945.

By now world leaders were changing. President Roosevelt died at Warm Springs, Georgia, on April 12, Mussolini was executed April 28 by his own people, and Hitler killed himself May 1 in Berlin. Germany surrendered on May 7. Japan continued to fight and rejected the first offer of surrender on July 29, after severe bombardment by U.S. Navy. President Harry Truman, not wanting more bloodshed of American forces, made a decision that ended the war. On August 6, the huge Superfortress, Enola Gay, took off from the island of Tinian, and dropped the first atomic bomb on Hiroshima.

The entire city was destroyed. The next day the second atomic bomb was dropped on Nagasaki, and on August 14, 1945 Japan finally accepted surrender terms and on September 2 signed the official surrender aboard the USS Missouri in Tokyo Bay. The war lasted six years and one day, and brought ruin and human suffering to the entire world. It also opened up the era of nuclear warfare. The 'greatest war in history' fought by the 'greatest generation' was now over. As the world began to rebuild, Russia and the United States faced each other as old friends and new enemies, and the Cold War began.

Of the approximately 2,900 men and women who served in World War II from Randolph County, more than 60 were killed in action. The events of this war were of such importance to the world, then and now, that it was hard to decide in writing this article just how many step by step details to include. The time factor and the massive area on both sides of the world in which the fighting took place were of such magnitude that research and writing could cover many pages.

Not long after World War II, hostilities began to flare between the people in Korea. Divided in half by Stalin and Churchill at the Yalta Conference, the Democratic People's Republic of Korea was created in the northern half of the country, with a large army trained and supported by Russia. While the southern half was largely unarmed and politically ill-equipped to deal with threats from the North. The U.S. encouraged the people of South Korea to create a republican form of government. When the U.S. withdrew their troops on June 29, 1949, 500 U.S. officers and men were left behind to train 65,000 men for the defense of South Korea, should it be needed. On January 26, 1950, the U.S. signed an agreement with South Korea to continue military and economic assistance to their country.

On October 17, and again on October 20, 1945, Ho Chi Minh of Vietnam sent telegrams to President Truman, requesting his country be allowed to participate in the newly established British-American, Russia-Chinese Advisory Commission for the Far East. Since he was a well-known communist, and the Cold War between former Allies was getting colder, Truman didn't reply to either telegram. He was hoping to buy enough time to give the seeds of independence and democracy in Korea and Indochina a chance to take hold. Truman had put pressure on France to set Vietnam free as we had the Philippines. He was also putting pressure on the Dutch to give Indonesia her independence. He could only go so far in these negotiations since France and the Dutch were needed in the continued defense of Europe. He was working feverishly to have Congress pass a bill he called the "five year plan for peace." This plan would rearm America and he believed that if the U.S. was strongly armed, Communists would not dare to attack any free world nation. Congress failed to act. On June 24, 1950, about 9 o'clock p.m. in the library of his home in Independence, Missouri, President Truman had a phone call from Secretary of State Dean Acheson, telling him North Korea had invaded South Korea. Truman feared the worst, but hoped it was just another raid such as the North had made numerous times in the year just past. The next morning his worst fears were realized when he received a cable from the South Korean Ambassador, John Muccio, saying, "the North had invaded South Korea at several locations in a manner which indicates an all out offensive." General Douglas MacArthur, who was in Japan, also sent a message to President Truman stating, "enemy actions are serious and strategic, and is an undisguised act of war subject to United Nation action, under the clause of the U.N. Charter." The clause referred to was: "Threats to peace, breaches of the peace and acts of aggression would not be tolerated." An immediate meeting of the U.N. Security Council was called and on a vote of nine to nothing it was decided to oppose North Korea's "unprovoked act of aggression."

President Truman then ordered General MacArthur to supply the South Korean army with whatever weapons and ammunition that was available and to evacuate families of the 500 military men who were stationed there, by using all Air Force planes at his disposal.

When he met with his Joint Chiefs of Staff, the President insisted each man give his opinion as to how this should be handled. No one suggested backing away.

Hoping to avoid sending U.S. ground forces to Korea, the order was given for the Air Force and Navy to provide any needed support to the South Korean army, so it would be their army that would do the fighting, and not U.S. troops. Only six days later Truman said he, "made the most difficult decision of my eight years in the White House," when on June 30, 1950, at 10 o'clock a.m. he advised his Cabinet that he was ordering U.S. ground troops into combat in Korea.

On September 15, 1950, the 7th Infantry Division and 1st Marine Division went ashore at Inchon in a surprise attack. At the same time troops inside the Pusan bridgehead went on the move and by September 29, Seoul had been retaken from the North Koreans. Many of them fled across the 38th Parallel back into North Korea. A decision now had to be made whether to cross the 38th Parallel and pursue the disarranged, but not destroyed army into North Korea or simply stop and keep them north of the 38th Parallel. The U.N voted to attempt the complete destruction of the army. It was their belief that complete destruction of North Korea's army was the only way to end the war. On October 7, they voted for a united, independent, and democratic government for Korea.

Reports were coming in to Washington from nations who were in contact with China that if U.S. troops crossed the 38th Parallel the Communist government in Peking would send troops into Korea. This was a major concern for the President and U.N. so Truman flew to Wake Island to discuss this with MacArthur first hand. He assured Truman there was no chance of Chinese or Russian interference. He said of the 300,000 men the Chinese had in Manchuria, not more than one third were stationed along the Yalu River and only one half of those could be gotten across should they try to attack. Since China had no air force and Russia had no place in Korea to station troops, there was no way they would intervene. How wrong this assumption was. On October 16, a Chinese prisoner told an interpreter they had crossed the Yalu River on a train. That was just one day after the Wake Island conference, where the possibility of this happening was dismissed by MacArthur.

American forces established and maintained by hard fighting and many enemy attacks, a perimeter around the port of Pusan at the lower tip of Korea. Six hundred thousand men were added to the fighting force, National Guard units were activated, the draft was extended and a massive effort to recruit more men into the military was launched. By November 30, the drastic impact of Chinese intervention was being realized. During the fight the Xth Corps evacuated 105,000 troops, 91,000 Korean refugees and 17,000 vehicles from the North Korean port of Hungnam, while the 8th Army fought a ferocious rear guard action that ended in defeat for the Americans, with 13,000 of our troops killed and wounded. A heavy price to pay.

Truman went on the radio on December 15, 1950 at 10:30 p.m. and informed the American people that the Chinese army had won a military advantage in Korea. He immediately made the decision to increase military strength by committing more troops into combat. By July 1951, U.S. hopes of quickly repelling the invasion of South Korea were not realized. The 90,000 troops brought in from Japan were not equipped nor did they have the combat experience needed. They were severely beaten by the well-trained North Korean troops and tank force.

On November 1, the 8th Cavalry Regiment was attacked by masses of Chinese after being fired on by mortars and Russian rockets. As U.N. troops pushed into North Korea, Chinese troops came swarming across the Yalu River and drove U.N. forces back, and Seoul fell once again to the North Koreans.

In December 1951, General Walton Walker, Commander of the 8th army was killed in a jeep accident. Within 24 hours General Matthew Ridgeway was in Korea and took charge of a confused and shaken army who had been faced with retreat after retreat. Within a month he had restored the fighting spirit of these American soldiers.

General MacArthur who was supposed to be in charge of military operations in Korea, kept himself in his Tokyo headquarters and continued to demand the authority to widen the war by bombing Manchuria and letting the Nationalist Chinese army under Chiang Kai-shek enter the fight against the aggressors. These opinions were taken very seriously in Washington, because early in January General Ridgeway's forces had to surrender Seoul. MacArthur believed if he were allowed to use his full military force without restrictions, he would be able to cross the 38th Parallel. This would enable him to not only save Korea, but also render a crashing blow to the possibility of Red China's waging an aggressive war for generations to come.

As he withdrew, General Ridgeway's forces took a heavy toll on the Chinese army. By mid-January, the Chinese offensive that was supposed to knock U.N. forces out of the war was a failure. The Chinese offensive was giving out. It was at this time that politics entered the picture. The U.N. General Assembly passed a peace plan on January 13, 1951 that offered Red China a seat on the U.N. and would hand over the Island of Formosa, if China would agree to a Korean settlement. The Chinese demanded immediate admission to the U.N., convening of a peace conference, Formosa, and the right to continue fighting. The U.N. rejected this demand. Much to Truman's relief the Chinese didn't sign the proposal. On February 1, U.N. members voted to regard China as an aggressor in Korea.

When this political phase didn't materialize, the 8th Army, which had been

197

nearly wiped out earlier in the war, began an offensive attack and the war started to take a turn for the U.N forces. A short time after February 1, the U.S. had the Chinese depending on a 260-mile supply line that ran back to Yalu, with every mile of it being pounded by American bombers. They soon ran short of food, medicine, equipment and ammunition. A terribly cold Korean winter had reduced their fighting force by sickness and death.

By the end of March Seoul was in possession of the U.N. forces. Our forces were once again at the 38th Parallel. In their advance they left behind thousands and thousands of dead Chinese soldiers. This major defeat was a hard lesson for the Chinese and not the reward they had anticipated when the war began.

With the U.N. firmly camped on the 38th Parallel and the Chinese Army battered and ready to collapse they surrendered by the thousands. Truman decided it was time to move forward and get an armistice in place to end the fighting as soon as possible. Truman and the State Department met for several hours writing a statement that would let the Chinese come to the negotiating table without loosing face. Truman felt the Chinese would be more likely to accept an agreement that did not humiliate them. MacArthur was informed of this decision, but issued a statement to the contrary, which was almost a threat, that the U.N may expand the war to other areas and expand military operations to coastal areas and interior bases. This would spell immediate doom for Red China's military. This was the last straw for Truman. Differences between him and MacArthur had been going on from the beginning. MacArthur had shown and voiced his contempt for the way the war was being fought, Truman was trying to confine the fighting to Korea to keep from drawing Russia and Japan into an all out war that the U.S. was not near ready for. On April 9, Truman decided to recall the WWII hero, a decision that made headlines and created an uproar on the homefront, with public opinion favoring MacArthur over Truman 69 to 29. Regardless of the uproar, Truman stuck to his guns, and the "old soldier just faded away." Negotiations continued for more than two years before a truce was agreed to. The U.S. had 132,000 Chinese and North Korean prisoners of war at the end of the fighting, and around 60,000 did not wish to return to their country in the prisoner exchange, which was included in the truce agreement. The Chinese did not want to admit their own people were not willing to return to North Korea. When Truman refused to, "buy an armistice by turning over human beings for slaughter or slavery," the Chinese became angry and refused to sign the armistice agreement. Had Truman given in and forced the prisoners and refugees to return, the war could have ended before November 1952.

When the U.S. went to the conference table to iron out a final agreement, the Chinese and North Koreans found the U.S. was no pushover. General Ridgeway carved a solid line across the peninsula of Korea and gave a sizeable chunk of North Korea to the South. He also ceded a small portion of South Korea at the other end to give the South higher ground for a military advantage to defend of the 38th Parallel, an advantage they had never had. After a lot of screaming and yelling by the Chinese, the U.S. terms were agreed to. A mutual defense treaty was signed with the Nationalist in December 1954. This war had claimed about four million lives, more than 15 of them from Randolph County.

Too soon after Korea came the jungles of Vietnam. Conflict between U.S. backed South Vietnam and the Viet Cong, who had the support of North Vietnam, got the U.S. involved in a situation in which they believed to be a fight against Communism. Vietnam was divided in 1954. Disagreement by the two sections concerning holding of elections, quickly escalated into a war between the two. Fearing the spread of communism, the U.S. supported South Vietnam, while China and the Soviet Union supplied the Viet Cong with needed material. The United States sent her first ground troops to Vietnam in 1961. It wasn't until 1965 that the U.S. began heavy bombing of North Vietnam. As fighting became more intense, more and more U.S. troops were committed to combat. By 1968, there were 500,000 U.S. soldiers in the Republic of Vietnam. This war claimed the lives of 50,000 American soldiers, around 25 of them from Randolph County. Many more returned home to experience health and personality problems that will never be healed.

U.S. involvement, heavy casualties, and daily television coverage, made this a very unpopular war for Americans. In 1973, Henry Kissinger helped to negotiate a peace agreement, which was signed in Paris. Shortly after U.S. troops left Vietnam, South Vietnam was overrun by North Vietnam and united under communist rule in 1975. Returning home, those who had fought in Vietnam, received very little thanks or recognition for the sacrifices they had made when called upon to serve their country. After years of being denied honor and recognition, a memorial was finally erected in honor of those who had given their lives. The huge black stone wall, inscribed with the names of comrades killed in action, was unveiled in Washington, D.C. in January 1983. A replica of this wall has traveled throughout the U.S. and some 35 years after the war, the names inscribed on this wall have made the American people realize the price veterans of the Vietnam War have really paid. The veterans of Vietnam had a long way home!

Since Vietnam the U.S. has had military peacekeeping forces in all parts of the world. Men and women have served in Bosnia, and Kosovo, keeping peace between minority Serbs and ethnic Albanians, in Korea and against terrorist activists in Somalia. The renown 10th Mountain Division, whose home base is Fort Drum, New York, has been on the scene in each of these places as well as the Persian Gulf.

The 100 Days War of the Persian Gulf began in 1990. The basic reason for this war had begun as far back as the 1930s, when oil was discovered in the region. World War II had kept the discovery from being explored and refined for use until 1946.

Iraq and Kuwait were both members of the original Organization of Petroleum Exporting Countries (OPEC), an organization formed to limit yearly oil production and control the price of oil. Iraq, formerly Mesopotamia, was a part of the Persian Empire. Britain invaded Mesopotamia in 1916, and in 1920 it was made a British-mandated territory, and renamed Iraq. The British-imposed monarchy was destroyed by the assassination of King Feisal II in 1958. A republic was established, but no elections were ever held. The renaissance party (Ba'ath Socialist Party of Iraq) overthrew the government of Prime Minister Kassem in 1968, and Saddam Hussein, an important member of the Ba'ath party for many years, became president in 1979.

Iraq has had border conflicts with all her neighbors, ranging from diplomatic accusations to sending in troops. She invaded Iran in 1979, starting the Iran-Iraq War. The Kurdish population of northern Iraq continued a rebellion and Hussein killed thousands of the Kurds instead of working with them to reach an understanding.

In 1990, Iraq demanded that Kuwait give its portion of the Rumaila oil field to them along with $2.5 billion for oil previously removed by Kuwait, and another $14 billion for income Iraq had lost. They also demanded Kuwait cancel $12 billion in loans which had been made to them during their involvement in the Iran-Iraq War. When Kuwait refused to bow to these demands, Iraq began assembling troops to force negotiations to this end. The negotiations lasted less than one hour, and it was believed by observers that Iraq made these excessive demands knowing Kuwait would reject them, and this gave Iraq an excuse for an invasion. On August 2, 1990, Iraqi troops entered Kuwait. Kuwait City fell to the invaders by noon and the Iraqi's began looting and plundering the country of Kuwait.

After the invasion, the carrier USS Independence was ordered to the Persian Gulf to lend support to the ships and military personnel in the area. The U.N sent the first armed forces in to protect the oil fields and to keep Hussein out of Saudi Arabia, and on August 8, F-15s and paratroopers were in position in Saudi. There were 600,000 military personnel eventually involved in Operation Desert Shield. An embargo was placed on Iraqi and Kuwait oil on August 4, and Iraq began to amass an army of 11 new divisions of troops for the conflict that was in the making. On August 6, the U.N. voted to impose worldwide economic and military sanctions against Iraq. On August 12, President George H.W. Bush ordered what amounted to a blockade against Iraq. Troops and armored divisions began the journey to Iraq. By September 6, the U.S. had 100,000 troops in the Gulf area. Hussein threatened, "thousands of Americans would return home in body bags."

In October, Iraq let it be known that they would withdraw from Kuwait if allowed to keep the islands of Warba and Bubiyan, which block Iraq access by water to the Persian Gulf. President Bush, in return made it clear, "Iraqi forces must withdraw from Kuwait before any negotiations would begin." Iraq responded by moving 250,000 more troops and mobilizing another 150,000 reserves into Kuwait on November 19. The next day, the U.N. passed a resolution for "limited military action" if sanctions previously imposed had no effect by January 15, 1991. The sanctions were not a success.

In mid-February, 1991, President George H. W Bush ordered the bombing of Hussein's forces. Operation Desert Storm forced the Iraqi troops from Kuwait, U.N. forces then crossed the border and charged into Iraq, driving the Iraqi troops toward Bagdad and overrunning Saddam's elite Republican Guard. After the withdrawal from Kuwait, the Kurdish population in the north and the Shiite faction in the south revolted. Many Kurds fearing for their lives fled to Iran and Turkey. In 1996, Iraqi troops invaded the region and thousands were brutally killed. The U.S. responded by forming a "no fly" zone.

The U.N. ended the war once they had Iraqi troops out of Kuwait, and Hussein agreed to never use weapons of mass destruction again. Four years after the war, Kuwait asked for a complete accounting of the 600 people who had disappeared from Kuwait during the war. Iraq has returned one set of remains and has done nothing more since 1998.

The next conflict that involved men and women from Randolph County involved the words: Al-Qaeda, World Trade Center, Osama Bin Laden, and Taliban. The mass killing and destruction on September 11, 2001 when Bin Laden sent his men to destroy the World Trade Center and its occupants, caused the U.S. to retaliate by sending troops to Afghanistan. Thousands of U.S. citizens were killed on their own soil and never had a chance to defend themselves. Bin Laden and his followers, members of Al-Qaeda, where determined to destroy the American financial network in hopes of causing a collapse of the country. Bin Laden was never located, but many members of Al-Qaeda were taken into custody. Many American troops were still in Afghanistan as of 2003.

The new millenium also ushered in renewed trouble with Saddam Hussein and was virtually a carry over from the 1990-1991 Persian Gulf War. Hussein had directly violated terms and sanctions placed on Iraq at the end of 1991. At home he ruthlessly suppressed and overcame all opposition. He took an aggressive stand toward the West and Israel, and was accused of stockpiling chemical weapons of mass destruction, as well as developing a nuclear capacity. At the beginning of 2003, President George W. Bush and Prime Minister Tony Blair of Britain led the way to disarm Iraq. In April the troops began Operation Iraqi Freedom, and after intense battles starting with the perimeter around Iraqi, moved into and took over Bagdad. Bagdad came under American control and the statutes of Hussein were collapsed and destroyed. British and American soldiers have remained in Iraq to help police the country until the newly freed Iraqi people can establish their new government.

It is hoped that the world can live in peace and no more young men or women will have to die for freedom. Randolph County has always given its best and if the need ever arises again Randolph Countians will again answer the call to arms. We have a proud heritage of service that is evident in the stories of this publication.

This article has been compiled from various research material written on these wars. Researched and written by Virginia Mansker.

INDEX

Note: The section "Served Our Country Too" is not included in this Index as it is listed in alphabetical order in its section starting on page 176.

A

Abbey, Harry 182
Acheson, Wilbur E. 172
Adams, Burnell 182
Adams, Clarence 182
Adams, Gilbert Kennedy 12
Adams, Harold W. 12
Adams, Robert and Mary McHenry 12
Agnew, John D. 12
Ahlheim, Fred W. 172
Ahrens, Bert and Hulda Winkleman 12
Ahrens, Roger 12
Ahrens, Roger L. 12
Aitken, Dean W. 172
Akin, Charles J. and Ernestine Moody 12
Akin, John R. 12
Allen, Andrew and Sarah Jane Hill 12
Allen, John R. 12
Allen, Mary McClinton 12
Allison, Dale 12
Allison, Harry J. 12, 172
Allison, John and Lizzie Smith 12
Allison, Reuel 12
Allison, Reuel and Ruby Jungwaelter 12
Allison, Richard 12
Allison, Royce and Loretta Jones 12, 13
Allison, Royce Briggs 13
Allmeyer, Frederick 13, 173
Allmeyer, Martin and Emma Ebers 13
Alms, Oliver 182
Alms, Elmer H. 13
Alms, Mr. and Mrs. William 13
Alms, Wilbert 182
American Legion 8
American Legion Auxiliary Post 487 8
American Legion BBK Post 480 8
American Legion Joseph Park Post 622 8
American Legion Post 396 8
American Legion Post 6632 8
Anderson, James H. 13, 172
Anderson, Noble and Elizabeth (Price) 13
Anderson, William Wesley 13, 171
Andrews, Chesteen 13
Andrews, Edward and Carrie Woods 13
Appel, Arnold and ___ Pierce 14
Appel, Lloyd T. 13
Armstrong, Glenn 182
Armstrong, Jack 69
Arnold, Ernest M. 172
Asbury, Albert R. 14
Asbury, Alto Harry and Cleva (Willis) 14
Asbury, Andrew C. 14
Asbury, Donald Raymond 14
Asbury, Donald T. 14
Asbury, Ervin Ray 14
Asbury, Harry Albert 14
Asbury, Howard and Ralph 15
Asbury, Howard Lavern 14
Asbury, Jack H. and Lela Hartman 14
Asbury, Jack Harold 14
Asbury, Kevin Bruce 14
Asbury, Mitchell William 14
Asbury, Murray Richard 15
Asbury, Ralph O. 15
Asbury, Roy Lee and Mabel Lorentz 15
Asbury, Samuel and Sarah Christian 14, 15
Asbury, Samuel Richard 15
Asbury, Thomas C. and Mattie Christian 14
Asselmeier, Herman 15
Asselmeier, Herman and Clara Fauss 15
Asselmeier, Vernon 15
Atchison, Jack 15
Atchison, Jackson 182
Atchison, Jerry (Jack) 172
Atchison, Milton 15
Atchison, Milton (Pete) Omer 15, 108
Atchison, Omer and Kate Holloman 15, 16
Atchison, Robert 182
Atchison, Thomas 15, 182
Athmer, Arthur F. "Art" 16
Athmer, Ben and Lena Johnson 16
Aubuchon, Dorothy Amsler 16
Aubuchon, Eli and Barbara 16
Aubuchon, Oliver 16

B

Bagwill, Edward and Martha Welch 16
Bagwill, Vernon L. 16
Baker, Albert 16
Bargman, Fred and Minnie Neely 16
Bargman, Henry 16
Bartens, Arnold and Sylvia (Roettjer) 16
Bartens, Glen M. 16
Bartens, Glen M. and Rose M. Liefer 16
Bartens, Norlyn B. 16
Bates, Tom, Sharon and Ashley 8
Bauer, Anton and Ida Gross 17
Bauer, Arthur M. 16, 17
Bauer, John H. 17
Bauer, Leora Becker 17
Bauer, Marilyn Burk 17
Bauer, Oliver I. 17
Bauman, John D. 17
Bauman, Louis W. and Veronica Schmerbauch 17
Beattie, Ernest J. 17
Beattie, Leon and Essie Smith 17
Beck, A. William 17
Beck, George and Hulda Caupert 17
Becker, Adam and Catherine Meier 18
Becker, Adam H. 17, 18
Becker, Douglas C. 18
Becker, Douglas W. 18, 172
Becker, Fred and Hilda Zippel 18
Becker, Fred W. 18
Becker, George and Anna Botterbrodt 18
Becker, George E. 18
Becker, George E. and Charleene Fehringer 18
Becker, Jennifer, Patricia, Brad and Katie 18
Becker, Kathy (Birk) 18
Becker, Ronald T. 18
Becker, Tyrus "Ty" 18
Becker, Tyrus and Lucille (Hunter) 19
Been, Ebenezer M. 19
Been, Eugene 172
Been, James Allen and Margaret Anderson Cox 19
Beisner, Herman and Linda 19
Beisner, Willard 19
Bel, William E. 19
Belcher, Carroll G. and Dorothy Lee (Conant) 19
Belcher, Stephen Carroll 19
Bell, Arthur and Lulu Moile 19
Bell, Nola V. Fucton 19
Bell, William E. 19
Bellman, Calvin 182
Bergfeld, Leland E. 19
Bergfeld, Rollie and Grace McIntyre 19
Bertram, Arthur J. and Pauline Meier 19
Bertram, Clarence L. 19
Besher, Glen M. 19
Besher, Robert H. and Fern (Gulley) 20
Best, Charles R. 20
Best, Van W. and Sarah Petty 20
Bierman, Alfred 182
Bierman, Hugo H. and Wynona L. (Bollman) 20
Bierman, Michael L. 20
Biesner, William 172
Bievenue, Elroy, Howard and Clinton 20
Bievenue, Ezra G. 20
Bievenue, Raymond and Jennie Thiery 20
Birchler, Gerald D. and Donna J. (Wingerter) 20
Birchler, Jarrod R. 20
Birke, Edward and Vera Laurent 20
Birke, Gary 2
Birke, Gary J. 20
Bivens, Everett F. and M. Lucille Newton 20
Bivens, Jack 9
Bivens, Jackie B. 20
BLair, Robert T. 20
Blasius, Ward H. 172
Blechle, Eddie 182
Blechle, Francis J. "Specs" 20, 21
Blechle, James C. 21
Blechle, Jim 182
Blechle, Theodore Sr. and Minnie Steinkeuhler 21
Bodeker, Arthur and Beulah Abel 21
Bodeker, Walter C. 21
Bogenpohle, Ralph 182
Bolino, Bert F. and Ruth V. Bourgeois 111
Bollinger, Floyd L. and Agnes Marie Bean 21
Bollinger, Gerald L. 21
Bollinger, Heinrich/Hennrich M. 21, 171
Bollman, Clemens 182
Bollman, Everett F. 21
Bollman, Fritz and Lena Waltemate 22
Bollman, Fritz and Mabel Rieckenberg 22
Bollman, Terry L. 22
Borgard, Fred 172
Born, John 172, 182
Bourner, Robert and Oleta Carlyle 22
Bourner, William Paul 22
Bowlin, John R. 22, 172
Bowlin, John R. and Wanda Rose 22
Bowlin, Robert J. 22, 173
Bowlin, Walter and Ella Mae Wilson 22
Boyd, Clyde B. and Marion Mae (Fulton) 22
Boyd, George S. 22
Boyd, George W. and Mary Ann Houston 22
Boyd, Jane and George 8
Boyd, Jane Wiley 22
Boyd, Roger 173
Boyd, Ruth Rachel Holmes 22
Boyd, William George 22
Boyster, Billy Joe Sr. 23
Boyster, Daniel and Ola Metcalf 23
Brandon, Harrel D. 172
Brant, Angela, Jackie and Donald Jr. 23
Brant Brothers 23
Brant, Donald 23
Brant, Donald R. Jr. 23
Brant, Donald R. Sr. and Phyllis P. Coleman 23
Brant, Howard N. 23
Brant, Phyllis 23
Brant, Richard D. 23
Brant, Roland E. 23
Breithaupt, Fredrick Charles 23
Breithaupt, Heinrich Dietrich Wilhelm and Catharina Maria Mehring 23
Bremer, Clinton F. 24
Bremer, Richard C. and Anna L. Albert 24
Brenning, ___ and ___ Harsman 24
Brenning, Albert and Oneta Eggemeyer 24
Brenning, Allen D. 24
Brenning, Elmer L. 24
Brockmeyer, Alfred O. 24
Brockmeyer, Delbert P. 173
Brockmeyer, Fritz P. Sr. and Anna Dierks 24, 25
Brockmeyer, Fritz E. 24
Brockmeyer, Irwin C. 24
Brockmeyer, William Sr. 25
Brown, Charles 182
Brown, David O. 25
Brown, J. Stanley and Geneva Stamm 25
Brown, John C. and Mary Short 25
Brown, Richard Lee 25
Brown, Richard Lee and Eva Morrison 108
Brown, Richard M. 182
Brown, Richard Morrison "Ping" 108
Brown, Sealsberry 27
Brown, Spencer F. 8, 25
Brown, W. John 25
Brown, W.C. and Jennie Smith 25
Brueggeman, Leroy 182
Brumester, Victor and Melba Schnepel 27
Brunhofer, Gerald M. 25
Brunhofer, Max and Estelle Brauer 25
Brush, Mike 8
Buatte, Charles and Grace Jungewaelter 25, 26
Buatte, Charles L. 25
Buatte, Dave 25
Buatte, Joe and Bessie Branom 25
Buatte, Phil 25
Bueckman Brothers 8
Bueckman, Earl L. 26
Bueckman, Henry and Sara Hartman 26
Bueckman, Lee 182
Bueckman, Melvin 26
Bueckman, Omer and Margaret Barger 26
Bueckman, Orville C. 26
Bueckman, William 182
Buena Vista Bank 8
Buescher, William and ___ Redecker 26
Buescher, William J. 26
Buhrmester, Christian H. 26
Burbes, Christian 26
Burbes, Mary Chardong 26
Burditt, Raymond 182
Burke, Dennis John and Mary Ellen O'Brien 26
Burke, Gary J. 20
Burke, John Warren 26
Burke, Patty 8
Burkhardt, Willard A. 172
Burmester, Harlan L., 27
Burmester, Harlen 27
Burris, William Lewis 27
Burris, Zebedee D. and Mary Polly Goodwin 27
Burton, Brandon L. 27
Burton, Larry R.
Burton, Larry A. and Gaye Irwin 27
Butler, James and Elizabeth Moore 27
Butler, James D. 172
Butler, John 27
Butler, Robert F. 27
Butler, William F. and Abigale L. Brown 27
Byrne, John 164

C

Caby, Billy Ray 173
Campbell, Charles F. and June L. Kroutter 28
Campbell, Charles Frederick 27
Campbell, Charles W. 27
Campbell, Craig Frederick 28
Campbell, John and Nancy 28
Campbell, Kenneth D. 28
Campbell, Laura R. Horn 27
Campbell, Samuel 28
Campbell, Verne and Blanche Hemphill 28
Caraway, Carl L. 28
Carlyle, William Louis 28
Carlyle, William Oscar and ___ Buatte 28
Carrico, Thomas 28
Carter, Willis and ___ Purdy 29
Carter, Willis C. Jr. 29
Casetta, Donald S. 29
Casetta, Donizio and Rosa 29
Casetta, Steve 29
Casetta, Steve and Ella Hoelscher 29
Cashion, G.W. 182

Cashion, John Boyd 29
Cashion, Robert and Jane Clifton 29
Castens, Arthur H. 29
Castens, Edith 29
Castens, Herman C. and Mary 29
Castens, Ivan L. 29
Castens, Paul W. 29
Castens, William and Ida Otten 29
Champman, Ralph T. 30
Chandler, Anita Bendorf 30
Chandler, James Clyde and Esther Wisdom 30
Chandler, James D. 29
Chandler, Jimmy and Bret 30
Chapman, Ralph Lloyd and Isabelle (Caskey) 30
Chapman, Ralph Thomas 30
Cheslick, George 172
Chester National Bank 8
Chester Rotary Club 9
Chester V.F.W. 8
Chester Women's Club 9
Choate, Albert H. 30
Choate, Albert Harold and Rosalee Draves 30
Choate, Dale and Jean Allen 30
Choate, George 172
Choate, George F. 30
Choate, Harold Alan and Tina J. Schultz 30
Choate, Jack R. 30
Choate, Jason D. 30
Choate, Lawrence and Lelia Smith 30
Choate, Linda Jean 30
Choate, Tavis M. 30
Chunn, Allan D. 31
Chunn, Allen A. 31
Chunn, Allen A. and Doris J. Bumann 31
Chunn, Don 32
Chunn, Herbert L. 31
Chunn, Ira Victor 31
Chunn, James Robert 31
Chunn, Jesse and Della Griffith 30, 31, 32
Chunn, Joseph A. 31
Chunn, Myron L. 31
Chunn, Sylvester Wayne 32
Chunn, Wayne 31
Cleary, Cleve C. 182
Cleland, Charles E. 32
Cleland, Robert James and Mary Margaret Ervin 32
Clendenin, Harry Burns 32
Clendenin, Harvey Jr. 32, 171
Clendenin, Harvey and Louracy Barber 32
Clendenin,Harvey and Maggie Morgan 32
Clendenin, James C. 32
Clendenin, John 27
Clendenin, John H. and Mary Elizabeth Vickers 32
Clendenin, Moses Walter 32
Clevenge, Homer and __ (Dyer) 33
Clevenger, Flora B. 32
Clevenger, Gary L. 32
Clevenger, Homer Lee 32
Clevenger, James A. and Bernice Lawder 32, 33
Clevenger, James L. 33
Clevenger, James L. and Shirley C. Andrews 32
Clevenger, Larry D. 33
Clevenger, Robert and __ Travis Dyer 32
Cluster, Roy Duane 33
Cluster, Roy E. and Effa Parker 33
Coats, James 33
Coats, Theodore and Erthabelle Lacefield 33
Coffee, Charles and Myrtle Nichols 33
Coffey, Charles H., Jr. 33
Coffey, Charles H. Sr 33, 34
Coffey, Charles Sr. and Myrtle Nichols 33
Coffey, Donald B. 33, 34
Coffey, William and Margaret Barrett 33
Cohen, Gordon Louis 172
Colbert, Daniel and Leila Barber 34
Colbert, Daniel N. 34
Colonna, Melton and Munroe 23
Colvis, Jean John Louis and Celestine Verlin 34
Colvis, Louis 34

Conway, Clement C. 34
Conway, James and Priscilla Coleburn 34
Coop, Edward C. and Elsie Pautler 34
Coop, James P. 34
Copple, Calvin and Donna Saul 34
Copple, Calvin Lee Jr. 34
Costliow, Gerald Thomas 34
Cotner, Jake 34
County Journal Newspaper 9
County Office Supply 9
Courier, Alva 172
Courier, Scott 182
Cowan, Curtis and Leona (Smith) 34
Cowan, Curtis E. Jr. 34
Cowan, Curtis E. Sr. 34
Cowan, Curtis R. and Essie M. Chitwood 34
Cowan, Ed Jr. 34
Cowell, Earl W. and Imogene Geppert 34
Cowell, James Earl 34
Cowell, James Edward 173
Cox, Edward Bernelle 35
Cox, W.A. Cox and Dora E. Preston 35
Craig, Esther E. Gerlach 35
Craig, Robert D. 35
Craig, Robert J. and Helen M. Hamilton 35
Crawford, Hugh and Annie Looney 35
Crawford, Samuel 35
Cressy, Rueben T. 172
Crippen, George 183
Crippen, Paul 183
Cronin, Dale W. 35
Cronin, John and Minnie Stevenson 35
Crow, Edward R. 35
Crow, Olen L. and Mary T. Schneider 35
Cundiff, Harry H. 35
Cundiff, Leo and Annie Colbert 35
Cunningham, Floyd L. and Pearl (Norvell) 35
Cunningham, William R. 35
Cushman, Joseph and Clara Lindner 36
Cushman, Louis J. 35
Cushman, Ludwig A. 36
Cushman, Ludwig "Louis" and Evelyn Novak 35, 36
Cushman, William W. 36

D

Danis, Michael 36
Danis, Michael and Marie Barbe Pilet dit LaSonde 36
Dannenbrink, Alfred 172
Dave's Food Center 9
Davis, Carl E. Jr. 36
Davis, Carl E., Sr. 36
Davis, Carl Eugene Sr. and Alberta (Gross) 36
Davis, James and Mae Schirmer 36
Dayton, Edward and Martha Johnson 36
Dayton, Orvil G. 183
Dayton, Orville C. 36. 172
Decker, Adolph C. and Maria Kipp 36, 37
Decker, Earl Paul 36
Decker, Edward V. 36, 37
Decker, George F. 37
Decker, Harvey H. 37
Decker, Vernon C. 37
DeFrenne, Joseph and Agnes LaChance 37
Defrenne, Preston J. 37
Degener, Alfred and Tillie Diechmann/Eichmann 37
Degener, Alfred H. 37
Degener, Alfred J. 37
Degener, Donald W. 37
Degener, Fredrich and Ida Kleeman 37
Degenhardt, Edward Valentine 38, 172
Degenhardt, John and Ida Niederbracht 38
Degenhardt, Ralph Frank 38
Dement, Bobby 2, 38
Dement, John and Anne Siler 38
Demick, Kenneth 183
Demick, Kenneth J. 172
Deppe, Ernest M. 172
Deppe, Roy 172
Derickson, Cardel/Cordell B. and Rose Mary Hauner 38
Derickson, Donald R. 38

Derickson, Frank E. 38
Derousse, Joseph S. and Bernice Chamberline 38
Derousse, Joseph S. Jr. 38
Dettmer, Herman and Louise Wolff 39
Dettmer, Raymond H. 38
Dettmer, Wilbert H. 172
Dienfenbach, William 172
Dierks, Ernest and Clara Ohlau 39
Dierks, Leonard A. 39
Dilday, Charles B. 183
Dilday, Henry 183
Dobyns, Arthur U. and Mary E. (Byers) 39, 40, 41
Dobyns, Arthur U. 40
Dobyns, Christopher Allen 39
Dobyns, Cletus R. "Buck" 39
Dobyns, Damon A. 39
Dobyns, Damon and Carol (Garner) 39
Dobyns, David R. 39
Dobyns, Don and Mildred 8
Dobyns, Donald D. "PeeWee" 39
Dobyns, Jerry D. 40
Dobyns, Joseph Lee 39
Dobyns, Mary Eliza (Byers) 40
Dobyns, Mildred (Midge) 7
Dobyns, Miles and Laura (Gowens) 40, 41
Dobyns, Otis Lee 40
Dobyns, Robert E. 40
Dobyns, Vernon A. "Pete" 40
Dobyns, Wayne Myles "Sonny" Sr. 41
Dobyns, Wayne Sr. and Sharon (Swartwood) 39, 40, 41
Dobyns, William David "Bill" 41
Dorf, Carolyn and Family 8
Dorf, Charles Ray 41
Dorf, Dr. & Mrs. Steven and Stefanie 8
Dorf, Earl E. 41
Dorf, Earl Sidney/Sydney and Anna Marie Miller 41
Dougherty, L.L. 183
Douglas, Lee 183
Douglas, Terry 173
Dowen, George 41
Dowen, George & Glenn 41
Downen, Snider and Clara Bunselmeyer 41
Downs, Arch and Annis Clark 41
Downs, James K. 41
Draves, Arnold G. 42
Draves, Edward and Anna Gray 42
Draves, Edward D. 42
Draves, Glenn 183
Draves, Harold 183
Dreczka, Eddie 42
Dreczka, John and Nathalie Williams 42
Dreczka, Stephen V. and Grace N. Leavitt 42
Dreczka, Virgil Ray 42
Duchinsky, Anthony Joseph 183
DuClos, Lemuel L. 42
Duclos, Louis and Pearl McClenahan 42
Duensing, Adolph and Emilie Brammer Sr. 43
Duensing, Adolph and Olga Knoke 43
Duensing, Clinton 42
Duensing, Elmer and Alma Siemers 42
Duensing, Lois Gillison 43
Duensing, Raymond H. 42, 43
Duensing, Wayne 43
Duffie, Charles Wilbert 43
Duffie, James Thomas 43
Duffie, Louise Cape 43
Duffie, Thomas and Mary Ann Watt 43
Dunn, Stephen Alexander 43
Durham, Walter A. and Rose Jung Durham 53
Durham, Walter F. 53
Durkee, Gary G. 43
Durkee, Louis and Naomi (Hermes) 43

E

Eagles Club 9
Easton, Shirley Ray 43
Easton, Thomas and Rosella Keeton 43
Eaton, George D. Jr. 43, 171
Eaton, George E. and Eliza Ann 43

Eaton, Margaret Grey 43
Ebers, Albert and Minnie Clasen 44
Ebers, Bill 183
Ebers, Bruce A. 43
Ebers, Edmund and Lena Dierks 44
Ebers, Fern Wolter 44
Ebers, Hilmer 43, 183
Ebers, Hilmer and Cleo Pautler 44
Ebers, Hilmer H. 43
Ebers, Norman A. 44
Ebers, Norman and Fern Wolter 43
Ebers, William L. 44
Ebert, Fred A. 183
Eggemeyer, Andrew Dean 44
Eggemeyer, Arthur and Cora Runge 45, 46
Eggemeyer, August and Minnie Dieckhoff 45
Eggemeyer, Clara Young 45
Eggemeyer, Clyde L. 44, 172
Eggemeyer, David P.H. 44
Eggemeyer, Dennis and Susan Springer 44
Eggemeyer, Donald D. 44
Eggemeyer, Donna, Joni and Tammy 44
Eggemeyer, Doris M. (Tockstein) Laurent 88
Eggemeyer, Eddie and Minnie Hapke 46
Eggemeyer, Edmund 44, 45, 183
Eggemeyer, Ernest 45
Eggemeyer, Floyd 45
Eggemeyer, Fritz and Caroline Rabe 44
Eggemeyer, Fritz and Frederick 46
Eggemeyer, Harold W. 45
Eggemeyer, Harvey F. 45
Eggemeyer, Henry and Pauline Gremmels 45
Eggemeyer, Herbert W. 45
Eggemeyer, James E. 46
Eggemeyer, Joseph and Theresa Rieckenberg 44, 45, 46
Eggemeyer, Lienald and Lydia (Eggemeyer) 46
Eggemeyer, Marlyss Blinn 45
Eggemeyer, Martin and Norma Degner 45
Eggemeyer, Melbert 46
Eggemeyer, Norma Jean Cotner 44
Eggemeyer, Otto and Grace Bockhorn 44, 45
Eggemeyer, Phillip 46
Eggemeyer, Raynold 46
Eggemeyer, Sylva L. 46
Eggemeyer, Wilbert 46
Ehlers, Herman Louis 46
Eichenseer, John and Mary Wierschem 47
Eichenseer, Vincent A. 46, 47
Eilers, Norman 187
Elsey, William 47, 171
Elzroth, Marilyn L. 47
Erdmann, Alvin H. 172
Erdmann, Arnold 47
Erdmann, Arnold and Lu 47
Erdmann, Rudolph and Caroline Hitzamen 47
Ervin, James H. 47
Ervin, Lionel H. 47
Ervin, Lionel H. and Margaret E. (Heppard/Hippard) 47
Ervin, Lionel Harry 47
Esselman, Donald Paul 47
Esselman, Lena Moranville 47
Esselman, Patrick Louis and Lillian Anderson 48
Esselmann, Donald P. 47
Ezekiel L. Holloman 71

F

Fadler, Andrew and Frances Brown 48
Fadler, Theodore W. 48
Falkenhein, Douglas 48
Falkenhein, Harold and Florentine (Koester) 48
Farmers National Realty 9
Favier, Clarence and Lillian Klien 48
Favier, Joseph C. 48
Feaman, Arnold and Aleda Ahrens 48
Feaman, Arnold Dean 48
Feaman, Carol P. 48
Feaman, Michael and Rita (Bryant) 117

201

Fey, Charles P. 48
Fey, Edward and __ Bollman 49
Fey, James J. 49
Fey, Oscar and Lydia Wolter 49
Fickles, Daniel F. 49
Fiechti, Rhonda Pautler 115
Fiechtl, Brenda and Brittany 115
File, John A. and Alice Potts 49
File, John A. and Helen M. Lamb 49
File, John W. 49
File, Lucien A. 49
Fink, Graydon M. "Frenchie" 49
Fink, John J. 49
Fink, Joyce and Bernice Louveau 49, 50
Fink, Richard D. 49, 50
Finley, John Melville and Mary Ethel Steele 50
Finley, Kenneth Olin 50
Finley, Robert H. 172
First National Bank 8
First State Bank 8
Fisher, Edward 8
Fisher, Edward J. 50
Fisher, Edward J. Sr. 50
Fisher, Vera Meyer 50
Flanigan, Robert and Ethel Jones 50
Flanigan, William E. 50
Floyd, Ralph and Clyde Linders 89
Ford, Judith (Rockwell) 126
Fortner, Bill 50
Fortner, Clay 50
Fortner, Sam Henry and Ida Mirtle Mounce 50
Foster, Alan "Izzy" 50
Foster, Harry G. and Catherine France 51
Foster, James and Allean (Lively) 50
Foster, James M. 51
Fowler, Hannah Tindal 51
Fowler, Rev. James and Mary Stephenson 51
Fowler, William 51
Fox, Dewayne L. 51
Fox, Doris M. Rust 51
Fox, Harold Oliver 51
Fox, Oliver M. and Edna Huff 51
Fox, Samuel and Taylor 51
Frager, Erwin A. 51
Frager, Morris J. and Kate S. Neuman 51
Franklin, Leo C. 51
Franklin, Harry and Agnes Braun 51
Fraze, Noah and Della Rice 51
Frazer, Alvin W. 51
Frazer, Alvin W. and Ruth N. Tiller 53
Frazer, Alvin Wilson 51
Frazer, Clifford 51
Frazer, David G. 51, 52
Frazer, Edward and Bertha Draves 52
Frazer, Ellen A. 52
Frazer, Frank D. 52
Frazer, Harry A. and Wanda M. Hasemeyer 52, 53
Frazer, Harry and Susan Belle Cashion 51
Frazer, Henry S. 52
Frazer, Ira and Grace G. Griffen/Griffin 52, 53
Frazer, Jamison 52
Frazer, Joe T. 52
Frazer, Kenneth C. 52, 173
Frazer, Marion 8, 9
Frazer, Michael W. 52, 53
Frazer, Mike and Sherri A. Linton 52
Frazer, Noah and Della Rice 51
Frazer, Terry W. 53
Frazer, Thomas and Mary Landis 52
Frazer, Walter Sidney 53
Frazer, William D. 8, 53
Frazier, Kenny 96
Fricke, Charles Wayne 53
Fricke, Fred and Emma Bell Krug 53
Fulford, Jewett and Lottie Mansker 53
Fulfors, John C. 53
Fulton, Dale 7
Fulton, Dale L. 53
Fulton, William Vernon and Florence Nitzsche 53

G

Gaertner, Lawrence Sr. and Susanna Hesse 54
Gaertner, Paul R. 53, 54
Gardiner, Gregory 54
Gardiner, Russell M. 54
Gardner, Geraldine Langwith 54
Gardner, James W. and Gertie Harrell 54
Gardner, Otis and Ruth Mann Langwith 54
Gardner, Willard 54
Geggie, Robert A. 54
Geggie, Robert J. and Myrtle Carns 54
Gendron, Jacques and Marie Francoise Emond 54
Gendron, Jean Baptiste 54
Gentsch, Donald 54
Gentsch, William and Alma Bewie 54
Gerlach, Albert and Lorene Modglin 54
Gerlach, Louis D. 54, 55
Gerlach, Richard F. and Lena Weberling 55
Gerlach, Richard W. 55
Gibbs, Arthur and Fannie Day 55
Gibbs, Donald 55
Gibbs, Jeffrey D. 55
Gibbs, Jesse and Evelyn (VanDer) Hyden 55
Gibbs, Jesse C. 55
Gibbs, Vincent and Marilyn Bodeker 55
Giffhorn, Rachel (Boyd) and Neil 22
Gilbert, Denise 55
Gilbert, Kevin L. 55
Gilbert, O.M. and Mary Maupin 55
Gilbert, Randy E. 55
Gilbert, Walter E. and Ruby Kirkover 55
Gilbert, Walter E. 55
Gilbreath, James 56
Gilbreath, John R. and Barton 56
Gilster, Henry Sr. and Dorothea Schrader 56
Gilster, Louis H. 56
Gilster-Mary Lee 9
Girard, Eric P. 56
Gischer, Gary and Linda Tindall 56
Gischer, Gary D., Jr. 56
Goessling, Lawrence W. 56
Goetting, Harry 173
Gordon, Lyle Norman 56
Gordon, Paul and Lydia Gardiner 56
Gordon, Stan 56
Gordon, Stephen E. 56
Graff, Carol Winn 57
Graff, Timothy A. 56
Grah, Donald R. 57
Grah, Eugene and Regina Casten 57
Grah, Harlan and Opal Marie Bollinger 57
Grah, William F. 57
Grau, Matthew A. 57
Grau, Norman and Thelma Schwenke 57
Gray, Albert and Melissa Armstrong 57
Gray, Charles Roy 57
Gray, George H. 57
Gray, Guy and Bertha Hindman 57
Gray, Robert W. 57
Grecco, Richard S. 57
Grecco, Samuel J. and Norma Petry 57
Green, Delbert L. 57
Green, Floyd R. 57
Green, Hugh and Eva Heinke 57, 58
Green, Ivan I. 58, 173
Green, Lawrence E. 58
Green, Russell 58
Green, Vernon H. 58
Greer, Barry J. 58
Greer, Bruce B. 58
Greer, David B. 58
Greer, Jimmie W. and Shirley Sebastian 58, 59
Grefe, Gerhard Wilbert 59
Grefe, Henry and Elfredia Trede 59
Gretzmacher, Emma Kirk 80
Griggs, Lloyd E. 59
Griggs, Lloyd O. and __ Lang 59
Grob, Frederick 59
Gross, Dennis E. 59
Gross, Henry and Violet Cassoutt 59
Gross, Herman E. 59
Gross, Lawrence A. 59
Gross, Lawrence and Helen (Bertholl) 59
Gross, Nicholas and Margaret Schoenberger 59
Grott, Gerald J. 59
Grott, Jerome and DeRousse 59
Grott, Jerome C. and Ursula M. 59
Grott, Reyburn J. 59
Guebert, Albert A. 60
Guebert, Albert C. and Marie (Mayme) Homrighausen 60
Guebert, Albert R. 60
Guebert, Albert R. and Adela Hartman 60
Guebert, August and Amanda Rathert 60
Guebert, Daniel L. 60
Guebert, Edwin A., Edwin F., Daniel L. 60
Guebert, Edwin F. and Nina M. Hanebutt 60
Guebert, Edwin F. Jr. 60
Guebert, Edwin H. 60
Guebert, Edwin H. and Anna Mueller 60
Guebert, Edwin H. Sr. 60
Guebert, Elvera 60
Guebert, Eugene 9
Guebert, Eugene T. 61
Guebert, Henry and Bertha Rosenburg 60
Guebert, Oliver T. 61
Guebert, Theodore and __ Blumenschein 61
Guebert, Walter and Alma Ohla 61
Gurley, Paul E. 61
Gurley, Ralph and Betty Brust 61
Guymon, John and Mary "Polly" Wright 61
Guymon, John Wesley 61, 171

H

Habermann, Albert and Lillie Liefer 61
Habermann, Clarence 61
Hagene, Jacob and Mary Mangin 61
Hagene, Lawrence J. 61
Hall, Barbara Schulein Lake 62
Hall, Dennis and Rene McDonough 62
Hall, Harvey 61, 62
Hall, Marvin B. 62
Hall, Noel and Pauline Watson 62
Hall, Rollie and Rose Pyle 62
Hall, Samuel L. 62
Hall, Warren D. 62
Hamer, Vicki McDaniel 98
Hamilton, Albert and Laura Bartlett 62
Hamilton, Archibald and Susanna Bridges 62
Hamilton, Archibald III 62
Hamilton, James 184
Hamilton, Myron 184
Hamilton, Oscar M. 28, 29
Hamilton, Rebecca Wells 62
Hamilton, Richard 184
Hamilton, Roger R. 62
Hamilton, Silas 28
Hamilton, Wilford "Pat" 62
Hamilton, William J. and Florence Reid 62
Hammack, Glennard 184
Hammel, Frederick 63
Hammel, J. George and Margaretha Blouth 63
Hammel, Marvin L. 63
Hammel, Otis L. 63
Hammel, Sam and Matilda 63
Hanebut, Henry 63
Hanebutt, Donald Dean 63
Hanebutt, Elroy 63
Hanebutt, Harry and Lottie (Stellhorn) 63
Hanebutt, Henry 63
Hanebutt, Henry and Mary Kueker 63
Hanebutt, Louis and Mary Liefer 64
Hanebutt, Louis H. and Clara Wolter 63
Hanebutt, Ralph L. 63
Hanebutt, William 63
Hanger, Lenard and Bessie Brewer 64
Hanger, Lenard L. 64
Hanson, J.R. 184
Happel, Leslie E. 64, 172
Happel, Richard and Edith Fairleigh 64
Hardy, William 184
Hargis, Gerald William 64
Hargis, William Lester and Marjorie Ellen Neisler 64
Harmon, David L. and Margaret E. Dean 64
Harmon, David N. 64, 184
Harmon, Dean O. and Gertrude Tanner 64
Harmon, John L. 64
Harmon, Joseph 64
Harmon, Michael and Catherine Ziegler 64
Harmsen, George and Grace Schilling 64
Harmsen, Harold 64
Harris, Doris Johnson 65
Harris, Gertrude 64
Harris, Ronald G. 64, 65
Harstick, Harry and Anna Illy 65
Harstick, Orville 65
Hartenberger, Carl and Ada (Stellhorn) 65
Hartenberger, Donald 65
Hartenberger, Lloyd H. 65
Hartenberger, Oscar and Laura Ebers 65
Hasemeyer, Courtland 66
Hasemeyer, Dale J. 65, 66
Hasemeyer, Ed and Mable Pariset 65
Hasemeyer, Ray 66
Hawkins, Evan and Clara Taylor 66
Hawkins, Milton C. 66
Hawthorne, David Emmett "Blackie" 66
Hawthorne, David McQuery 66
Hawthorne, James C. and "Josie" Blair 66
Heaton, Clifford E. 172
Hedrick, William T. 184
Hein, Robert 136
Heines, Craig 66
Heins, Kyle C. 66
Heires, Paul A. 66
Heires, Walter and Rose Burch 66
Heizer, Charles William 66, 67
Heizer, Leo J. 67
Heizer, Leo J. and Rosalie A. (Heck) 67
Heizer, Robert L. 67
Heizer, William A. 67
Heizer, William and Elizabeth G. Shea 67
Helmers, Harry and Gladyus Hathaway 67
Helmers, Russell A. 67
Henderson, Arnold 172
Henderson, "Junior" Clarence 136
Henson, Harley 185
Herrell, Elmer and LeeElla Hendrix 67
Herrell, Herbert and Burnie (Wilson) 68
Herrell, Herbert L. 67
Herrell, Jeffrey M. 67
Herrell, Seth Adam 67
Herrell, Steve and Donna Rinehart 67
Herrell, Steve L. 67, 68
Herring, Benjamin Clay and Edith Johnson 68
Herring, H.O. 184
Herring, Herbert J. 68
Herring, James C. 68
Herring, Walter and Eva B. Crittenden 68
Herschbach, Charles H. and Sophie Schrader 68
Herschback, William F. 68
Herzog, Brian P. 68
Herzog, Craig R. 68
Herzog, Henry and Barbara Wipfler 69
Herzog, Jarret O. 69
Herzog, Paul A. 69
Herzog, Paul A. and Carol F. Bievenue 68
Herzog, Thomas and Mary Detering 69
Herzog, Thomas H. 69
Higgins, Charles R. 69
Higgins, Raymond and Imogene Lipe 69
Hill, Charles, Jr. 172
Hillyard, Jewell H. 69
Hillyard, Madison (M.M.) and Bertha A. (Riley) 69
Hindman, James Harve and Fannie Shelby 69
Hindman, John 69
Hirte, Charles and Lois (Mueller) 69
Hirte, Terry L. 69
Hitzemann, Eenst 69
Hitzemann, Friederich and Wilhelmine 69
Hoenig, Harry 184
Hohgrefe, Hugo and Margaret Zimmer 69
Hohgrefe, Robert D. 69
Holcomb, Evelyn Schulze 70
Holcomb, F.R. and Mary Jane Klee 70
Holcomb, Ralph R. 70
Holder, Donald and Carolyn 8
Hollaway, Dalton and Minnie Lee 70
Hollaway, Eugene L. 70
Holley, Gordon V. 70

Holley, Gordon V. and Rosanna Korando 70
Holley, Newton and Lucy Gordon 70
Holley, Richard D. 70
Holley, Roger and Connie Pautler 70
Holley, Ron T. 70
Holloman, Dale 70
Holloman, Ezekiel Brown 71
Holloman, Ezekiel J. 71
Holloman, George H. 71, 173
Holloman, Jesse M. "Mack" and Elisabeth Cushman/Cushmann 70, 71
Holloman, John P. 71
Holtz, Lester P. 172
Holub, Dr. Michael P. 8
Homan, Ernest and Frieda Fromeling 71
Homan, Wilbert 71
Hood, Roger E. 71
Hoops, Ervin C. 71
Hoops, Harley 184
Hoops, William and Matilda Kueker 71
Hopkins, Albert 71
Hopkins, Albert and Rose Harbor 71
Hopkins, Robert 184
Hoppel, William H. 184
Hornberger, Donald 184
Hornberger, Walter 184
Hornberger, Walter Edwin and Iola Bell Durkee 72
Hornberger, Walter Eugene 72
Horrell Distributing Company 9
Horrell, Gerald F. 72
Horrell, Henry A. and Josephine M. Levery 72
House, Ray 184
Howie, Ann (Edwards) 72
Howie Brothers, James, Everett and Herbert 72
Howie, David and W.D/Adele D. Rickenberg/Rieckenberg 72, 73
Howie, Eddie and Elsie Bendorf 72
Howie, Emerson T. 72
Howie, Everett D. 72
Howie, Harold T. 72
Howie, Herbert F. 72
Howie, James M. 172
Howie, James Willard "Whimpy" 73
Howie, William Emerson and Edith L. Ledbetter 72
Hubert, Bernie L. 73
Hubert, Lawrence and Amelia (Walta) 73
Huey, Floyd 184
Huey, John and Jennie 73
Huey, Lloyd 184
Huey, Willard M. 73
Hughes, James 73
Hughes, Thomas and Martha 73
Hunter, Sylvester J. 73
Huntley, Eddie 173
Hutchison, Burdett Watson and Mytle E. (Harvey) 73
Hutchison, James D. 73

I

Irose, Andrew and Mary Washichek 74
Irose, John W. 73
Irose, Joseph L. 73
Irose, Leo and Jessie 73

J

Jackson, Harry Michael 74
James, Austin G. and Violet M. Dorway 74
James, Danny 7
James, Danny and June 8
James, Danny D. 74
James, June 7
James, Stephen Robert 74
Jany, Andrew 74
Jany, Delbert L. 74
Jany, Donald J. 74
Jany, Donald J. and Nedra Casetta 74, 5
Jany, Douglas R. 74
Jany, Frank W. and Mary Petrowske 75
Jany, George 75

Jany, Herman J. 75
Jany, Herman Michael 75
Jany, Kevin 75
Jany, Lawrence R. 75
Jany, Melvin M. 74
Jany, Roman and Stephanie Bert 74, 75
Johanning, Marvin 75
Johanning, Theodore and Anna Buettner 75
Johnson, Bartholomew and Alice (Eliza) Darwin 76
Johnson, Charles T. and Katherine L. Godier 76
Johnson, Claude B. 75
Johnson, Earnest 75
Johnson, Evelyn Spurgeon 76
Johnson, Gerald Melvin "Red" 76, 172
Johnson, Herman Clyde 76
Johnson, Hurd and Jessie (Husband) 76
Johnson, Hurd H. 76
Johnson, Jana and Richard 76
Johnson, Joel C. 76
Johnson, Kerry L. 76
Johnson, Margaret Mansker 76
Johnson, McKinsey and Minnie Cashion 76
Johnson, Richard S. and Mollie Moss 76
Johnson, William and Alma Jean Smith 76
Johnson, William Lester 76
Jokerst, Ken and Wilma Staffen 76
Jokerst, Kevin G. 76
Jones, Cadwallader and Martha Ham 77
Jones, Franklin 77
Jones, Franklin and Ellen Webb 77
Jones, Fred 77
Jones, Gabriel 171
Jones, J.R. Strother 171
Jones, Lowell L. 77
Jones, red and Marjorie Campbell 77
Joost, Elmer A. 77
Joost, Herman and Emma Meyerhoffe 77
Jordan, Cynthis Steibel 144
Jordan, Ken 144
Jung, Henry and Margaret Muerer 77
Jung, Henry John 77
Jung, Henry John and Virginia Schulein 77
Jung, Loren Boniface 77
Junge, Arlin L. 184
Junge, Edgar F. 77
Junge, Henry G. 77
Junge, Henry H. and __ Luebkemann 77
Junge, Vernon F. 77
Junge, Vernon J. 77
Jungewaelter, Clyde 77
Jungewaelter, Earl 77
Jungewaelter, John 78
Jungewaelter, John Sr. and Sylvia Medcalf 77, 78

K

Karsten, Harry G. and Hulda A. Fischer 78
Karsten, Leroy H. 78
Kasten, Henry 172
Katz, Adolph 184
Katz, Allen 184
Keeton, Donald Allen 78
Keeton, Vearl Lee 78
Keeton, Virgil 184
Keller, Claude M. and Lizzie Manis 78
Keller, Jacob 78
Keller, Mary Glore 78
Keller, Melvin Lee 78
Kelly, Clarien G. and Ethel Frazier 78
Kelly, Dewey R. 78
Kelly, Marland R. 78
Kempfer, Albert F. 78
Kempfer, Ivan J. 78
Kempfer, Paul E. 78
Kempfer, Roy and Minnie Keller 78
Kempfer, Vernon C. 79
Kempfer, Vernon W. and Elva Sassanger 78, 79
Kempfer, William H. and Ruth 116
Kent, John 79
Kent, Thaddius and Johanna Johnson 79
Kerkhover, James T. and Amelia VanVooren 79

Kerkhover, Jeffrey 8
Kerkhover, Louis Joseph 79
Kessler, Frank Paul 79
Kessler, John and Helen O'Sullivan 79
Kiehna, Dennis 79
Kiehna, Heinrich August Wilhelm and Margaretha Mohr 79
Kiehna, Henry and Bessie Egbert 79
Kiehna, Melvin and Nathalie (Des Rocher) 79
Kiehna, Melvin L. 79
Kiehna, William G. 79, 168
Killion, Jimmie Dean 79
Killion, Lon and Geneva Eggemeyer 79
King, James "Ernie" 80
King, Noah and Martha Boyles 80
Kipp, James E. 80
Kipp, Ralph and Bonnie 8
Kipp, Victor and Beatrice Bean 80
Kirk, Albert E. 80, 172
Kirk, John S. and Emma Sauerhage 80
Kirk, Kenneth Smith 80
Kirk, Stephen and Addaliza Mansker 80
Kirkland, George Lee 80
Kirkland, Jesse and Geraldine Apple 80
Kirkpatrick, Alberta "Bert" James and Nettia/Nettie Lou (Harris) 80
Kirkpatrick, Bruce Wayne 80
Kirkpatrick, Harold V. 80
Kirsch, Osmond J.G. 81
Klingman/Klingmann, Donald R. 81
Klingmann, Harry and Gladys Gnaegy 81
Klingmann, Marilyn 81
Kloepper, Albert and Olga Harms 81
Kloepper, Oliver A. 81
Klot, Henry and Emma Grefe 81
Kloth, Albert H. 81
Kloth, Ardell Eggemeyer 81
Kloth, Clarence 81, 184
Kloth, Clarence and (Lorenz) 82
Kloth, Clarence and LaVerne Lorentz 81
Kloth, Gary R. 81
Kloth, George H. 81
Kloth, Herman and Bertha Eilers 81
Kloth, Lauren O. 81
Kloth, Otto and Violet Schultz 81, 82
Kloth, Ronald D. 82
Kloth, Terry Lee 82
Kloth, Wilbur 82
Kluba, David J. 82
Kluba, Steven and Clara Probst 82
Knigge, Louis and Minnie Junge 82
Knigge, Theodore H. 82
Knope, Louis and Mayme Schaffer 82
Knope, Merle 82
Knott, Dillon and Mae McKinney 82
Knott, Harold 184
Knott, James D. 82
Knowles, William 184
Koch, Alfred and Malinda (Castens) 83
Koch, Delphine J. 56
Koch, Gary 173
Koch, Leland P. 83
Koehler, Alfred 172
Koeneman, Don and Paul, Attorneys at Law 9
Koeneman, Roy B. 185
Koenig, Heinrich 83
Koening, Edward and Eva Eliza Engelhardt 83
Koening, Edward William 83
Koester, Fred 185
Koester, Fred C. and Mina Rowold 83
Koester, Fred W. 83
Koester, Glenn W. 83
Koester, Paul 83, 185
Koester, William and Ella (Hartmann) 83
Kontz, Donald R. 83
Kontz, Donald R. and Marcella Hohgrefe 83
Kontz, Jacob and Melissa Holland 84
Kontz, Michal D. 83
Kontz, Robert F. 83
Kontz, Robert F. and Clara Runge 83
Koopman, Walter 172
Korando, Andy and Myrtle Wilson 84
Korando, Charles and Rosa Shields 84
Korando, Fred W. 84
Korando, Glenn R. 84

Korando, Joseph and Philomena Bert 84
Korando, Michael and (Rodely) 84
Korando, Michael Thomas 84
Korando, Michael T. JR. 84
Korando, Patrick Thomas 84
Korando, Raymond 84
Korando, Thomas and Ella Shields 84
Kraft, Floyd 172
Kraft, John Henry and Mary Caroline Meyer 85
Kraft, William H. 84
Krause, Gustav 85
Krause, Martin and Caroline Buse 85
Krause, Victor H. 85
Krug, Casper and Viola Moore 85
Krug, Charles Ellsworth 85
Kruse, Ernst and Minna Liefer 85
Kruse, Victor H. 85
Kuehne, Albert and Emma Childers 85
Kuehne, Charles A. 85
Kueker, Alvin C. 172
Kueker, Archie Dean and Alice Marie Eggemeyer 86
Kueker, Clarence A. 85, 172
Kueker, Delbert G. 85
Kueker, Donald and Eloise Becker 85
Kueker, Edward and Frieda 85
Kueker, Elisabeth, Noah and Jacob 85
Kueker, Gregory D. 85
Kueker, Jonathan R. 86
Kueker, Leslie Segelken 85
Kueker, Martin and Frieda Behman 85
Kueker, Martin and Frieda Schenck 86
Kueker, Robert L. 86
Kueker, Robert Lee and Carol Ann Suhre 86
Kueker, Wilbert F. 86

L

Lafferty, James J. 86
Lafferty, John Marshall and Julia Jordan 86
Lafferty, John W. 86
Lahr, Alvin Elsworth and Pearl Catherine Ruppert 86
Lahr, Donald McClelland 86
Lake, Bobbie and Blaise 142
Lambert, Dale Allen 86
Lambert, Richard and Patricia Schumaker 86
Landmann, Frank C. 86
Landmann, Frank J. and Madeline Dickey 87
Lang, Leslie Charles 87
Lang, William P. and Mary Josephine Yankey 87
Lange, Donald F. 87
Lange, Lorenz F. and Ester Pearson 87
Langin, Dean 185
Langrehr, Charles and Caroline Hanebutt 87
Langrehr, Stanley W. 87
Langrehr, Walter 87
Langrehr, Walter and Anita Liefer 87
Laramore, Jerry R. 87
Laramore, Malcom and Juanita Mines 87
Laramore, Ronald 87
Laramore, Wayne H. 87
Laurent, Michael 88
Laurent, Michael D. 87, 88
Laurent, Robert A. and Mabel Carr 88
Laurent, Robert J. 88
Lawder, Henry and Annie Pinkerton 88
Lawder, James Leslie 88
Lawder, Ray Austin 88
Lawder, Samuel and Sarah Malone 88
Ledbetter, Everett E. 88
Ledbetter, Mr. and Mrs. (nee Saal) Lewis 88
Lemburg, Edward H. 185
Lessley, J. Vernon and Mabel Brown 88
Lessley, Norris Brown 88
Levery, Boniface L. 88
Levery, Lawrence and Olga Zipfel 88
Lewis, Loren and __ Kearbey 88
Lewis, Robert Loren 88
Liefer, Edward and Rosina Gielow 89
Liefer, Herbert E. 89
Liefer, Louis and Mary Hanebutt 63
Liefer, Maureen K. 89

Liefer, Maureen K. Casetta 89
Limbaugh, Daniel 8
Limbaugh, Daniel B. 89
Limbaugh, Manley and Mary Jane (Heagler) 89
Linders, Clyde 89
Linders, Edward and Tillie Hecke 89
Linders, Floyd L. 89
Linders, Ralph 89
Linders, Vernon 89
Lindsey, Clarence and Loretta Jett 89
Lindsey, Jackie W. 89
Ling, Daniel Bishop 89
Ling, Rolla Clendenin 90
Ling, Walter Sidney 90
Ling, William Sherman and Dora Belle Thompson 90
Link, Boniface and Grace Ragsdale 90
Link, Doris Word Jackson 90
Link, Robert S. 90
Little, Claude 90
Little, Delbert and Bertha Freemann 90
Lively, A. and Anna Sitkoskie 91
Lively, Alonzo and Frances East 91
Lively, Nora Hood 91
Lively, Ralph Willard 90, 91
Lively, William J. 91
Lochhead, Dale R. 91
Lochhead, David Albert and Nora Fey 92
Lochhead, Dean L. 91
Lochhead, Donald J. 91
Lochhead, James F. and Lizzetta/Lizzie Pick 91
Lochhead, James H. and Hilda D. Knigge 91
Lochhead, Leonard and Donald 91
Lochhead, Leonard C. 91
Lochhead, Melvin 91
Lochhead, Vernon Chester 92
Lohman, Donald and Deborah (Brueggemann) 92
Lohman, Jason P. 92
Lohrdine, Dorian H. 92
Lohrdine, George Henry and Henrietta Priebe 92
Long, Charles and Vera (Wiley) 92
Long, Robert J. 92
Lorentz, Slyvester 92
Lorentz, Sylvestor 172
Lorenz, Hugo and Pauline Schneider 92
Lorenz, Slyvester J. 92
Loveland, John V. 172
Lunsford, Robert V. 186
Lybarger, Charles 185
Lyle, James 28, 29
Lynch, Joe 186
Lynch, Maurice 172, 186

M

Maasberg, August and Maggie Wine 92
Maasberg, Frederick D. 92, 173
Mabe, Cicero 92
Mabe, Vernon F. 92
Mabuce, Eddie 172
Macieiski, Stanley 93
Macke, John Jr. 93
Macke, John Sr. and Anna Marie Dehn 93
Maes, Arthur 93
Maes, Leo 186
Maes, Louis and Anna Postman 93
Magany, Michael 93
Magany, Sarah Donald 93
Magers, Dan L. 93, 186
Magers, Henry and Lucy Lohrding 93
Malone, George 186
Mann, Arthur C. and Ida A. Stumpe 94
Mann, John Preston 93
Mann, Richard 8
Mann, Richard J. 94
Mansker, Adam 94
Mansker, Arthur Vernon 94
Mansker, Bernard Cole and Iva Pearl Dunn 94, 95
Mansker, Henry Clay 171
Mansker, Herbert Lloyd 94
Mansker, Howard 94

Mansker, Ira (Jack) 94
Mansker, Ira Warren 94
Mansker, John 186
Mansker, John and Margaret Robinson 95
Mansker, Joseph H. 94
Mansker, Kirby and Carolyn Devall 94
Mansker, Noah Edward and Mary Louise Warren 94, 95
Mansker, Paul B. 95
Mansker, Samuel 95
Mansker, Samuel and Elizabeth Bartley 95
Mansker, Samuel and Nancy Crawford 94
Mansker, Sherry J. 8
Mansker, Thaddeus C. 95
Mansker, Virginia 5, 7, 8
Manwaring, Albert and Ephemia McMurtrie 95
Manwaring, Albert W. 95
Manwaring, Raymond and Cazzie Sheets 95
Manwaring, Ronald S. 95
Marcinkowska, Augustine 186
Marlen, Richard B.S. 95, 171
Marlen, William C. 95, 171
Marlen, William Riggs and Jane Gant 95
Marlin, Leslie 186
Martin, John M. 95
Massie, Charles and Anita Mullins 95
Massie, Charles E. 95
Mathewson, James 172
Mathis, Bruce L. 96
Mathis, Clarence A. and Ramona (Steele) 96
Mayo, Scott E. 96
McAdams, Donald Ray 96
McAdams, Jesse Daniel and Adeline (Baum) 96
McAdoo, Michael 173
McCarty, Everett and Minnie Stipe 96
McCarty, Paul Henry 96
McCauley, Henry 96
McCauley, Henry and __ Frieman 96
McCauley, Hugh and Mary 96
McCauley, Noral A. 96
McClinton, John 96
McClinton, John and Elizabeth Anderson 96
McClinton, John F. and Mary Orr 96
McClinton, Samuel 96
McClinton, William P. 96
McConkey, James 97
McConkey, James Lee 96
McConkey, James William 97
McConkey, Robert and Sarah 97
McConkey, William R. and Florence Frazer 97
McCormick, Cliff and Pam Jordan 97
McCormick, Clifford L. 97, 185
McCormick, Dale E. 97, 185
McCormick, Donald R. 97, 185
McCormick Family 185
McCormick, Gerald D. 97
McCormick, Herbert and Edith Stewart 97
McCormick, Herbert R. 97, 185
McCormick, Jerry 185
McCormick, Johnathan F. 97
McCormick, Michael B. 97
McCormick, Michael Bradley 185
McCormick, Roger 97, 185
McCormick, Roger and Charlotte Robbins 97
McCormick, Ross and Gettie Asbury 97
McCormick, Wanda 185
McCree, Lowell and Marie Ashoff 98
McCree, William A. 98
McDaniel, Charles C. and Carolyn Myers 98
McDaniel, June Word 98
McDaniel, Richard 98
McDaniel, Roy E. 98
McDaniels Bookbinding 9
McDaniels, Jack F. 98
McDaniels, Roy E. 98
McDonald, Bill 186
McDonald, Emmett 186
McDonald, Myrl T. 172
McDonald, Paul 186
McDonald, Waldo 186
McDonald, W.O. 186
McDonald, Waldo D. 98
McDonald, William Perry and Laura Belle Voelker 98

McDonough, Donald L. 98
McDonough, Jerald Peters and Viola (Pierce) 99
McDonough, Joe and Hester Sipole 98, 99
McDonough, Joseph B. 98
McDonough, Joseph Neal 98
McDonough, Larry S. 99
McDonough, Larry S. and Imogene Bierman 99
McDonough, Shannon T. 99
McGee, Armstrong 99, 171
McGee, George and Nellie Johnson 99
McGee, George and Thomas 99
McGee, Glennard S. 99
McGee, Thomas 171
McGee, Walter G. 100
McGuire, Byron H. 100
McGuire, Earl F. and Martha Schlimme 100
McGuire, Fern 100
McGuire, Fredrick L. 100
McGuire, Harry B. 100, 172
McGuire, J.H. 100
McGuire, William and Willadean Hendricks 100
McGuire, William Earl 100
McGuire, William J. 100
McIntyre, Albert and Mildred Leadbetter 100
McIntyre, Jerry R. 100
McKelvy, Hugh 100
McKelvy, James and Margaret 101
McKenzie, Carl R. 101
McKenzie, Grace Ratliff 101
McKenzie, Loren D. 101
McKenzie, R.H. and Grace Ratliff 101
McKenzie, Robert H. 101
McKinle, William A. 101
McKinley, Dwight C. 101
McKinley, Lee A. 101
McKinley, Ralph and Mary (Aitken) 101
McKinley, Roy L. 101
McKinley, William A. 101
McLaughlin, Harry W. 101, 168
McLaughlin, Sam W. and Elizabeth Dickey 101
McMichael, Roy Lee 102
McMichael, Hugh and Mary Krull 102
McMichael, Marvin 102
McMichael, Marvin and Maxine Petty 102
McMichael, Marvin Dale 102
McMichael, Roy Lee 102
Mehre, Oscar and Stella Valleroy 102
Mehrer, Donald Walter 102
Mehrer, Elmer Pete 102
Meier, Donald Walter 102
Meier, Edgar and Erna Donaldson 102
Meierhoff, Leo 186
Meister, Christopher A. 102
Meister, Donald E. and Teresa A. (Miller) 102
Menke, Burdell G. 103
Menke, Otto and Adeline Veath 103
Mennerich, Albert Charles 103
Mennerich, Albert Charles and Helen Jany 103
Mennerich, Elizabeth Horschmann 103
Mennerich, Franz John and Anna Catharina Goedeke 103
Mennerich, Henry and Franz 103
Mennerich, Vincent James 103
Mennerich, William 103
Mennerich, William C. and Louisa Rall 103
Mennerich, William C., Frank, Elizabeth, Margaretta, Wendell, Mary, Emma Gertrude, August and Mathilde 103
Meyer, Frederick Ludwig 103
Meyer, Frederick Ludwig and Hulda Schaack 103, 104
Meyer, Harold A. 103
Meyer, Heinrich and Mary Rabe 103
Meyer, Raymond F. 103
Miller, Arthur 186
Miller, Clifford D. 172
Miller, Herman and Anna L. Rice Ralston 104
Miller, Jack and Ellen 104
Miller, John Henry 104, 186
Miller, Paul 186

Miller, Udell 104
Miller, Walter and Nettie Mansker 104
Miller, William 104
Misselhorn, Edgar A. 104
Misselhorn, William and Hulda Ruback 104
Modglin, Myron and Arlene Albers 104
Modglin, Timothy L. 104
Moffat, Robert A. and Dorothy Bertram 104
Moffat, Robert A. JR. 104
Moffat, Robert Andrew 104
Moffat, Robert E. and Henrietta Clyde Edwards 104
Mohr, Henry and Anna Lisch 105
Mohr, Leonard and Anna Brecht 105
Mohr, Leonard H. 104
Mohr, Victor 8
Mohr, Victor L. 105
Moll, Delbert J. 105
Moll, Ferd W. and June J. Eggemeyer 105
Moll, Ferdinand W. 105
Moll, Steven William 105, 173
Moll, Theodore and __ Hunter 105
Moll, William and Ella Mattingly 105
Monroney, Garry R. 105
Monroney, Gerald D. and Glenna (Dregke) 105
MontreuilL, Jean Baptiste 105
Montreuil, Marie-Josephe LaLonde 105
Montreuil, Michael Sedilot dit 105
Montroy, Armin J. 105, 106
Montroy, Denis R. 106
Montroy, Francis and Florence Sisson 106
Montroy, Francis W. 106
Montroy, Harry 8
Montroy, Harry E. 106
Montroy, Harry H. and Hazel Andrews 106
Montroy, J.L. Montroy and Cecelia Moskop 105
Montroy, James and Tammy Blum 106
Montroy, Kenneth 186
Montroy, Lawrence and Ethel Hennrich 106
Montroy, Scott A. 106
Moor, Albert and Louvisa Payne 107
Moore, Arthur I. 106
Moore, Daymon 106
Moore, Damon and Leona Kohlhaas/Kuhlhaas 107
Moore, Grover and Kate Williams 106, 107
Moore, Grover Lloyd 106
Moore, Harvey and Mary Henson 107
Moore, Ira Murel 107
Moore, Ira Porter 107
Moore, John and Elizabeth Laugton 106
Moore, Lonnie 107
Moore, Olin E. 107
Moore, Robert and Millia Inman 106
Moore, Robert I. 107
Moore, Ronald 107
Moore, Sidney Smith 107
Moore, Vince James 107
Moore, Virgil E. 107
Moore, William H. and Grace Martin 107
Moore, Wilson and Vashti Skipworth 107
Morgan, James 172
Morris, Samuel and Lucy Stevens 107
Morris, William 107
Morrison, Michael and Lillian Bradley 107
Morrison, Norman J. 107
Morrow, Charles Lonnie "Termite" 108
Morrow, John William 108
Morrow, Samuel A. Jr. 108
Morrow, Samuel A. Sr. 108
Morrow, Samuel A. Sr. and Marie E. Foertsch 108, 109
Morrow, William M. and Lula (Kirkland) Oglesby 108
Mudd, Alfred and Eolalia E. Simpson 109
Mudd, Charles D. 109
Mudd, Emory James and Anna E. Peyrot 109
Mudd, Harold Francis 109
Mudd, Larry 9, 109
Mueller, Dietrich Friedrich and Anna Maria Ebers 109
Mueller, Edward and Carolina 109
Mueller, Fred H. and Frieda Hornbostel 110
Mueller, Friederich H. 109

Mueller, Henry O. and Josephine Bollman/Bollmann 110
Mueller, John Fredrich 109
Mueller, Louis 109
Mueller, Louis and Emma (Bollmann) 109
Mueller, Melvin 109, 186
Mueller, Milton 109, 186
Mueller, Ralph B. and Susan (Bradley) 110
Mueller, Raymond C. 109
Mueller, Robert H. 110
Mueller, Walter C. 110
Mueller, William C. 110
Mueth, Clement 172
Mulholland, Albert and Mayme Marshall 111
Mulholland, J. Earl and Edna McKee 110
Mulholland, Joe and Pearl Hemphill 110
Mulholland, John 110
Mulholland, Joseph 110
Mulholland, Leonard L. 110
Mulholland, Lyle 186
Mulholland, Travis C. 111
Mulholland, Travis, Loyd and Melvin 111
Muller, Johann Freidrich and Ilsa Margreta Rajas 109
Murer, George A. 27

N

Nagel, Elmer 186
Nance, Earl Burdette 111
Nance, Forrrest B. 111, 173
Nance, Jesse B. and Effa Parker 111
Nance, Russell Parker 111
Neisler, Edwin Burrell and Winifred Ethel Stump 111
Neisler, Gordon Stump 111
Nelson, Raymond 172
Nelson, Russell J. 186
Nevois, Edgar W. 172
Niblock, Morris 186
Niehaus, Gweneth Jeanne Bolino 111
Nitzsche, C.S. "Bud" and Marjorie (Rockwell) 111
Nitzsche, Leonard A. 111, 173
Norman, Herbert 111
North County News 9
North County Savings Bank 8
Nurnberger, Casper 111
Nurnberger, Dan 112
Nurnberger, Harry 112
Nurnberger Insurance 9
Nurnberger, Kent 112

O

O'Brien, Harvey and __ Brayfield 112
O'Brien, Myron H. 112
Odle, William J. 112
Ohlau, Arnold and Alwine Meierhapp 112
Ohlau, Betty Runge 112
Ohlau, Betty Wucher 113
Ohlau, Melvin H. 112
Ohlau, Roger W. 112, 113
Ohlau, Walter and Dorothy Fricke 112
O'Rear, Donald 113
O'Rear, Wiley S. and Hattie M. Smith 113
Oser, Albert J. 113

P

Papenberg, Harold A. 113
Papenberg, Oscar and Ella Luebkemann 113
Park, Mary 8
Parker, John W. and Ada Ward 113
Parker, Shirley Ward 113
Parrish, Ben R. 113
Parrish, George R. and Claudia Johnson 113
Partington, Gene and Leota (Colbert) 114
Partington, Roger D. 113, 114, 173
Patterson, Gilbert 114
__ M 114

Pautler, Anthony M. and Margaret G. Heuman 114
Pautler, Ben and Marcella Gaertner 115
Pautler, Brian J. 114
Pautler, Brian P. 114
Pautler, Bryce 115
Pautler, Clyde W. and Anna Marie Parker 114, 115
Pautler, Daniel J. 114
Pautler, Edward and Carla Pinter 114
Pautler, Edward B. 114
Pautler, Edward Phillip 114
Pautler, Ezra and Bertha Stork 115
Pautler, Kevin 115
Pautler, Lawrence and Gertrude Young 114, 115
Pautler, Margie Walter 115
Pautler, Michael and Edna Ross 115
Pautler, Norman A. 114, 115
Pautler, Paul A. 115
Pautler, Robert G. 115
Pautler, Ross L. 115
Pautler, Roy 115
Payne, Charles L. 115
Payne, Samuel and Emma 115
Perzia, Guy and Angeling Russo 115
Perzia, Leonard A. 115
Pestor, Henry Sr. and Caroline Messenbrink 115
Pestor, Willaim J. 115
Peters, Fred J. 115, 116
Peters, Harry M. 116
Peters, William and Ruth Kempfer 115
Petrowsk, Theophile and Magdalene Kloss 116
Petrowske, Delmar L. 116
Petrowske, Delmer 173
Petrowske, Donald R. 116
Petrowske, Elroy J. 116
Petrowske, Herman A. 116
Petrowske, Herman and Florence Singer 116
Petrowske, Jesse and Mildred Alms 116
Petrowske, Raymond and Dorothy (Bodeker) 116
Petrowske, Roger L. 116
Phegley, Burton W. 172
Phegley, Harold 186
Phillips, Thomas W. 116
Phillips, Thomas W. and Mary Florence Weir 116
Phillips, Willis Allen and Amanda Webb 116
Phoenix, Joseph E. 117
Pierce, Jack B. 169
Pierce, James Thomas and Anna R. Honeycutt 117
Pierce, John William 117
Pierce, Roy E. Sr. and Rosa P. (Morrow) 117
Pierce, Rufus 117
Pierce, Warren David 117
Pinkerton, Roy D. 117
Pinkerton, Isaac and Harriet Gilchrist 117
Pirkle, Theodore T. 117
Pirtle, Henry Clay and Eliza Thornton 117
Pirtle, Klondis R. 117
Pittman, Jack Lee 117
Pittman, John Irvin and Roxie Tindall 118
Poenitske, Andrew and Josephine Shemonic 118
Poenitske, Joe 118
Pohle, Kurt H.H. 172
Poniske, Richard A. 118
Poniske, Thomas and Anna M. Grott 118
Porter, Charles W. 172
Powderly, Vernon 172
Powley, A.E. and Nora Welten 118
Powley, Edward H. 118
Preston, John C. 118
Preston, Scherer 118
Preston, Wahneta Roehrkasse 118
Price, Howard and Beulah (Pflasterer) 118
Price, John D. 118
Priestley, Harry and Emma Norman 118
Priestley, Harry W. 118
Prosek, George D. 118
Prosek, George D. and Theresa E. Grott 119
Prosek, Gilbert Goerge 118, 138, 172
Prosek, Joseph and Francis Paulus 118

R

Rabe, Dorothy R. (Ivanouk) 119
Rabe, Frederick L. 119
Rabe, Henry and Mary Fortmann 119
Rader, Charles 96
Rader, Charles W. 119, 173
Rader, George and Sylvia (Neihouse) 119, 120
Rader, George E. 119
Rader, Jacob and Della Boyd 119, 120
Rader, Jake B. 119
Rader, Paul A. 119, 187
Rader, Russel A. 119, 187
Rader, Wilbur E. 120, 172
Rader, Wilbur P. 120
Ragland, Kenneth W. 120
Ragland, Mason C. 120
Ragland, Norman H. and Callie Crain 120
Ragland, Ron K. 120
Ragland, Roy K. and Audrey Kempfer 120
Ragland, Roy K. 120
Rahlfs, Clarence H. 121
Rahlfs, Harry A. 121
Rahlfs, Harry H. and Clara Gentsch 121
Rahn, Orvile Jr. 121
Rahn, Orville and Lena Mae Kirkley 121
Rahn, Orville Jr. 121
Rahn, Orville Sr. 121
Rahn, William and Freida Eggers 121
Ralston, George and Nellie Brown 121
Ralston, Luke and Bessie Darnell 121
Ralston, Raymond Luke 121
Ralston, William 121
Ramsey, Ben 150
Ramsey, Ben and Fleta (Hathaway) 121, 122
Ramsey, Charles D. 121
Ramsey, Darrel L. 121
Ramsey, Donald E. 122
Ramsey, Fleta Hathaway 150
Ramsey, Wayne E. 122
Randolph County Board 9
Randolph County Clerk's Office Staff 9
Randolph County Farm Bureau 9
Randolph County Genealogical Society 9
Randolph County Tribune 9
Rather, Friederike Heuer 122
Rather, Heinrich 122
Ratz, A.J. and Ella Dinges 122
Ratz, Raymond C. 122
Ray, Bert and Nancy NcNew 122
Ray, Lyman Wade 122
Reed, Robert B. 122
Reed, Roger S. and Barbara Brown 122
Reeder, James Leonard 122
Reeder, Raymond G. and Minnie G. Stone 122
Rees, Dallas K. 122, 123
Rees, Harlan and Vera Vancil 122
Rehmer, Fredrich 123
Reid, Arthur Cornelious "Connie" 123
Reid, Harry DeRose and Cora E. Frazer 123
Reid, Harry G. 123, 169
Reid, James D. 124, 171
Reid, Joseph and Margaret Ann Ryan 124
Reid, Joseph D. 123
Reid, Martha Bowman 123
Reid's Harvest House 9
Reimer, Albert 124
Reimer, Albert and Marie Heinke 124
Reimer, Roger & John 187
Res, Charles A. 124
Res, Joseph and Etta Murden 124
Rheinecker, George W. SR. 124
Rheinecker, George W. and Bertha Clendenin 124
Rheinecker, Joseph and Clara Bergfeld 124
Rheinecker, Joseph Paul 124
Rhodes, Kieth 187
Richardson, Glenn 173
Richeson, Edwin F. 172
Rickenberg, Chad A. 88, 124
Rickenberg, Morris and Linda (Laurent) 124
Riddle, Don 124, 125
Riddle, Harry 124, 125
Riddle, Jewell (Bob) and Evelyn (Neely) 125
Riddle, Richard Karry "Rick" 125

Riecan, Joseph Sr. 187
Ried, Arthur 187
Ried, Glenn 187
Riester, Jerry and Reta Radford 125
Riester, Mark C. 125
Rigdon, George and Florence Hiller 125
Rigdon, Ruth Victoria Ralston 125
Rigdon, Virgil G. 125
Rinne, Edwin and Elda Duensing Brammer 125
Rinne, Lester 125
Ritter, Heinrich 125, 171
Robert, Donald L. 125, 126
Robert, Henry and Ethel K. Johnson 126
Robert, Jim and Rose Kessler Hutchison 162
Roberts, Walter Yourtee 187
Rockwell, Albert G. 126, 171
Rockwell, Emma Marlen 126
Rockwell, Ephraim 126
Rockwell, Justus T. Jr. 126
Rockwell, Justus T. Sr. and Judith Cornelius 126
Rockwell, Justus T. Sr. and Sallie Perkins 126
Rockwell, Ozella Clore 126
Rockwell, Robert 126
Rockwell, Sarah Cole 126
Rodely, Bert and Marie Short 126
Rodely, Richard C. 126
Rodely, Thomas D. 126
Rodewald, Daryle G. 126
Rodewald, Omer H. 126
Rodewald, Omer H. and Ruth (Meyerhoff) 126
Rodewald, Rudolph and Blanche Eggers 126
Rodewald, Wilbert H. 127
Roehrkasse, Arthur 127
Roehrkasse, Hugo and Bertha Busse 127
Roesemeier, Edwin 172
Rogers, Gene 127
Rogers, George Therman 127
Rogers, Irvin Earl and Hattie Casey 127
Rohlf, Herman Christian and Ida Josephine Deichmann 127
Rohlfin, Henry F. and Frieda Luehr 127
Rohlfin, Henry Fredrick Sr. and Emma C. Breithaupt 127
Rohlfing, Christian Heinrich 127
Rohlfing, Herman Christian 127
Rohlfing, Howard William 127
Rohlfing, LaVerna Bruns 127
Rohlfing, Marvin W. 127
Rohlfing, Mary Anna Louise Linders 127
Rohlfing, Robert Ernst 127
Rohlfing, Robert L. 128
Rohlfing, Theodore and Bernice Schrieber 128
Rohlfling, Marvin W. 127
Roscow, Ann Aubuchon 128
Roscow, Eldon and Sarah 128
Roscow, Ervin and Ann 128
Roscow, Ervin P. 128
Roscow, James and Thelma Hunter 128, 129
Roscow, James E. 128
Roscow, Jason P. 128
Roscow, Jeffrey M. 128
Roscow, Jennifer Becker 128
Roscow, Michael P. 128
Roscow, Roger and Bonita Rosenberg 128
Roscow, Roger L. 128, 129
Rosenberg, Henry C. and Effie Davis 129
Rosenberg, Marvin 129
Rowald, Conrad and Emmeline Goetting 130
Rowney, Charles E. and Mayme Arnett 129
Rowney, Charles Lee 129
Rowold, August and __ Laramore 129
Rowold, Harold 129
Rowold, John David 129
Rowold, Ken 129
Rowold, Ken and Virginia Welge 129
Rowold, Walter F. 129
Rowold, Walter F. and Marcella A. Lindner 89
Roy, Aaron and Lucille Blow 130
Roy, Dale W. 130

205

Rozier's Country Market 9
Rubach, Herman and Emma Pinkerton 130
Rubach, Homer H. 130, 187
Ruebke, Fritz and Clara Hartmann 130
Ruebke, Larenz 130
Runge, Earl J. 130
Runge, Henry F. and Ruth E. Hapke 130
Runge, Leonard L. 130
Runge, Leonard R. 130
Runge, Richard L. "Dick" 130
Runge, Roy F. and Velma Leonard 130
Ruroede, Clarence M. 130
Ruroede, Edward E. 131
Ruroede, Ernest C. 131
Ruroede, Martin and Dora Hartmann 131
Rushing, John Cameron 131
Rushing, Kenneth and Melodie Mansker 131
Rushing, Kurt W. 131
Rutherford, Ted R. 172

S

Saak, Charles William "Bill" 131
Saak, Jacob 131
Saak, Robert W. 131
Saak, Wilbert 131
Saak, Wilbur and Edna Baughman 131
Saak, Wilbur M. 131, 132
Saak, Wilbur M. and Edna G. Baughman 131
Saak, William F. and Jennie C. Marlow 132
Saddler, Edwin Gary 132
Saddler, Hueston 132
Saddler, Hueston and Alberta (Neely) 132
Saddler, John E. and Lavilla Rader 132
Saddler, John Larry 132
Salger, Edwin and Bernice (Stellhorn) 132
Salger, Edwin Gary 132
Salger, Glenn A. 132
Salger, Harvey P. 132
Salger, Herbert M. 132
Salger, Joan Green 132
Salger, Leonard Salger and Doris E. (Brelye) 98
Salger, Paul H. and Leona Schoenbeck 132
Salger, William and Amanda Alms 132
Sauer, Benjamin P. 132, 133
Sauer, Bonnie M. Roscow 133
Sauer, Lesley (Smith) 133
Sauer, Milton T. and Almaneda Becker 133
Sauer, Page and Alexis 133
Sauer, William "Bill" Fred 133
Sauer, William F. and Bonnie M. (Roscow) 133
Sauer, William J., Bradley T., Benjamin P. and Amanda R. 133
Sauerhage, James W. 133
Sauerhage, Louis and Alice Hefner 133
Schaffner, Edith Fredericka 133
Schaffner, Herbert J. 133
Schaffner, James Homan 133
Schaffner, William F. 133
Schaffner, William F. and Ethel Anita Thompson 133
Schaffner, William H. and Mary Elizabeth Homan 133
Scherle, Peter H. 134
Schirmer, Bertram I. 134
Schirmer Brothers 134
Schirmer, John W. 134
Schirmer, John W. and Caroline C. Sprengel 134
Schirmer, Paul, Bertram and John 134
Schirmer, Paul E. 134
Schirmer, Paul E. and John F. 134
Schmerbauch, Fred 134
Schmerbauch, John Louis and Charlotte Buatte 134, 135
Schmerbauch, Otis C. 134, 187
Schmerbauch, Paul 150
Schmerbauch, William A. 134, 135, 170
Schmidt, Eugene J. 135
Schmidt, George 135

Schmidt, Oscar J. and Emma Mae Du Frenne 135
Schmitz, Earl 135
Schmitz, George and Mary 135
Schmitz, John and Helena Hoeft 135
Schmitz, Robert J. 135
Schmoll, John A. 135
Schmoll, John A. and Caroline Petzinger 135
Schmoll, Louis H. 135
Schnepel, Friedrich 135
Schnepel, Johann Cord Dietrich and Christine 135
Schnoeker, Dean 136
Schnoeker, Dennis 136
Schnoeker, Dennis Earl and __ (Schutz) 136
Schnoeker, Dennis Jr. 136
Schnoeker, Earl J. 136
Schnoeker, Earl J. and __ (Bollmann) 136
Schnoeker, Edmund and __ Sickmeyer 136
Schobe, Harvey and Mable Tatum 136
Schobe, Harvey W. 136
Schoenbeck, Emma Wettig 136
Schoenbeck, Fred and Louise Nagel 136
Schoenbeck, Wilbert H. 136
Schott, Alvin John 137
Schott, Clyde Eugene 136
Schott, Goldie Lilly (Howie) 137
Schrader, Clarence W. 137
Schrader, William H. and Clara Caupert 137
Schram, Scot 56
Schram, Susan Clinken Beard Gordon 56
Schroeder, Ludwig and Emma Hartenberger 137
Schroeder, Roger A. 137
Schuchert, E. Fred 137
Schuchert, John F. and Anna Schemmer 137
Schulein, Cletus and Mary Petry 137
Schulein, Elroy A. 137
Schulein, Robert C. 137
Schulein, Thomas H. 138
Schulte, August and Emma Gosejohann 138
Schulte, Lester G. 138
Schultz, Kenneth and Debbie Pierottie 138
Schultz, Kenneth L. 138
Schultz, Otto G. and Violet 82
Schupbach, Fred A. and Anna Porter 138
Schupbach, Fred P. 138
Schuwerk, Brown and Arbeiter 9
Schuwerk, William A. Sr. 138
Schuwerk, William H. 138
Schuwerk, William H. and __ Crisler 138
Schuwerk, William M. and Hoffman 138
Scott, A.F. and Vergie Reves 137
Scott, Charlie T. 137
Sebastian, Benjamin A. 138
Sebastian, Benjamin and Lillian/Lilie Montroy 138
Sebastian, Charles C. 138, 187
Secor, Arthur E. 172
Seeman, Harold Carl 139
Seeman, Henry D. 139
Seemann, Fredrich and Margareta Dreyer 139
Seemann, Henry D. 139
Seemann, Henry D. and Augusta Wolters 139
Segar, Robert 187
Seljc, Capt. 3
Served Our Country, Too 176
Seymour, Arthur H. and Millie Ennis 139
Seymour, Arthur Q. 139
Seymour, Gerald E. 139
Sharette, Bill 109
Shaw Brothers 139
Shaw, Dennis L. 139
Shaw, Kenneth "Shorty" 139
Shaw, Lynn 139
Shaw, Lynn H. and June McIntyre 139
Shaw, Stanley 139
Shaw, Wayne 139
Sheeler, Charles C. 139
Sheeler, Franklin D. 140
Sheeler, Leola Koester 140

Sheeler, Scott, Keith, Kristen and Kathleen 140
Sheeler, Thomas E. 140
Sheeler, William C. and Margaret O'Neill 139, 140
Shemonic, Elmer 2
Shemonic, Elmer J. 140
Shemonic, Jacob and Mary ? 140
Shemonic, John 140
Shemonic, John II and Sadie Harmon 140
Sheppard, Jack, WHCO 9
Sickmeyer, Adolph and Selma Vieregge 140
Sickmeyer, Donald A. 140
Siemers, Ed and Leona Bockhorn 141
Siemers, Edward J. 140, 187
Siemers, Leonard 172
Simmons, Dean 187
Simpson, Claude Henry and Nathalie Rosa Kennedy 141
Simpson, Daniel M.H. 141
Simpson, Eddie 173
Simpson, Orville 141, 172
Singer, Harry R. 141
Singer, Jeremiah and Alice Crowe 141
Sipole, Emmett S. and Selma Hall 141
Sipole, Malden E. 141
Sipole, Percel E. 141
Sippel, Heinrich 171
Slack, Victor E. 141
Slack, William and Clara Breithaupt 141
Smith, Augustus 141
Smith, Edwin R. 141, 142
Smith, Francis and Agnes Adams 142
Smith, George and Harriet Pinkerton 143
Smith, Henry Salkeld and Juliana "Eula" Gaertner 142
Smith, Ignatius and Theresa 141, 142
Smith, James A. 142
Smith, Janice Steele 142
Smith, Joseph 142
Smith, June Heuman 142
Smith, Lisa (Jeff Lake) and Perry (Jennifer) 142
Smith, Mary Dailey 141
Smith, Norman A. 142
Smith, Paul 142
Smith, Powell 142
Smith, Renwick and Ella Phegley 142
Smith, Richard 171
Smith, Roger W. 142
Smith, Salkeld and Eula (Gaertner) 142
Smith, Virgil K. 142
Snider, Brian, KSGM 9
Snodgrass, Archibald and Isabella Blair 143
Snodgrass, Daryl Leslie 143
Snodgrass, Everett C. and Florence Morton 143
Snodgrass, Everett Clarence 143
Snodgrass, Isaac Everett 143
Snodgrass, Martin L. and Mary Jane McIntyre 143
Snyder, Vincent 187
Sparta Chamber of Commerce 9
Sparta News Plaindealer 9
Sparta Rotary Club 9
Sparta V.F.W. 8
Spier, Erhardt and Dorothy Eggerding 143
Spier, James A. 143
Spitzmiller, Ethel F. "Babe" Dobyns Gardiner 54
Sprengel, Arthur and Hildegard Moll 143
Sprengel, Oscar W. 143
Springer, Louis and Gertrude Good 143
Springer, Norbert G. 143
Spurgeon, Lewis 143
Stallman, Paul C. 143
Stallman, Paul C. and Henrietta Beck 143
Stallman, Paul E. 143
Stallman, Rudolph and Emilie Koopman 143
Stanley, Murray 143
Stanley, William and Cora Pait 144
Steele, Charles R. 144
Steele, John 144
Steele, Noah Luther and Hattie Benson 144
Steele, Samuel 144
Steele, Sarah Hunter 144
Steeleville Ledger 9

Steeleville Pharmacy 9
Stefani, Ernest and Dolores (Wittenbrink) 144
Stefani, Richard T. 144
Stegman, Martin W. 144
Stegmann, Herman and Alma Rubach 144
Stegmann, Martin W. 144
Steibel, Charles J. 144
Steibel, Charles J. and Mary F. (Pautler) 144
Steibel, Colin J. 144
Steibel, Corey J. 144
Steibel Family 144
Steibel, George and Wilmarth (Sis) (Dufrenne) 144
Steiner, Andrea 145
Steiner, Brenda 145
Steiner, Julius and Edith (Hood) 145
Steiner, Larry D. 144, 145
Steiner, Ryan 145
Stellhorn, Alfred A. 145
Stellhorn, Conrad and Wilhelmina Kloepper 145
Stellhorn, Conrad H. 145, 172
Stellhorn, Edgar H. 145
Stellhorn, Edward and Elma Lucht 145
Stellhorn, Gilbert P. 145
Stellhorn, Oscar and Erna Harms 145
Stepanek, Frank A. 172
Sternberg, Clyde F. 172
Stewart, Ames H. 146
Stewart, Armond L. 173
Stewart, Eugene S. and Anna Rodewald 145, 146
Stewart, Glenn R. 145
Stewart, James E. 146
Stewart, James H. 146
Stewart, James H. and Ruth 146
Stewart, Marvin L. 146
Stewart, Netter and Laura (Brenning) 146
Stewart, Roy L. 146
Stipe, Benjamin F. 146
Stipe, John and Susanna H. Thurman 146
Stirnaman, Archie and Mildred Longlois 147
Stirnaman, Boniface G. 146
Stirnaman, Clement and Emma Bessen 146
Stirnaman, Courtland E. 146
Stirnaman, Courtland E. and Phyllis (Simpson) 147
Stirnaman, Delbert R. 147
Stirnaman, Earl W. 147
Stirnaman, James Douglas 147
Stirnaman, Marcella 147
Stirnaman, Nevlin and Irene McFaddin 147
Stirnaman, Roy and Bernice Davis 147
Stirnaman, Wayne Edward 147
Stork, Gary L. 147
Stork, George J. 147
Stork, Gerald L. 147
Stork, Harold and Elizabeth Roche 147
Stork, Lawrence and Hazel Heinz 147
Stork, Lawrence J. and Bertha Wesbecher 148
Stork, Lawrence N. 148
Stork, Ron 148
Straight, Charles and Leta Mae Skinner 148
Straight, Charles Donald 148
Straight, Charles Donald and Dorothy Braun 148
Straight, Robert C. 148
Stumpe, Alan George 148
Stumpe, David 148
Stumpe, George H. 148
Stumpe, Henry 148
Stumpe, Henry and Mary Pick 148
Stumpe, John D. and Marie G. Weber 148
Stumpe, John H. 148
Stumpe, Norbert G. and Martha Bauer 148
Stumpe, Norbert P. 148
Stumpe, Roger William 148
Stumpe, Rudolph and Josefeane Molly 148
Stumpf, Arnold and Elizabeth Reger 148
Stumpf, Paul E. 148
Suhre, Billy, Charles and Vernon 149
Suhre, Billy F. 148
Suhre Brothers 149
Suhre, Charles H. 149

Suhre, Earnest Hugo and Louise Catherine Brugert/Burgret 148, 149
Suhre, Hugo and Charles 149
Suhre, Hugo and Vernon 149
Suhre, Richard Joseph 149, 173
Suhre, Rovbert Lee 149
Suhre, Robert Lee and Violet R. (Jordan) 149
Suhre, Vernon H. 149
Suhre, Vicki 149
Suhre, Violet 149
Summers, Phillip Paul 149, 173
Summers, Robert and Teresa Colvis 149
Sunderman, Fred F. 172
Surman, Daniel and Marcella (Eggemeyer) 150
Surman, Larry G. 149
Sutton, Lisa Darnstaedt Heines 66
Swinferd, Edwin and Marie Knigge 150
Swinferd, Henry C. 150, 169

T

Taggart, John and Clara Jostes 150
Taggart, John Q.C. 150
Taggart, Kenneth Sidney 150
Taggart, Thurston T. 150
Taylor, Arthur and Grace Mizer 150
Taylor, George E. and Helen M. Gibbs 150
Taylor, George R. 172
Taylor, Jesse L. 150
Taylor, Roy Logan 150
Taylor, Warren Rankin 150
Thieret, James H. 150
Thies, Harold H. 150
Thies, Henry C. and Dorothea Fuhrhop 151
Thies, Lillian Vallery 150
Thies, Sigmun and Clara Rubach 150
Thies, Sigmund H. 150, 151
Thimming, Charles J. 172
Thomas, Albert Desper and Lola A. (Hillyard) 151, 156
Thomas and Alice Richmond Martin 95
Thomas, Brunhilda Noke 151
Thomas, Carl E. 2, 151
Thomas, Clinton O. 151
Thomas, Howard Leroy 151
Thomas-VanSant, Nadean N. 155
Thompson, Lyle A. 172
Thurau, Emil and Lula Milligan 151
Thurau, Lester F. 151
Tiller, Benjamin Roy and Lydia Watkins 152
Tiller, Bobby Lee 151
Tiller, Charles Harold 152
Tiller, Herschel W. 152
Tiller, James Lloyd 152
Tiller, William Archie 152
Tilton, Charles O. 152
Tilton, Claude and Estella Etter 152
Tilton, Herman 188
Tilton, Wesley 188
Tindall, James and Maggie Lorentz 153
Tindall, Charles and Elizabeth Holley 153
Tindall, Genevieve Petrowske 153
Tindall, Isaac and Lorna Stamm 153
Tindall, Isaac C. 152
Tindall, James A. 153
Tindall, James and Maggie Lorentz 152
Tindall, Jerry D. 153
Tindall, Mark A. 153
Tindall, Reggie and Kathryn Layne 153
Tindall, Willaim 153
Tope, Jesse 153
Toulouse, Blaise Barutel dit 153
Toulouse, Joseph Barutel dit 153
Toulouse, Marie Ann Giar 153
Trieb, Hugo and Georgianna Christophersen 153
Trieb, Robert J. "Bob" 153
Trost, Leroy R. 153
Trost, Walter and Alma Kraemer 153
Troue, Herbert and Ethel (Meyerhoff) 154
Troue, Leslie J. 153, 154
Trucano, Alan D. 173
Tudor, Douglas A. 154
Tudor, Maurice and Frieda Mansker 154
Tudor, Phillip L. 154
Turnage, William 188

U

Uebel, Johann "John" 154
Uebel, Mary A. Trout 154
Uffelman, Henry B. and Matilda Paperberg 154
Uffelman, Vernon J. 154

V

Valentine, John and Sophie Baer 154
Valentine, John J. 154
Valentine, Welton 188
Van Meter, Charlie and Minnie Tindall 155
Van Meter, Elva "Red" 155
Vancil, Ed 154
Vancil, Ed & Varlan 154
Vancil, France E. 154
Vancil, Varlan D. 155
Vancil, Willis E. and Wilma Glenn 155
VanMeter, Elva 188
VanSant, Brian and William Jr. 156
VanSant, Carlin R. 155
VanSant, Charles Boynton "Chuck" 155
VanSant, Horace and Mozelle (Chism) 156
VanSant, Lauren and Kelly 156
VanSant, Lisa King 156
VanSant, Louise Hartmann 156
VanSant, NaDean N. (Thomas) 155
VanSant, Thomas A. 156
VanSant, William Eugene "Gene" 156
VanSant, William Horace and Mozelle (Chism) 155, 156
Vasquez, Peter and Rosalie Sills 156
Vasquez, Richard G. 156
Venuti, Pat 169
Vickers, Marvin 156
Vickers, Maurice 156
Vickers, Melvin D. 156
Vickers, Michael 157
Vickers, William C. and Emma E. McKenzie 156, 157
Victor Drugs 9
Village of Ellis Grove 9
Village of Prairie du Rocher 9
Village of Rockwood 9
Village of Ruma 9
Viner, George and Gene Whitaker 157
Viner, Jack P. 157
Viner, Mary Schmoll 157
Von Bey, Ernst B. 157
Von Bey, Ernst F. and Lyda J. Herr 157
Voss, Fred 173
Vuichard, Charles D. 157
Vuichard, Charles F. 157
Vuichard, Charles P. and Martha Hillyard 157
Vuichard, Charles R. and Betty (Church) 157
Vuichard, George W. and Margaret Coppman 157

W

Wagner, Alva and Olinda Eggemeyer 158
Wagner, Betty Mennerich 158
Wagner, Erich R. 157
Wagner, Ernst and Marie Springer 157
Wagner, Karen Athmer 9
Wagner, Roland L. 157, 188
Wagner, Ronald and Rhonda 158
Wagoner, Lydia 32
Waldron, Edward F. 158
Waldron, Edward J. and Elizabeth Mennarigh 158
Waldron, Harold S. 158
Wall, Ardell Merle 158
Wall, J. and Edna Goudier 158
Walter, Jerald L. 158
Walter, William and Ruth Schulein 158
Ward, Charles C. 158
Ward, George 158
Ward, John J. and Edith Garris 158
Watson, Bill and Patti Martin 159
Watson, Jack 9
Watson, Jack and Mary M. Cleland 159
Watson, John "Jack" 158, 159
Watson, John H. and Florence 159
Watson, John Kyle 159
Watson, Kory W. 159
Watson, William H. 159
Weaver, Edwin and Ella Dagner 159
Weaver, Kenneth "Bud" 188
Weaver, Orville 159
Wegener, Henry and Minnie Hanebutt 159
Wegener, Otis C. 159
Wehrenberg, Ralph W. 159
Weir, John E. 159, 172
Welge, Albert and Anna Hogrefe 160
Welge, Bruce L. 96, 159, 173
Welge, Conrad 188
Welge, Donald E. 160
Welge, Edgar 160
Welge, Elaine 160
Welge, Michael W. 160
Welge, Pechacek, Schroeder, McClure 9
Welge, William H. and Rudelle Fritze 159, 160
Welten, Edith 160
Welten, Louis and Alma Schnoeker 160
Wente, Donald A. 160
Wente, Guido E. 160
Wente, Merle W. 160
Wente, William C. 161
Wente, William C. and Caroline Gray 160
Wente, William C. and Caroline Griese 160
Wente, William C. and Ruth Elsey 160
Wente, William C. Jr. 160
Werner, John L. 188
Wesbecher, Harold 161
Wesbecher, William L. and Leona Krull 161
Wesbecker, Cyril "Zip" 161
Wesbecker, Frances Roth 161
Wesbecker, William L. 161
Whitcher, Stella 78
White, Kenneth 188
Wicklein, Glen and Linda Gietz 161
Wicklein, Roger G. 161
Wiley, Albert Lawton 161
Wiley, Clement O. and Margaret J. Skinner 161
Wiley, Fowler and Clara May Adams 161
Wiley, John and Mary "Polly" Little 162
Wiley, John Orval 161
Wiley, Wilbur A. 161
Wiley, William 162
Wiley, William Fowler and Clara May Adams 161
Williams, Albert 172
Williams, David and Rena Moore 162
Williams, Derrick 162
Williams, Kenneth F. 162
Williams, Westley and Anna Neighmeyer 162
Williamson, Roger 172, 188
Willis, Charles and Lulu 162
Willis, Edmund L. 162
Willis, Woodrow "Woody" 162
Wilsey, Julie (Robert) 162
Wilson, Albert and Alma Dierks 162
Wilson, Anna Patterson 114
Wilson, Gilbert A. 162
Wilson, Melvin 162
Wilson, Norman B. 172
Wilson, Ralph W. 162
Wilson, Rudolph and (Beisner) 162
Wingerter, Donald A. Sr. 163
Wingerter, Donald L. 163
Wingerter, Jerry Dean 163
Wingerter, Joe and Iona (Tindall) 163
Wingerter, Lenus and Eleanor Braun 163
Wingerter, Robert C. 163
Wingerter, William and Mildred Dallas 163
Witbart, Albert and Anna D. Leaders 163
Witbart, Richard W. 9, 163
Wittbracht, Lee A. and Mona Fuhrhop 164
Wittbracht, Lee Andrew 163
Wittbracht, Warren 163
Wittenbrink, Anthony A. 164
Wittenbrink, Donald Richard 164
Wittenbrink, Elmer Robert 164
Wittenbrink, Fred H. and Eva Asbury 164
Wittenbrink, Fred H. Sr. and Edith Carroll 164
Wittenbrink, Fred Harding 164
Wittenbrink, Fred Henry and Eva Asbury 164
Wittenbrink, George E. 164, 172
Wittenbrink, Joe W. 164
Wittenbrink, John Henry 164
Wittenbrink, Vernon O. 164
Witthoft, Carl 188
Witthoft, H.A. 188
Wolff, Leo N. and Eleanor Schittendecker 164
Wolff, Nicholas and Jacque Louvier 165
Wolff, Nicholas W. 164
Wolff, Omer and Gloria (Saak) 164
Wolff, Omer W. "Tony" 164
Wolff, Reynold J. 164
Wolff, Shannon L. 165
Wolshock, Edward J. and Mamie Rahlfs 165
Wolshock, Jerome J. 165, 172
Wolshock, Sylvester 188
Wolter, Louis C. and Edna Goedelmann 165
Wolter, Oliver H. 165
Wolters, Elmer and Marie Bierman 165
Wolters, Louis and Anna Kothe 165
Wolters, Martin H. 188
Wolters, Norlyn R. 165
Wolters, Richard L. 165
Woods, Cecil F. and Emma Sykes 166
Woods, Harold Merle 165
Woods, John H. 165
Woods, John Vance and Elveretta Mansker 165
Woodside, Clyde H. 166
Woodside, Clyde H. and Loraine Schekel 166
Woodside, Irl H. 166
Woodside, John E. 166
Woodside, Rolland D. 166
Woodside, Samuel Harold and Anna M. Heinike 166
Woodside, William C. 166
Woodside, Wilmer G. 166
Word, Carlos and Agnes Beveridge 166
Word, James H. 166
Wright, Edward and Mae Sutherland 167
Wright, Raymond Earl 166
Wunderlich, John P. and Kate Klein 167
Wunderlich, Vernon M. 167, 188

Y

Yankey, Charles and Flora Holley 167
Yankey, Harold J. 167
Yankey, Jesse C. 167, 172
Yankey, June (Mehrtens) 167
Yankey, Roy Lee 167
Yankey, Shirley "Peck" 167
Yankey, William G. 167
Yates, Walter D. 172
Young, Cole R. 167
Young, Donald R. and Sue Gardner 167

Z

Zellar, Robert 188
Zimmer, Carlisle and Joyce (Kreyer) 168
Zimmer, Edwin F. and Emma A. Luebkemann/Lueblemann 167, 168
Zimmer, Edwin J. 167
Zimmer, Gerard A. 168
Zimmer, James A. 168
Zimmer, Michelle (Stiebel) 144
Zimmer, Ralph and Irene Duhigg 168
Zimmer, Ralph R. 168
Zimmer, Richard and Meta Beisner 168
Zimmer, Wilbert F. 168
Zimmerman, Gustav and Esther Alms 168
Zimmerman, Melvin A. 168

THESE BOYS

Robert Adger Bowen

Published in Chester Herald Tribune, May 16, 1918

They are not heroes in their own esteem,
These boys whose souls with patriotism glow,
Whose steadfast eyes so clearly see below
The semblance and the glamour of the dream.
Yet not the less upon their spirit gleam
The joys and splendors of young life's bright glow,
The ardent flame, the keen desire to know,
And love's right royal guerdon to redeem.

Will they come back? We ask with quivering breath,
Nor dare to show the very dread we feel,
So calm and bravely unafraid are they;
As though the challenges they make to Death
The purposes divine of Life reveal
'Tis we who falter at the price they pay!

www.ingramcontent.com/pod-product-compliance
Lightning Source LLC
Chambersburg PA
CBHW081920180426
43200CB00032B/2880